THE NEW JEWISH DIASPORA

THE NEW JEWISH DIASPORA

Russian-Speaking Immigrants in the United States, Israel, and Germany

EDITED BY
ZVI GITELMAN

RUTGERS UNIVERSITY PRESS
New Brunswick, New Jersey, and London

Library of Congress Cataloging-in-Publication Data
The new Jewish diaspora : Russian-speaking immigrants in the United States, Israel, and Germany / edited by Zvi Gitelman.
pages cm
Includes bibliographical references and index.
ISBN 978–0–8135–7629–9 (hardcover : alk. paper)—ISBN 978–0–8135–7628–2 (pbk. : alk. paper)—ISBN 978–0–8135–7630–5 (e-book (epub))—ISBN 978–0–8135–7631–2 (e-book (web pdf))
1. Jews, Russian—Israel—Ethnic identity. 2. Jews, Russian—United States—Ethnic identity. 3. Jews, Russian—Germany—Ethnic identity. 4. Russia (Federation)—Emigration and immigration. I. Gitelman, Zvi Y., editor.
DS113.8.R87N49 2015
305.892'4—dc23   2015032494

A British Cataloging-in-Publication record for this book is available from the British Library.

This collection copyright © 2016 by Rutgers, The State University
Individual chapters copyright © 2016 in the names of their authors
All rights reserved

No part of this book may be reproduced or utilized in any form or by any means, electronic or mechanical, or by any information storage and retrieval system, without written permission from the publisher. Please contact Rutgers University Press, 106 Somerset Street, New Brunswick, NJ 08901. The only exception to this prohibition is "fair use" as defined by U.S. copyright law.

Visit our website: http://rutgerspress.rutgers.edu

Manufactured in the United States of America

"These are the travels of the children of Israel...."
                                                Numbers 33:1

CONTENTS

	List of Figures	xi
	List of Tables	xiii
	Acknowledgments	xv
	Introduction: Homelands, Diasporas, and the Islands in Between ZVI GITELMAN	1
	PART I. DEMOGRAPHY: WHO ARE THE MIGRANTS AND WHERE HAVE THEY GONE?	21
1	Demography of the Contemporary Russian-Speaking Jewish Diaspora MARK TOLTS	23
2	The Russian-Speaking Israeli Diaspora in the FSU, Europe, and North America: Jewish Identification and Attachment to Israel UZI REBHUN	41
3	Home in the Diaspora? Jewish Returnees and Transmigrants in Ukraine MARINA SAPRITSKY	60
	PART II. TRANSNATIONALISM AND DIASPORAS	75
4	Rethinking Boundaries in the Jewish Diaspora from the FSU JONATHAN DEKEL-CHEN	77
5	Diaspora from the Inside Out: Litvaks in Lithuania Today HANNAH POLLIN-GALAY	89
6	Russian-Speaking Jews and Israeli Emigrants in the United States: A Comparison of Migrant Populations STEVEN J. GOLD	103

PART III. POLITICAL AND ECONOMIC CHANGE 123

7   Political Newborns: Immigrants in
    Israel and Germany   125
    OLENA BAGNO-MOLDAVSKI

8   The Move from Russia/the Soviet Union
    to Israel: A Transformation of Jewish
    Culture and Identity?   139
    YAACOV RO'I

9   The Economic Integration of Soviet
    Jewish Immigrants in Israel   156
    GUR OFER

PART IV. RESOCIALIZATION AND THE MALLEABILITY OF ETHNICITY 171

10 Russian-Speaking Jews in Germany   173
    ELIEZER BEN-RAFAEL

11 Performing Jewishness and Questioning the
    Civic Subject among Russian-Jewish
    Migrants in Germany   186
    SVETA ROBERMAN

12 Inventing a "New Jew": The Transformation of
    Jewish Identity in Post-Soviet Russia   196
    ELENA NOSENKO-STEIN

PART V. MIGRATION AND RELIGIOUS CHANGE 211

13 Post-Soviet Immigrant Religiosity:
    Beyond the Israeli National Religion   213
    NELLY ELIAS AND JULIA LERNER

14 Virtual Village in a Real World:
    The Russian Jewish Diaspora Online   229
    ANNA SHTERNSHIS

PART VI. DIASPORA RUSSIAN LITERATURE 247

15 Four Voices from the Last Soviet Generation:
    Evgeny Steiner, Alexander Goldshtein,
    Oleg Yuryev, and Alexander Ilichevsky   251
    MIKHAIL KRUTIKOV

16	Poets and Poetry in Today's Diaspora: On Being "Marginally Jewish" STEPHANIE SANDLER	266
17	Triple Identities: Russian-Speaking Jews as German, American, and Israeli Writers ADRIAN WANNER	286
	Afterword: The Future of a Diaspora ZVI GITELMAN	299
	Notes on Contributors	303
	Index	307

FIGURES

I.1	USSR Mean Numbers of Annual Jewish Emigrants	10
1.1	Out-Migration of FSU Migrants from Israel, 2000–2009	31
7.1	Trust, Efficacy, and Protest in Germany, Israel, and Ukraine	134

TABLES

1.1	Emigration of Jews and Their Relatives from the FSU, 1970–2009, in Thousands	24
1.2	Emigration of Jews and Their Relatives from the FSU to Israel, the U.S., and Germany, by Republic (Country)/Region, 1970–1988 and 1989–2001, in Thousands	26
1.3	Emigration from the Russian Federation to Israel, by Area, 1990–2009, Percentages	27
1.4	Age Distribution of Jews and Their Relatives Who Migrated from the FSU to Three Main Destinations, 1990/1991–2004, Percentages	28
1.5	Departures from and Returns to Israel of FSU Immigrants Who Arrived in Israel since 1990, in Thousands	29
1.6	Immigration from Israel to the Russian Federation and European FSU Countries, 1997–2009	30
1.7	Dynamics of the "Core" Jewish Population Originating from the FSU, 1970–2010, in Millions	34
1.8	Distribution of the "Core" Jewish Population in the FSU, by Country, 2010, in Thousands	35
1.9	Distribution of the Post-Soviet Jewish Diaspora Population, by Country, 2010, in Millions	35
6.1	Persons Naturalized during Fiscal Years 2006–2010 by Region/Country of Birth and Selected Characteristics. Region/Country: Russia	110
6.2	Persons Naturalized during Fiscal Years 2006–2010 by Region/Country of Birth and Selected Characteristics. Region/Country: Israel	111

7.1	Legal and Socio-Political Background in Germany, Israel, and Ukraine	129
9.1	General Characteristics: The Jewish Population and Immigration Waves	159
10.1	The Age Factor	176
10.2	RSJs' Integration into German Society	177
10.3	Feeling Part of/Solidarity with Given Collectives (%)	180
10.4	Exogamy and Jewishness—Selected Items	182
10.5	The Importance of Giving Children a Jewish Education	183
12.1	What Can You Say About Your Jewish Roots?	197
12.2	Religiosity among Russian Jews	204
12.3	If You Believe in God, What Religion Do You Choose?	204
12.4	What Movement in Judaism Do You Prefer?	206

ACKNOWLEDGMENTS

This book is based on a selection of papers presented at a conference on the contemporary Russian-speaking Jewish diaspora held at the Kathryn W. and Shelby Cullom Davis Center for Russian and Eurasian Studies, Harvard University, in November 2011. The papers were rewritten, edited, and updated for publication. This was a truly international conference, bringing together participants from Canada, France, Germany, Great Britain, Israel, Russia, and the United States. It was co-sponsored by the Kathryn W. and Shelby Cullom Davis Center for Russian and Eurasian Studies, and the Jean and Samuel Frankel Center for Judaic Studies at the University of Michigan. Additional generous support was provided by the American Councils for International Education, Aquidneck Foundation, Mr. Fredo Arias-King in honor of Rabbi Leonardo Libersohn of Monterrey, Mexico; Blavatnik Family Foundation; Center for Jewish Studies at Harvard University; Centre for Diaspora and Transnational Studies at the University of Toronto; Consulate General of France in Boston; Frankel Family Foundation; Genesis Philanthropy Group; Lucius N. Littauer Foundation; Mr. Eugene Mercy; Russkiy Mir Foundation; and the Russian Foundation for Humanities.

I wish to express my profound gratitude to Dr. Lisbeth Tarlow, my co-organizer of the conference. At the time she was Associate Director of the Davis Center and had conceived and administered a program on Soviet/Russian Jewry for several years. Always of good cheer and amazingly efficient, Lis made everything run smoothly with her remarkable diplomatic skills and good sense. We were ably assisted by Matt Weinberg, coordinator of the Russian-Jewish Diaspora Project.

We all benefitted from the participation in the conference of: the late Svetlana Boym, Barry Chiswick, Timothy Colton, Alanna Cooper, Natasha Gellman, Olga Goldberger, Rabbi Pinchas Goldschmidt, Jerry Goodman, Boris Gorbis, Brian Horowitz, Anna Wexler Katznelson, Samuel Kliger, Rebecca Kobrin, Vladislav Kurske, Sergey Lagodinsky, Serhii Plokhii, Larissa Remmenick, Alla Rosenfeld, Gabriel Sheffer, Barry Shrage, Maxim Shrayer, Thomas W. Simons, Jr., Lisa Vapné, Lenore Weitzman, and Ruth Wisse.

Thanks also to Prof. Timothy Colton who was director of the Davis Center when the project was conceived and to Prof. Terry Martin who succeeded him. Their support, advice and encouragement was most valuable. Maria Altamore at the Davis Center insured that the finances and logistics of the project were in good order. At the University of Michigan I have been greatly assisted in preparing this volume by Sarah Garibova. Marlie Wasserman of Rutgers University Press has been a very helpful critic and guide. To all of these people, my deepest gratitude.

THE NEW JEWISH DIASPORA

INTRODUCTION

Homelands, Diasporas, and the Islands in Between

ZVI GITELMAN

"Diaspora" is a commonly used word without precise definition.[1] Sometimes it is a synonym for ethnic group. It is often associated with "globalization" and "transnationalism," though these two concepts are distinct phenomena.[2] William Safran notes that "the label [diaspora] has been stretched to cover almost any ethnic or religious minority that is dispersed physically from its original homeland, regardless of the conditions leading to the dispersion and regardless of whether, and to what extent, physical, cultural or emotional links exist between the community and the home country."[3] Some have tried to differentiate "diasporas" from migrant or ethnic groups, or transnational and globalized groups. Others have despaired of the enterprise and suggested that "there are no diasporas, only different ways of constructing, managing, and imagining the relationships between homelands and their dispersed peoples."[4] For our purposes, we need not belabor the definition. This book deals with a population that is scattered in many different countries, originates from a state that no longer exists, but to varying extents clings to a culture, or subculture, emotionally and instrumentally. Is it a diaspora? If so, what is its homeland? The Soviet Union that no longer exists? The USSR's successor states, to which few return?[5] Israel—a place to which almost anyone in this group could go but many choose not to? Their countries of immigration? Do they feel themselves "at home" there?

Two young women living in the United States, one born in the USSR, the other born in the U.S. to Soviet-born parents, reflect ruefully on this question. Alina Dizhik, born in Kharkov, is often identified as "Russian," though she was born in Ukraine and lives in the United States. "Enough with Russia, Already: I Want to Be an American" is the title of her essay in which she observes, "It's been 24 years since I left the Soviet Union to come to America, and I hadn't settled on a single answer [to 'where are you from?'] that feels right.... Today, I'd rather be defined by being American."⁶ American-born Samantha Shokin finds herself "consistently gravitating toward Russian expats," much to the chagrin of her parents. "It became clear by the time I entered college that my parents' hopes of raising an all-American daughter with zero ties to the Old Country had largely backfired."⁷ Polina, one of the characters in David Bezmozgis's *The Free World*, captures the dilemma when she observes, "Wherever we go we will be among strangers."⁸

Whether Russian-speaking Jews constitute a diaspora or a transnational entity, what defines the entity is neither a territory—"homeland" or otherwise—nor institutions, nor an aspiration, such as establishing a state or returning to a home territory. The connective tissue of the group is its highly valued language and culture, or, more precisely, a subculture. The subculture includes specific values and common experiences. This entity is currently populated by two or three generations and will likely be transformed out of existence in the not-too-distant future. It is not the first such group in Jewish history, not even in the modern period.

The Russian-speaking Jewish diaspora, if it is that, is a link in history's longest diaspora chain. After all, it was the Jewish/Israelite/Hebrew god who invented diaspora. In the *tochacha* [admonition] in Leviticus 26:14–45, God tells the Jewish people (v. 33): "I shall scatter you among the nations ... and your land shall be desolate." But in v. 44, God says He will not abandon the Jews and hints at return to the land, but only hints. The second version of the *tochacha* (Deuteronomy 28:15–68, v. 64) reads: "God shall scatter you among all the peoples/nations [*amim*] from one end of the earth to the other and you shall worship different gods there whom neither you nor your ancestors knew, trees and stones." Here there is no promise of return. Yet, the prospect and promise of return is taken up by the Hebrew prophets: Zechariah, Isaiah (ch. 40 and later, Isaiah 43:5).⁹

According to the biblical narrative, diaspora is punishment for deviating from God's word. Hence, it is an abnormal situation that can be rectified by returning to His ways. As the liturgy for Jewish pilgrimage festivals says, "Because of our sins we have been exiled from our country and distanced from our land." The scheme is clear: evil-doing leads to exile, repentance leads to return. The modern Zionist, secular version of this concept is that diaspora is abnormal, whatever its causes may have been, and it should be rectified by creating a state that will serve as a homeland. All variants of Zionism share the postulate that the Jews are a nation; every normal nation has its own state; therefore, Jews must be normalized and have their own state, that is, a homeland. *Where* the homeland should be located became a matter of debate, though the Zionists quickly settled on the ancient Land of Israel rather than the African territory offered by the British.¹⁰

Beginning in the eighteenth century, some Jews, mostly in Western Europe and North America, asserted that their present countries of residence were their homeland. Many German Jews thought of themselves as *Deutsche staatsburger Mosaischen Glaubens*, others as Magyars or Poles of the Israelite faith. Some thought that no homeland was needed as long as national-cultural autonomy would be provided within whichever state Jews lived. Others believed that a distinctly Jewish space, wherever it was, would become a *kind* of homeland, and so they established Jewish colonies in western Canada, Argentina, and the United States. In 1934, the Soviet government decreed the formation of a "Jewish autonomous oblast' [region]" in Birobidzhan, a region in southeastern Siberia. In the early twentieth century, there were diaspora affirmationists such as Shimon Dubnov, Bundists, and Territorialists. But Zionists repudiated the viability and desirability of the diaspora. They called it *galut*, or exile, and rejected it contemptuously, along with its languages, values, and mores. Only in recent decades has that negation been softened, perhaps because Zionism has emerged triumphant from the battle of ideological movements. The term *tfutsot*, or dispersion, has taken the place of *galut*, the more pejorative and value-laden "exile."[11] Ideology, demographics, and catastrophe combined to make Israel the Jewish homeland, in the eyes of most Jews and many non-Jews. The poet Robert Frost famously observed, "Home is the place where, when you have to go there, they have to take you in." In that sense, alone among the states of the world, Israel has defined itself and has acted as the Jewish homeland and has never placed restrictions on immigration by Jews.

Though most Jews the world over were not Zionists before World War II, after the Holocaust the establishment of a Jewish state emerged as the consensus solution to "the Jewish problem," and not among Jews alone. Speaking at the United Nations exactly a year before the State of Israel was proclaimed, Soviet representative Andrei Gromyko, not a sentimental man, representing a state not noted for its Zionist sympathies, invoked the Holocaust and urged the General Assembly to support the establishment of a Jewish state. He said, "It would be unjustifiable to deny this right to the Jewish people, particularly in view of all it has undergone during the World War."[12]

The lessons derived by many from World War II were that dispersal, acculturation, and even assimilation did not guarantee acceptance and that Jews could count only on themselves for defense. However, in the late twentieth and early twenty-first centuries, there has been a fashionable "turn" in academia toward embracing diaspora and exile, and perhaps not just as subjects of study. While most ordinary people who are homeless or in exile are not happy about their condition, some academics, perhaps longing to fit into the mold of the alienated, marginalized intellectual (who nevertheless draws a nice university salary), have become preoccupied with diaspora literatures, the politics of exile, and memoirs of expulsion and rootlessness. Jonathan and Daniel Boyarin proposed that Zionism was "the subversion and not the culmination of Jewish culture," and so they advocated "a privileging of Diaspora, a dissociation of ethnicities and political hegemonies as the only social structure that even begins to make possible the maintenance of cultural identity in a world grown . . . thoroughly interdependent."[13] Perhaps this would work in Berkeley, Chapel Hill, or Ithaca; it did not work in Europe.[14]

Israel is on the way to becoming the single largest concentration of Jews in the world, if it is not already that. Six million Jews in Israel represent about 43 percent of world Jewry.[15] In 1900, there were 5.2 million Jews in the Russian empire; today, there are fewer than 400,000 in the territories of the former Soviet Union.[16] They are now 2.2 percent of world Jewry. The changes in Jewish populations have been dramatic and dynamic, nowhere more so than in the Russian Empire and the Soviet Union. Almost two million Jews emigrated from the Russian Empire in the late nineteenth and early twentieth centuries. In 1931, it was estimated that "as a result of post-war and post-revolutionary changes to state frontiers, about 55 per cent of the Jews of the empire became citizens of other states."[17]

In chapter 1 of this book, Mark Tolts carefully delineates the dynamics of RSJ migration; subsequent chapters explore the perceptual changes that have accompanied it. In light of high Jewish intermarriage rates and low birth rates in all countries, and a steady, if recently modest, immigration to Israel, it is not unimaginable that in the foreseeable future the majority of the world's Jews will live in the self-defined Jewish state. How will that affect Israel's relations with the Jewish diaspora, if at all? Rather than speculate, we can with greater assurance describe how Israel-Diaspora relations have changed over the years:

1. A shift from stand-offishness among non-Zionists to a close embrace of Israel, especially after 1945 and again after 1967;
2. A change from Israeli dependence on the diaspora for economic and political support to the diaspora's reliance on Israel as a means of maintaining or even creating Jewish—not necessarily Israeli—identity and consciousness. "Operation Birthright" has brought hundreds of thousands of young diaspora Jews to Israel for brief visits, a "gap year" spent in Israel is popular among the Orthodox, while others go for "fun 'n' sun," or secular and religious study;
3. Some Jews are distancing themselves from Israel—partly because of Israeli policies, partly because Israel is no longer a miracle but at times an embarrassment, and partly because of Jewish assimilation. There is a debate among sociologists on whether young people are becoming more distant from Israel; data from the United States and United Kingdom seem to point in that direction;[18]
4. More Jews in the diaspora are willing to criticize Israel;[19]
5. Israelis have accepted the permanence of the diaspora.

Another, more general change is that the term "diaspora" used to imply the existence of a territorial homeland but no longer necessarily does. For the purposes of this volume, it generally does not. "The nation-state container view of society does not adequately capture the complex interconnectedness of contemporary reality."[20] Since it is not clear what a territorial homeland [*rodina*] for Russian-speaking Jews (RSJs) would be, as vividly exemplified by the chapters on Lithuanian Jews and RSJs in Germany and in Israel (chapters 7, 10, 12, and 13), it might be more useful to think of a *culture* than of a *place* as the nexus of the diaspora. The cultural tie that binds is a variant of Russian culture, the kind of "thin" Russian-Jewish culture that developed among Soviet Jews over the course of seven decades. This culture has specific values—urbanity, education, fear of "socialism," among others—and a distinct sense of humor. It is based on experiences shared by Soviet Jews and not by other Soviet citizens. The chapters on Russian literature by Krutikov, Sandler, and Wanner explore different manifestations of the multifaceted RSJ culture. The connection among Russian-speaking Jews is a compound of place of origin, shared experiences and collective memories, and a distinct subculture that is mainly Russian. As Robin Cohen observes, "In a global age where space itself has become reinscribed by cyberspace, a diaspora can, to some degree, be cemented or recreated through the mind, through artifacts and popular culture, and through a shared imagination." Cohen calls this "deterritorialized disaspora."[21]

Russian-speaking Jews are concentrated overwhelmingly outside their birthplaces or the birthplaces of their parents. Today almost two million Russian-speaking people, most of them Jews, live outside the Former Soviet Union (FSU). In January 1989, when the last Soviet census was taken, 1,449,000 people identified themselves as Jews. Now there are probably no more than 300,000–400,000 Jews living throughout the former Soviet territories, about 250,000 of them in Russia itself. Mark Tolts (chapter 1) calculates that between 1989 and 2009 about 1.6 million Jews and their non-Jewish relatives left the FSU, with nearly a million going to Israel (61%) and about 326,000 immigrating to the United States and 224,000 to Germany.[22] Add to that approximately 290,000 Russian-speaking Jewish émigrés from 1970 to 1988, and we get 1,890,000 émigrés between 1970 and 2009, roughly the same number of Jews who left the Russian Empire between 1881 and 1914, when the population base was nearly five times as great. Thus, today there are between four and five times as many Jewish native speakers of Russian outside the borders of the FSU as within them. Zionists may regard them as people returning to their ancestral home; Russians may regard them either as traitors or ambassadors of Russian culture; and RSJs may see themselves in many different ways. Elena Nosenko-Stein shows that even those remaining in the former Soviet Union vary in their understandings of what being a Russian-speaking Jew means (chapter 12).

RSJs do not fit easily into the "expatriate" category since they have formally adopted new *patrias* by becoming citizens of their host countries. "By shaping new shades of belonging and their legal expression," diasporas have affected definitions of citizenship,[23] as we shall see below. Beyond citizenship, we may reasonably argue that in the multicultural, multiethnic societies of Israel and the United States they are Israelis or Americans, and their children will certainly be so culturally and socially. But one wonders about the Jews of Germany: only in a formal sense are they "German Jews" since their culture is not that of the prewar "Yekkes," and Germany in general is only very slowly defining itself as a society in which people of non-German descent may be considered "Germans." As one researcher observes, "The majority of German participants [in a study of RSJs] reported feeling like outsiders both in Germany and in Russia."[24] Sveta Roberman and Eliezer Ben-Rafael (chapters 10 and 11) explore the complexities of RSJ identities in Germany, the former using survey data and the latter ethnographic study. For now, perhaps the people they study are better described as "Russian-speaking Jews living in Germany," just as many of the over one million Arabs living in Israel increasingly see themselves as "Palestinian Arabs living in Israel."

A third general change is that "homeland" and "diaspora" are no longer dichotomous categories. The fluidity of populations, the globalization of the economy, and the erosion of borders, at least in some parts of the world, have made the categories ambiguous.[25] A few examples are Russian-speaking Jews; Mexican Americans; Europeans born in one country, working in a second, and residing in a third; and Overseas Chinese. RSJs living in one country have family in several others, whom they visit; they tour those countries; do business or study or work in another RSJ center; read, watch, and hear RSJs living in other countries.

This illustrates the ambiguities, ambivalences, and realities of the mental and physical states of increasing numbers of people the world over. We can think of those realities as islands on an archipelago that has a putative homeland at one point of the chain, linked to islands at greater or lesser distances. The imaginary typical immigrant anywhere inhabits an island in the archipelago, neither fully at home in the new country nor any longer fully at home in the old one—and even "feeling at home" is not necessarily the same as "belonging."[26] Some become fully assimilated, at least to their own satisfaction, while others remain entirely at the margins of their adoptive society. Most immigrants and often their children live in at least two cultures, to one extent or another. Usually, the dual cultures yield to acculturation and even assimilation.

HOMELAND-DIASPORA RELATIONS

Exploring the relations between "homelands" and "their diasporas," we raise several questions.

1. How do states relate to the diasporas of their peoples?[27]
   A. *Hostility and rejection*: Israel and the Soviet Union considered those who left their respective countries traitors, or, at best, weaklings (the late Israeli Prime Minister Yitzhak Rabin called them "dregs and weaklings" [*nipolet shel nemushot.*]) For decades, the Soviet government considered émigrés traitors to the homeland. Only during perestroika were some voices heard urging a more tolerant view of emigration, suggesting that it could be an asset to Russia. After the collapse of the USSR, some Russian commentators lamented the "brain drain" caused by emigration.[28] However, Valery Tishkov, former minister of nationality affairs of the Russian

Federation and longtime head of the Institute of Ethnology and Anthropology of the Russian Academy of Sciences, considers diasporas "spoilers" of normal interstate relations and points to the "German-Jewish roots of H. Kissinger or the Polish-Jewish roots [sic!] of Z. Brzezinski" as having interfered with their analyses of foreign policy issues.[29] Nevertheless, "both the liberal regime of Yeltsin and the more strong-handed one of Putin pursued a deliberately nonethnicized vision of who should be taken as 'our own people' in the post-Soviet states . . . a very loose concept of 'compatriots' was created; by this the Russian state started to make welcoming gestures (though mainly on paper) towards an amorphous conglomerate of former Soviet citizens speaking the Russian language and retaining some emotional links to Russia."[30] As far as Jews are concerned, in one view "Russia resorts to diasporization practices toward Russian-speaking Jews in an attempt to re-define its national identity as a homeland for all former citizens of the Soviet Union."[31] Language seems decisive here. The Russian Federation under Vladimir Putin has made no such gestures toward Central Asians, Baltic people, or Romanian/Moldovan-speaking Moldovans. Fellow Slavs, Belarusians, and Ukrainians have been embraced with varying degrees of enthusiasm and insistence.[32]

B. *Ambivalence*: The other post-Soviet states have had a complex relationship with their diasporas. Ukraine and the Baltic diasporas include a high proportion of nationalists who saw Soviet rule as an unmitigated disaster. These diasporas have tried to influence their former homelands to be suspicious of, if not hostile to, Russia. Some younger people resent the influence of émigrés and their politics, but the war between Russia and Ukraine has given them pause. Tensions between Belarus and Russia, and the firm commitment of the Baltic States to NATO and the EU, complicate the Russian Federation's relations with those states. On the other hand, Belarus and Kazakhstan have joined a Russian-sponsored customs union.

C. *Embrace*: At least seven postcommunist states (Bulgaria, Slovenia, Slovakia, Ukraine, Romania, Hungary, and Russia [1999]) have adopted diaspora laws that "define the target group in ethno-cultural terms,"[33] rather than by their country of residence. "The Russian law 'On Compatriots' defines compatriots as those . . . born in the same state, who live there or used to live there, and who share a common language, religion, culture, traditions and customs, as well as their direct descendants." Russian law "specifically names tsarist Russia, the USSR, and the Russian Federation as states from which compatriots originate." The government of the Russian Federation has a "Federal Agency for the Commonwealth of Independent States, Compatriots Living Abroad and Inter-cultural Cooperation."

"The Hungarian, Croatian and Romanian constitutions address co-ethnics residing outside the boundaries of the state."[34] Some Hungarians see Hungary as the natural guardian and protector of ethnic Magyars everywhere. The first Hungarian postcommunist prime minister, Jozsef Antall, said upon his election in 1990 that he felt himself to be "in spirit" the prime minister of fifteen million Hungarians, five million more than lived in Hungary at the time. Thus, he appeared to "define nationhood in cultural/ethnic rather than political/civic terms—which, in turn, gave rise to claims in the neighboring countries [particularly Romania and Slovakia] of a revival of Hungarian revisionism."[35]

In 2006, Russian President Vladimir Putin remarked that "what is important to us is that our compatriots abroad have the possibility of preserving their ethnic and cultural identity, be able to protect their lawful rights and interests, and, if they wish, return to their homeland."[36] Even a former Soviet city has reached out to its "translocality." Odessa has established a special department for relations with its worldwide diaspora. Its slogan is: "Odessans of the world, unite!"[37] Poland, Italy, Greece, Israel, and Hungary are among many countries that promote cultural programs, mostly aimed at young people, among their coethnics abroad. Summer language courses, tours, and specialized projects take place in the ancestral homeland. Until the 1970s, India and China encouraged their émigrés to integrate into their host countries. Chinese law still requires Chinese naturalized abroad to give up their Chinese citizenship, but since 2005 India has created an "Overseas Citizenship of India." More states now allow voting from abroad. "Multiple and dual citizenship in the past decades have become widely accepted worldwide," and some states have used this to promote their interests abroad through their diasporas.[38]

2. How do members of the diaspora relate to the homeland and to the state that runs it? These may be separate issues.[39]

   A. *With hostility and disgust*: I recall older people saying to their children, "Why do you want to go to Europe? I ran away from there!" Sometimes, people are ashamed of the place they came from and change their names and habits to disguise their origins.

   B. *With ambivalence*: Some in diasporas regard the "homeland" as "the place we came from and we feel positive about it but we would not want to live there—we did leave, after all." Politically, some émigrés believe that the homeland is a wonderful place but the state is illegitimate or has ruined it. This is the stance taken by many who fled communist countries. They formed the "Assembly of Captive European Nations" (1954–1972) and created a counter-narrative of national history and culture. Ukrainians in Canada are a striking example. Per Rudling asserts that "'community leaders,' claiming to speak on behalf of Ukrainians in Canada, have often taken political positions more radical and nationalistic than popular opinion in Ukraine proper."[40]

   C. *Indifference*: It's where "we" came from, but why would it matter now?

D. *Involvement*: support for the homeland in the new country—politically, philanthropically, economically. The head of the post-Soviet Estonian military, Aleksander Einseln, was a former U.S. Army colonel. The former foreign minister of Armenia, Rafi Hovanissian, was born in the United States; Vaira Vīķe-Freiberga, president of Latvia from 1999 to 2007, lived in Canada from 1954 to 1998. Émigrés' involvement may be oppositionist, trying to change the government, or partisan, supporting a particular party or ideology.

SOVIET EMIGRATION AND DIASPORA

The emigration of large numbers of Soviet Jews was unanticipated and uneven in volume. It was ecstatically welcomed by some and forcefully opposed by others. Its composition, volume, and direction were determined for the most part by governments that sent and received the immigrants, and by the migrants themselves. Four governments (USSR, Israel, U.S., and Germany) were the primary regulators of the emigration. Israel has been the most consistently welcoming and, at some points, insisted that it had an exclusive right to the migrants. The Soviet government consistently opposed the emigration of any of its citizens until the end of the 1980s. In the preceding decade, it had experimented with emigration as a political and social safety valve that would release pressure in an increasingly assertive society by ridding it of dissenters and malcontents. However, the safety valve turned into a boiling cauldron, and attempts to put the lid on the cauldron—through "education taxes," visa denials, exile and imprisonment, and social condemnation—ultimately failed.

The United States favored Jewish emigration from the USSR because it fit perfectly with several aims: 1) it would weaken the Soviet image because mass migration raised doubts about the perfection of Soviet society and the contentment of its citizens; 2) it served the cause of human rights, taken seriously by the administrations of Presidents Ford and Carter, including the right of emigration as delineated in Basket Three of the 1975 Helsinki Accord of the Conference on Security and Co-operation in Europe; 3) it pleased Israel, many Western countries, and a broad domestic constituency, as American Jews had succeeded in linking the cause of Soviet emigration to that of civil and human rights. Soviet Jewry was the one issue that united all American Jews when fissures began to develop in support for Israeli policies. It drew support from the left, focused on human rights, and from the anti-Soviet right.

But in October 1989, U.S. Attorney General Edwin Meese ruled that Soviet Jews were no longer endangered and should not be granted refugee status. It remains a matter of speculation whether this channeling of Soviet Jews to Israel was the result of a deal concluded between an Israeli government—embarrassed by the fact that by 1989, 90 percent of all Soviet émigrés were choosing not to go to Israel—and an American government anxious to force the Israelis to negotiate with the Palestinians. Whatever the reason, the policy change ultimately brought 1,052,747 Jews and their non-Jewish relatives to Israel in the decade between 1989 and 1998, the largest single immigration in Israeli history.

The Federal Republic of Germany, burdened by guilt for the near-total destruction of its historic Jewish population and the murder of 2.7 million Soviet Jews during World War II, saw Soviet Jewish immigration as a way of strengthening a fragile Jewish population and community. There was an ironic echo of *Sonderbehandlung* [special treatment] in the establishment of a separate queue of Jewish visa applicants at the German Embassy in Moscow. Germany offered some attractions to Jewish emigrants that Israel or the United States did not. German authorities were not overly concerned with the Jewish status of the immigrants or their families, and they provided a strong network of social supports. Only because of domestic political and economic pressures Germany changed its generous immigration policies around 2006, cutting social services and requiring that immigrants know some German.

The emigration of Jews from the USSR and its successor states came in several waves. There was a wavelet in 1968–1971 of 17,257 people.[41] Mass emigration began in March 1971 as a result of a decision by the Soviet leadership, and by 1980 (inclusive) 233,788 Jews had emigrated, about 155,000 to Israel and the rest mostly to the United States, with a strong trend after 1974 toward the U.S.[42] Relations between the USSR and the West deteriorated following the Soviet invasion of Afghanistan in December 1979. As a consequence, between 1981 and 1986, only 16,400 Jews were allowed to leave. Clearly, the volume of emigration—which increased when relations with the West were good and decreased as a sign of displeasure with the West—was driven much more by Soviet policy than by Jewish preferences.

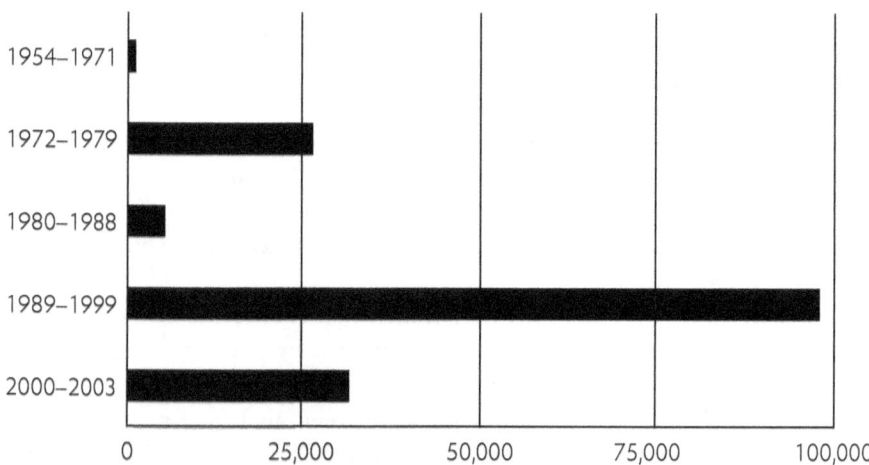

FIGURE I.1. USSR Mean Numbers of Annual Jewish Emigrants

In the early twenty-first century, the number of RSJs immigrating to Israel plummeted by 75 percent, from an average of 45,000 a year between 1997 and 2000, to about 11,000 in 2001–2007. The average number immigrating to the United States dropped from 8,500 a year in 1997–2001 to about 1,500 thereafter. The annual average going to Germany declined from about 15,000 (1995–2005) to less than a thousand after Germany changed its immigration policy in 2005. The drop in immigrants is due to a combination of American and German policies and the emptying of the reservoirs of potential migrants, changes in Israel's image, and the comparative economic situations in countries of origin and destination.

THE DIRECTION OF THE EMIGRATION

In the twentieth century, the direction of the emigration was determined mostly by the aspirations and preferences of emigrants, which were closely associated with their experiences and situations in their native lands. Between 1971 and 1973, 98 percent of emigrants initially went to Israel. By the late 1980s, the majority of Jewish émigrés did not go to Israel. In 1987–1989, when Soviet immigration policy was relaxed due to perestroika, of 98,000 émigrés, only 16,000 went to Israel (17 percent).[43] I attribute the change in the direction of the majority of émigrés to their perception after the October 1973 Middle East war that Israel was in a precarious military, economic, and political situation. Moreover, the first wave of emigration came disproportionately from the Baltic States, the western peripheries of the USSR, and Georgia (a quarter of the immigrants came from Georgia where they were only 2.5 percent of the Soviet Jewish population), areas in which Jewish secular and religious traditions remained relatively strong. Many of the émigrés, especially Georgian Jews, seemed more "pulled to Israel" than "pushed" from the USSR. The change in direction of the émigrés was due not only to their perceptions of Israel, but to their cultures and experiences. The *Zapadniki*, or Westerners, that is, those who had become Soviet citizens as a result of the annexation in 1939–1940 of the Baltic republics, eastern Poland, and Bessarabia-Bukovina (from Romania), were less acculturated than those living under Soviet rule since 1917 or 1921. They had stronger memories of and commitments to Judaism, Hebrew, Yiddish, and Zionism. About a third of the *aliyah* of the 1970s came from these areas, whereas they were probably no more than 10 percent of the Jewish population. Only about 40 percent of the *olim* came from Russia, Belorussia, and Ukraine, which together contained 81 percent of the 1970 population.

The second wave of immigrants came largely from the three Slavic republics and headed for America. From 1975 to 1989 (inclusive), 68.6 percent of the émigrés did not settle in Israel. This wave of émigrés was more "pushed" from the USSR than "pulled to Israel." There was a direct relationship between involvement in Jewish culture and the propensity to immigrate to Israel. The Jews of the Slavic republics, many of them third-generation Soviet citizens, had been cut off from Jewish culture for decades, and had little reason to go to Israel. They sought political and cultural freedom, economic opportunity, and social equality in the West. Since they left on Israeli visas, "dropped out" in Vienna, and transferred to Rome where American Jewish organizations facilitated their entry to the United States, they became a bone of contention between the Israeli government and the Jewish Agency for Israel, on one hand, and the American Jewish community, on the other. Frustrated by the general lack of aliyah, and embarrassed by the fact that tens of thousands of Soviet Jews chose not to go to Israel, Israelis charged that American Jewish organizations were seducing the immigrants in order to justify their staffs and budgets. In turn, most of the American Jewish community declared their support for freedom of choice for the émigrés. American Jews were fascinated, energized, and mobilized by the immigration of tens of thousands of people from the territories from which most of their ancestors had come. Soviet Jewry became the consensual issue for American Jews, even more than support of Israel whose economic problems and policies began to divide American Jewry.

The direction of emigration abruptly reversed in October 1989, when the American government decided that Soviet Jews no longer qualified for refugee status since the Soviet government had ceased to persecute them. They would have to enter the United States under the established immigrant quotas. This policy changed the direction of immigration sharply. Whereas in 1989, 59,024 Soviet immigrants had settled elsewhere than Israel, almost all in the United States, in 1990, 97 percent of the largest single emigration in Russian Jewish history went to Israel. Not just the destination, but the nature of the immigration, had changed again. These were not "born again" Zionists but panicky refugees who viewed with dismay the economic deterioration of the USSR, growing ethnic strife, and the emergence of public, virulent, grassroots anti-Semitism. But now they had to go to Israel, which accepted them unconditionally.[44]

Since September 11, 2001, American restrictions on immigration have been so tightened that only an average of 1,600 RSJs a year arrived in 2002–2005. In fact, for some time Germany became the preferred destination of the émigrés. From 1993 to 2004, an average of 16,000 Jews and their non-Jewish relatives immigrated to Germany every year. Between 2002 and 2004, more Russian Jews went to Germany than to Israel.[45] In January 2005, Germany passed a new immigration law requiring all immigrants to meet some educational and language requirements in order to reduce the burden on the welfare system. German policy even toward its own diaspora shifted from welcoming ethnic German immigrants to supporting their culture abroad.[46] The number of Jewish immigrants to Germany fell to 1,100 in 2006, as compared to an average of 15,000 annually between 1995 and 2005. All in all, by about 2007 emigration from Russia and Ukraine had slowed to a trickle.

The RSJs arrived in the three main receiving countries when those countries were moving away from assimilationist, melting-pot ideologies toward cultural and ethnic pluralism. This worked in favor of their acceptance and, at least in some circles, of their culture, though there was plenty of anti-immigrant animus. In addition to the changing postures of the host countries, a few other factors worked to preserve the distinctiveness of the RSJs: 1) their sheer mass; 2) residential concentration; 3) pride in their culture rather than the embarrassment immigrants often feel; 4) the distance of their cultures and mentalities from those of their host cultures and societies.

What is the future of the Russian-speaking Jewish diaspora? As one wag observed, it's very hard to predict—especially the future. But perhaps the precedent of the pre–World War II, East European, Yiddish-speaking diaspora is instructive, and Jonathan Dekel-Chen (chapter 4) usefully places the recent immigration in historical context. The links of family, friends, acquaintances, shared experiences, and cultures were the same. There was a Yiddish and East European "way of life," defined by language, religious practices, food, humor, customs, and clothes. It connected the Jews of Argentina, Belgium, Brazil, France, England, Lithuania, Mexico, Palestine, Poland, the United States, and to the extent politics permitted, the USSR. Actors, writers, tourists, businessmen, and students traversed "Yiddishland" with ease, as did those visiting relatives. World War II and the Holocaust ruptured these connections and weakened the connective power of the Yiddish language, perhaps fatally. But even without the war, there were indications that Jewish immigrants were settling in to their new cultures and societies and felt less of a connection to their places of origin. An activist in a *landsmanshaft* (immigrant association) in New York, observed that early immigrants

> cursed Columbus for having discovered such a country where it's so hard to earn a piece of bread . . . and though all knew that the *alter haym* [old home] was cut off and one must adjust to America, one looked for a *haymishe* [warm, intimate, homelike] atmosphere among one's own *landsleit* . . . . The leadership of the organization stated emphatically that the organization must always be connected to the *alter haym*, so that, if for example, a fire broke out . . . Heaven forbid, our duty would be to rebuild the town as quickly as possible.
>
> Despite all our efforts . . . we have not succeeded in attracting our sons [*zin*] as members of our *landsmanshaftn* . . . . This problem occupies all existing *landsmanshaftn* . . . . The reason is clear, they are in a far better position than we were as newcomers. The present-day immigrant has someone to turn to, he has established relatives, etc. He seeks to forget the *alter haym* which is associated with horrible memories. The longing for a *haymisher* environment has been extinguished.[47]

Émigrés from the Former Soviet Union may be more attached to the dominant culture and the Soviet mores of their native lands than were the earlier Jewish immigrants from the same territories, perhaps with the exception of some earlier intelligentsia and highly politicized émigrés from Eastern Europe and Jews who fled Nazi Germany. Why is this the case? 1) The earlier immigrants had no part in the tsarist state, whereas Jews had helped build the Soviet state, economy, culture, military; 2) they spoke a minority language, Yiddish, whereas the present immigrants speak Russian, the language of the general population and of the dominant culture; 3) many of the earlier immigrants came with few skills and little education but moved up rapidly socially and economically, reinforcing negative feelings about the "old country," whereas present-day migrants are generally highly educated and skilled and often experience downward mobility, arousing skepticism about the "new country's" appreciation of them; 4) the older emigration was more attached to a "thick" Jewish culture, religious and secular, whereas the new emigration has only a "thin" distinctive culture and can more easily identify with the dominant non-Jewish culture; 5) the older immigrants who mostly identified themselves with the religious tradition, though many threw it overboard, came to societies that valued religion and disparaged ethnicity. They could present themselves as Jewish religionists, not another ethnic group, especially since they did not come from a single country. As Eli Lederhandler puts it, "Their 'country of origin' is a transnational, religio-cultural diaspora, abounding with more than the usual assortment of language/dialect groups, but professing only one religion.... Official non-recognition of American Jews as an ethnicity is an established tradition."[48] Today's migrants are mostly secular but, if they are associated by others with any religion, it is Judaism.

Another major difference in the two Jewish diasporas is the nature of international communications. Letters that took weeks to arrive have been replaced by e-mail and the Internet that provide instant, more intense communication. As one researcher puts it, "Cyberspace, the 'nowhere' land, is the most appropriate realm for expressing migrant cultural mobility and repositioning."[49] The World Wide Web is precisely that for many of the Russian-speaking Jews, as Anna Shternshis demonstrates in chapter 14. It connects them more rapidly, frequently, and intensely than was the case with the Yiddish-speaking diaspora.

It is not only the new technologies that bind people together more intensely. Larissa Remennick surveyed 800 Russophone immigrants in Israel. She found that 20 percent made annual trips to their original homes; 40 percent made such trips every few years. Half the interviewees reported calling friends and family, and over three-quarters had hosted someone from the FSU in their homes. Fifteen percent own a small business with ties to the FSU.[50]

These connections, both virtual and face-to-face, do not necessarily indicate attachment to the *countries* from which the immigrants came. In fact, like their Yiddish-speaking predecessors, many have negative feelings about those countries. Some of the present émigrés display "nostalgia for birch trees" [the Russian landscape] but not for their former states. Perhaps, like American Jews of later generations, their children will have more neutral feelings but some curiosity about their parents' countries and cultures of origins.

An indicator of the present generation's fealty to their culture and, specifically, Russian or Russian-Jewish identities, is that they retain their first and last names. In the past, in America, Yitzchoks became Irvings, Moishes became Morrises,

Gitls became Gertrudes, and Shprintsehs were transformed into Shirleys. In the 1970s, in Israel, there was some tendency for Vladimir to become Ze'ev, and Ilya to become Eliyahu, or Natasha became Nili and Iulia or Elena morphed into Ilana. Later, it seems, in all the countries of immigration, including Israel, Boris and Efim, Masha and Anya remain as they were. This may be because those societies have become more tolerant of ethnic and nominal pluralism, so that attempts at symbolic acculturation are not seen as necessary, but it may also indicate pride in one's origin and culture. Does this mean that "straight-line theory" whereby acculturation leads to assimilation will not hold true among RSJs? I think it will. What are Vadim and Ksenia naming their children? And when Vadim marries a Melissa, or Ksenia marries a Yoram, what will they name their children?

My impression is that the proportion of RSJ–RSJ marriages is high among first-generation immigrants, just as it was in earlier times in Israel and the United States. But as marriages increasingly cross ethnic lines, linguistic acculturation goes on, and ways of life come to resemble those of the larger society, what will remain of Russian-speaking origin will be the kind of symbolic ethnicity that Herbert Gans famously discussed.[51] I notice fewer Soviet-origin students knowing how to read and write Russian, though they continue to speak it, some with American accents.

The Holocaust dried up the stream of international connections and mutual reinforcement based on Yiddish and shared East European cultures. Parallel processes will occur as the number of Russian-speaking Jews in the Former Soviet Union and of emigrants continues to shrink. Of course, should there be a drastic deterioration in the polities, societies, and economies of Russia and Ukraine, emigration may resume, though never in its previous dimensions. The "sending" population has shrunk enormously.[52]

LIVING IN THE ARCHIPELAGO

In the past, people felt constrained to declare one homeland and pledge exclusive allegiance to it. Today, people can "feel at home" in several countries, particularly if they are bound together in an entity like the European Union. Some people feel they have a "motherland" and a "fatherland." For a while, it was believed that technology and the diffusion of innovation would bring the world together, homogenize it, and erase the boundaries that set people apart from each other. This would be a good thing, it was thought, for familiarity would breed tolerance, similarity would engender understanding, homogeneity would eliminate rivalry. It turns out that technology and sameness do not eliminate emotions. People feel something about their homes. Home is a mental construct, not only a physical place. But the human mind can inhabit more than one home at a time. Yet, one may not be fully "at home" in any. There are immigrants who, having left the old home, do not see themselves as living in a new one. The first generation of immigrants might be sojourners mentally, for the most part. They may not be completely at home and might even be psychologically homeless. They are at one end of a spectrum of relationships people have to homes: some have several, some one, and some none. Life can be lived in any of them. There are many islands in the archipelago that link the homeland or homelands with the diasporas. Perhaps, as John Donne put it, "no man is an island," but each of us inhabits a specific place, as another English writer centuries later put it, in a room or rooms of our own. To change the metaphor, if "home is where the heart is," we should remember that the heart has four chambers.

NOTES

1. "The notion of diaspora is often used casually, in an untheorized way [and] seems now loosely to refer to any communities in the world living far from their natal homelands." Robin Cohen, *Global Diasporas: An Introduction* (Seattle: University of Washington Press, 1997), x, quoted in William Safran, "Comparing Diasporas: A Review Essay," *Diaspora* 8.3 (1999): 264. Stephane Dufoix observes, "In the space of about fifteen years, 'diaspora' has evolved into an all-purpose word used to describe a growing number of populations." *Diasporas* (Berkeley: University of California Press, 2008), 30. There are many citations to the literature on diasporas in a study of Russian-speaking intellectuals who emigrated. See Irina Isaakyan, "'Platoon' Friendship of the Soviet Academic Disapora," *Studies in Ethnicity and Nationalism* 10.2 (2010): 271–289.
2. "Globalization" means the process of international integration through the interchange of ideas, products, and perhaps values. Cristina Bradatan and her coauthors argue that "transnationals" are those who not only master the languages of their countries of origin and immigration, but can operate socially among people in both. See Adrian Popan, Cristina Bradatan, and Rachel Melton, "Transnationality as a Fluid Social Identity," *Social Identities* 16.2 (March 2010): 174. See the introduction in Eliezer Ben-Rafael and Yitzhak Sternberg, eds., *Transnationalism: Diasporas and the Advent of a New (Dis)order* (Leiden-Boston: Brill, 2009), 1–28.
3. William Safran, "Deconstructing and Comparing Diasporas," in *Diaspora, Identity and Religion*, ed. Waltraud Kokot, Khachig Tololyan, and Carolin Alfonso (London: Routledge, 2004), 9.
4. Roger Waldinger, introduction to Dufoix, *Diasporas*, xvi.
5. According to Mark Tolts, "Of all FSU immigrants to Israel since 1990, 125,100 had left the country by the end of 2009 and stayed abroad continuously for one year or more. However, a sizable number (23,700) of these have since returned to Israel, and this return is continuing. . . . About 10 percent . . . left Israel without returning." See "Demography of the Contemporary Russian-Speaking Jewish Diaspora" (paper presented at the Conference on the Russian-Speaking Jewish Diaspora, Davis Center for Russian and Eurasian Studies, November 13–15, 2011), 17.
6. Alina Dizik, "Enough with Russia, Already: I Want to Be an American," *Tablet*, July 3, 2014, http://www.tabletmag.com/jewish-life-and-religion/175857/russian-american?print.
7. "Family: The Refusenik That Wasn't," *Jewcy*, October 7, 2013.
8. David Bezmozgis, *The Free World* (Toronto: HarperCollins, 2011), 58.
9. "Do not fear for I am with you, from the east I shall bring your descendants and gather you from the west." Ezekiel 36:19: "I scattered them among the nations, and they were dispersed among the countries. . . . But I had pity . . . And will take you from among the nations and *bring you to your own land. . . . and you shall dwell in the land I gave to your fathers.*"
10. See Gur Alroey, "Angolan Zion: The Jewish Territorial Organization and the Idea of a Jewish State in Western Africa, 1907–1913," *Journal of Modern Jewish Studies* 14.2 (July 2015): 179–198, and the works by Bar-Yosef, Heyman, Rovner and Weisbord cited therein.

11. Ephraim Nimni, "From Galut to T'futsoth: Post-Zionism and the Dislocation of Jewish Diasporas," in *The Challenge of Post-Zionism: Alternatives to Israeli Fundamentalist Politics*, ed. E. Nimni (New York: Palgrave, 2003), 117–152.
12. United Nations General Assembly, 1st Special Session, 77th Plenary Meeting, quoted in Yaacov Ro'i, ed., *From Encroachment to Involvement* (New York: John Wiley, 1974), 38.
13. Daniel Boyarin and Jonathan Boyarin, "Diaspora: Generation and the Ground of Jewish Identity," *Critical Inquiry* 19.4 (Summer, 1993): 712, 723. The essay is reprinted in *Theorizing Diaspora*, ed. Jana Evans Braziel and Anita Mannur (Malden, MA: Blackwell, 2006), 85–118.
14. See Irving Zeitlin, *Jews: The Making of a Diaspora People* (Cambridge: Polity, 2012), 26–28.
15. Sergio DellaPergola, *World Jewish Population 2010* (North American Jewish Data Bank, University of Connecticut, Current Jewish Population Reports no. 2), 10.
16. Ibid., "Our 2010 assessment of the total *core* Jewish population for the 15 republics of the FSU is 330,000, of whom 311,400 lived in Europe and 18,600 in Asia" (50).
17. "Emigration from and Immigration to Russia," in *International Migrations* 2, ed. W. F. Willcox (New York, 1931), quoted in Anatoly Vishnevsky, "The Dissolution of the Soviet Union and Post-Soviet Ethnic Migration: the Return of Diasporas?" in *Diasporas and Ethnic Migrants*, ed. Rainer Munz and Rainer Ohliger (London: Frank Cass, 2003), 157.
18. The debate is joined in Steven M. Cohen and Ari Y. Kelman, "Thinking about Distancing from Israel," *Contemporary Jewry* 30.2–3 (October 2010): 287–296; and, by contrast, in Theodore Sasson, Charles Kadushin, and Leonard Saxe, "Trends in American Jewish Attachment to Israel: An Examination of the 'Distancing' Hypothesis," *Contemporary Jewry* 30.2–3 (October 2010): 297–319. See articles by Ariela Keysar and Ron Miller in the same issue.
19. Gabriel Sheffer, "Loyalty and Criticism in the Relations between World Jewry and Israel" (paper presented at the 2011 Israeli Presidential Conference, Jerusalem, Israel, July 2011).
20. Ben-Rafael and Sternberg, *Transnationalism*, 5.
21. *Global Diasporas*, 2nd ed. (London: Routledge, 2008), 8. Central Asian, Georgian, and Mountain Jews represent subcultures within the subculture.
22. Mark Tolts, "Demography of the Contemporary Russian-Speaking Jewish Diaspora," 2–3.
23. Elena Barabantseva and Claire Sutherland, "Diaspora and Citizenship: Introduction," *Nationalism and Ethnic Politics* 17.1 (2011): 2.
24. Ludmila Isurin, *Russian Diaspora: Culture, Identity and Language Change* (New York: deGruyter, 2011), 202.
25. "We must escape the facile opposition between national societies and transnational society, reminiscent of those binary oppositions that encumber sociological thought in the style of primitive society vs. modern society, Gemeinschaft vs. Gesellschaft." See Dominique Schnapper, "From the Nation-State to the Transnational World: On the Meaning and Usefulness of Diaspora as a Concept," *Diaspora* 8.3 (1999): 250. "Just like diaspora, homeland . . . is a dynamic, fluid, and contingent concept that does more to organize the world than to describe it." See Illa Ben-Porat, "Perpetual Diaspora, Changing Homelands: the Construction of Russian-Speaking Jews as a Diaspora of Both Israel and Russia," *Nationalism and Ethnic Politics* 17 (2011): 76. "The nation-state container view of society does not adequately capture the complex interconnectedness of contemporary reality." See Ben-Rafael and Sternberg, *Transnationalism*, 3–4.
26. Isurin finds that RSJs in Israel consider Israel their "home" but "admit feeling like outsiders." Op. cit., 202.
27. Brandy Jones discerns five types of "models of diaspora-homeland relations engaged [*sic*] by sending countries and their diasporas. . . . Economic collaboration, Transitional, Global nation-state, Dissident, and Crisis relations." See "Bringing Africa into the Study of Transnationalism: The Senegalese Global Nation-State" (PhD diss., University of Michigan, 2007), 73.
28. Otto Latsis, "Who Is Leaving Russia and Why," *Noviye Izvestia*, July 5, 2002, transl. in *Current Digest of Post-Soviet Press* 54.28 (2002): 7. See also Mora Flynn, "Returning Home?

Approaches to Repatriation and Migrant Resettlement in Post-Soviet Russia," in *Diasporas and Ethnic Migrants: Germany, Israel and Post-Soviet Successor States in Comparative Perspective*, ed. Rainer Munz and Rainer Ohliger (London: Frank Cass, 2003), 173–187.

29. Valery Tishkov, *Rekviem po etnosu* (Moscow: Nauka, 2003), 468.

30. Natalya Kosmarskaya, "Russia and Post-Soviet 'Russian Diaspora': Contrasting Visions, Conflicting Projects," *Nationalism and Ethnic Politics* 17.1 (2011): 59–60.

31. Barabantseva and Sutherland, "Diaspora and Citizenship: Introduction," 11.

32. The evolution of post-Soviet Russian governmental attitudes toward the Russian diaspora is traced by Igor Zevelev, "Russia and the Russian Diasporas," in *Race and Ethnicity: Comparative and Theoretical Approaches*, ed. John Stone and Rutledge Dennis (Oxford: Blackwell, 2003). Dual citizenship was encouraged in the early 1990s but was seen as threatening those states in which a Russian diaspora lived. The "compatriot" idea has pretty much replaced it. "Compatriots" are not only ethnic Russians but all nationalities whose "roots" are in the former Soviet Union.

On Russian policy toward its diaspora, see also V. S. Buyanov, R. G. Gadzhieva, and L. O. Ternovaia, *Russkaia identichnost' v usloviiakh globalizatsiii* (Moscow: Izdatel'stvo RAGS, 2008). On dual citizenship policies, see Thomas Faist, Jurgen Gerdes, and Beate Rieple, "Dual Citizenship as a Path-Dependent Process," *International Migration Review* 38.3 (Fall 2004): 913–944; and Marc Morje Howard, "Variations in Dual Citizenship Policies in the Countries of the European Union," *International Migration Review* 39.3 (Fall 2005): 697–720.

33. Oxana Shevel, "The Post-Communist Diaspora Laws," *East European Politics and Societies* 24.1 (Winter 2010): 160.

34. Bill Kissane and Nick Sitter, "The Marriage of State and Nation in European Constitutions," *Nations and Nationalism* 16.1 (January 2010): 62.

35. Agnes Batory, "Kin-State Identity in the European Context: Citizenship, Nationalism, and Constitutionalism in Hungary," *Nations and Nationalism* 16.1 (January 2010): 39. When the socialists came to power in 1994, Batory states, their leader, Prime Minister Gyula Horn, "promptly declared himself to be the prime minister of 'only' ten million Hungarians—signaling that the Socialist-liberal concept of political community was defined by citizenship rather than blood or language."

36. *Russkaya mysl*, quoted in Dufoix, *Diasporas*, 86.

37. Vera Skvirskaja, "New Diaspora in a Post-Soviet City: Transformations in Experiences of Belonging in Odesa, Ukraine," *Studies in Ethnicity and Nationalism* 10.1 (2010): 76–91. The organization is called the "Worldwide Club of Odessa." It publishes a newspaper and raises funds for the city's cultural needs. Cities often generate a kind of *lokal-patriotismus*. Parisians, Berliners, New Yorkers, Jerusalemites, Muscovites, and St. Petersburgers, among others, will attest to that.

38. Szablocs Pogonyi, "Dual Citizenship and Sovereignty," *Nationalities Papers* 39.5 (September 2011): 685.

39. Long ago a prominent Jewish sociologist observed that "The nature of the émigré's ties with his native land varies. . . . The paradox [is] that immigrants from highly developed countries, Swedes, Englishmen, Norwegians, Danes are less closely attached to their mother country than immigrants from backward, impoverished lands, Poles, Ukrainians, Lithuanians, Letts, etc. Apparently, the former, children of rich and free peoples, are confident of the survival of their original national groups . . . the latter emigrants . . . take with them the unrest of their early homes and even in their new country bear for quite a long time the yoke of battle for freedom of the native land." See Jacob Lestchinsky, "Jewish Migrations, 1840–1946," in *The Jews: Their History, Culture and Religion*, ed. Louis Finkelstein (Philadelphia: Jewish Publication Society, 1949), 4:1199.

On the different ways Arab-Americans relate to the Middle East, see Kenneth Wald, "The Diaspora Project of Arab Americans: Assessing the Magnitude and Determinants of Politicized Ethnic Idntity," *Ethnic and Racial Studies* 32.8 (October 2009): 1304–1324.

40. See Per Rudling, "Multiculturalism, Memory, and Ritualization: Ukrainian Nationalist Monuments in Edmonton, Alberta," *Nationalities Papers* 39.5 (2011): 756. Rudling writes that "Official multiculturalism has given Ukrainian nationalists a new lease on life, assisted them in raising new generations in an authoritarian, illiberal and intolerant political tradition."

41. Based on a table in Baruch Gur, *Le-akhar Gorbachev* (Jerusalem: World Zionist Organization, 1995), 112. Other sources differ slightly.

42. For documentation of Soviet decisions on emigration issues, see Boris Morozov, *Evreiskaya emigratsiia v svetle novykh dokumentov* (Tel Aviv: Tel Aviv University Press, 1988).

43. Calculations based on figures in Baruch Gur, *Le-akhar Gorbachev*.

44. For an analysis, see Zvi Gitelman, "Glasnost, Perestroika and Antisemitism," *Foreign Affairs* 70.2 (Spring 1991): 141–159.

45. Based on data in Mark Tolts, "Post-Soviet Aliyah and Jewish Demographic Transformation" (Paper presented at the 15th World Congress of Jewish Studies, Jerusalem, Israel, August 2–6, 2009), table 1.

46. See, for example, James Koranyi and Ruth Wittlinger, "From Diaspora to Diaspora: The Case of Transylvanian Saxons in Romania and Germany," *Nationalism and Ethnic Politics* 17:1 (2011): 106–107.

47. Azriel Galai, "Musher un Baranovitsher farayn in Niu-York," in *Baranovits: sefer zikaron* (Tel Aviv: Irgun yotsai Baranovits be-Yisrael, 1952), 648, 656.

48. *Jewish Immigrants and American Capitalism, 1880–1920: From Caste to Class* (Cambridge: Cambridge University Press, 2009), xiii.

49. Ruxandra Trandafoiu, *Diaspora Online: Identity Politics and Romanian Migrants* (New York: Berghahn, 2013), 150. See chapter 14 of this book for an elaboration of the role played by the Internet among migrants.

50. Larissa Remennick, "Transnatsional'nye tendentsii v zhizni Russkoiazychnoi obshchiny Izralil'ia," in *'Russkoe' litso Izrail'ia: cherty sotsial'nogo portreta*, ed. Moshe Kenigshtein (Moscow: Mosty, 2007), 429.

51. Herbert Gans, "Symbolic Ethnicity," *Ethnic and Racial Studies* 2.1 (1979): 1–20.

52. Myria Georgiou postulates that community is based on "a) co-presence, which might be real, virtual or tele-presence . . . b) memory, which is communal and selective and relates to the imagined We, the imagined Others and the common myth of roots and routes . . . c) future outlook, which is necessary for existence." In *Diaspora Identity and the Media* (Creeskill, NJ: Hampton Press, 2006), 51. "Virtual" and "tele-presence" depend on a person's desire to connect; memories fade or disappear; "future outlooks" may well have nothing to do with the "old country."

William Safran lists "many factors" that determine the survival of a diaspora and concludes that "the collective identity of a diaspora and its long-term prospects depend above all on the political context of the host country and, albeit to a lesser extent, on conditions in the homeland." See "Democracy, Pluralism, and Diaspora Identity: An Ambiguous Relationship," in *Opportunity Structures in Diaspora Relations: Comparisons in Contemporary Multilevel Politics of Diaspora and Transnational Identity*, ed. Gloria Totoricaguena (Reno: Center for Basque Studies, University of Nevada, 2007), 157. Safran asks, "Does a politics of inclusion of immigrants and their descendants secure the maintenance of diaspora identity, or does it distill and weaken such an identity? The evidence is ambiguous" (178).

PART I DEMOGRAPHY

Who Are the Migrants and
Where Have They Gone?

Not since the late nineteenth century have as many Jews migrated as the nearly two million Jews who left the Soviet Union between 1971 and 2009. Soviet authorities made emigration well-nigh impossible for citizens of the USSR until early 1971 when they permitted a few, highly selected Jews to leave for other countries. Nearly 300,000 left—more than half of them to Israel—between 1971 and the end of 1988. In the 1970s and 1980s, emigration was carefully restricted to ethnic Jews, Germans, some Armenians, and Christian evangelical groups. But as Mikhail Gorbachev changed the Soviet system with his policies of *glasnost* [openness] and *perestroika* [reconstruction] emigration became a realistic option for a broad swath of Soviet citizens. Economic instability and social unrest propelled over a million and a half Jews and their non-Jewish close relatives to emigrate. Nearly a million went to Israel, constituting the single largest immigration (*aliyah*, in Israeli parlance) in its history. The rest went mostly to the United States and Germany.

No one has studied the composition and direction of this mass migration more closely than Mark Tolts, himself a native of the Soviet Union. In his chapter, he lays out the most important contours of the migration, showing where in the USSR the migrants originated, which countries they immigrated to and when. Tolts argues that the "push" factors propelling them to leave played a greater role than the "pull" factors attracting them to the particular countries to which they immigrated. He also illuminates the domestic and international considerations that affected each country's migration policies.

As with all international migrations, some immigrants return to their countries of origin. Tolts estimates that about 10 percent of the Russian-speaking immigrants to Israel have done so—a low proportion compared with other migrations to Israel and to other countries of immigration. This chapter analyzes the demographic changes that have taken place among the immigrants in Israel, and the impact of this mass migration on Israel's present and future.

Demographer Uzi Rebhun's chapter deals with Russian-speaking Jews who immigrated to Israel and later returned to the former Soviet Union (FSU) or moved to a third country. He describes and seeks to account for the patterns of religious and ethnic identification and attachment to Israel among Russian-speaking Israelis (RSIs) abroad. Rebhun addresses three questions: 1) what are the patterns of Jewish identification and attachment to Israel among RSIs? 2) how do *return* migrants (those who immigrated to Israel and later returned to their country of origin) differ from *repeat* migrants (those who immigrated to Israel and later moved to a third destination)? and 3) how do key migration factors (such as duration in Israel and time elapsed since leaving Israel), as well as demographic and socioeconomic characteristics, affect Jewish identification and attachment to Israel? Using data from an online survey, Rebhun finds that RSIs in the FSU have the strongest group identification, followed by their peers in North America. Those settling in West-Central Europe have the weakest identification. He attributes much of this to the differing environments in which the migrants find themselves. The FSU environment is most supportive of Jewish group identity, for reasons Rebhun details. RSIs who settled in West-Central Europe are repeat migrants. They are challenged to adjust to a new place and its culture, and face a strong national ethos of clear, unequivocal local commitment. While the ethos of North America is civic nationality, wherein people are connected through a common polity rather than common ethnicity and religion, many European countries are ethnic nations, rooted in shared history, religion, customs, and the culture of its inhabitants, thus making it difficult for newcomers to maintain distinct group affiliation.

Focusing on a particular group of migrants, those who returned to Odessa (Ukraine) from Israel, Marina Sapritsky uses an ethnographic approach to capture the variety of motivations and behaviors that might characterize the small proportion of those RSJs who returned from Israel to the places from which they emigrated. "The actual experiences of returnees displayed a mosaic of different orientations, attachments, and associations constructed by returnees about their past and present locations and homes." Some throw themselves into local Jewish life, while others distance themselves from it, even converting to Christianity. The ambivalences displayed by her interviewees illustrate the complexity of the concepts "home" and "diaspora," made even less clear by the current fluidity of populations across international borders. The blurred lines between homeland and diaspora will appear in subsequent chapters. Massive movements across political and national borders, with many people moving from country to country several times, do not render "home" and "diaspora" meaningless, as some would have it, but the categories are less sharply defined and may have shifting meanings. Migration is as challenging and complicated as ever, primarily to migrants themselves, to sending and receiving states and societies, and to those who would analyze it.

1 · DEMOGRAPHY OF THE CONTEMPORARY RUSSIAN-SPEAKING JEWISH DIASPORA

MARK TOLTS

In the course of the 1990s, most of the second largest Jewish Diaspora population, which resided in the former Soviet Union (FSU), changed their places of residence. The majority immigrated to Israel; the rest were divided mostly between the United States and Germany. This was a continuation of the mass migration that started in the 1970s, and was temporarily halted in the 1980s. However, the emigration of the 1990s was much larger than that of the 1970s. This chapter describes the Soviet and post-Soviet Jewish migration and resettlement as well as its demographic dynamics, and estimates the worldwide size and distribution of the contemporary post-Soviet Jewish Diaspora.[1] In studying the demography of this diaspora population, we use data from very different statistical sources collected from the many countries where these Jews live.[2]

RECENT MASS MIGRATION

For many years, Soviet Jews, like all other citizens of the USSR, had no real possibility to emigrate in sizable numbers, but this changed in the 1970s. Between 1970 and 1988, a total of roughly 291,000 Soviet Jews and their relatives emigrated from the country, the majority of whom—approximately 165,000—came to Israel (see table 1.1).

However, only after 1989 did mass emigration, in particular, to Israel, play a decisive role in the fate of Jews in the FSU. Estimates are that between 1989 and 2009, more than 1.6 million Jews and their relatives emigrated from the FSU. Approximately 61 percent of this migration (about 998,000 people) went to Israel; the rest went mostly to the United States and Germany. During this period the number of Jews and their relatives who emigrated from the FSU to the U.S.

TABLE 1.1. Emigration of Jews and Their Relatives from the FSU, 1970–2009, in Thousands

Year	Total	Israel	U.S.[a]	Germany	Percent of total to Israel
1970–1988	291	165	126	...	57
1989	72	12.9	56[b]	0.6	18
1990	205	185.2	6.5[b]	8.5	90
1991	195	147.8	35.2	8.0	76
1992	123	65.1	45.9	4.0	53
1993	127	66.1	35.9	16.6	52
1994	116	68.1	32.9	8.8	59
1995	114	64.8	21.7	15.2	57
1996	106	59.0	19.5	16.0	56
1997	99	54.6	14.5	19.4	55
1998	83	46.0	7.4	17.8	55
1999	99	66.8	6.3	18.2	67
2000	79	50.8	5.9	16.5	64
2001	60	33.6	4.1	16.7	56
2002	44	18.5	2.5	19.3	42
2003	32	12.4	1.6	15.4	39
2004	25	10.1	1.1	11.2	40
2005	18	9.4	0.9	6.0	52
2006	10	7.5	0.6	1.1	75
2007	10	6.5	0.3	2.5	65
2008	8	5.6	0.2	1.4	70
2009	9	6.8	0.2	1.1	76
1989–2009	1,634	998	326[c]	224	61
1970–2009	1,925	1,163	...	...	60

SOURCE: Mark Tolts, "After the Exodus: Post-Soviet Jewry in the Contemporary World," in *International Migration: Economics and Politics*, ed. V. A. Iontsev (Moscow: TEIS, 2006), 70 [updated].
[a] Data for 1970–1988 include all destinations other than Israel for those who emigrated with Israeli visas; annual data for 1991–2009 cover only those immigrants who were assisted by the Hebrew Immigrant Aid Society (HIAS).
[b] Departures from the Soviet Union.
[c] Including migrants who were not assisted by HIAS.

is estimated at about 326,000, while the number emigrating to Germany was about 224,000.

This emigration peaked in 1990–1991—the last two years of severe crisis preceding the dissolution of the Soviet Union—when about 400,000 Soviet Jews and their relatives left the USSR; of these, 333,000 (83 percent) went to Israel. The rate of this great exodus was significantly higher than the mass Jewish emigration from the Russian Empire around the turn of the twentieth century.[3] Between 1992 and 1998, slightly more than half of those who emigrated from the FSU chose Israel. Only in 1999 did Israel's share of the emigrants jump to 67 percent when immigration to Israel temporarily increased after the Russian financial crash in the previous year. On the other hand, since 2000, significant economic growth has resumed in the FSU countries and emigration to Israel has decreased rather steadily. These data clearly illustrate the decisive role of the "push" factor in this migration movement. Our findings coincide with the generally decisive role of push factors in global Jewish migration.[4]

In the 1990s, the United States introduced quotas that limited the possibility of ex-Soviet Jewish immigration to only those persons who had close relatives already living in the country.[5] Nevertheless, between 1991 and 1996, the United States ranked second as a receiving country. Between 1997 and 2001, more emigrants went to Germany than to the United States. In the early 1990s, Germany introduced a special program for Jewish immigration from the FSU, which eventually made it the second-ranking receiving country.[6] After September 11, 2001, the United States ceased to be a major destination for ex-Soviet Jewish emigration as immigration rules tightened greatly. From 2002 to 2004, more emigrants went to Germany than to Israel, and Germany temporarily became the first-ranking receiving country. Since 2005, after Germany's admission policy became much more restrictive,[7] the number of Jews and their relatives who immigrated to Germany dropped dramatically, and Israel again became the first-ranking receiving country for ex-Soviet Jewish emigration. Israel keeps its borders open unselectively to Jewish immigration in accordance with the Law of Return, enacted in 1950 by the Israeli parliament (the Knesset) and amended in 1970 to include Jews, their children and grandchildren, and all spouses of persons eligible for immigration to Israel (*aliyah*).

In 2009, a severe global economic crisis affected all FSU states; however, its impact on the Israeli economy was much more moderate. In 2009, the gross domestic product in all eleven FSU countries that are members of the Commonwealth of Independent States (CIS) fell by 6.9 percent.[8] This decrease was even more pronounced in the principal country of concentration of Jews still in the FSU—the Russian Federation—where GDP declined 7.8 percent.[9] In striking contrast, Israel's gross domestic product increased in 2009 by 0.8 percent.[10] The decrease in emigration from the FSU to Israel reversed, and in 2009, the number of immigrants from FSU countries as a whole increased by 21 percent and by 25 percent from the Russian Federation alone. In that year, Israel's share among all the emigrants returned to the level of 1991—76 percent. This recent reversal of migration dynamics again confirms the decisive role of the push factor in the migration of Jews from the FSU.

During the years of mass migration, 1989–2001, Israel was the predominant receiver for each sending region. Among FSU immigrants to Israel, the proportion of those who originated in Ukraine and the Russian Federation was about equal—33 and 32 percent, respectively.[11] Jews and their relatives from Transcaucasia and Central Asia were especially inclined to migrate to Israel. About 13 percent of the newcomers from the FSU in Israel were from Central Asia, making them the third largest subgroup among the ex-Soviet migrants. During the period 1989–2001, the recorded number of immigrants to Israel alone from each formerly Soviet region (except the Baltic States) was higher than the entire emigration from the entire Soviet Union over the previous nineteen years, 1970–1988 (see table 1.2).

According to estimates for 1989–2001, among those who immigrated to the United States, the absolute number of Ukrainian Jews and their relatives was 1.6 times higher than that from the Russian Federation. The absolute number of Ukrainian Jews and their relatives who immigrated to Germany was double the number of those from the Russian Federation. Consequently, among FSU emigrants to the United States, and even more so to Germany, the share of those originating in Ukraine was dominant—41 and 56 percent, respectively. The share of those immigrating to these two countries from the Russian Federation was much lower—26 and 27 percent, respectively. Among migrants to Germany, the number of those originating in Transcaucasia and Central Asia was very low, approximately equal to that of the Baltic States, despite the tremendous discrepancy in the sizes of the Jewish populations in these regions at the start of this migration.

According to the results of the 1989 Soviet census, 31 percent of the Jews in Russia lived in Moscow, 19 percent in St. Petersburg, and half in the "provinces." The data show that the share of migrants to Israel from St. Petersburg among the total number of emigrants from the Russian Federation peaked in 1990

TABLE 1.2. Emigration of Jews and Their Relatives from the FSU to Israel, the U.S., and Germany, by Republic (Country)/Region, 1970–1988 and 1989–2001, in Thousands

Republic (country)/region	Total, 1970–1988[a]	To Israel, 1989–2001	To the U.S., 1989–2001[b]	To Germany, 1989–2001[b]
Russian Federation	50.4	291.2	81.1	45.0
Ukraine	106.7	299.8	128.5	92.7
Belorussia/Belarus	13.8	70.4	34.4	6.1
Baltic States	27.3	21.4	8.0	7.2
Moldavia/Moldova	29.4	48.3	15.7	8.1
Transcaucasia	41.5	56.5	10.8	2.2
Central Asia	21.7	114.7	35.5	5.0
Unknown	0.0	18.8	0.0	0.0
Total	290.8	921.1	314.0	166.3

SOURCES: Mark Kupovetsky, "K otsenke chislennosti evreev i demograficheskogo potentsiala evreiskoi obshchiny v SSSR i postsovetskikh gosudarstvakh v 1989–2003 gg.," *Evroaziatskii evreiskii ezhegodnik 5765 (2004/2005) god* (Kiev: Dukh i Litera, 2005), 89; Mark Tolts, "Demography of the Jews in the Former Soviet Union: Yesterday and Today," in *Jewish Life After the USSR*, ed. Zvi Gitelman, with Musya Glants and Marshall I. Goldman (Bloomington: Indiana University Press, 2003), 178; Mark Tolts, "Migration since World War I," in *The YIVO Encyclopedia of Jews in Eastern Europe*, ed. Gershon D. Hundert (New Haven, CT: Yale University Press, 2008), 1438; Table 1.1 of this chapter.
[a] Including all destinations for those who emigrated with Israeli visas.
[b] Estimate for republic/region is based on the known distribution of emigrants which was adjusted for the total number for the FSU in this period.

(31.7 percent), and from Moscow in 1991 (31.6 percent). By 1994, these shares had declined to 11.0 percent from Moscow and to 9.7 percent from St. Petersburg, and in 1998 they were as low as 5.0 percent for each city (see table 1.3). In the same period, the percentage of emigrants from outside Moscow and St. Petersburg ("the provinces") increased steadily until 1998. In 1990–1991, this group's share of the migration was about half; by 1994, it reached 79 percent, and in 1998, it peaked at 90 percent—much greater than the percentage of these Jews among all of Russian Jewry, which was around 50 percent.

However, in the second half of the last decade, the trend reversed. By 2009, Moscow's share of migration from the Russian Federation to Israel increased to 22.0 percent, and it was 4.4 times more than its share in 1998 (5.0 percent). In fact, it had returned to its level in 1992. St. Petersburg's share increased to 10.8 percent in 2009, even higher than that in 1992 (10.6 percent). At the same time, the majority (67.2 percent) of immigrants to Israel from Russia originated from the provinces.

The data show that age distribution of the migrants to their three main destinations were very different (see table 1.4). The stream to Israel was the youngest.

TABLE 1.3. Emigration from the Russian Federation to Israel, by Area, 1990–2009, Percentages

Year	Total	Moscow	St. Petersburg	Provinces
1990	100	21.7	31.7	46.6
1991	100	31.6	13.7	54.7
1992	100	22.1	10.6	67.3
1993	100	14.1	9.5	76.4
1994	100	11.0	9.7	79.3
1995	100	9.0	8.8	82.2
1996	100	9.0	8.0	83.0
1997	100	6.6	5.9	87.5
1998	100	5.0	5.0	90.0
1999	100	7.8	7.9	84.3
2000	100	8.3	7.3	84.4
2001	100	7.8	7.1	85.1
2002	100	6.9	6.5	86.6
2003	100	8.0	6.8	85.2
2004	100	8.4	7.6	84.0
2005	100	10.9	8.4	80.7
2006	100	12.5	9.0	78.5
2007	100	18.0	8.2	73.8
2008	100	20.3	9.3	70.4
2009	100	22.0	10.8	67.2

SOURCES: Computation based on Israel Ministry of Immigrant Absorption data for 1990–1993; Rosstat data for 1994–1998; and data on Jewish Agency assisted flights of migrants to Israel for 1999–2009.

TABLE 1.4. Age Distribution of Jews and Their Relatives Who Migrated from the FSU to Three Main Destinations, 1990/1991–2004, Percentages

Age group	Israel, 1990–2004	U.S., 1991–2004	Germany, 1991–2004
Total	100.0	100.0	100.0
0–14	20.1	16.9	12.1[a]
15–29	24.3	18.7	15.0[a]
30–44	22.3	21.0	22.2
45–64	21.0	26.5	28.1
65+	12.3	16.9	22.6
Median age	33.6	40.2	45.5

SOURCES: Computation based on Israel CBS data, Moscow IOM office data recorded for Jewish emigration to the U.S., and the German Federal Office for Migration and Refugees (BAMF) statistics on authorized applications.
[a] 0–17 and 18–29 age groups, respectively.

The most numerous among these migrants were fifteen to twenty-nine years old—24.3 percent—and only 12.3 percent of them were sixty-five and above. Among the migrants to the United States and Germany, the most numerous age group was fifty-five to sixty-four years old: 26.5 and 28.1 percent, respectively. The share of those sixty-five and above was much higher to these two countries than immigrants to Israel—17 percent in the stream to the United States and 23 percent to Germany. At the same time, the share of children among migrants to Israel was higher than that to the United States and Germany. Children under fifteen made up 20 percent of the migrants to Israel, whereas the broader age group under eighteen numbered only 12 percent among migrants to Germany.

In 1990–2004, the median age of the immigrants to Israel was 33.6 years. In 2009, with a new increase in FSU immigration to Israel, it was even lower—33.1 years.[12] In 1991–2004, this indicator was much higher for migrants to the United States and even more so to Germany: 40.2 and 45.5 years, respectively. This very large differentiation in age structure of the migrants in their three main destinations should have many implications for their absorption experiences in their receiving countries and for the future development of the three branches of the contemporary post-Soviet Jewish Diaspora.

OUT-MIGRATION FROM ISRAEL OF FSU IMMIGRANTS

Debates about the size of out-migration of Jews from Israel "tend to be more pervasive and heated than those linked with most other groups,"[13] and there are many unsubstantiated statements concerning "huge" numbers of Jews, in particular those from the FSU, emigrating from Israel.[14] Using a demographic approach to this problem,[15] we shall base our analysis of out-migration from Israel by FSU immigrants on data from official statistical sources. In order to evaluate these dynamics, we shall study the appropriate Israeli statistics, as well as those from FSU countries.

Data collected by the Israel Central Bureau of Statistics (Israel CBS) on FSU immigrants who arrived since 1990 make it possible to study their annual out-migration as a whole (see table 1.5). These data are presented as numbers of immigrants who left Israel for all destinations in a designated year and stayed abroad continuously for one year or more ("departures"), and numbers of immigrants who returned to Israel in a designated year among all those who had previously left Israel for all destinations and stayed abroad continuously for one year or more ("returns").[16]

TABLE 1.5. Departures from and Returns to Israel of FSU Immigrants Who Arrived in Israel since 1990, in Thousands

Year	Departures[a]	Returns[b]	Balance	Departures, per 1,000 FSU immigrants[a,c]
1990	0.4	0.0	0.4	6
1991	3.1	0.0	3.1	12
1992	5.8	0.1	5.7	16
1993	5.3	0.3	5.0	13
1994	5.3	0.5	4.8	11
1995	6.3	0.6	5.7	12
1996	6.2	0.9	5.3	11
1997	6.0	1.3	4.7	10
1998	6.2	1.2	5.0	10
1999	5.6	1.5	4.1	8
2000	6.9	1.5	5.4	9
2001	8.0	1.2	6.8	10
2002	9.7	1.2	8.5	12
2003	9.4	1.5	7.9	12
2004	8.7	1.9	6.8	11
2005	7.5	2.1	5.4	9
2006	7.4	1.9	5.5	9
2007	6.7	2.0	4.7	8
2008	6.0	1.9	4.1	8
2009	4.6	2.1	2.5	6
1990–2009	125.1	23.7	101.4	–

SOURCES: Israel CBS data.
[a] Immigrants who left Israel for all destinations in the designated year and stayed abroad continuously for one year or more.
[b] Immigrants who returned to Israel in the designated year of all those who had previously left Israel for all destinations and stayed abroad continuously for one year or more.
[c] The rate is per 1,000 FSU immigrants who arrived in Israel since 1990 and were still living there by the designated year, not including children born in Israel; computed by the author [Mark Tolts, "Post-Soviet Jewish Demography, 1989–2004," in *Revolution, Repression, and Revival: The Soviet Jewish Experience*, ed. Zvi Gitelman and Yaacov Ro'I (Lanham, MD: Rowman & Littlefield, 2007), 298 (updated)], except 1998–2001 [Israel CBS, *Immigrant Population from the Former Soviet Union: Demographic Trends, 1990–2001* (Jerusalem: Central Bureau of Statistics, 2006), 146].

We can compute the annual rate of out-migration for FSU immigrants who arrived in Israel since 1990 and were still living there for each year up to 2009. This indicator is based on the number of FSU immigrants who left Israel for all destinations in any given year and stayed abroad for more than one year. According to these data, the rate of out-migration was highest in 1992, shortly after the greatest wave of FSU immigrants arrived in Israel during the previous two years, 16 per 1,000. Over the following years, the rate decreased rather steadily, and in 1999, it fell to 8 per 1,000. By 2002, it had returned to the level of 1995—12 per 1,000—and remained at the same level in 2003. From 2004, the rate fell and by 2009, it had returned to its lowest level of 6 per 1,000.

For our study of the distribution of out-migration from Israel of FSU immigrants, we rely on statistics from the receiving countries.[17] We assembled data on immigration from Israel to the Russian Federation and six European FSU countries (table 1.6).[18] The most sizable FSU return migration flow has been to Russia. Immigration from Israel to the Russian Federation was registered in Russian statistics, and these data have been available since 1997 for analysis. We can use these statistics to study the relationship between return migration and economic dynamics.

The statistics of Rosstat are based on data provided by the neighborhood passport office that registered immigrants who resumed residence in Russia.[19] In 1997, there were 1,626 registered immigrants from Israel to the Russian Federation. In 1999, a period of severe economic crisis in Russia, the number of immigrants from Israel decreased to about 1,400.

TABLE 1.6. Immigration from Israel to the Russian Federation and European FSU Countries, 1997–2009

Year	Russian Federation	Ukraine	Belarus	Moldova[a]	Latvia	Lithuania	Estonia
1997	1,626	1,045	...	...	51	...	...
1998	1,528	1,193	230	...	50	...	...
1999	1,425	1,098	214	9	38	12	...
2000	1,508	1,019	198	12	28	9	...
2001	1,373	898	207	38	36	77	...
2002	1,670	1,003	233	40	51	94	...
2003	1,808	1,164	361	68	58	94	...
2004	1,486	1,411	283	90	75	117	13
2005	1,004	1,281	227	94	58	88	14
2006	1,053	1,372	271	72	32	87	17
2007	1,094	1,381	297	131	47	59	22
2008	1,002	1,205	257	95	54	54	29
2009	861	885	268	109	15	33	18

SOURCES: Compilation based on data of the national statistical services of the respective FSU countries.

[a] Immigrants with Israeli citizenship, 1999–2006; repatriates from Israel, 2007–2009.

In 2003, in a period of recession in the Israeli economy, the registered number of immigrants to Russia from Israel reached its maximum to date—1,808. However, in 2004, the number of immigrants decreased to fewer than 1,500. In 2005, the registered number of emigrants from Israel to Russia fell even more noticeably to about 1,000. This coincided with the improvement in Israel's economy after 2004.

At the same time, even a short-term worsening of the situation in Israel (e.g., the recession caused by the Second Lebanon War) led to an increase in the numbers of out-migrants from the country in 2006 and 2007 as shown by the Rosstat data: 1,053 and 1,094, respectively. However, in 2008, only 1,002 immigrants from Israel were registered by Rosstat. This coincided with the strong performance of the Israeli economy in this period. As noted, in 2009 a world crisis affected the Russian economy even more severely than the CIS countries as a whole. At the same time, its impact on the Israeli economy was much more moderate. In 2009, the registered number of immigrants to Russia from Israel reached its minimum to date, 861. Thus, our findings based on the recent data confirm the previous analysis that found that emigration from Israel is largely dependent on the dynamics of the country's business cycle.[20]

Before 2005, in Ukraine, the registered number of immigrants from Israel was consistently lower than that in the Russian Federation (see table 1.6). In 2004, the registered number of immigrants to Ukraine from Israel reached its peak to date—about 1,400. However, in 2005, despite the euphoria after the Orange Revolution, the registered number of these immigrants was lower. In Belarus, as in Russia, the registered number of immigrants from Israel reached its peak in 2003. At the same time, in Latvia and Lithuania these respective numbers reached their zenith in 2004. For the Russian Federation and European FSU countries as a whole, the registered number of immigrants from Israel peaked in 2003—about 3,600. This picture corresponds rather well with the dynamics of out-migration according to Israeli statistics (cf. table 1.5; see figure 1.1), which inevitably lagged behind statistics of the FSU countries. Of course, there were some immigrants from Israel who officially resumed residence status in the other FSU countries,[21] and we may conservatively estimate that in 2003, the total number of such immigrants from Israel to the FSU as a whole was almost 4,000.

A comparison of Israeli data for all destinations with statistics of Russia and European FSU countries as a whole clearly shows that a sizable part of FSU out-migration from Israel went to Western countries (see figure 1.1), mostly to North America. However, we have no appropriate statistical data for the United States. At the same time, according to the 2001 Canadian census, "8,030 individuals born in the Former Soviet Union... came from Israel to Canada after June 1996";[22] that is, about 1,600 per year. Therefore, in this period, the average annual number of FSU immigrants from Israel to Canada was higher than in the Russian Federation (cf. table 1.6).

Of all FSU immigrants to Israel since 1990, 125,100 had left the country by the end of 2009 and remained abroad continuously for one year or more. However, a

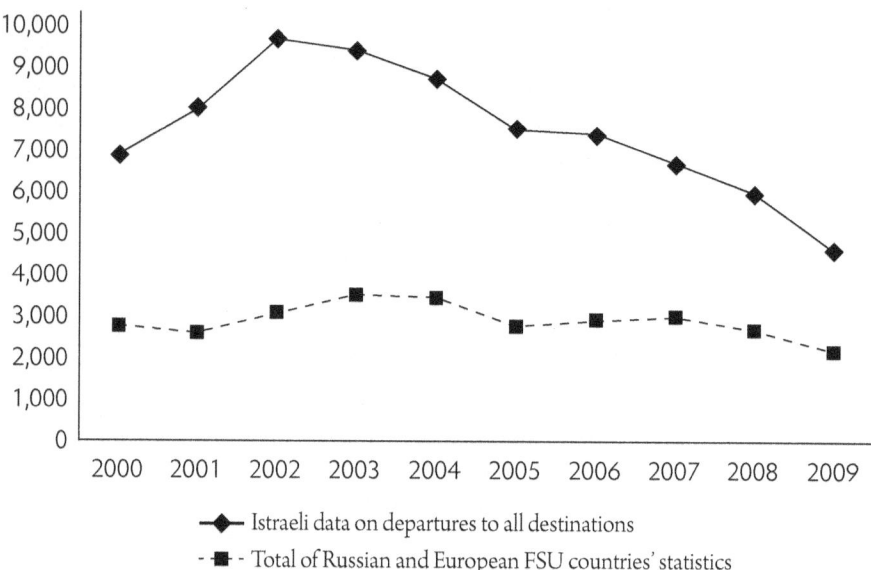

FIGURE 1.1. Out-Migration of FSU Migrants from Israel, 2000–2009

sizable number (23,700) of these have since returned to Israel, and this return is continuing. Thus, at the end of 2009, the registered number of FSU immigrants who left Israel and had not returned to the country was actually 101,400 (see table 1.5). In 1990–2009, about 985,100 immigrants arrived in Israel from the FSU. Thus, about 10 percent of this number left Israel without returning.

WORLDWIDE SIZE AND DISTRIBUTION

The 1970 Soviet census, conducted around the time that mass Jewish emigration began, showed that there were about 2.15 million self-identified "core" Jews in the Soviet Union.[23] To evaluate their subsequent dynamics, we must estimate the respective balance of births and deaths, plus additions to the "core" Jewish population as a result of ethnic re-identification in the process of migration. Other factors are not as influential as these two dynamics, including ethnic re-affiliation of people of mixed origin remaining in the FSU. Based on this approach we estimate that at the beginning of 2004, there were about 1.6 million self-identified "core" Jews worldwide who had originated from the FSU.[24]

For the period 1970–2003, the negative vital balance of this population was tentatively estimated at about -700,000. For an update of our previous estimated figure for the worldwide number of "core" Jews originating from the FSU at the beginning of 2010, we surmise that in the subsequent six years, the negative vital balance of this population was about 60,000 which gave us -760,000 for the total forty-year period between 1970 and 2009. However, this decrease was partially offset by additions to the "core" Jewish population as a result of ethnic re-identification in the process of migration. This phenomenon of re-identification may be tentatively calculated based on the discrepancy between the percentages of Jews among the immigrants to Israel according to the Russian/FSU and Israeli definitions.

Israeli official statistics are based on the Ministry of Interior's Population Register whose definition of "who is a Jew" is according to Orthodox Jewish religious (*halakhic*) criteria. At the same time, "Jews," according to the official Russian/FSU definition, were only those emigrants (aged sixteen and over) designated as such in their internal passports. For children without passports, ethnicity was determined by the parents' ethnicity. If the parents belonged to different ethnic groups, preference was given to the mother's ethnicity, although even in the post-Soviet era, non-Jewish ethnic affiliation was clearly preferred by the offspring of such couples.[25]

One consequence of the post-Soviet Jewish vital crisis and of rising mixed marriage is the recent and pronounced decrease in the number of Jews among the FSU immigrants to Israel. According to official Israeli data, they constituted 96 percent in 1990, 72 percent in 1995, 45 percent in 2000, and only 41 percent in 2009. These proportions were almost the same as those immigrating from the Russian Federation.[26] According to official Russian data, the proportion of Jews among all those who immigrated to Israel fell from 64 percent in the second half of 1992 to 53 percent in 1995, 27 percent in 2000, and 22 percent in 2007—the last year for which such data were processed by Rosstat.[27] The different standards for defining Jewishness in Israel and the FSU explain the divergence in the respective percentages. Obviously, some of the immigrants, who were considered Jews according to their former Soviet internal passports (as well as in population censuses), are counted as non-Jews by Israeli statistics, which are based on *halakhah*.[28] Nonetheless, many more immigrants are counted as Jews in Israel than were registered as such in the FSU, and many of these had never identified themselves as Jews before.

By the start of 2004, based on the data above, the number of such immigrants was estimated at about 150,000, a number that we now know was too conservative. Moreover, we based our previous analysis on partial sources concerning the role of formal conversions to Judaism in Israel and surmised that this was a rather minor phenomenon. However, by the start of 2010, the total number of formal conversions among FSU immigrants from the last wave to Judaism reached about 19,000.[29] Therefore, the total number of additions to the "core" Jewish population, including formal conversions to Judaism in Israel, in connection with migration may be tentatively placed at about 210,000. This recognition of the Jewish religious and/or ethnic identity of individuals who had previously neither identified themselves nor been seen by FSU authorities as Jews somewhat slowed the decline of the "core" Jewish population originating from the FSU, and contributed to the Jewish population in Israel.

Thus, at the beginning of 2010, according to our updated estimates that use the 1970 Soviet census as a baseline, there were about 1.6 million "core" Jews worldwide who had originated from the FSU (see table 1.7). In 2010, the number of remaining "core" Jews in the FSU was estimated at about 327,000, of whom 205,000 lived in the Russian Federation and 71,500 in Ukraine. The October 2009 census of Belarus recorded 12,900 Jews and we adjusted this figure upward to 13,300 to include some people of unknown/unstated ethnicity (see table 1.8).

In the Russian Federation, the October 2010 census recorded 157,763 Jews as compared with our core Jewish population estimate of 200,000 for the same year (a number derived from the February 1994 Russian microcensus estimate of 401,000 Jews and subsequent vital and migration dynamics). Thus, there were possibly additional Jews (approximately 42,000) among people whose ethnicity was unknown/unstated in the census. This gap clearly demonstrates a growing process of Jewish ethnic assimilation in contemporary Russia and shows that a sizable group of Jews do not want to be recorded as Jews in the census.

Ample data on the demographic history and the contemporary situation of the Jews in the FSU have been collected that clearly demonstrate their demographic decline.[30] However, wishful thinking is not uncommon among some segments of the post-Soviet Jewish community in the FSU and so their demographic collapse is often denied. For the Russian Federation alone, highly inflated figures claiming that the "real" number Jews falls between one or two million are in circulation, and there are even fantastic figures as high as ten million.[31] At the same time, the demographic decline of this Jewry has been confirmed by the recent decrease in the number of pupils in Jewish schools and the groups served by Jewish charities there.[32]

A contrasting, positive demographic situation is characteristic of FSU immigrants in Israel.[33] According to the Israel CBS data, based on the last 2008 census, by mid-2009 there were 892,400 Jews born in the FSU living in Israel, including their Israeli-born children.[34] However, among these offspring, 45,000 were born

TABLE 1.7. Dynamics of the "Core" Jewish Population Originating from the FSU, 1970–2010, in Millions

Dynamics	Number
"Core" Jewish population in the Soviet Union, 1970	2.15
Vital balance, 1970–2009[a]	−0.76
Accession to "core" Jewish population in connection with migration[b]	+0.21
"Core" Jewish population originating from the FSU, 2010	1.6

SOURCES: 1970 Soviet census; author's estimates.
[a] "Effectively Jewish" births minus Jewish deaths. "Effectively Jewish" births are newborns who are identified as Jews.
[b] Mostly in Israel; figure based on the discrepancy between percentages of Jews among immigrants to Israel according to Russian and Israeli definitions, including also formal conversion to Judaism in Israel (about 19,000), see text.

TABLE 1.8. Distribution of the "Core" Jewish Population in the FSU, by Country, 2010, in Thousands

Country[a]	Number	Country	Number
Entire FSU	327	Kazakhstan	3.6[d]
Russian Federation	205[b]	Georgia	3.2
Ukraine	71.5	Lithuania	3.05[e]
Belarus	13.3[c]	Estonia	2.0[e]
Azerbaidzhan	9.1[d]	Kirgizstan	0.6[d]
Latvia	6.4[e]	Turkmenistan	0.2
Uzbekistan	4.5	Tadzhikistan	0.0
Moldova	4.1	Armenia	0.0

SOURCES: Author's estimates.
[a] FSU countries are listed in the order of the number of "core" Jews.
[b] Estimate derived from the February 1994 Russian microcensus estimate of 401,000 Jews and subsequent vital and migration dynamics; for the data of the 2010 Russian census and their evaluation, see text.
[c] According to the data of the October 2009 census of Belarus (12,900) adjusted upward to include some people of unknown/unstated ethnicity.
[d] According to the data of the 2009 national census.
[e] According to the data of the 2011 national census.

in Israel before 1970, and thus should be excluded from our evaluation. Clearly these are children of the (unknown) number of Jews born to Russian and Soviet immigrants who arrived in the country before 1970. Of course, if they are still alive, these veteran immigrants are also included in the aforementioned total figure. Moreover, some of their children were born after 1970 as well. At the same time, CBS provides no data for the third generation—mostly grandchildren of the immigrants of the 1970s—and this factor somewhat offsets the above-noted exclusions. Thus, our estimated figure of fewer than 850,000 ex-Soviet Jews living in Israel is quite conservative (see table 1.9).

In the United States, the estimated number of 300,000 is only a small fraction of the total "core" Jewish population, which numbered 5.275 million.[35] Our figure

TABLE 1.9. Distribution of the Post-Soviet Jewish Diaspora Population, by Country, 2010, in Millions

Country	"Core" Jews	Total[a]
Israel	Fewer than 0.85	More than 1.1
FSU	0.327	Fewer than 1.0
U.S.	0.3	Fewer than 0.5
Germany	0.1	0.2
World[b]	1.6	2.9

[a] For Israel, FSU immigrants, their children and grandchildren. For all other countries, mostly people eligible to immigrate to Israel according to the Law of Return.
[b] Including other much smaller ex-Soviet Jewish immigrant communities, see text.

for the "core" Jewish population in the United States originating from the FSU remained the same as earlier estimates for 2004. After September 11, 2001, the United States was no longer a major destination for post-Soviet Jewish emigration (see above), and the balance of births to deaths is negative among American Jewry as a whole.[36]

In 1990–2009, 102,533 FSU immigrants joined Germany's Jewish communities.[37] Of course, there are some "core" Jews who are unaffiliated with any official Jewish institutions. At the same time, there is a disproportionate number of the elderly among FSU immigrants to Germany (see table 1.4), so the balance of births and deaths among the FSU immigrants there was decisively negative. These two factors somewhat offset each other. In Germany, we estimated the number of "core" Jews originating from the FSU at around 100,000. It is a predominant fraction of the total German "core" Jewish population, which numbered 119,000 in 2010.[38]

Our analysis shows that today, Israel, the United States, Germany, the Russian Federation, and Ukraine are the main centers of Jews originating from the FSU. To this, we must add information on two overseas countries. The 2011 census shows 8,395 Jews from the FSU living in Australia.[39] According to a revised estimate,[40] in 2011 in Canada, there were about 28,000 "core" Jews born in the FSU who immigrated there since 1970.

Finally, let us try to estimate the total number and distribution of the post-Soviet Jewish diaspora population in the world. According to Israel CBS data, there were 926,500 FSU immigrants who arrived in Israel since 1990 and who were still there at the end of 2009 (including their children born in Israel). In the previous twenty years, from 1970 to 1989, about 178,000 immigrants arrived in Israel from the Soviet Union (see table 1.1). Although some of them subsequently emigrated, this decrease was somewhat offset by their decidedly positive vital balance. Moreover we have also included in our evaluation the third generation of FSU immigrants—their grandchildren—for which Israel CBS provides no data. Thus, we arrived at a figure of more than 1.1 million for Israel (see table 1.9).

According to an authoritative estimate, in 2007, in the FSU, there were about one million people eligible to immigrate to Israel according to the criteria of the Israeli Law of Return.[41] Our figure for 2010 is less than one million. Since 1989 more than 220,000 FSU Jews and their relatives have migrated to Germany. Their vital balance was decisively negative and some of these people subsequently re-emigrated. Thus, our estimate for Germany is about 200,000.

Since 1970, about 450,000 FSU Jews and their relatives have migrated to the United States (see table 1.1). We may surmise that during this period, about 50,000 people joined them who had first migrated from the FSU to Israel.[42] As noted above, the balance of births and deaths is negative among U.S. Jewry as a whole. Thus, our estimated figure for the United States is less than half a million.

All in all, we estimate the total size of the global post-Soviet Jewish diaspora at 2.9 million, which includes, in addition to the numbers for Israel, the FSU, the United States, and Germany, an additional 100,000 people in all other countries.

CONCLUDING REMARKS

The results of our study allow us to better understand some aspects of the post-Soviet Jewish diaspora and its identity. The discrepancy between the estimated number of emigrants when calculated according to self-identification (1.6 million) and the total number of people belonging to the post-Soviet Jewish diaspora (2.9 million) is instructive. In countries outside Israel, many individuals who fall into this gap number of 1.3 million are practicing Christians, even without Jewish parentage. Moreover, some scholars have proposed the formation of a paradoxical, Russian Orthodox Christian Jewish identity, especially among baptized Jews living in Russia.[43]

At the same time, our analysis clearly reveals sizable additions to the "core" Jewish population as a result of the official recognition of Jewish religious/ethnic identity in addition to the self re-identification of many immigrants in Israel who had previously neither identified themselves as Jews nor had been seen by FSU authorities as such. In Israel, all FSU immigrant children are educated in Jewish schools, and the vast majority of the non-Jewish segment of these immigrants does not have an affinity for Christianity. In the first decade of the recent migration wave, 1990–1999, in Israel only a small minority (8,700) of the FSU newcomers who were classified as non-Jews chose to be registered as Christians.[44] In the following decade, 2000–2009, this number was as low as 2,100. The overwhelming majority of FSU immigrants classified in Israel as non-Jews preferred to be registered as having "no religion," and they may be seen as a potential addition to the Israeli Jewish population.

NOTES

1. Our demographic study covers the post-Soviet Jewish Diaspora as a whole rather than just its Russian-speaking segment, for which we have insufficient data for a separate treatment. The most serious obstacle is that the Israeli censuses of 1995 and 2008 collected no information on spoken languages. Thus, we have no data concerning Russian fluency for a sizable portion of this diaspora. Moreover, in some parts of the FSU, Russian fluency among Jews has fallen dramatically. For example, the last Azerbaijani census, conducted in 2009, shows that only a small minority of Jews (19.3 percent) in that country speak Russian fluently.

2. To analyze migration flows, we assembled and utilized data from the statistical services of FSU states and statistical information from the destination countries: the Israeli Central Bureau of Statistics [Israel CBS], the Hebrew Immigrant Aid Society [HIAS, USA], the German Federal Office for Migration and Refugees [BAMF], as well as international organizations (Council of Europe, Eurostat, International Organization for Migration [IOM]). We have also utilized

some unpublished tabulations from the Israel CBS. For other published and unpublished sources, see below.

3. Zvi Gitelman, "'From a Northern Country': Russian and Soviet Jewish Immigration to America and Israel in Historical Perspective," in *Russian Jews on Three Continents*, ed. Noah Lewin-Epstein, Yaacov Ro'i, and Paul Ritterband (London: Frank Cass, 1997), 21–41.

4. See Sergio DellaPergola, "International Migration of Jews," in *Transnationalism: Diasporas and the Advent of a New (Dis)Order*, ed. Eliezer Ben-Rafael and Yitzhak Sternberg (Leiden and Boston, MA: Brill, 2009), 213–236.

5. Fred A. Lazin, *The Struggle for Soviet Jewry in American Politics: Israel versus the American Jewish Establishment* (Lanham, MD: Lexington Books, 2005), 270–279.

6. The best publication based on official German statistics concerning the recent FSU Jewish immigration, whose data we use in our analysis, is Sonja Haug and Michael Wolf, *Soziodemographische Merkmale, Berufsstruktur und Verwandtschaftsnetzwerke jüdischer Zuwanderer: Projekt Zuwanderer aus Russland und anderen GUS-Staaten-Jüdische Zuwanderer* (Nürnberg: BAMF, 2007). For updated information in a general publication, see: German Federal Ministry of the Interior with German Federal Office for Migration and Refugees, *Migrationsbericht 2009* (Berlin: BMI, 2010).

7. For example, see German Federal Office for Migration and Refugees, *Evaluierungsbericht: Aufnahmeverfahren für jüdische Zuwanderer aus der ehemaligen Sowjetunion* (Nürnberg: BAMF, 2009).

8. These data do not include the Baltic States and Georgia, which are not CIS members.

9. The Interstate Statistical Committee of the Commonwealth of Independent States, "CIS in Figures: Annual Data" [online data-base], http://www.cisstat.com/eng/index.htm.

10. Israel CBS, *Statistical Abstract of Israel 2010* (Jerusalem: Central Bureau of Statistics, 2010), 622.

11. In 1991–1994 and since 2003, the number of migrants from the Russian Federation to Israel exceeded that from Ukraine, and overall, 1989–2010, more migrants arrived in Israel from the Russian Federation than from Ukraine: 32.5 and 32 percent of all FSU migrants, respectively.

12. Israel CBS, *Statistical Abstract of Israel 2010*, 236.

13. Steven Gold, "The Emigration of Jewish Israelis," in *Jews in Israel: Contemporary Social and Cultural Patterns*, ed. Uzi Rebhun and Chaim I. Waxman (Hanover, NH: Brandeis University Press, 2004), 448.

14. For example, Radio Tehran (Farsi broadcast, January 29, 2008, 14:00 local time; communicated to the author by Vladimir Mesamed, an Israeli expert on Iranian affairs) stated: "Thousands of former citizens of the Soviet Union, who moved to the Zionist state over the last 15–20 years, leave it monthly, returning to their old places of residence, to the USA or to European countries. According to various estimates, the number of respective returnees fluctuates from 300 to 400 thousand."

15. See: Sergio DellaPergola, "Migration: Israeli Emigration," in *Encyclopaedia Judaica*, 2nd ed., ed. Michael Berenbaum and Fred Skolnik (Detroit: Macmillan Reference USA, 2007), 14:218–219.

16. For details on the method for counting out-migration in Israeli statistics, see: Marina Sheps and Ahmad Hleihel, "The Challenge in Creating a Stock of Emigrants from Israel" (paper presented by the Israel Central Bureau of Statistics at the Joint UNECE/Eurostat Work Session on Migration Statistics organized in collaboration with UNFPA, Edinburgh, Scotland, November 20–22, 2006). According to an assessment of organizations responsible for international statistical cooperation, "[T]his method has produced very promising results on emigrant stocks, thanks to the possibility of linking accurate and individual data on population stocks and flows." (United Nations Economic and Social Council, "Report of the Meeting of Group of Experts on Migration Statistics," Summary of Joint UNECE/Eurostat Work Session on

Migration Statistics organized in collaboration with UNFPA, Edinburgh, Scotland, November 20–22, 2006, 4).

17. According to an official responsible for Israel CBS migration statistics, the national statistical service has no information on distribution of out-migration by country of destination, and therefore does not present such data (author's conversations with Marina Sheps).

18. For Estonia, we found no data on migration flows for the period before 2004 on either national or international online databases. However, migration from this country to Israel was the smallest among all FSU countries, making the absence of Estonian data unimportant. For a review of international migration statistics in the CIS countries, see Olga Chudinovskikh, "Comparability and Exchange of International Migration Statistics in the CIS Countries" (paper prepared for the Joint UNECE/Eurostat Work Session on Migration Statistics, Geneva, Switzerland, March 3–5, 2008).

19. These data also include some individuals who previously immigrated to Israel from other parts of the FSU.

20. For comparison, see: Sergio DellaPergola, *World Jewry Beyond 2000: The Demographic Prospects* (Oxford: Oxford Centre for Hebrew and Jewish Studies, 1999), 35, 37.

21. In 2000, 80 immigrants were registered from Israel in Kazakhstan and 69 in Uzbekistan. See IOM, *Migration Trends in Eastern Europe and Central Asia: 2001–2002 Review* (Geneva: International Organization for Migration, 2002), 96, 165.

22. Charles Shahar and Howard Magonet, "Part 5: Immigration & Language," in *The Jewish Community of Canada: 2001 Census Analysis* (Toronto: UIA Federations Canada, 2005), 8.

23. The "core" Jewish population is the aggregate of all those who, when asked, identify themselves as Jews or, in the case of children, are identified as such by their parents. It does not include persons of Jewish origin who reported another ethnicity in the census.

24. Mark Tolts, "The Post-Soviet Jewish Population in Russia and the World," *Jews in Russia and Eastern Europe*, 1.52 (2004): 52–58.

25. For comparison, see: Andrei Volkov, "Etnicheski smeshannye sem'i v SSSR: dinamika i sostav," *Vestnik statistiki*, 8 (1989): 8–24; Mark Tolts, "The Jewish Population of Russia, 1989–1995," *Jews in Eastern Europe* 3.31 (1996): 15.

26. For the detailed annual data, see: Mark Tolts, "Sources for the Demographic Study of the Jews in the Former Soviet Union," in *The Social Scientific Study of Jewry: Sources, Approaches, Debates*, vol. 27 of *Studies in Contemporary Jewry*, ed. Uzi Rebhun (New York: Oxford University Press, 2014), 168.

27. Ibid.

28. According to Jewish law (*halakhah*), a Jew is defined as a person born to a Jewish mother or who converts to Judaism through a formal religious procedure.

29. According to the database of the Israel Ministry of Immigrant Absorption, whose information is drawn from the data of the competent governmental sources (communicated to this author by a Ministry official). For detailed annual data since 1999, see: Chaim I. Waxman, "Multiculturalism, Conversion, and the Future of Israel as a Modern State," *Israel Studies Review* 28.1 (2013): 43.

30. Mark Tolts, "Demography of the Jews in the Former Soviet Union: Yesterday and Today," in *Jewish Life After the USSR*, ed. Zvi Gitelman, Musya Glants, and Marshall I. Goldman (Bloomington: Indiana University Press, 2003), 173–206.

31. For example, see: "Evrei vozvrashchaiutsia v Rossiiu," *BBC Russian Service*, October 25, 2004, http://news.bbc.co.uk/hi/russian/russia/newsid_3952000/3952609.stm. See also: Anna Rudnitskaya, "Fishing for Jews in Russia's Muddy Waters," *JTA*, February 23, 2010, http://www.jta.org/news/article/2010/02/23/1010779/fishing-for-jews-in-russias-muddy-waters.

32. For example, see: Zvi Gitelman, "Do Jewish Schools Make a Difference in the Former Soviet Union?" *East European Jewish Affairs* 37.3 (2007): 377–398; Betsy Gidwitz, "Post-Soviet

Jewry on the Cusp of Its Third Decade—Part 2," *Changing Jewish Communities* 69.15 (June 15, 2011).

33. Mark Tolts, "Demographic Transformations among Ex-Soviet Migrants in Israel," in *Research in Jewish Demography and Identity*, ed. Eli Lederhendler and Uzi Rebhun (Boston: Academic Studies Press, 2015), 146–168.

34. Israel CBS, *Statistical Abstract of Israel 2010*, 156.

35. For comparison, see Sergio DellaPergola, "World Jewish Population, 2010," *Current Jewish Population Reports* 2 (2010): 32.

36. Ibid., 41.

37. ZWST, *Mitgliederstatistik der jüdischen Gemeinden und Landesverbände in Deutschland für das Jahr 2009* (Frankfurt am Main: Zentralwohlfahrtsstelle der Juden in Deutschland, 2010), 3.

38. Cf. DellaPergola, "World Jewish Population, 2010," 49.

39. David Graham, *The Jewish Population of Australia: Key Findings from the 2011 Census* (Darlinghurst, NSW: Australian Centre for the Study of Jewish Civilisation, Monash University, 2014), 23.

40. This estimate is based on data from the Canadian National Household Survey of 2011, kindly prepared at our request by Robert J. Brym, the leading expert on FSU Jews in Canada (Robert J. Brym, e-mail message to author, February 13, 2015).

41. Sergio DellaPergola, *Jewish Demographic Policies: Population Trends and Options in Israel and in the Diaspora* (Jerusalem: Jewish People Policy Institute, 2011), 116–117.

42. On this group, see Uzi Rebhun and Lilach Lev Ari, *American Israelis: Migration, Transnationalism, and Diasporic Identity* (Leiden and Boston, MA: Brill, 2010), 31.

43. See Elena Nosenko-Stein, "Aliens in an Alien World: Paradoxes of Jewish–Christian Identity in Contemporary Russia," *East European Jewish Affairs* 40.1 (2010): 19–41; see also Anna Shternshis, "Kaddish in a Church: Perceptions of Orthodox Christianity among Moscow Elderly Jews in the Early Twenty-First Century," *Russian Review* 66.2 (2007): 273–294.

44. Mark Tolts, "Jewish Demography of the Former Soviet Union," in *Papers in Jewish Demography 1997*, ed. Sergio DellaPergola and Judith Even (Jerusalem: Avraham Harman Institute of Contemporary Jewry, The Hebrew University; World Union of Jewish Studies; Association for Jewish Demography and Statistics, 2001), 117.

2 · THE RUSSIAN-SPEAKING ISRAELI DIASPORA IN THE FSU, EUROPE, AND NORTH AMERICA

Jewish Identification
and Attachment to Israel

UZI REBHUN

Migration across international boundaries is a common phenomenon in the late twentieth and early twenty-first centuries.[1] Over the last two decades, the number of international migrants—persons born in a country other than that in which they live—increased by more than one-third from 1990 to 2010 (155 million to 214 million).[2] Complementary push-and-pull factors may explain such migrations. These include, among other things, political turnovers; the reorganization of the geopolitical order by dismantling states into smaller sovereign entities; the unification of countries on the basis of economic and cultural cooperation, or ad-hoc agreements between countries; and demographic trends such as aging populations and the need for labor. In addition, aspirations to improve standards of living, the exploitation of economic opportunities for industrial and technological development,[3] and ideological and religious considerations affect these migrations.[4] The "flattening of the world" facilitates reactions to these forces. Cyberspace allows for the free flow of information, money, and communication from place to place. Under such new conditions of "communicating vessels," people interact easily between any two points on the globe.

The dynamics of transnational migration, which are motivated by structural considerations and individual aspirations along with multiple identities, are such that they may engender another move, either back to the country of origin or another migration to a third country. These patterns are also relevant for Jewish immigration from the Former Soviet Union (hereafter FSU) following perestroika. This migration is comprised of three geographic pillars—the FSU as the region of origin, Israel as the (Jewish) homeland, and other diaspora countries. With this approach, we may develop a typology of several types of migration that form different sub-populations which we define as:

1. Non-migrants: Jews who stayed in the FSU
2. Immigrants: moved from the FSU to Israel
3. Return migrants: moved to Israel and later returned to the FSU
4. Early migrants: left the FSU to Israel and later moved to a third country
5. Late migrants: left the FSU to a diaspora country and later relocated to Israel
6. Emigrants: departed the FSU and settled in a diaspora country
7. Repeat migrants: emigrated from the FSU to another diaspora country and later moved to a new diaspora country
8. Circular migrants: moved from the FSU to a diaspora country but later decided to migrate back to the FSU.

This detailed typology can be re-grouped into four major segments of Russian-speaking Jews:

A. Non-migrants (1)
B. Russian Jews in Israel (2 and 5)
C. Russians Jews abroad with no experience of living in Israel (6, 7, and 8)
D. FSU Jews abroad with an experience of living in Israel (3 and 4).

Although the latter group is the smallest among the four—constituting approximately only 100,000 people[5]—it expresses most powerfully the meaning of diaspora, which, according to William Safran, is people or their ancestors who were dispersed from their original center to several other areas.[6] It is likely that they are the only FSU Jews in the diaspora who hold Israeli citizenship. Among the four major segments of FSU Jews, those who immigrated to Israel and later returned to the FSU or moved on to another country have received the least attention in scholarly literature. Hence, this study describes and seeks to account for the patterns of religious and ethnic identification and attachment to Israel among Russian-speaking Israelis (hereafter RSIs) abroad. Specifically, I address the following three questions: 1) what are the patterns of Jewish identification and attachment to Israel among RSIs? 2) how do return migrants (Russian Jews who immigrated to Israel and later returned to their country of origin) differ from repeat migrants (Russian Jews who immigrated to Israel and later moved to a third destination)? and 3) how do key migration factors (such as duration in Israel and time elapsed since leaving Israel), along with demographic and socioeconomic characteristics, affect Jewish identification and attachment to Israel? Findings from this investigation should contribute to our knowledge of the FSU Jewish diaspora and to the wider literature on contemporary transnationalism and diasporas.

THEORETICAL CONSIDERATIONS

The contemporary movement of people involves a large number of developed and developing countries.[7] Although most migration moves from areas in the early stages of modernization to more advanced and developed countries, there are also movements in the opposite direction.[8] Some immigrants intend from the outset to stay only temporarily and return to their country of origin after acquiring human and economic capital.[9] Many of those who stay permanently maintain close contacts with their home country. This has political, economic, and cultural implications for the individual migrants and their families, as well as for the origin and destination societies.

Such migrations are also defined as transnational, and they create ethnonational diasporas.[10] These diasporas establish organizational and communal infrastructures. They maintain group cohesion through residential segregation, informal social networks, political and cultural activities, and economic niches, and remain in close contact with their immigrant peers who settled in other destinations. Through these organizations and relationships, the immigrants maintain the values, social norms, and narratives of their homeland and communicate among themselves in their national language.[11] Ethnic diasporas may have strong emotional attachments to the homeland that are based on primordial social-psychological elements of their group identity.

Members of diasporas may also have a strong political consciousness, which is expressed by lobbying for their homeland in their country of immigration and, if granted the right, by participating in their homeland's political elections. Some homelands even permit representatives of the diaspora to join their parliament.[12] Furthermore, migrants traveling from developing countries to developed countries often send remittances to family, which help strengthen the economy of the origin country.[13] Under certain circumstances and at different times, the emigrants' identification with the homeland might strengthen,[14] often when there is unrest or a security crisis overseas.[15]

Thus, immigrants may develop a double identity. This identity involves relationships and commitments to the new "here" of the host society and to the old "there" of the origin country. The intensity of the identity is not split equally between the two places, and over time it often shifts in favor of the new locality. The spaces that accommodate the connections are further ramified and comprise relations of migrants with coethnics who live in other diasporas as well as with local veteran ethno-religionists.[16] Accordingly, the image of "home" blurs and may include several places: some are personally experienced and have intimate connections to the migrants, while others are imagined, virtual communities linked, inter alia, by the Internet and other technologies.[17]

Immigrants respond to this array of identities in different ways depending on the origin and destination countries, the size of the immigrant population, their socioeconomic stratification, family patterns, and religious and national identification. The type and intensity of transnational activities may also vary among political, economic, or cultural subgroups.[18] A multiple identity is possible today since many host countries tolerate particularistic ethnic and religious identifications, including transnational connections. Likewise, countries of origin and governments have transformed their attitudes toward those who left into more constructive and even sympathetic views.[19]

THE EMPIRICAL FOUNDATION

In order to investigate RSI identification, I used data culled from a diaspora-wide survey, conducted in 2009–2010, among Israeli émigrés.[20] The study was based on a questionnaire on the website of the Israeli Ministry of Immigrant Absorption. It included twenty-five questions that covered demographic characteristics, social and economic attainment, migration and settlement, Jewish identification, and relationships with Israel. The questionnaire was available in Hebrew, English, Russian, French, and Spanish.

Efforts were made to capture the attention of Israelis abroad and to encourage them to fill in the questionnaire. This was done on the home page of the Ministry of Immigrant Absorption, as well as through major search engines (in Hebrew). Overall 2,002 respondents answered the questionnaire. Of these, 209 indicated that they had been born in the FSU. Indeed, this is a rather small sample. It reflects the resources that were available for the study and the number of Russian Israelis abroad who could be conveniently reached. Even if it does not represent precisely the Russian-speaking Israelis diaspora, we believe it provides important insights into the characteristics and determinants of their ethno-religious identification and variations across major areas of settlement.

To be sure, this is not a random sample of Israelis abroad in general, or of the RSI, in particular. I assume that people surfing the website of the Ministry of Immigrant Absorption, whether as a practice or following information on the study, form a selective group. Since the introduction to the questionnaire indicated that its aim was to strengthen the relationship between the State of Israel and its citizens abroad, it stands to reason that the findings reflect the characteristics of those with strong Israeli identification. Nevertheless, several comparisons between our data and results from other studies on Israelis abroad reveal considerable similarities in key demographic and socio-economic characteristics.[21]

THE CREATION OF THE RUSSIAN-SPEAKING ISRAELI DIASPORA

The RSI diaspora developed from two major subgroups. One group consists of Jews who moved from the FSU to Israel and later returned to one of the now independent republics of the FSU. The other group consists of Jews of Soviet background who immigrated to Israel and, after some time, moved to a third country. Our research population is almost equally divided between these two groups: 45.1 percent reside in the FSU (mostly in the European republics), and 54.9 percent, in other countries. Among the latter, the largest concentration is in North America, divided between the United States and Canada (two-thirds and one-third, respectively); another 15 percent resides in West-Central Europe. Nevertheless, RSIs are dispersed, though in small numbers, across the globe (aggregated here under the rubric "rest of world"), which includes Latin America, East Asia, and Oceania.

Attention is now directed to place of birth and place of current residence of the RSIs while also remembering that they lived in Israel prior to their return to the FSU or their onward migration to a new destination. At the outset of the analysis it should be observed that nine of every ten RSIs were born in the European part of the FSU. The largest segment is that of Russian-born Jews (46.1 percent), followed by those born in Ukraine (27.2 percent).[22] The settlement preferences of the RSIs vary according to their place of birth. Russian-born immigrants and those from the Asian part of the FSU exhibit the greatest inclination to return to the FSU; slightly more than half of each of these groups resettled in the FSU. The Russian-born population returned to the European part of the FSU, settling primarily in Russia, their republic of birth. By contrast, those born in the Asian republics are fairly evenly dispersed throughout the Asian and European parts of the FSU.

The geographic dispersion of the Russian-born migrants and those born in the Asian republics who chose not to return to the FSU is very similar. Approximately 20 percent of each group lives in the United States today, about 10 percent in Canada, and close to 15 percent in West-Central Europe. Among those from the Asian FSU, some migrated to different areas of the globe after spending time in Israel. Compared to the Russian-born population, a smaller proportion of those born in Ukraine returned to the FSU (42.9 percent). However, most of the Ukrainian Jews who migrated from Israel back to the FSU returned to Ukraine. The rest of those born in Ukraine settled, in similar numbers, in the United States and Canada, and a lower proportion in West-Central Europe. More than any other group, the "Ukrainians" tend to resettle in the "rest of the world." Among those born in Moldova and the rest of the FSU, 20 percent and 25 percent, respectively, returned to their area of birth. The majority of the people in both groups preferred to move to the United States.

Interestingly, the RSIs resided in Israel for a fairly long period of time. Their average stay in Israel was 11.5 years. More than one-half of the RSIs resided in Israel for eleven years or more, and 20 percent resided there between six and ten years. The proportion that lived in Israel for eleven or more years is especially high among Moldovans and those born in the rest of the European FSU. As shown above, these two groups are characterized by a low rate of migration back to the FSU. Repeat migration involves a long, complicated process of adjustment to a new social and cultural environment, and thus requires more consideration and planning. Such a decision would be more difficult than that of return migration.

Tenure in the current place of residence offers a complementary look at the process of migration. The average tenure of RSIs in their place of residence in the diaspora is about 5.5 years. About 25 percent of them arrived in their place of residence over the last two years and a similar proportion has a tenure of three to five years. Slightly more than one-third have a tenure of six to ten years and approximately 15 percent have resided in their current locality for eleven or more years. The distribution of tenure in current place of residence is quite similar across the various destination areas. Nevertheless, a significant proportion of RSIs in the United States have a long tenure in the country as compared to a much smaller proportion of veteran RSIs in Canada and West-Central Europe.

Overall, the RSI diaspora is concentrated in three major areas: the FSU, North America, and West-Central Europe. Their preferred destination, following temporary residence in Israel, varies by place of origin in the FSU. Likewise, their tenure in Israel is also associated with their place of birth. Slightly less significant is the variation in tenure in current place of residence by place of birth. The two major components involved in the making of the RSI diaspora are place (of birth and current) and time (in Israel and in current place). These are likely to play an important role in shaping their Jewish identification and attachment to Israel.

Overall, the RSIs share a high socioeconomic status and are highly educated. The majority holds academic diplomas—65 percent in the FSU, 69 percent in North America, and 74 percent in West-Central Europe. While in each of the two former areas more than half have a graduate degree (master's or PhD), this is true for only about one-fifth of their counterparts in West-Central Europe. Naturally, the occupations of most of the RSIs are mainly white-collar positions—67 percent in the FSU, 84 percent in North America, and 78 percent in West-Central Europe. In the FSU, there is a clear preference for working in management, while in North America—and to a somewhat lesser extent in West-Central Europe—a large proportion are scientists. These socioeconomic characteristics will be taken into consideration when assessing the determinants and differences in Jewish and Israeli identification of the RSIs in their different areas of settlement.

JEWISH IDENTITY AND IDENTIFICATION

Religious Identity and Denominational Preference

The two complementary dimensions of the ethno-religious orientation of RSIs in the diaspora are Jewish identity and Jewish identification. As explained above, identity reflects the individual's own definition of the nature of his group belonging and his location within social or religious categories. Identification, on the other hand, is the translation of identity into tangible behavioral patterns. This identification consists of different elements particular to the local Jewish milieu and may reflect the status of Judaism in the diaspora as both a religion and an ethnicity.[23] Most of our respondents (70.2 percent) defined themselves as secular, an additional 22.7 percent as traditional, and less than a tenth as religious or ultra-Orthodox. Indeed, in all three geographical areas, most respondents defined themselves as secular. However, it is striking that the proportion of the secular is smallest among the return migrants to the FSU, whereas traditional and religious Jews constitute 36.3 percent of the returnees. By contrast, a high proportion of the RSIs who settled in West-Central Europe are secular, and the rest define themselves as "traditional." The distribution of the religious identities of the RSIs in North America is somewhere between those of their counterparts in the FSU and West-Central Europe.

Despite the low proportion of RSIs who regard themselves as traditional or religious/ultra-Orthodox, they exhibit a preference for one of the religious denominations within Judaism. One of every ten reported his/her denominational preference to be Orthodoxy, but three of ten identified with another denomination—Conservative, Reform, or other. Among the RSIs in the FSU there is much overlap between the distribution of their religious identities and denominational preference. The proportion of the Orthodox (12 percent) is similar to the proportion who defined themselves as religious or ultra-Orthodox, while the proportion who defined themselves as Conservative, Reform, or Other (26.3 percent) resembles the proportion who defined themselves as traditional. The remaining proportion of those with no religious preference overlaps with the proportion who identify themselves as secular. Perhaps because of the availability of synagogues belonging to various denominations, close to half of the RSIs in North America reported a denominational preference. Especially salient is the high rate of Orthodox (12.5 percent—three times higher than the proportion who defined themselves religious/ultra-Orthodox). The rest who expressed a denominational preference indicated Conservative or "other." Very few defined themselves as Reform. By contrast, in West-Central Europe, among those who listed a denominational preference (32 percent) the Reform movement scored highest (16 percent), perhaps because, outside of England, the Conservative movement hardly exists. Interestingly, about half the religious do not identify with any of the three major denominations. It is possible that some of those who indicated "other" identify or are affiliated with Chabad, or other hasidic groups, and regard this sect as different from the "Orthodox" denomination. The traditionalists are dispersed quite evenly across all denominations. The largest category consists of those with no denominational preference.

Jewish Identification: Ritual Observance, Communal Involvement, and Jewish Education

In exploring patterns of Jewish identification, I focus on the observance of key religious practices and holidays, communal involvement, and the experience of children in formal and informal Jewish education.[24] The first category is a composite of prescriptive rituals such as keeping Jewish dietary laws (kashrut), fasting on Yom Kippur, lighting Chanukah candles, and attending Passover seders. The most common behavior, as is true of most Jews around the world, is attendance at a Passover seder. This is practiced by about 75 percent of all RSIs in the diaspora. A similar number celebrate Chanukah by lighting candles, whether during all eight days or only for part of the holiday. About six of every ten respondents fast on Yom Kippur. The least popular behavior is the observance of kashrut; only about a quarter of our respondents claim to observe Jewish dietary laws.

RSIs in West-Central Europe score the lowest on all four indicators of religious practices and holidays. They differ substantially from their counterparts in the other two areas. RSIs in the FSU are characterized by the highest rate of kashrut observance at home. However, they exhibit low levels of observance, as compared to RSIs in North America, in their fasting on Yom Kippur, lighting Chanukah candles all eight days, and seder attendance. The patterns of religious and holiday rituals of RSIs in North America and the FSU present two rather different approaches to group commitment. Among the former, little importance is attached to the private observance of the rigorous daily ritual of kashrut, but there is a relatively strong tendency for intermittent observance of major Jewish holidays which center around family gatherings. These patterns largely coincide with Herbert Gans's concepts of symbolic religiosity and ethnicity.[25] By contrast, in the FSU, the differentials between the rates of those observing the various rituals are much smaller; there is more harmony among the four rituals; and Jewish identification seems more coherent and systematic. Although they exhibit the lowest rates of observance, the outlook of the RSIs in West-Central Europe regarding the organization and interrelations of ritual practices more closely resembles that of their peers in the FSU than of those in North America.

Approximately 10 percent of the RSIs in the diaspora claim to attend synagogue at least once a week and another 5 percent do so on a monthly basis; slightly less than one-third visit the synagogue on the High Holy Days and on special occasions associated with family events. A quarter say they never attend synagogue during the year. The RSIs in West-Central Europe have the weakest affiliation with the synagogue as reflected by the one-third who never visit the synagogue during the year. Furthermore, while about half of all RSIs participate in the social and cultural activities of the local Jewish community, this is true for only 39 percent among those who live in West-Central Europe.

Unlike rituals practiced within the family or community involvement in the public sphere—both of which foreground the adult population—parochial education is aimed at children. Our questions on this matter were also answered by respondents with adult children since we inquired about current as well as past Jewish education. The findings below should be regarded with some caution since they might reflect, among other things, differences in the availability of various types of Jewish education by area of residence. Generally speaking, parochial education for children highlights the importance that their parents attach to Jewish identification and continuity. About a quarter of the RSI respondents enrolled their children in a Jewish day school; another 15 percent sent their children to supplementary Jewish school. However, the overwhelming majority (59 percent) did not provide their children with any Jewish education at all. This high rate contrasts sharply with the likely exposure of these children to Jewish educational content had their parents remained in Israel. The proportion of respondents in West-Central Europe who enrolled their children in all-day Jewish schools is half that of each of the other two areas; this differential is added to by Jewish supplementary education. (The situation is complicated by the different number of day schools in each European country.) As for informal Jewish education, approximately one-fourth of all the children are in a Jewish youth movement. Substantial differences exist between RSIs in the FSU and North America (33 percent and 17 percent, respectively) with West-Central Europe being somewhere between with 29 percent. This wide gap between the FSU and North America may be due to the very small number of Jewish youth groups in the United States. RSIs in all three places express a preference for formal Jewish education over informal Jewish education.

DETERMINANTS OF JEWISH IDENTIFICATION

The Jewish identification patterns of RSIs are determined by many factors. Besides differences in current place of residence, there are demographic and individual socioeconomic characteristics (e.g., age, gender, marital status, education, and occupation) and migration characteristics (e.g., place of residence, number of years in Israel, age at emigration from Israel, tenure in current place of residence, and local citizenship) that may explain variations in Jewish identification. Since these characteristics are probably interrelated, one should isolate each of them in order to evaluate its net effect by keeping all other characteristics constant. This can be achieved through multivariate analysis.

To simplify the impression from the results, I established three indices of Jewish identification. Each index is a composite of several of the detailed practices discussed above. The ritual index is a composite of kashrut observance, fasting on Yom Kippur, lighting Chanukah candles, and attendance at a Passover seder. The community index includes synagogue attendance and participation in Jewish communal, social, and cultural activities. The Jewish education index considers both formal and informal Jewish educational variables. All variables were recoded as 0 (no) or 1 (yes).[26] Thus, the ritual index has a range of 0 to 4, and the community index and the Jewish educational index are both ranked from 0 to 2.

Multivariate analysis (ordinal logistic regression) suggests that, when all other variables in the model are held constant, women have a stronger commitment to ritual practices than men. Educational attainment, especially a post-secondary degree, increases the probability of observing major religious rituals. Regardless of differences in demographic, socioeconomic, and migration factors, RSIs who live in West-Central Europe tend to practice religious rituals less often. Leaving Israel between ages thirty and thirty-nine is negatively associated with ritual observance as compared with those who emigrated at older ages. Finally, holding citizenship in the current country of residence is also associated with weak religious behaviors.

Place of residence itself is not a significant determinant of communal involvement or Jewish education for children. Like the ritual index, communal involvement is stronger among women. It is negatively associated with a managerial occupation, as well as with emigration from Israel at older ages. The sole, but very powerful, determinant of providing a Jewish education for children is the educational attainment of their parents; for each level of education completed beyond secondary school—namely, some college, a college degree, or a graduate degree—we expect an increase of about 20 in the order log odds of the Jewish educational index. Overall, a relatively small number of variables explain the differences in levels of Jewish identification among the RSI diaspora. Still, these variables explain the fair amount of variation in the religious, communal, and Jewish education indices of 16 percent, 21 percent, and 31 percent, respectively.

ISRAELI IDENTIFICATION AND ORIENTATION

Fluency in Hebrew

A major dimension of adaptation to a given society, which contributes to the individual's attachment to it, is proficiency in its language. Language proficiency allows a wide range of exposure to the society through newspapers, literature, and other materials in the society's language; listening to the media in the particular country; consumption of its culture; and the ability to communicate with local people. It should be emphasized that there is a great difference between Russian, a Slavic language that is the mother tongue of most Soviet Jews, and Hebrew, a Semitic language. The proficiency of the RSIs in Hebrew is dependent, among other things, on their knowledge of Hebrew prior to their immigration to Israel, their acquisition of Hebrew in Israel, and the duration of their stay in Israel. It is also influenced by their age of immigration to Israel, as learning a new language is easier at younger ages.

Unsurprisingly, the ability to speak Hebrew is more common than the ability to read or write. A high proportion (83 percent) of the respondents reported that their ability to speak Hebrew was either "good" or "very good." The parallel rates for reading and writing in Hebrew are 76 percent and 72 percent, respectively. If we add those who reported little knowledge of Hebrew, it can be stated that almost all of the RSIs have some knowledge of Hebrew.

However, we cannot generalize to the entire population. There are differences according to place of residence. The North Americans and West-Central Europeans have much better knowledge of Hebrew than their counterparts who returned to the FSU. About three times as many of the former two groups reported very good knowledge in speaking, reading, and writing Hebrew as compared to the RSIs in the FSU. Those who settled in North America exhibit the highest levels of Hebrew in all its three dimensions. In fact, about nine of every ten RSIs in North America and West-Central Europe report good or very good fluency in speaking, reading, and writing Hebrew. By contrast, only two-thirds of the RSIs in the FSU indicated that their spoken Hebrew is good or very good, and for reading and writing the parallel rates were less than one-half. Multivariate analysis should show whether this is associated with socio-demographic variation and emigration variables, or with other factors not indexed by the survey data.

Relationships with Israel

There are tangible expressions of attachment to a homeland. These include visits to the country and the intensity of contacts with family and friends. Furthermore, it stands to reason that there is some correlation between the different forms of relationships with the homeland and those having family or friends visiting Israel more often. We should also take into account that distances between the current area of residence and Israel affect the cost of travel; hence, RSIs in North America will travel less often compared to those residing in West-Central Europe or in the FSU.

We found that 80 percent of the RSIs are "always" in contact with family in Israel and another 8 percent have such contact "often." Slightly more than 80 percent are always or often in contact with friends in Israel. A high proportion (about half) of the RSIs visit Israel at least once a year and, with the addition of the next two categories, seven out of every ten visit Israel at least once every three years. These indicators attest to a strong relationship of diaspora RSIs with Israel.

RSIs in West-Central Europe are the most frequent visitors to Israel. The proportion among them who visit Israel at least once a year—73 percent—is substantially higher than among their counterparts in the other two areas—43 percent of those residing in North America and 39 percent of those in the FSU. Indeed, the former are those who have the most intensive ties with family in Israel, which could explain a strong desire to visit the country; yet, the differences in the intensity of family ties by area of residence are not as significant as the difference in visits to Israel. Somewhat surprisingly, RSIs in the FSU visit Israel less frequently than those who reside in North America. Besides the distance, visits to Israel may be affected by key individual demographic and socioeconomic characteristics that will be adjusted later in the multivariate analysis. Meanwhile, I suggest that perhaps because of strong familial ties among RSIs in the FSU, there are more reciprocal visits, namely of family in Israel who travel to the FSU, which can then include gatherings with friends in the old country, nostalgic visits to certain sites, and a vacation in a familiar landscape and climate. This would be much less common among relatives travelling from Israel to North America.

Approximately two-thirds of the RSIs in the FSU are always in contact with friends in Israel. The parallel figures among their counterparts in West-Central Europe and North America are lower—57 percent and 51 percent, respectively. However, if we combine those who keep friendship contacts "always" and "often," the differentials diminish substantially.

Consumption of Israeli Culture

Israelis abroad have a variety of means through which they can obtain information and culture from Israel. The availability of such channels may vary by place. Likewise, the consumption of some of the available cultural products requires knowledge of Hebrew—which, as shown above, is not evenly distributed among the RSIs—and hence may contribute to spatial variations. I examine the frequency in the consumption of three cultural products: the press (written or electronic) in Hebrew, Israeli websites (other than newspapers) in Hebrew; and watching Israeli movies that may include translations into the local language.

News is the most frequently consumed product among RSIs abroad. More than half of our respondents report that they read Israeli newspapers very often, and another 20 percent read them to some extent. News can be obtained by purchasing Israeli newspapers abroad or through the Internet. Thus, it seems that RSIs abroad are well aware of what is happening in Israel. The Internet was found to be a source of information on Israel; slightly more than one-third surf Hebrew sites "very often" and another quarter do so "sometimes." Movies rank a distant the third as a source of cultural contact with Israel: only about one-third watch Israeli movies "very often" or "to some extent."

This ranking of the means of consuming information and culture resembles the characteristics of RSIs in North America and West-Central Europe. In the FSU, the frequency of reading newspapers and surfing the Internet is very similar. Accordingly, while the rate of RSIs in the FSU who read Israeli newspapers is significantly lower than among their counterparts in North America and West-Central Europe, the RSIs in the FSU surf Israeli websites most intensively. Following an approach of looking at the two highest frequency categories together ("very much" and "somewhat") respondents in West-Central Europe have the highest rate of reading Israeli newspapers; respondents in the FSU have the highest rate of surfing the Internet for Israeli content, whereas the highest rate of watching Israeli movies is among respondents in North America.

DETERMINANTS OF ISRAELI IDENTIFICATION

Multivariate analysis can offer deeper insight into the determinants of the level of Israeli identification. To this end, I created four indicators of Israeli identification: a Hebrew proficiency index, an index of visits to Israel, an Israeli contact index, and an Israeli cultural index. Each index includes one or more of the detailed Israeli identification variables discussed above. The index of Hebrew proficiency is composed of the variables related to speaking, reading, and writing the language. The second index—visits to Israel—is the original variable of this behavior. The third index—Israeli contacts—is composed of the variables of familial and social relationships. The last index—Israeli culture—takes into account the consumption of press in Hebrew, Internet sites in Hebrew, and Israeli movies. Each of the original variables of Israeli identification has values from 0 to 3. Hence, the first and the fourth indices are in the range of 0 to 9, the second index ranges from 0 to 3, and the third index ranges from 0 to 6. The appropriate multivariate technique for these dependent variables is ordinal logistic regression.

When all other factors are held constant, work in management is positively associated with proficiency in Hebrew. Unlike blue-collar professions and some other white-collar jobs, management involves considerable use of the local language. To the extent that present occupation outside of Israel is a good proxy for the respondent's occupation in Israel, it can explain the direction and significance of this relationship. One may further postulate that respondents who indicated that they work in management take advantage of their acquaintance with Israel to establish business and other professional relationships with people and companies there, which help them to maintain their knowledge of Hebrew. The number of years that RSIs lived in Israel is also positively associated with proficiency in Hebrew. Likewise, being between eighteen and thirty-nine years old is a significant predictor of high proficiency in Hebrew as compared to older age cohorts. In agreement with the descriptive findings, respondents who reside in North America exhibit better knowledge of Hebrew than do their counterparts who returned to the FSU. The explanatory power of the model is very impressive; it reached a level of nearly two-thirds (63 percent).

The tendency to visit Israel, as well as maintain contacts with Israeli family and friends, is stronger among women than among men. This may reflect differences in gender roles, with women taking more responsibility for familial and social matters. The longer the RSIs lived in Israel, the more often they visit the country. Interestingly, tenure abroad is also positively associated with visits to Israel. It is possible that after the formative years abroad—adjusting to the new environment, finding a job, and gaining some disposable income—there are more opportunities for trips and vacations, with Israel as a serious option. Yet, citizenship in the present country of residence inhibits visits to Israel, attesting to the strengthening of local ties over relationships with the homeland. In fact, longer tenure in Israel is also consistently and positively associated with the Israeli contact index and Israeli cultural index, while local citizenship has the opposite relationships. When demographic, socioeconomic, and migration characteristics are held constant, RSIs in West-Central Europe and in North America have weaker Israeli contacts; they also consume Israeli culture less intensively than do their counterparts in the FSU. These two expressions of Israeli orientation increase commensurate with education, and working in professional and managerial occupations also positively influences the consumption of Israeli culture.

In comparison with proficiency in Hebrew, the independent variables are less robust for explaining visits to Israel, Israeli contacts, and the consumption of Israeli culture. The explanatory variance for each of these three identification indices is less than half that for proficiency in Hebrew. Nevertheless, an explanatory power of 31 percent for visits to Israel, 25 percent for Israeli contact, and 28 percent for consumption of Israeli culture may be regarded as satisfactory.

SUMMARY AND DISCUSSION

This chapter has examined the patterns and determinants of ethno-religious identification and attachment to Israel among Russian-speaking Israelis (RSIs) in the diaspora. It has also provided a comparative examination of these issues in three of their major areas of settlement—the FSU, North America, and West-Central Europe. RSIs in the FSU are migrants who returned to their country of origin while their counterparts in North America and West-Central Europe are repeat migrants. There are important studies on the Soviet Jewish diaspora, including those in the FSU or elsewhere abroad as well as those who live in Israel, but to the best of my knowledge this is the first attempt to examine Russian-speaking Jews who lived in Israel and later left.

Results from a worldwide survey of Israelis abroad conducted in 2009–2010 indicate that RSIs in West-Central Europe observe fewer Jewish rituals than their counterparts who returned to the FSU. They also maintain weaker contacts with family and friends in Israel, and are less inclined to consume Israeli culture. These latter two expressions of Israeli identification are weak among RSIs in North America. By contrast, for reasons not immediately apparent, RSIs in North America scored highest in Hebrew proficiency. I did not find significant regional variations for other indicators of Jewish identification—communal involvement, parochial education for children, and visits to Israel. Based on this empirical evidence, it would seem that the RSIs in the FSU have the strongest group identification, followed by their peers in North America, with those settling in West-Central Europe having the weakest identification. Other factors involved in the dynamics of the RSI migration are tenure in Israel, which is positively associated with the various dimensions of Israeli identification; tenure abroad, which did not play a significant role in determining either Jewish or Israeli identification and did not distance respondents from particularistic group behaviors; and citizenship in present country of residence, which had a significant negative relationship with four of the seven expressions of group identification examined here.

Thus, environment is an important element of religious and ethnic behavior. The environment embodies a general social and cultural ethos, including the nature and role of group identity, the opportunities that communal infrastructure provides for exercising group identification, and the presence of a critical mass of co-ethno-religionists, which shapes the cohesion and commitment of minority groups. Return migrants are well acquainted with their "new" old home, including their ethno-religious community, and are likely to have relatives and friends in the area. Their familiarity with the local language and culture further eases the maintenance of group behaviors. RSIs who returned to the FSU are exposed to changes in the general atmosphere that allow religious worship as well as numerous Jewish activities and services. After decades of religious and national oppression during the communist era, Jews (and other ethnic groups) have an intensified desire to express group consciousness and individual identity. Together with strong confidence about their status in Russian society, which is anchored in the citizenship they often continued to hold while residing in Israel, they exhibit high levels of Jewish identification and attachment to Israel.

North America has absorbed large numbers of Russian-speaking immigrants. The multi-cultural societies of Canada and the United States are sympathetic toward new immigrants' desires to maintain ties with their homelands. The two countries also have strong and developed Jewish infrastructures. Beside their large Jewish populations, they also have sizable numbers of Soviet Jews from the pre-perestroika immigration, as well as Soviet Jews who arrived after 1990. Such conditions encourage affiliation and group cohesion. Still, this is not a return to their homes. The RSIs who have settled in North America have to learn the local language and culture, seek local citizenship, and devote more effort to finding employment and living arrangements than if they had returned to the FSU. Moreover, repeat migrants who lived relatively briefly in three countries, namely the FSU, Israel, and the United States/Canada, are likely to encounter stronger obstacles to integration into the new community than migrants who return to a familiar environment. In this regard, the RSIs who settled in West-Central Europe are also repeat migrants. In addition to the need to adjust to the new place, they face a strong national ethos of clear, unequivocal local commitment. That is, while the model of the United States and Canada is essentially one of civic nationality in a united political framework with unanimity among the inhabitants on key social and cultural principles, many European countries are ethnic nations. Each is rooted in the shared history, religion, customs, and culture of its inhabitants, making it difficult for newcomers to maintain distinct group affiliation. From the point of view of ethno-religious belonging, the Jewish communal infrastructure, attachment to Israel, and the size of the Jewish population in Europe, although these vary from country to country, are nevertheless weaker than in the United States and, quite often, than those in Canada.

We should think of the environment not only as the current place of residence but also as a mediating entity between the country of origin and the final destination country. In the case of the RSIs, Israel was that environment that we label their "homeland." Here, the environment, on one hand, and duration of residence in Israel, on the other, intertwine to positively affect attachment to Israel. This dimension of time also determines, albeit indirectly, attachment to the current place of residence (FSU, North America, or West-Central Europe) and shapes an identity that involves two countries: homeland and host country.

RSIs who moved to a third country, namely North America or West-Central Europe, are very mobile geographically. The large number of moves among new areas may betray a lack of confidence or decisiveness as to the appropriate place to live. It is also possible that no final decision has been made regarding the current residence and it is only an exploration of another alternative. Economic opportunities or chain migration to follow other family members may also explain such intensive mobility. Such circumstances make it difficult and unprofitable for immigrants to plant deep roots in a local community, which is likely to involve membership fees and efforts to develop social ties. As far as the United States is concerned, following the initial settlement, the RSIs may undertake an internal move to a different region or state which, according to the "disruption" model of migration-identity relationships—quite robust among the wider American Jewish population[27]—would further distance them from affiliation with the Jewish community. This may also be true for West-Central Europe, given the ease of movement between countries in the European Union.

Likewise, leaving Israel, on the one hand, and not returning to an environment of mutual familiarity of the individual and the Jewish community in the FSU, on the other, may reflect a desire to maintain distance from intensive Jewish life. This is better facilitated after citizenship is acquired and settlement becomes permanent because there is much less need for assistance and welfare services from the Jewish community. Here, the distinction suggested in the theoretical literature between transnational communities and trans-state diasporas is relevant.[28] The notion of transnational communities emphasizes the stream of people, ideas, and goods across borders in a way that negates nationality and nationalism as the paramount sources of identity and identification. "Trans-state diasporas" attaches great importance to ethno-national identity, which is associated with a real or imagined country of origin, whose members have memories of their homeland and are strongly involved in social, cultural, and political matters regarding that homeland. The RSIs, by virtue of their voluntary participation in this study (perhaps like any other study which defines its target population according to self-definition), largely correspond to the concept of a trans-state diaspora. Indeed, like trans-state entities more generally, the RSIs are not a homogenous group;

they have a core of members with strong identification, and peripheral members who display weak ethno-religious behaviors and maintain few contacts with the organized community. Still, both the core and peripheral members share a common ethno-national origin. Judging by their consciousness and self-definition, they are people who belong to a distinctive diasporic entity.

Future investigations of RSIs whose historical homeland served as a temporary place of residence should seek to rely on a random sample. They should locate Soviet-born Jews who lived for some time in Israel; inquire into their national and ethno-religious identities; define more accurately the nature of this diaspora and how its members fit the concepts of transnational and trans-state diasporas; identify the determinants of their group identity; and demonstrate how this identity is associated with behaviors and attitudes. Special attention should be directed to understanding where the "homeland" is for these migrants and the meaning and attachment they attribute to the other areas involved in their migrations. Such a sample should include a larger number of respondents. Ideally, it would be possible to break down the categories of "West-Central Europe" and "FSU" into individual countries. It would also be beneficial to add other areas of settlement for repeat migrants, which would have a sufficient number of cases. Such studies should inquire more deeply into the motivations for the different types and directions of migration. In the meantime, I hope the present study provides valuable insights into a relatively new diaspora that has evolved due to geopolitical changes in the FSU. This diaspora can serve as an important case for understanding the nature and dynamics of present-day international migrants and their group identification.

NOTES

Due to space limitation this chapter does not includes tables. Upon request, I will be happy to provide detailed tables of both descriptive and multivariate analyses (uzi.rebhun@mail.huji.ac.il). I wish to thank Maya Malach for her helpful assistance in data analysis and Judith Even for editorial assistance.

1. Charles Hirschman, "The Role of Religion in the Origins and Adaptation of Immigrants Groups in the United States," *International Migration Review* 38.3 (September 2004): 1206–1233; Gabriel Sheffer, "A Reexamination of the Main Theoretical Approaches to the Study of Diasporas and their Applicability to the Jewish Diaspora," in *Transnationalism: Diasporas and the Advent of a New (Dis)Order*, ed. Eliezer Ben-Rafael and Yitzhak Sternberg, with Judit Bokser Liwerant and Yosef Gorny (Leiden and Boston: Brill, 2010), 375–396; Steven Vertovec, "Migrant Transnationalism and Models of Transformation," *International Migration Review* 38.3 (September 2004): 970–1001.
2. United Nations, Department of Economics and Social Affairs, Population Division, http://esa.un.org/migration/p2kodata.asp.
3. Stephen Castles and Mark J. Miller, *The Age of Migration*, 2nd ed. (New York: Guilford, 1998).
4. Ludger Pries, "New Migration in Transnational Spaces," in *Migration and Transnational Social Spaces*, ed. Ludger Pries (Aldershot, UK: Ashgate Publishing Company, 1999), 1–35.

5. Mark Tolts, *Some Demographic and Socio-Economic Trends of the Jews in Russia and the FSU: Final Report* (Jerusalem: The Hebrew University, The Harman Institute of Contemporary Jewry, Division of Jewish Demography and Statistics, 2009), 16.
6. William Safran, "Diasporas in Modern Societies: Myths of Homeland and Return," *Diaspora: A Journal of Transnational Studies* 1.1 (1991): 83–99.
7. Thomas Friedman, *The World is Flat: A Brief History of the Twenty-First Century* (New York: Farrar, Straus & Giroux, 2005).
8. Douglas S. Massey, "Why Does Immigration Occur? A Theoretical Synthesis," in *The Handbook of International Migration: The American Experience*, ed. Charles Hirschman, Philip Kasinets, and Josh DeWind (New York: Russel Sage Foundation, 1999), 34–51.
9. Linda Basch, Nina Glick Shiller, and Cristina Blanc-Szanton, *Nations Unbound: Transnational Projects, Postcolonial Predicaments, and Deterritorialized Nation States* (Basel, Switzerland: Gordon and Breach, 1994); Leonard Dinnerstein, Roger L. Nichols, and David M. Reimers, *Native Strangers: Blacks, Indians, and Immigrants in America* (New York: Oxford University Press, 1990); Luis E. Guarnizo, "The Economics of Transnational Living," *International Migration Review* 37.3 (September 2003): 666–699.
10. Stephane Dufoix, *Diasporas* (Berkeley: University of California Press, 2008).
11. Peggy Levitt, Josh Dewind, and Steven Vertovec, "International Perspectives on Transnational Migration: An Introduction," *International Migration Review* 37.3 (September 2004): 565–575; Michael P. Smith, "Transnational Urbanism Revisited," *Journal of Ethnic and Migration Studies* 35.2 (March 2005): 235–244.
12. Peggy Levitt and B. Nadya Jaworsky, "Transnational Migration Studies: Past Development and Future Trends," *Annual Review of Sociology* 33 (2007): 129–156; Michael P. Smith, *Transnational Urbanism: Locating Globalization* (Malden, MA: Blackwell, 2000).
13. Yossi Shain, *Marketing the American Creed Abroad: Diasporas in the U.S. and Their Homelands* (New York: Cambridge University Press, 1999).
14. Levitt and Glick Schiller, "Conceptualizing Simultaneity: A Transnational Social Field Perspective," *International Migration Review* 38 (2004): 1002–1039; Smith, *Transnational Urbanism*.
15. Yossi Shain, *Kinship and Diasporas in International Affairs* (Ann Arbor: University of Michigan Press, 2007); Matthew F. Jacobson, *Special Sorrows: The Diasporic Imagination of Irish, Polish, and Jewish Immigrants in the United States* (Berkeley: University of California Press, 2002).
16. Eliezer Ben-Rafael and Yitzhak Sternberg, "Debating Transnationalism," in Ben-Rafael et al., *Transnationalism*, 1–25; Levitt and Jaworsky, "Transnational Migration Studies."
17. Robin Cohen, "Solid, Ductile and Liquid: Changing Notions of Homeland and Home in Diaspora Studies," in Ben-Rafael et al., *Transnationalism*, 117–133; Dufoix, *Diasporas*.
18. Nadia Y. Kim, "Patriarchy Is So Third World: Korean Immigrant Women 'Migrating' White Western Masculinity," *Social Problems* 53.4 (November 2006): 519–536; Levitt and Glick Schiller, "Conceptualizing Simultaneity"; Sarah J. Mahler and Patricia R. Pessar, "Gender Matters: Ethnographers Bring Gender from Periphery toward the Core of Migration Studies," *International Migration Review* 40.1 (February 2006): 27–63.
19. Gabriel Sheffer, "Israelis, Israel, and the Jewish Diaspora in the Last Decade," *Kivunim Hadashim (New Directions): Journal of Zionism and Judaism* 5 (October 2001): 148–170 (in Hebrew).
20. Uzi Rebhun and Israel Pupko, *Far but Home: Migration, Jewish Identification, and Attachment to Homeland among Israelis Abroad (A Research Report)* (Jerusalem: The Hebrew University of Jerusalem, Israel Ministry of Immigration Absorption, and the Jewish Agency for Israel, 2010) (in Hebrew).
21. Yinon Cohen, *Size and Selectivity Patterns among Israeli Born immigrants in OECD Countries* (Florence: European University Institute, 2009).
22. There were not enough people from Belarus and the Baltic countries to form a separate category.

23. Alan J. Winter, "The Transformation of Community Integration Among American Jewry: Religion or Ethnoreligion? A National Replication," *Review of Religious Research* 33.4 (June 1992): 349–363; Jonathan S. Woocher, *Sacred Survival: The Civil Religion of American Jews* (Bloomington: Indiana University Press, 1986).

24. There are important differences in the structure of Jewish communities of the three destination areas. To a large extent, each area (or country) has its own communal characteristics. Jewish communities in the United States are built on an associational base (See Daniel J. Elazar, *People and Polity: The Organizational Dynamics of World Jewry* [Detroit: Wayne University Press, 1989]). The connections with organized Jewish life are based on voluntary association with particularistic organizations or institutions. The most frequent pattern of the affiliated Jew is that of multiple memberships which strengthen each other and reinforce the overall group identity. The synagogue and Jewish Communal Center (JCC) are the focal points of communal affiliation and encompass different types of activities—religious, social, educational, or cultural. These communities operate largely at the local level and are rather independent. There is much fluidity and transition among congregations.

In Western Europe, the organization of Jews is much more centralized (Sergio DellaPergola, "Jews in the European Community: Sociodemographic Trends and Challenges," *American Jewish Year Book* [1993], 93: 25–82; Elazar, *People and Polity*). There are integrative organizational structures that have not only religious meanings but also salient social and political roles. Organizational affiliation is viewed in terms of position and needs of the Jewish group vis-à-vis the general society. The national Jewish community is afforded some type of official recognition by the host governments. In some West European countries Jews are automatically registered as members of the Jewish community unless they opt out. These patterns reflect the civil and national nature of European society and the tension that exists between Jews and their general society in each country. In the last few years, following the geopolitical changes associated with the formation of the European Union, some European-wide roof organizations have been established but their overall influence is insignificant.

Jewish communal structures in the FSU somewhat resemble that of the United States in that they are split into independent communities (Semen Charnyi, "Judaism Across the Commonwealth of Independent States," in *Religion and Politics in Russia: A Reader*, ed. Marjorie M. Blazer, [Armonk, NY: M. E. Sharpe, 2010], 182–190; Betsy Gidwitz, *Post Soviet Jewry on the Cusp of Its Third Decade—Part 1* [Jerusalem: Jerusalem Center for Public Affairs, 2011 http://www.jcpa.org/JCPA/indexPH.asp]). These communities are often affiliated with a certain denomination or religious sect. Nevertheless, membership does not involve fees, or at least only minimal payment, and unlike in the United States membership is often aimed at receiving material assistance and support. Multiple memberships are common, which increases the sources of support for the individual.

25. Herbert J. Gans, "Symbolic Ethnicity: The Future of Ethnic Groups and Cultures in America," *Ethnic and Racial Studies* 2.1 (January 1979): 1–20; Herbert J. Gans, "Symbolic Ethnicity and Religiosity: Towards a Comparison of Ethnic and Religious Acculturation," *Ethnic and Racial Studies* 17.4 (October 1994): 577–592.

26. The variables which originally had more than two values and had to be recoded are "Chanukah candles," which here distinguishes between those who do not light Chanukah candles at all (0) and those who do light a few days or all eight days. Synagogue attendance regrouped those who do not attend at all or only on special occasions into one category (0) and those who attend synagogue on High Holy Days, once a month, or once a week (1); formal Jewish education differentiates between those whose children did not attend a Jewish school (0) and those whose children were enrolled in either day or supplementary education (1).

27. Sidney Goldstein and Alice Goldstein, *Jews on the Move: Implications for Jewish Identity* (Albany: SUNY Press, 1996).

28. Sheffer, "A Reexamination."

3 · HOME IN THE DIASPORA?

Jewish Returnees and
Transmigrants in Ukraine

MARINA SAPRITSKY

> "Jewish is not a nationality, it is a mode of transportation."
> —Popular Soviet joke

Jewish citizens of the USSR emigrated with great difficulty during some periods of Soviet rule and more freely following its fragmentation into independent states. The breakup of the USSR paved the way for one of the largest waves of Jewish emigration. Suddenly, the possibility of leaving—to a myriad of destinations—became a reality for ex-Soviet Jews. However, not everyone took the opportunity to emigrate and, for those who did, Israel was by no means the obvious place to go. The choice of the Jewish population that remained in the Former Soviet Union (hereafter, FSU) baffled many human rights crusaders who, ever since the Soviet borders opened slightly in the 1970s, had seen themselves as liberating Jews from communist repression and anti-Semitism. According to one source addressing the Jewish diaspora, "Emigration from the 'land of state-sponsored anti-Semitism' has been the dominant lens through which everyone has seen Jewish life in Russia."[1] The fact that at one point the majority of emigrating Jews chose destinations other than Israel was also highly disappointing for Zionists. Emigration from the former Soviet states has slowed down greatly and, as Uzi Rebhun shows in chapter 2, we can now analyze a new dimension of ex-Soviet Jewish migration: their return.

DEBATES ON EX-SOVIET JEWISH RETURN MIGRATION

The emigration of Israeli citizens from Israel to the United States and Europe has been described previously,[2] yet the out-migration of FSU-born Jews from Israel has only recently captured the attention of politicians, scholars of Russian-speaking Jewry, and journalists. The fact that, for the first time in the history of

Russian Jewish migration, "more Jews [were] migrating *to* Russia from Israel than the other way around"[3] has elicited concern in Israel.

Statistics related to Jewish migration from Israel back to the FSU vary greatly. According to research conducted in Israel in 2004, between 2001 and 2003 alone, nearly 50,000 ex-Soviet Jews returned from Israel to Russia and other independent countries.[4] A report released by the Federation of Jewish Communities of Russia stated that while about 50,000 Jewish former emigrants to Israel returned to Russia since 2001, only about 30,000 Russian Jews left for Israel.[5] Meanwhile, Yevgeny Satanovsky, former president of the Russian Jewish Congress, noted that over the same period, 100,000 Russian Jews returned to their countries of origin or other industrial centers and capital cities in the FSU.[6] The number of Israeli returnees in Moscow alone is estimated at 50,000.[7] However, as Mark Tolts notes, "There are a lot of ungrounded statements concerning huge numbers of FSU outmigrants from Israel."[8] Relying on the official statistics of the Russian and Ukrainian governments, Tolts reports in his chapter that there were 17,438 registered returnees to the Russian Federation from 1997 to 2009 and 14,955 returnees to Ukraine. Because many returnees do not register with the local passport office and hold on to their Israeli passports, the number of registered returnees (and hence the number who show up in official statistics) is much smaller than the mass of returnees who typically opt to hold on to their foreign passports. Many of the so-called "returnees" also frequently travel back and forth to Israel and are therefore automatically excluded from the statistics of out-migrants calculated by the Israeli state.[9] Nonetheless, Israeli officials expressed concern about a possible Russian "brain drain" and the general increase in Russian out-migration from Israel. In a 2007 survey of 4,214 Russian-speaking Jewish respondents, 90 percent of whom resided in Israel, 81 percent said they had thought about leaving Israel.[10] Some Israeli sociologists, including Elizar Feldman, insist that many of the returnees are not "failed cases of *aliyah*" (individuals who were unable to adapt to an Israeli way of life) but, rather, young, well-educated, and capable individuals whose skills could not be accommodated in Israel's limited employment market and who had reached a "glass ceiling."[11] Other specialists in Russian Jewish migration insist that, due to the nearly identical characteristics of emigrants *from* Russia to Israel and immigrants *to* Russia from Israel, the recent developments "do not cause a 'brain drain' in either place."[12] Together with other groups of Israelis who choose to live outside Israel, the outflow of Russian-speaking Jews could be perceived as undermining the "Zionist assertion that Israel is the best place for Jews to live."[13] Some social scientists, journalists, and their readers have expressed "surprise" at this development.[14] Evidently, the old narratives of Soviet repression still lingered. In response, Satanovsky warned Western audiences not to read too much into this trend and to look beyond the Soviet days of repression. "There is no Iron Curtain anymore, and that's what the phenomenon is. . . . Nobody is surprised when an American Jew goes to Nepal for a work contract and then returns to visit his aunt in New Jersey. . . . All these are simply signs that Russia is a normal country now."[15] While the old narratives of Soviet repression and anti-Semitism are still very much in force in the media,[16] new stereotypes are also being propagated in which "returnees galvanize Jewish community life"[17] and "revive Jewish culture."[18] Those who have experienced life in the Jewish "homeland" are thus perceived as having become active and knowledgeable Jews who have something to teach local Jews in the old homeland about Judaism and Jewish community.[19]

In this chapter, I attempt to grapple with return migration and transnational patterns among Jewish ex-Soviet emigrants and their family members who have recently returned from Israel, either to their place of origin or to another location in the FSU to take advantage of new entrepreneurial, professional, educational, and personal opportunities, or just to feel "at home." Going beyond the debated statistics and the stereotypes promoted by the media, I aim to present material about the everyday reality of returnees, including the motives for their return and the various ways they adjust to their home environments following a prolonged period of absence. I analyze the ways in which returnees to Odessa, Ukraine, forge and dissolve ties within their social environments in order to construct and negotiate their sense of belonging. I argue that most ex-Soviet Jewish returnees do not envision their return as permanent. They entertain the option of an eventual return to their original emigration destination or relocation to yet another destination. The freedom of choice guaranteed by a foreign passport allows returning Jews to approach "home" as both a place of familiarity and a place of discovery.[20] Placing my research within the larger context of diaspora studies, I end this chapter with an analysis of the homeland-diaspora dichotomy, which is significantly complicated by the case of Odessan Jews and their patterns of migration.

WHO RETURNS AND WHY

Israeli returnees had different reasons for leaving Israel and for choosing to return to Odessa, whether on a permanent, undefined, or temporary basis. These included family obligations, career development, the danger of living in the Middle East, and improving economic and social prospects in Ukraine. For the most part, the returnees I met were from Israel; a smaller percentage migrated from Germany, and a few from Australia and the United States. This pattern may be explained by the fact that "migration to the USA and Germany usually entails inter-generational families, rather than individual Jewish youth and young couples, as is frequently the case with Israel."[21] Another explanation of the low frequency of returns from the United States and Australia is the distance and cost of travel. While visits from Germany were very common,[22] permanent returns were less frequent. European citizenship and the accompanying social benefits are some of the main reasons "Germans" visiting Odessa gave to explain this pattern.

Among the returnees I met were people who had simply never managed to find their way in Israel and, facing economic, social, or personal constraints, decided to return home. Among such so-called "failed cases of *aliyah*" were young Jews who had set off on their own and found it difficult to survive without family support.²³ In other instances, elderly Odessans had found themselves too dependent on others for communication and everyday tasks, and middle-aged migrants struggled to make a living. There were also well-to-do migrants lured back to Odessa by business opportunities. To this particular group of "opportunity seekers," life in Israel presented no obstacles of acclimatization; instead, they chose to leave because of better prospects abroad. These returns were often impermanent, with individuals frequently traveling back and forth. This group, whom I call "transmigrants," divided their time between multiple locales with split business and family commitments.

Some Israelis in Odessa moved to the city to study or work for one of the local Jewish organizations.²⁴ The returnees, transmigrants, and long-term visitors whom I met were not all originally from Odessa. In some cases, returnees were natives of other cities in the FSU but were drawn to Odessa by a personal or professional connection.

NARRATIVES OF RETURNEES

Nina and her son Kostia were among the first returnees from Israel I met in Odessa. They were not acquainted with others who had returned.²⁵ Leaving Odessa in 1989, Nina had returned in 2000, and her son followed a year later. In our initial conversations, it had already become obvious that Nina's decision to immigrate to Israel had not been driven by Zionist ideology or by a desire to live in the Jewish homeland. She did not see her move to Israel as "going home." On the contrary, she described leaving Odessa as "a difficult decision of leaving my native home." At the same time, she told me she had been comforted by the idea that she was going to a place where no one would call her *zhidovka* [yid] and, in that sense, she would feel *more* at home.

She reflected on her time in Israel with mixed emotions. Nina had struggled economically for the eleven years she spent in Israel as she and her son changed jobs, apartments, and cities in order to make ends meet. She also faced other social problems associated with immigrant life, including nostalgia and the unfamiliar local climate. At the same time, she spoke of Israel as a "holy place" where she could feel history, see breathtaking landscapes, and sense the presence of God. In Israel, Nina started attending religious services, not at a synagogue but at a Russian Orthodox Church, which she described as being "culturally close" to her. She recalled meeting a number of other Jews during services who were *vykresty* [baptized Jews].²⁶ It was during her years in Israel that Nina claims to have become closer to Jesus Christ, a relationship she still maintained through regular prayer and conversations with evangelical missionaries who visited her home. Other than occasional visits to the Jewish Club for the Elderly, Gmilus Hesed, Nina did not take part in Jewish activities in Odessa nor identify herself as being Jewish through any of the new avenues available to Jews in the city.

Though Nina had formed some attachment to Israel, in the end it was not enough to make her stay. She was one of the few returnees I met who, on coming home, opted to change her Israeli passport for a Ukrainian one, which she needed in order to receive a pension and acquire a *propiska* [certificate of residency]. Most returnees held tight to their Israeli passports for travel purposes, and for the advantages of having an alternative country of residence.[27] "I came back to a lot of new things," she explained, "but I still came back home." When I asked Nina how others in the city responded to her return, she had little to say. "I don't tell many people about it," she explained, adding, "I don't want to brag about living abroad." Referring to a painful incident after her return when one of her neighbors called her a *zhidovka*, Nina said that ordinary Ukrainians (especially newly arrived migrants to the city from other parts of Ukraine) were jealous of the opportunities available to Jews. Her son, Kostia, had never experienced any such negative reactions as a returnee. Rather, "the people [he] told about Israel were always curious to know more."

Kostia was nearly eighteen when he followed his mother to Israel. This was the first time he and his mother had left the Soviet Union. Soon after his arrival, he was admitted to one of Tel Aviv's leading art institutes, which he attended for several months but eventually left because he needed a job. Despite his efforts, Kostia never managed to obtain a degree or master Hebrew well enough to use it on a professional level, which greatly limited his employment opportunities. Nonetheless, he saw his time in Israel positively, as extremely meaningful. His return to Odessa was dictated primarily by his inability to support himself financially in Israel after his mother's departure. Four years after returning, Kostia still defined Israel as his *rodina* [homeland] and retained his Israeli passport. The idea of eventually going "home" (to Israel) was a recurrent theme in his conversation. His long absence from Odessa meant that Kostia felt little, if any, connection to the city, the place where he was born and partially raised.

During the year before I met him, Kostia had become more observant of Jewish religious laws, had started wearing a *kippah*, and regularly attended the synagogue—none of which had been part of his life in Israel. Once back in Odessa, however, he found that he wanted to lead an active Jewish life. While some returnees had become religiously observant during their time in Israel, for Kostia and some others it took returning to Odessa from Israel to develop a desire to be part of an organized Jewish community. Kostia felt a sense of connection within Odessa's religious organizations where he could practice his Hebrew and discuss Israeli life. He also hoped that participation in local Jewish organizations would provide an opportunity to return to Israel. I was told that Kostia did return to Israel a couple of months after I left Odessa, although without any definite prospects there.

Other young returnees behaved similarly, although with a less religious pattern of affiliation. Marat, a young entrepreneur in his mid-thirties, explained that in Israel he did not follow any religious traditions: "You don't need to do anything in Israel to feel Jewish." However, when he came back to Odessa he occasionally visited the Chabad congregation where his friends go for the major holidays and occasional *shabbatot*. He illustrated his participation in the religious congregation with the old quip: "Rabinovich goes to the synagogue to talk to God and I go to talk to Rabinovich." Marat had initially immigrated to Israel in the early 1990s when he could not get a visa to move to the United States. Thus, Israel was not his primary choice for immigration; rather, he explained, it was a way to leave Odessa and its stagnant economic and political situation at the time. He first returned to Odessa in 2002 for an experimental year and, subsequently, having returned to Israel for a short time, he made the decision to move back to Odessa permanently in 2004. Marat still considered Israel his historical homeland but felt that the life of an immigrant was difficult to cope with. Back in his native city, he started a construction company with another Israeli returnee. Marat enjoyed working as a manager as opposed to the manual labor jobs he had held in Israel. Although he did not imagine himself returning to Israel, other destinations such as Canada or, potentially, the United States, where his father lived, were not out of the question if Odessa's economic situation became difficult in the future.

REINTEGRATION AND BELONGING IN ORGANIZED JEWISH LIFE

As I alluded to in the introduction, some argue that Jewish returnees play a central role as religious and cultural experts in re-energizing Jewish communities outside Israel. With regard to Odessa, this image of returnees actively reviving local Jewish life is a considerable oversimplification. The generational differences in affiliation with Jewish Odessa that we saw between Nina, her son Kostia, and Marat were not atypical. Most older returnees tried to ease back into their old lives unnoticed and usually avoided official affiliation (except for the sake of social benefits such as pensions). Younger returnees strove to practice their Hebrew, took part in Jewish holiday celebrations, and often found employment in Jewish organizations, although others chose to remain on the periphery of Jewish activities. The behavior of middle-aged returnees was largely determined by the nature of their employment and family circumstances. Some, seeking career benefits, used Jewish organizations to "network," especially for potential clients. Others, seeing no advantages, did not include Jewish gatherings in their busy routines. For families whose children were enrolled in Jewish schools, occasional Jewish activity was the norm, which sometimes led to more extended involvement, while others felt too constrained by lack of time or lack of interest.

One of my informants, Dina, who had returned after nine years living in Tel Aviv, said that she could not relate to Jewish life in Odessa, as it was "too religious."[28] A young woman in her late twenties, she had moved back in late 2006 primarily to live closer to her family who had decided against moving to Israel. Her first encounter with Israel had been on a study abroad program and, immediately, she decided to emigrate. At the age of fifteen she had made *aliyah*, leaving her sister and parents behind in Odessa. Prior to her move Dina was an active participant in numerous Jewish programs in the city. However, during her years in Israel, she drifted away from Jewish practices, and her passion for being an active Jew had slowly faded. As Dina put it, "When you actually live in Zion, you don't need to do anything else to feel Jewish." Returning to Odessa, she had chosen not to revive her old relationships with Odessa's Jewish circles. She looked down on the Jewish Agency's policy of, as she put it, "feeding Jews fairytales" about their "home." Similarly, nothing about the religious observance of her friends struck a chord with her present Jewish identification. The new outlook she had adopted abroad now made them seem "narrow and old-fashioned in their understanding of Jewish identity."

Even outside the city's Jewish circles, Dina struggled to find her way among old friends. Most of her peers who had stayed in Odessa had graduated from college and found employment. Many of her old girlfriends were also married and starting their own families. By contrast, Dina was single, had "lost two years to the army" and, despite her sustained efforts to work and study at the same time, had not managed to complete her college education in Israel. In Odessa, where most education is still free of charge, continuing higher education appeared more feasible. Within a month of her return, Dina had managed to register for several classes at the Engineering Institute of Odessa, which she attended with great interest. Despite her plans to remain in Odessa, after six years, Dina returned to Israel, where she lives today. In our latest correspondence, she explained that living in Ukraine, a place she described as a "country of fools," proved more difficult than she had imagined.

While some returnees intended their re-migration to be permanent or at least long term, others did not. This group of transnational migrants, or "transmigrants" as I call them, define their relationship with Odessa as one of partial belonging and residency. Genady, his wife Luba, and their two children came to Odessa in the last two months of my fieldwork, having previously lived in Israel for ten years. They decided to move to Odessa in order to grow their business of selling Herbalife products: Israeli-made food supplements and skin care goods. They traveled regularly to and from Israel, as well as across Ukraine, in order to satisfy work and family obligations. They missed Israel for its food, music, and natural beauty. Genady and Luba retained their Israeli citizenship, with Ukrainian resident visas securing permission to work. Although their primary identification was Israeli—a title they gave themselves and that others used to describe them—Odessa, Genady's native city, served as a convenient business base in the region. The fact that Genady's mother lived in Odessa and was available to babysit their children made it easier for them to manage. As Genady put it: "It is easy for me to come back to Ukraine as opposed to moving to Canada, which is where my wife and I originally wanted to go once we decided to expand our business. In Odessa,

I know everyone that I need for any given situation and I feel free. In Israel, starting your own business is difficult, especially as an immigrant."

Other entrepreneurs I met had similar experiences of conducting business overseas. Vova, a returnee from Haifa, told me, "You can't trust anyone in Israel: I had a business with a Moroccan guy but he tried to cheat me out of all my money." Describing his motivation for coming to Odessa and his plans for the future, he was clear: "I am here to make money." Two months into his stay, Vova was following his passion for Israeli food, working hard to open a hummus restaurant in the city. To that end, he had attended a number of Jewish functions in the city and approached the Chabad rabbi to for help in pursuing his entrepreneurial efforts. According to Vova, the rabbi knew a number of local businessmen to whom he could turn for funding. Similarly, Vova approached other Jewish organizations in the city where he hoped to meet other Israelis and potential sponsors for his business. Vova was originally from St. Petersburg, while his wife, Nadya, was a native of Odessa. The deciding factor between the two cities was that, in Odessa, there was an apartment available for their use. I also sensed from our conversation that Vova's determination not to return to St. Petersburg sprang from the fact that he had missed out on opportunities that his friends there had made use of during his absence. "Those people [in St. Petersburg] were really able to grow and make something of themselves. I have been watching clouds and picking my nose for the last ten years living in Israel." In addition, Nadya, having visited Odessa many times during the time they lived in Israel, assured Vova that she would be able to get a job in one of the city's Jewish organizations where her Hebrew language skills would be in demand and that he, too, would find interesting entrepreneurial opportunities in the city.

Like Nadya, Nina, and Marat, many people who consider returning from Israel first make a number of preliminary visits to their potential destination. Yulik, originally from the Ukrainian city of Dnepropetrovsk and currently living in Israel, was on such an exploratory visit to Odessa when I met him. Like Genady, Vova, and Nadya, he was attracted to Ukraine for its business potential, in his case, in IT. Originally planning to relocate to Kiev, Yulik was now leaning toward a smaller city such as Dnepropetrovsk or Odessa, where the IT industry was not nearly as saturated as it was in Ukraine's capital. Yulik's family in Ukraine had offered to help him get started, if he were able to provide the finances. Unfortunately, when visiting his "hometown," he had found that Dnepropetrovsk did not feel anything like home. Having spent most of his life in Israel, he felt like a foreigner. He spoke Russian with a Hebrew accent and knew no Ukrainian. His diet, dress, and mannerisms were all marked by his experience abroad. Nonetheless, Yulik felt a sense of curiosity in experiencing a life that was both familiar and foreign for him.

HOMECOMINGS AND OTHER PROJECTS OF RETURN

The same tone inflected the stories of many other returnees. Those coming back to Odessa described it as a place simultaneously known and unknown. During their extended absence, their home had undergone significant changes while they, too, had formed new habits and ways of thinking in the context of different resources and realities. For some, this made living in Odessa interesting; for others it was difficult to cope. "Homecoming often contains elements of rupture, surprise, and perhaps disillusionment, besides the variety of practical problems that returnees usually confront."[29] In *Coming Home*, Lynellyn Long and Ellen Oxfeld similarly point out that, "as the act of returning unfolds, the specific experiences often contrast with the returnee's original dreams."[30] George Gmelch describes how Barbadian returnees "feel that their own interests are more cosmopolitan and transcend [those of] the local community... the place now appears as 'narrow.'"[31]

Returning to Odessa was a complex and ambivalent process. On the one hand, returning often signaled that it was Odessa that ultimately "was home." On the other hand, some Ukrainian and other FSU returnees (Odessans and non-Odessans) moved in order to follow their families or enhance their chances of prosperity without necessarily thinking of themselves as coming home. In general, when I would ask someone why he or she returned from Israel, many would respond that they did not necessarily "come back." In other words, their locational identity was still in flux. In fact, many returning Jews continued to define themselves as Israelis both legally and socially.[32] Still other ex-FSU Israelis considered other destinations, such as Canada or the United States.[33] The actual experiences of returnees displayed a mosaic of different orientations, attachments, and associations constructed by returnees about their past and present locations and homes.

For older returnees, the decision to move back was typically a response to obstacles in Israel that younger or middle-aged immigrants did not encounter. They usually envisaged their return as permanent and experienced it as more rooted. In other words, they felt it was a homecoming. Younger returnees still felt strong ties to Israel, where (although born in Odessa or the FSU) many had been raised and educated, and some had served in the army. Thus, they felt acculturated to the Israeli way of life. For these returnees, Israel remained a place that partially defined them, even in Odessa. The orientations of middle-aged returnees were also mixed and largely depended on their familial and professional needs. However, in nearly all cases, returnees came to Odessa seeking to "create better, more satisfying future lives" and thus, were more likely to be engaged in "feasible projects of homecoming" than those "aiming at resurrecting a golden, but lost past."[34]

CONCLUSION

The experiences of Israeli Russian-speaking Jewish returnees in Odessa are important to consider in analyzing "home" and "diaspora." Their patterns of migration and practices of homebuilding challenge the traditional model of Jews as a diaspora population connected to Israel as their "homeland" and cradle of Jewish identity and offer more nuanced ways of approaching the question of belonging. Diaspora, defined by the *Oxford English Dictionary* as the "dispersion of the Jews beyond Israel" and in its more contemporary context the "dispersion of any people from their traditional homeland," ultimately assumes a link between people and their "*proper* place" (emphasis in the original).[35] Within diaspora studies, Jews have been identified as an "ideal type,"[36] a "classic 'old diaspora'"[37] whose dispersal exemplifies them as a prototypical case of a diaspora population. Recent scholarship has challenged the negative conflation of diaspora with exile by viewing diaspora in a "positive light."[38] Daniel Boyarin and Jonathan Boyarin have even proposed to "privilege Diaspora" as a structure of "dissociation of ethnicities and political hegemonies" which they regard as the "most important contribution that Judaism has to make to the world."[39] Together with its popularity, the term "diaspora" has nonetheless been questioned for becoming a "catch-all phrase" that "presumes that there is a single center of a given community"[40] defined by the "natural bond" that people supposedly have with their native home.[41] As a critique, many works on diaspora populations have highlighted the multiple homelands that exist for and ultimately define any one group of people;[42] others point to the fact that people are no longer defined by places and "identities have become deterritorialised."[43] Within Jewish studies, this shift in analysis has challenged the perception of Jews as a "classic" diaspora.[44] In many accounts of Jewish life outside of Israel we can see how the supposed diaspora countries and various cities within those countries are perceived and experienced as homelands, and Israel is regarded as a place of spiritual, religious, and communal importance but not necessarily as a "home" or "homeland." The importance of the State of Israel and its claim to be *the* Jewish homeland has been questioned by a number of scholars and, in some cases, subject to political criticism.[45]

Research on "Russian" Jews and other minority populations who have faced difficulty adapting within Israeli society or have been reluctant to let go of their cultural capital brought from overseas has also been instrumental in transforming the idea of Israel as a Jewish home.[46] The experiences of Israelis who choose to live outside of Israel exhibits another level of ambivalence between Jews and Israel, apparent in the literature on *yeridah* [emigration from Israel].[47]

The material in this chapter allows us to move beyond traditional assumptions regarding Jewish loyalties, attachments, and orientations and offers a more nuanced, multifaceted way of understanding concepts of home and diaspora in today's global environment through the experiences of ex-Soviet Jewish returnees. On one hand, returnees who choose to leave Israel and return to Odessa might be seen as challenging the supposedly fundamental connection between Jews and their ancient homeland, returning to the so-called diaspora both as a place of familiarity and roots and as a new center of professional activity and personal growth. On the other hand, many returnees express strong ties to Israeli culture, defining themselves as Israeli through self-identification as well as through citizenship, language, dress, music, food, worldview, and even the idea of eventual return. Many transmigrants continue to travel back to Israel and build their businesses, some utilizing Israeli products and services. Israel is undoubtedly regarded as an important place on the Russian-speaking Jewish map even for those who choose to leave it behind. Israel has the largest Russian-speaking population outside the FSU and a growing network of economic, social, and political linkages with Russian speakers worldwide.

For many returnees, the question of belonging remains tied into their economic and social situations. The future for most returnees will be dictated to a large extent by the type of personal and professional opportunities available to them. Now part of the global post-Soviet Jewish population spread over many continents and countries, the returnees described in this chapter are as much part of the Russian-speaking diaspora as they are of the Israeli and Jewish diasporas whose "cultural, geographic, and national boundaries are blurred and in flux."[48] We can even add "religious" to the list, as seen in our case studies. The overlapping worlds that define ex-Soviet Jewish returnees and transmigrants through the process of migration and remigration account for multiple understandings of home and ultimately transcend the common distinction of "old" and "new" diasporas of traditional diaspora discourse. Returnees, in effect, take up the role of being both transnational and Jewish, albeit in different ways.

Multilocal life and work patterns in the context of globalized and neoliberal economies challenge the empirical reality of "home" as a single location. The attitudes of Odessa's returning Jewish population toward "homeland" and "diaspora" were far from fixed. Similar to other migrant populations, their identity as a "diasporic imagined community" is "constituted within the crucible of the materiality of everyday life."[49] Contingent, negotiated, and reflecting the socioeconomic and political circumstances of home and abroad, where one feels "at home" or "away from home" is a function of an individual's experiences. In some instances, the notion of home or homeland may be applied to more than one destination or, in the process of disorientation, may even cease to exist. This is particularly true for returnees who, having shared the experience of living as a Russian-speaking diaspora member in Israel, possibly viewed themselves on their return, or were viewed by others, as "Israelis" and, in effect, as part of an Israeli diaspora in Odessa. As James Clifford notes, "At different times in their history, societies may wax and wane in diasporism, depending on changing possibilities, obstacles, openings, antagonisms and connections—in their host countries and transnationally."[50]

Thus, "home" and "diaspora" are not ideologically driven constants associated with the center (life in Israel) and periphery (life outside of Israel). Rather, they should be conceptualized as variable locations infused with memories and attachments that social actors inhabit and relate to through everyday experiences and life circumstances, which, in turn, shape their imagined reality and sense of attachment. If home, as Stephan Feuchtwang has defined it, is "a reference to a territory of belonging,"[51] then ex-Soviet Jewish returnees have multiple and interconnecting homes that encompass their "cultural norms and individual fantasies"[52] and bring together their diverse experiences as locals, migrants, repatriates, and returnees.

NOTES

1. Caryn Aviv and David Shneer, *New Jews: The End of the Jewish Diaspora* (New York: New York University Press, 2005), 29, 49.
2. See, for example, Rina Cohen, "From Ethnonational Enclave to Diasporic Community: The Mainstreaming of Israeli Jewish Migrants in Toronto," *Diaspora* 8.2 (1999): 121–136; Yinon Cohen and Yitzchak Haberfeld, "The Number of Israeli Immigrants in the United States in 1990," *Demography* 34.2 (1997): 199–212; Steven Gold, "The Emigration of Jewish Israelis," in *Jews in Israel: Contemporary Social and Cultural Patterns*, ed. Uzi Rebhun and Chaim Waxman (Hanover, NH: Brandeis University Press, 2004), 445–464; Calvin Goldscheider, *Israel's Changing Society: Population, Ethnicity and Development* (Boulder, CO: Westview Press, 1996); Mira Rosenthal and Charles Auerbach, "Cultural and Social Assimilation of Israeli Immigrants in the United States," *International Migration Review* 99.26 (1992): 982–991.
3. Alexander Osipovich, "Reverse Exodus," *Russian Profile*, 2004, http://russiaprofile.org/culture_living/a2473.html, quoted in Aviv and Shneer, *New Jews*, 49. See also Evgeny Finkel, "Na dvukh stulyakh," *Otechestvenye Zapiski: Migratsia: ugroza ili blago* 4.19 (2004): 329.
4. Lucy Ash, "Israel Faces Russian Brain Drain," *BBC News*, November 24, 2004, http://news.bbc.co.uk/1/hi/programmes/crossing_continents/4038859.stm.
5. Osipovich, "Reverse Exodus." I am not aware of a similar report produced in Ukraine.
6. Yevgeny Satanovsky, "Russian Jews the Variant of the Future" (paper presented to the Euro-Asian Jewish Congress, November 19, 2009), http://eajc.org/page34/news14038.html.
7. Theodore H. Friedgut, "The Problematics of Jewish Community Development in Contemporary Russia," in *Revolution, Repression, and Revival: The Soviet Jewish Experience*, ed. Zvi Gitelman and Yaacov Ro'i (Lanham, MD: Rowman & Littlefield, 2007), 239–272.
8. Mark Tolts, "Post-Soviet Aliyah and Jewish Demography Transformation" (paper presented at the 15th World Congress of Jewish Studies, Jerusalem, Israel, August 2–6, 2009).
9. According to Israeli authorities, the term "out-migrants," otherwise referred to as *yordim*—those who descend from the Promised Land into the diaspora—refers to Israelis who have left Israel and who have stayed abroad for a year or more.
10. See "Otiezd iz Izrailia. Za i protiv [Emigration from Israel. For and against]," *Newsru*, February 4, 2007, http://www.newsru.co.il/info/bigpoll/yerida2007.html. A smaller survey of over 100 Russian Israelis (currently residing in Israel as well as abroad) conducted by Evgenyi Finkel on *LiveJournal* indicated that 20 percent of his respondents have left Israel—27 percent returned to their countries of origin; 24 percent left for the U.S.; 14 percent to Canada; 23 percent to Europe; and 7 percent to Australia. Another 25 percent of Finkel's respondents who have not left Israel have entertained the idea of leaving Israel (Finkel, "Na dvukh stulyakh," 327).
11. Author's notes from the conference "Russian-Speaking Jewry in the Global Perspective: Power, Politics, and Community," Bar Ilan University, October 17–19, 2014. See also http://www.jewishtimes.com, subheading "Israel News," on October 27, 2006 (last accessed 12/01/2009); Finkel, "Na dvukh stulyakh," 324–328.
12. Tolts, "Post-Soviet Aliyah," 15.
13. Gold, "The Emigration of Jewish Israelis," 445.
14. For an extended list of articles dealing with ex-Soviet Jewish remigration from Israel to the FSU, see http://www.ncsj.org/AuxPages/080404_return.shtml; also http://www.jewishla

.org/federationinforcus/html/apro5_jfishel.html; http://www.nysun.com/article14147. For returnees from the U.S., see http://www.businessweek.com/1997/25/b353252.html.
15. Osipovich, "Reverse Exodus," 1.
16. See, for example, "Return of the Jews: For Decades the Story of Russia's Jews Has Been One of Fear and Flight to Israel. Now Many Are Coming Home," *Newsweek International*, August 9, 2004, and "Once Desperate to Leave, Now Jews Are Returning to Russia, Land of Opportunity," *The Times*, April 28, 2005.
17. *Jewish Telegraph Agency*, August 26, 2004.
18. *Los Angeles Times*, February 3, 2005.
19. Perhaps this stereotype is linked to the diaspora discourse discussed by Aviv and Shneer that "envisions the Jewish world hierarchically with Israel on top: 'the diaspora' on the bottom" (*New Jews*, 19–20).
20. Data for this chapter was collected during fieldwork in Odessa, Ukraine, in 2005–2007 and includes in-depth interviews and participant observation with short-term and long-term returnees engaged in both provisional and permanent returns, as well as "transmigrants" who regularly move between Odessa and Israel and other destinations. I interviewed thirty-two returnees for this research. For the most part, I met returnees through other Jewish locals in the city who knew of my interest in return migration. I also met returnees in more organized settings of the local Jewish cultural center Migdal, the two orthodox synagogues, the Jewish Agency (Sokhnut), Beitar Camp, the Medical Institute, the Israeli Cultural Center, and communal Shabbat events organized by religious families in the city. While I draw mainly on the experiences of returning migrants in Odessa in my analysis, I have also included interviews with returnees I met in Kiev.
21. Rebecca Golbert, "Constructing Self: Ukrainian Jewish Youth in the Making" (D.Phil. diss., Oxford University, 2001), 347.
22. Belensky and Skolnik document that 92 percent of ex-Soviet Jews in Germany have traveled back to their hometowns, compared with 9 percent in the United States and 19 percent in Israel. They provide no data on permanent returns from Germany to the FSU. Misha Belensky and Jonathan Skolnik, "Russian Jews in Today's Germany: End of the Journey?" *European Judaism* 31.2 (1998): 37.
23. A number of younger returnees I met had initially moved to Israel on their own initiative, often following their involvement with the Jewish Agency (Sokhnut), Betar, or other Zionist organizations in the city. Many of them had taken part in a three-year study abroad program, *Na'aleh*, which invited Jewish youth to experience life in Israel with the ultimate goal of *aliyah* (see Fran Markowitz, "Cultural Change, Border Crossings and Identity Shopping: Jewish Teenagers from the CIS Access their Future in Israel," in *Russian Jews on Three Continents: Migration and Resettlement*, ed. Noah Lewin-Epstein, Paul Ritterband, and Yaacov Ro'i [London: Frank Cass, 1997], 344–363).
24. Odessa was home to a number of Russian-speaking Israelis who had come to the city to study medicine and other professions. A small number of returnees are affiliated with one of the two Orthodox movements in the city and the local branch of the Jewish Agency, an Israeli organization that operates in the FSU to educate Jews about Israel and assist them in making *aliyah*. These individuals and families usually stay in the city for a limited duration defined by their contract or length of course.
25. Returning Israeli Odessans did not form any sort of an organized network or community as they did in Moscow or in Kiev. However, Israeli students in Odessa's Medical Institute (including some ex-FSU residents) did organize events with each other on a regular basis.
26. For more on Russian-speaking Jews who have converted to Christianity or are attracted to the Christian faith, see Judith Deutch Kornblatt, *Doubly Chosen: Jewish Identity, the Soviet Intelligentsia, and the Russian Orthodox Church* (Madison: University of Wisconsin Press, 2004);

Mark Tolts, "Demography of the Jews in the Former Soviet Union: Yesterday and Today," in *Jewish Life after the USSR*, ed. Zvi Gitelman, Musya Glants, and Marshall Goldman (Bloomington: Indiana University Press, 2003), 201–202; Elena Nosenko-Stein, "Aliens in an Alien World: Paradoxes of Jewish Christian Identity in Contemporary Russia," *East European Jewish Affairs* 40.1 (April 2010): 19–41.

27. Citizens of Ukraine need a visa for most destinations outside the FSU, which can involve a time-consuming and costly application process. Israeli citizenship facilitates less restricted travel and an easier visa application process.

28. Chabad and a group affiliated with Ohr Sameach—both organizations that encourage Jews to become more religious—are highly visible in the city.

29. Anders H. Stefansson, "Homecomings to the Future: From Diasporic Mythographies to Social Projects of Return," in *Homecomings: Unsettled Paths of Return*, ed. Fran Markowitz and Anders Stefansson (Lanham, MD: Lexington Books, 2004), 4.

30. Lynellyn D. Long and Ellen Oxfeld, "Introduction: An Ethnography of Return," in *Coming Home? Refugees, Migrants, and Those Who Stayed Behind*, ed. Lynellyn Long and Ellen Oxfeld (Philadelphia: University of Pennsylvania Press, 2004), 10.

31. George Gmelch, "West Indian Migrants and Their Rediscovery of Barbados," in *Coming Home?*, ed. Long and Oxfeld, 213.

32. All the returnees I met, except Nina, who had reverted to a Ukrainian passport, could easily have opted to go back to Israel on their retained citizenship and legal documents.

33. In an online survey begun on February 4, 2007, 43.9 percent of the respondents said that, if they left Israel, they would like to live in Canada; 39.7 percent, the U.S.; 25.1 percent, Australia; 13.3 percent, the UK; 12.2 percent, Russia; 10.4 percent, Germany; and only 5.8 percent named Ukraine. "Otiezd iz Izrailia. Za i protiv [Emigration from Israel. For and against]," *Newsru*, February 4, 2007, http://www.newsru.co.il/info/bigpoll/yerida2007.html.

34. Stefansson, "Homecomings to the Future."

35. Eftihia Voutira, "Post Soviet Diaspora Politics: The Case of Soviet Greeks," *Journal of Modern Greek Studies* 24.2 (2006): 380.

36. William Safran, "Diasporas in Modern Societies: Myths of Homeland and Return," *Diaspora* 1.1 (1991): 83–99.

37. Andre Levy and Alex Weingrod, "On Homelands and Diasporas: An Introduction," in *Homelands and Diasporas: Holy Lands and Other Places*, ed. Andre Levy and Alex Weingrod (Stanford: Stanford University Press, 2005), 4.

38. Howard Wettstein, "Introduction," in *Diasporas and Exiles*, ed. Howard Wettstein (Berkeley: University of California Press, 2002), 2; Erich S. Gruen, "Diaspora and Homeland," in *Diasporas and Exiles*, ed. Wettstein, 18–46; Larry Tye, *Home Lands: Portraits of the New Jewish Diaspora* (New York: Henry Holt and Company, 2001), 3.

39. Daniel Boyarin and Jonathan Boyarin, "Diaspora: Generation and the Ground of Jewish Identity," *Critical Inquiry* 19.4 (Summer 1993): 723.

40. Aviv and Shneer, *New Jews*, 22.

41. Eftihia Voutira, "Post Soviet Diaspora Politics," 380.

42. James Clifford, "Diasporas," *Cultural Anthropology* 9.3 (1994): 302–338; James Clifford, *Routes: Travel and Translation in the Late Twentieth Century* (Cambridge, MA: Harvard University Press, 1997); Markowitz and Stefansson, *Homecomings*; Levy and Weingrod, "On Homelands and Diasporas."

43. Robin Cohen, *Global Diasporas: An Introduction*, 2nd ed. (London: Routledge, 2008), 2. See also Smadar Lavie and Tel Swedenburg, *Displacement, Diaspora, and Geographies of Identity* (Durham, NC: Duke University Press, 1996).

44. Among others see Pollin-Galay's chapter in this volume; Aviv and Shneer, *New Jews*; Levy and Weingrod, "On Homelands and Diasporas;" Laurence J. Silberstein, *Mapping*

Jewish Identities (New York: New York University Press, 2000); Tye, *Home Lands*; Wettstein, "Introduction."

45. Among others see Boyarin and Boyarin, "Diaspora;" Aviv and Shneer, *New Jews*.

46. Specifically for the Russian case, see Dina Siegel, *The Great Immigration: Russian Jews in Israel* (New York: Berghahn Books, 1998); Larisa Fialkova and Nina N. Yelenevskaya, *Ex-Soviets in Israel: From Personal Narratives to a Group Portrait* (Detroit: Wayne State University Press, 2007).

47. *Yeridah* is translated from Hebrew as descent and refers to the "stigmatized path of Israelis who descend from the promised land into the Diaspora" (Gold, "The Emigration of Jewish Israelis," 445). Emigrants from Israel are thus referred to as *yordim*. See endnote 2 for relevant literature.

48. Olga Gershenson and David Shneer, "Soviet Jewishness and Cultural Studies," *Journal of Jewish Identities*, special edition on Russian Jewish identity, 4.1 (January 2011): 141.

49. Avtar Brah, *Cartographies of Diaspora: Contesting Identities* (London: Routledge, 1996), 183.

50. Clifford, *Routes*, 249.

51. Stephan Feuchtwang, "Theorising Place," in *Making Place: State Projects, Globalisation and Local Responses in China*, ed. Stephan Feuchtwang (London: UCL Press, 2004), 7.

52. N. Rapport and J. Overing, *Migrants of Identity: Perceptions of Home in a World of Movement* (Oxford: Berg, 1998), 8.

PART II TRANSNATIONALISM AND DIASPORAS

Though Jews, along with Armenians, were long considered the prototypical diaspora, recent writings on diasporas have mostly ignored them. In chapter 4, Jonathan Dekel-Chen argues that, on one hand, the study of diasporas should include contemporary Jewry and that, on the other, studies of contemporary Jewish migration could benefit from some of the recent scholarship on diasporas in general. For example, rather than following the traditional "push-pull" framework for analyzing migration, the study of population movements would benefit from the application of network analysis. Dekel-Chen emphasizes the roles of domestic and international politics in migration and, specifically, in the formation of diasporas. He points to the often fraught relations between "host" societies and migrants and the tensions that exist between new arrivals and receiving Jewish communities, even in the State of Israel.

Dekel-Chen suggests that the frequent migration of modern Jews complicates their identities. This complexity is explored among Lithuanian Jews by Hannah Pollin-Galay. She interviewed Jews who lived in prewar Lithuania, survived World War II, and returned there. They would like to think of their small republic as "home" but cannot deny that the majority of Jews who originated in Lithuania now live elsewhere. Moreover, while they are proud of their "Litvak" heritage and would like "to embrace Lithuania and elevate it to a Jewish-home symbol, since they remember the place as it once was," they have strong reasons to revile Lithuania "and render it an anti-home, recalling the downfall of Jewish life there, both during the Holocaust and in subsequent decades." The attachment of foreign Jews to the place their ancestors lived complicates further the nuanced, highly ambivalent attitudes of those still living in Lithuania. One might add that many Jews the world over whose ancestral roots are in Europe, especially Eastern Europe, are conflicted by curiosity about the lands and cultures of their increasingly remote origins and, at the same time, the assumption, often confirmed by historical research, that their non-Jewish neighbors had been hostile to their ancestors and in World War II had even participated in the murder of local and other Jews.

Exploring even more dimensions of migration, Steven Gold finds that the experiences of Israelis and RSJs who come to the United States are quite different. He compares systematically the family lives, cultural adaptation, relations with American Jews, and communal institutions of the two immigrant groups. Gold finds that the Israeli Americans are far more involved with their country of origin than are the RSJs, but, after facing initial suspicion and occasional hostility, both groups have made their mark on American Jewry demographically, economically, and culturally. Clearly, far more Israeli Americans return to Israel, either as family visitors, entrepreneurs, or re-migrants, than do those from the FSU to their countries of origin. But both groups of immigrants are part of an increasingly fluid movement of Jews back and forth between their places of birth and of immigration. Whether this enhances the sense of commonality and kinship among Jews in various parts of the world is a question that should be addressed.

4 · RETHINKING BOUNDARIES IN THE JEWISH DIASPORA FROM THE FSU

JONATHAN DEKEL-CHEN

This chapter is constructed from many parts in hopes that its "whole" will offer a coherent map of the "ins" and "outs" of the the study of the Jewish diaspora from the FSU (former Soviet Union). I also suggest what could be added to our research agenda on the Russian-speaking diaspora in order to engage more fruitfully with general migration and diaspora studies. The complexity and connectivity of the Russian-speaking Jewish diaspora make it a potentially attractive subject for the wider scholarly community. Although dwarfed by mass migrations such as the Irish or Chinese migration of the nineteenth century, the movement of Jews from Soviet space and the establishment of its diaspora communities parallel the migration of other ethnic groups in recent decades. It should therefore be relevant to discussions of geography, politics, economics, and identity in general migration and diaspora studies.

I begin with a brief historiographic overview. Jews were among the first groups analyzed by the pioneers of diaspora studies in the 1960s and 1970s. Since then, the range of communities examined by the field has expanded exponentially. Recent scholarship reveals growing interest in émigré communities and homelands both within and beyond Europe, the Far East, the Indian subcontinent, and Africa. Most recently, scholars have begun to examine the relationship between Muslim homelands and their diasporas in Europe and the Americas.[1] By contrast, barring token references to Jews as a "classic" diaspora, recent scholarship has largely ignored the Jewish diaspora—in particular, its East European offshoots.[2] It is time to examine whether newer analytical models in diaspora studies can be applied to Russian-speaking Jewish émigrés. Given that recent demographic studies are already eulogizing the depleted and aging Jewish community in the former

Soviet Union,³ we might also ask whether there is any point making comparisons with or among its progeny in Israel, North America, Germany, and elsewhere.

APPLYING NETWORK METHODOLOGY TO THE JEWISH CASE

We need more explicit assessments of the transnational networks linking the Russian "motherland" with its offspring abroad.⁴ Both older and more recent studies on modern Jewish migration have proposed linear interpretations to the mass westward movement of Jews from the 1880s until the enactment of the Reed-Johnson Act in 1924.⁵ A common image emerged from these works in which a mix of economic, social, demographic, and political factors "pushed" and "pulled" millions of Jews from East to West, primarily to the "New World." Younger historians and sociologists have explained how the diaspora communities of the time expended considerable energy endeavoring to make themselves, and in particular their most recently arrived members, more American, French, Argentine, etc. While individuals and organizations in these Jewish communities in the West mobilized periodically to aid their brethren in the East, they were focused primarily on being loyal citizens of their homelands. Consequently, the Alliance Israelite Universelle, formed in 1860 as an international organization to intervene on behalf of embattled Jewish communities in the East, splintered along national lines shortly after its establishment.

"Fast-forwarding" to the post-1988 wave of migration from Soviet space suggests a rethinking of this linear interpretation of migration and diaspora. Rather than emphasizing national models of advocacy and absorption, an alternative interpretive prism would show that recent migrations can be better understood as a series of diaspora networks. These networks are visible in post-perestroika migrations, in which the diaspora "wheel" centers on the axis of the USSR and FSU with spokes reaching to Israel, the Americas, Europe, and elsewhere. In many respects, this model resembles the mass migrations and resulting diaspora communities of the period 1881–1921, but the rate of connectivity among the contemporary sites of diaspora has accelerated. Today, they communicate regularly around media, cultural, business, and travel interests. Moreover, some official data and informal observations show that the patterns of migration from the late 1980s were not unidirectional. Rather, serial migration was not uncommon, starting with *aliyah* [immigration to Palestine/Israel] but often continuing with migration to another country. There are signs of part-time or full return migration by thousands of *olim* back to the FSU from Israel today.⁶

Echoes of the contemporary network model can be found in earlier diasporas from the Russian Empire. If we set aside the technological possibilities of twenty-first-century communication, the *fin-de-siècle* diaspora exhibited a comparable level of networking, at least in the cultural and economic realms. Judging from the frequency and depth of transnational activity by *landsmanshaftn* in the

West around the turn of the last century, it is clear that networking must be part of any study of the Russian Jewish diaspora.[7]

However, these networks contain a theoretical conundrum. In short, the series of modern Jewish diasporas from Eastern Europe can be described as a recurring cycle of migration and more durable settlement. But when and where does one end and the next begin? We must remember that Eastern Europe itself was a site of diaspora—Jews were not native to the area and were usually considered "outsiders" by both locals and the ruling regimes, even if Jews themselves often came to regard the region as their homeland. Their process of arrival and absorption into East European states (culminating in the Russian annexations during the partitions of Poland) ended by the early nineteenth century. However, many of these same Jews continued to migrate within Russian space or attempted to leave it, departing for other regions in Europe and beyond. Hence, at around the same time that some formerly Polish Jews found themselves living in a new "homeland"—Russia—other "Russian" Jews were moving elsewhere within the Russian empire or beyond.

Another theoretical conundrum provoked by a network approach to migration and diaspora concerns identity. Physical migration from Eastern Europe had unpredictable results for the émigrés' identity. For example, while most young "greenhorns" in New York in 1899 or 1989 tried to become "more American," others were content living within Yiddish- or Russian-speaking enclaves. Perhaps more than other ethnic groups, serial migration has been a frequent trend in the Jewish world, complicating identity issues. Temporary sojourns in less desirable lands were often followed by migrations to perceived "golden lands" in North America or Western Europe.

The study of serial migration should not be confined to post-Soviet Jews making a pragmatic "pit-stop" in Israel before moving on to seemingly greener pastures. Even though this pattern of migration was established by Russian Jews a century earlier, it still surprises many to learn that a notable number of migrants in these earlier waves of migration returned to their points of origin in Eastern Europe. During the mass migrations of the late nineteenth into the early twentieth century, the rate of return from the United States to the Russian Empire may have reached as high as 15–20 percent.[8] A considerably higher rate of return, albeit in relatively tiny absolute numbers, characterized the seemingly more ideologically motivated *aliyot* from the Russian Empire to Ottoman-controlled Palestine.[9] Then, as now, remigration is difficult to track because returnees often do so "off the books," without formally declaring their return.

REMEMBERING POLITICS

Judging from the titles of publications in recent decades, the theme of "Russian Jews on Three Continents" has become popular. In 2011 alone, two special issues of scholarly journals appeared on this topic,[10] reflecting the new emphasis within diaspora studies on sociology, culture, and gender. Without discounting these studies' importance, I would nevertheless argue for the enduring centrality of politics in the general scheme of migration and diaspora.

The interwar period is an optimal case study for this argument. From 1921 to 1924, international immigration laws changed radically, almost depriving East European Jews entirely of access to their traditional receiving countries in the Americas and Europe. The rise of fascism and ultra-nationalism in Central and Eastern Europe in subsequent years created great anxiety as increasing numbers of Jews frantically sought alternative sites of refuge. Initially, this was a grassroots process without much assistance from Jewish organizations. Not surprisingly, many young Jews in Eastern Europe were drawn to Zionism since Mandate Palestine seemed to be a sole remaining site of refuge.[11] Sensing the political dangers spreading across Europe, non-Zionist organizations in the early 1930s began to see resettlement of these endangered European Jewish communities as their central mission. In a parallel development, the liberal and fascist governments in Europe began to discuss the transfer of unwanted populations to distant lands.[12] This should remind scholars of diasporas that, despite the relevance of social and cultural methodologies for the field of diaspora studies, we cannot overlook the importance of political history.

Politics are important not just for the study of refugees and their lives in the diaspora but also for Jewish communities in the receiving countries. Only by understanding the trauma of the interwar years for Jews in the West and its continued reverberations for their descendants can we conceptualize what Henry Feingold refers to as the diaspora's "soft" political power from the Roosevelt through the Ford administrations.[13] Domestic and foreign politics, of course, also played a significant role in the formation of the Soviet Union's emigration policy. It is equally true that immigration and absorption policies in the West over the past 150 years have been linked as much by internal politics as by governmental relations with regimes in the East.

Economic issues must also be factored into any analysis of the politics of migration and diaspora. For example, Jewish organizations in the West bartered with Nazi Germany to rescue European Jews; paying governments to secure freedom of movement for East European Jews did not end with Hitler. Two secret deals and two resettlement operations enabled the flight of 29,000 Jews from communist Poland to Israel between 1949 and 1951 because of the latter's willingness to pay for their exit, a financial deal underwritten mostly by third parties in the West. Tectonic shifts in East-West politics pushed tens of thousands more Jews out of Poland by the end of the 1960s.[14] Similar arrangements were in place to facilitate the movement of Romanian Jews to Israel as well as the return of ethnic Germans to Germany starting in the 1960s.[15]

We should bear in mind that the role of money in resettlement politics is also crucial *within* the Jewish world. For example, one cannot properly gauge interwar

Jewish politics without taking into account the bitter struggles between Zionist and non-Zionist organizations; these conflicts hinged heavily on the distribution of scarce financial resources in the West. Prominent Jewish leaders of the time argued furiously about whether this money should be invested in the "redemptive" resettlement of European Jews in Palestine or in rescuing them by whatever means available to whichever location was most economically viable.[16]

Because they create "push" and "pull" factors, the actions of states must serve as a central axis of general and Jewish diaspora studies, especially with regard to forced migration. Admittedly, a direct connection cannot be drawn between the forced migrations of ethnic groups in Eastern Europe and Jewish migration.[17] Neither can we chart a direct link between forced migrations within Eastern Europe and the formation of new Jewish diaspora communities outside of the region.[18] Nonetheless, it is clear that forced migrations of Jews and other groups during the tsarist and Soviet eras destabilized these societies and promoted conditions that launched or accelerated mass Jewish emigration. Moreover, from the perestroika period (1985–1991) onward, the instability caused by the return of some of these ethnic groups to their national homelands (e.g., Crimean Tatars) contributed to Soviet and post-Soviet Jews' decisions to emigrate since they felt vulnerable to nationalist pressures both as Jews and as people perceived by the returnees as "Russians."

The role of political regimes and Jewish organizations in the formation of modern diaspora communities and group identities requires further exploration. Seen over time, the mass movement of Jews out of Russian-speaking space fed, and was fed by, the establishment of transnational Jewish philanthropic organizations. Their philanthropic intercession was formalized with the creation of the Alliance, whose first major test was the migration and resettlement resulting from the refugee crisis in Memel in 1869–70.[19] The work of such organizations continued to expand until the turn of the twenty-first century. Throughout, their focus was where and how "Russian" Jews could be resettled after their rescue from Eastern Europe. From the Memel crisis onward, Jewish transnational aid organizations began envisioning reconstructive resettlement projects, not just the relocation of destitute refugees.

Philanthropic organizations attempted to fashion individuals and communities in the East European diasporas of the "new" worlds of the Americas or in the "new/old" world of the Holy Land.[20] With the start of mass migration from Eastern Europe in the 1880s, individual *shtadlanim* [intercessors] such as the Rothschilds and Jacob Schiff, as well as organizations such as the Hebrew Immigrant Aid Society (HIAS), deliberated over which types of candidates were most suited for resettlement. In these early formative years, even liberal humanists in the West, like Emma Lazarus, pondered the degree to which the receiving communities should select and train the newcomers based on their potential to become self-supporting, assimilated citizens. By the late 1880s, a clear gap had emerged in the philanthropic orientation of receiving agencies in the West and those in

Palestine.²¹ In the former, organizations such as HIAS, ORT, the Jewish Colonization Association, and the Industrial Removal Office supported vocational training and productivized resettlement. For the better part of the period between 1881 and the immediate post-Holocaust era, agricultural settlement was a major component of the philanthropic program for immigrants in the West. These programs, whether or not they created multigenerational farming families, left a significant imprint on the profile of immigrant communities in the receiver countries, particularly in Argentina where the ethos of the Jewish *gaucho* is still part of the communal legacy, even if nowadays only a small segment of Argentinian Jews have actual familial roots on the *pampas*.²² In Palestine, these sorts of mass productivization efforts were delayed for a couple of decades, though the Zionist historical narrative often ignores these facts. In the meantime, Baron Rothschild dispensed aid akin to a "dole" to much of the Jewish community in Ottoman and Mandatory Palestine.

Differences between these philanthropic approaches may explain longer-term tendencies. In the *Yishuv*—the Jewish community of pre-state Palestine—fairly traditional charitable practices resulted in an unfortunate propensity among large parts of the population to rely on handouts from the international Jewish community. Among East European Jewish communities in North America, no such expectation developed and it remains relatively rare today, even among the ultra-Orthodox. Of course, these generalizations must be balanced with some historical perspective. Clearly, the first waves of *aliyah* to the *Yishuv* could not have survived without external support, whereas the resources and opportunities available in North America allowed for a relatively autonomous process of absorption. Later, during the mass immigration of Soviet and post-Soviet Jews, governmental and communal agencies in North America, Germany, and Israel provided relatively few social welfare benefits. Given the relatively high socioeconomic status of the immigrants, they needed only language training or professional equivalency tutoring in order to enter the local workforces in their new homelands.

ACCOUNTING FOR UNPLEASANT FACTS

A troubling and largely undiscussed feature of absorption politics is the uneasy, often paternalistic, relationship between immigrants from Eastern Europe and Jewish "veterans" in the receiving countries.²³ *Shtadlanim* and communities in the West repeatedly mobilized on behalf of the rights of Jews in the East, campaigning vigorously for free emigration from imperial Russia and the USSR.²⁴ It is equally true that many of these Western Jews were ambivalent toward the idea of multitudes of East European Jews actually landing on their shores.²⁵ Even those Jewish "natives" who initially welcomed Russian or Soviet-Jewish refugees to the West often lost their positive orientation toward their new countrymen, regarding them as "un-Jewish" or ungrateful.²⁶ This may help explain why some activists in the

Soviet Jewry movement in the United States felt alienated from Soviet Jews once they arrived in the West.[27] It may also help account for the continuing trend of separation between the "native" Jewish communities and much of the post-Soviet diaspora in New York and Germany, despite ongoing efforts to bring the communities together through inclusion programs at synagogues, schools, Jewish community centers, and local federations. Looking back to the period 1881–1924, similar ambivalences and class-based tensions underlay relations between the German-speaking *yahudim* in the United States and the arriving waves of Russian or Yiddish-speaking *yidn*.[28] In much smaller numbers and with a greater degree of ethnic variance, social tensions were, and to a degree still are, evident in the reception of repeated waves of *aliyah* to the *Yishuv* and the State of Israel.

The challenge of absorbing Russian-speaking immigrants from the 1970s to the present has attracted considerable attention and resources from the receiving states and multiple Jewish communal organizations. With the annual arrival of tens, and then hundreds of thousands, of Russian-speaking immigrants in Israel, the United States and, eventually, Germany, conflicts inevitably arose regarding dependence and integration. One source of friction today related to the absorption of Russian-speakers, particularly in Israel, can loosely be referred to as the hotly debated "Jewishness" of the immigrants. The issue of "non-Jewish Jews" had little resonance during the mass emigrations from 1881 to 1924 and in the formative years of the *Yishuv* and early state. By contrast, with the onset of mass emigration from the Soviet Union during the 1970s, Jewish activists in the receiving countries were disturbed by the immigrants' lack of a conventional religious identity.[29] While disquieting to some in the West, this issue has come to be a political and social powder keg in Israel. Although opinions regarding the issue vary widely, a large proportion of the emigrants departing from the FSU in the late 1980s and purporting to be Jews were, in fact, not Jewish, either according to Israel's Law of Return or, especially, according to *halakhah*. Moreover, in the late 1990s and thereafter a significant number of the FSU immigrants—perhaps as many as 300,000—laid no claim to Jewish identity. Under the Law of Return they became Israeli citizens by virtue of family ties to Jews. The long-term implications of this state of affairs are unknown, but given the large numbers of these immigrants and their families residing in Israel, this issue promises to remain in the public eye. Absorption efforts by the Israeli government and the Israeli military have resulted in many Orthodox conversions for these immigrants, but a large number have not undergone conversion. As we will see, questions of "personal status" in Israel create difficulties at crucial life-cycle junctures—particularly marriage and death—and feed mercurial media polemics. Most observers would agree that these non-Jewish immigrants have integrated into Israeli society at nearly the same pace as their Jewish counterparts. They serve in the Israel Defense Forces, enter professional life, and remain virtually indistinguishable from their Jewish peers. Until tragic moments, such as the deaths of Russian-speaking, non-Jewish soldiers in the line of duty, the comparable level of "Israeliness" among Jews and non-Jews may suggest that the Jewish component in the identity of the immigrant pool is less important than the Russian part.

DILEMMAS OF IDENTITY AND GEOGRAPHY

In order to address these issues of identity and integration, new ways of analyzing immigrant life emerge. To what degree are individual Russian speakers in diaspora communities culturally and socially insular? If general insularity persists, how does this occur despite the purported globalization/homogenization of culture everywhere else? Furthermore, we must also account for internal Jewish diasporas or migrations *within* Russian-speaking space. More concretely, what are the conceptual and practical comparisons to be drawn between the movement of Russian or Yiddish-speaking Jews from Kovno in 1899 or 1999 to Canada versus their neighbors who migrated in 1939 to Karaganda and established a new Jewish community there?[30] One must also wonder, given the frequent insularity of Russian-speaking diaspora communities, what are the implications of migration between territorially distant communities if individual migrants continue to live their daily lives primarily within a Russian-speaking bubble, no matter where they reside?

Although not unique in this regard, Russian-speaking Jews are among recent immigrant groups who have maintained a strong sense of their cultural identity. How is this manifested in their contemporary sites of diaspora? Daniel and Jonathan Boyarin present an argument regarding the link connecting monotheism, diaspora, and territory, and illustrating how these interact with identity.[31] Although I disagree with much of their argument, it remains a striking proposal. Using a *longue durée* lens to examine the East European Jewish diaspora as it has developed on at least three continents over the past forty years, it seems reasonable to argue that the "glue" of identity that continues to bind these communities is more tribal than religious, ethnic, or territorial. The overwhelmingly nonreligious, Russian-speaking diaspora communities, including those in Israel, are largely islands unto themselves, not because of religion but because of cultural commonality based on an abstract kinship and shared experience. In many cases, sizeable post-Soviet Jewish communities have become self-sustaining cultural hubs in their new homes in Berlin, Brighton Beach, and Bat Yam.

As the Boyarins suggest,[32] our conception of diaspora should no longer be based merely around a single territorial axis (i.e., the Land of Israel) as the sole means of determining what constitutes a diaspora. To move beyond their hypothesis, I would suggest that diaspora is no longer about geography but rather, a state of mind. If an immigrant community's cultural baggage or sense of group identity is strong enough, and the community is sufficiently large, that community can legitimately view itself—no matter where it resides—as a "center" that no longer longs for a distant homeland, whether Israel or Russia. This model of diaspora is available to Russian-speaking diaspora communities more than any other community in the modern Jewish world because of its overwhelming secularism and strong, language-based cultural heritage, which almost entirely bypasses the importance placed by individuals and groups on religious-based redemption in the Land of Israel.

Furthermore, there are multiple post-Soviet Jewish identities in each diaspora community, contained in generational or sub-ethnic groups. In Israel, for example, the meaning of being "Russian" is fundamentally different for older *olim* compared with younger people who have already undergone some level of socialization in the Israeli educational system, during their mandatory army service, or in the workplace. The intra-diaspora gaps in identity are even more noticeable when comparing the relative position of Ashkenazi versus non-Ashkenazi communities among the Russian-speaking *olim*.

A daunting challenge in the study of identity among FSU immigrants is to compare emigrants who, in some way, could be defined as ideologically motivated as opposed to those who left for other reasons. The "right to choose" or "dropout" crisis, which began in the mid-1970s, generated great tension among diaspora communities, the Israeli establishment, and Zionist activists in the Soviet Union. Decades later, we are in a position to compare the identities exhibited by communities in North America versus Israel. Those who arrived in Israel may now exhibit a stronger "Jewish" identity than their counterparts in North America or Germany. Most of these *olim* did not come to Israel entirely out of ideological conviction. Nevertheless, they and their children may appear to be more "Jewish" than their counterparts in the West by virtue of living in a Jewish state with a Jewish calendar, national symbols, and language. It is perhaps more surprising that these *olim* do not seem to be any more or less "Russian" than their seemingly less "Jewish" counterparts in the United States or Western Europe.

I am struck by an apparent contradiction in our perceptions of identity within the contemporary Russian-speaking diaspora. A generation ago, when very few people foresaw the disintegration of the Iron Curtain, let alone a vibrant, global diaspora of Russian-speaking Jews, scholars and activists in the West struggled to formulate a coherent and workable definition for Soviet-Jewish identity after decades of antireligious persecution and voluntary acculturation. At the time, the concept of a "thin" but resilient Jewish culture seemed to best capture the nuances of Jewish life in the USSR.[33] Today, one cannot help but marvel as we observe the strengthening of culture and identity among post-Soviet Jewish communities, in the FSU and abroad.[34] These same Jews, some of whom have left Minsk for Mannheim, Manhattan, and Maaleh Adumim, now exhibit what appears to be a "thicker" Russian-Jewish culture. Still, given the "thin" culture of the Soviet era, combined with the relative secularism of most post-Soviet Jews, might this current state of affairs suggest that we are not talking about a Russian-Jewish identity as much as a simpler Russian identity that has traveled with these emigrants to their diaspora communities?

CONCLUSION

In calling for the application of network analysis as well as analyzing political history and the role of organizations, and rethinking conventional approaches toward identity issues, I hope we can begin to reinsert the study of Jewish migration and diaspora into the rapidly expanding general scholarship on diasporas. Admittedly, the application of new approaches, such as network theory, is not for everyone and carries its own problems. What might be the lasting value of studying modern Jewish migrations, particularly the post-*perestroika* exodus from the former Soviet Union, for non-Jewish scholarship? Can we make our work relevant to a more general audience? Can we engage in more holistic research about interactions between East European diaspora communities and the receiving societies? The answers rest almost entirely in our hands.

NOTES

1. See, for example, Eva Østergaard-Nielsen, "Diasporas in World Politics," in *Non-State Actors in World Politics*, ed. Daphné Josselin and William Wallace (Houndsmills, UK: Palgrave, 2001), 218–234.
2. See Jennifer M Brinkerhoff, ed., *Diasporas and Development: Exploring the Potential* (Boulder, CO: Rienner, 2008); Nancy Foner, Rubén G. Rumbaut, and Steven Gold, eds., *Immigration Research for a New Century: Multidisciplinary Perspectives* (New York: Russell Sage, 2000); Nicholas Van Hear, *New Diasporas: The Mass Exodus, Dispersal and Regrouping of Migrant Communities* (Seattle: University of Washington Press, 1998). In the edited volume, *Theorizing Diaspora*, ed. Jana Evans Braziel and Anita Mannur (Malden: MA: Blackwell, 2005), there is no mention of the Jewish diaspora other than in a chapter by Daniel Boyarin and Jonathan Boyarin, "Diaspora: Generation and the Ground of Jewish Identity," 85–118.
3. See Mark Tolts, "Post-Soviet Jewish Demography, 1989–2004," in *Revolution, Repression, and Revival: The Soviet Jewish Experience*, ed. Zvi Gitelman and Yaacov Ro'i (Lanham, MD: Rowman & Littlefield, 2007), 283–312; Sergio DellaPergola, "The Demography of Post-Soviet Jewry: Global and Local Contexts," in *Revolution, Repression, and Revival*, ed. Gitelman and Ro'i, 313–330.
4. In doing so, it is helpful to draw on the broader scholarship on networks. For example, see Margaret E. Keck and Kathryn Sikkink, *Activists beyond Borders: Advocacy Networks in International Politics* (Ithaca, NY: Cornell University Press, 1998).
5. Mark Wischnitzer, *To Dwell in Safety: The Story of Jewish Migration since 1800* (Philadelphia: Jewish Publication Society, 1948), 37–157; Simon Kuznets, "Immigration of Russian Jews to the US: Background and Structure," *Perspectives in American History* 9 (1975): 35–98; Arcadius Kahan, *Essays in Jewish Social and Economic History*, ed. Roger Weiss (Chicago: University of Chicago Press, 1986), 102.
6. Ofer Matan, "Ha-aliyah ha-rusit nimshechet, le-Moskva," *Haaretz* supplement, February 14, 2014, 45–48.
7. Rebecca Kobrin's *Jewish Bialystok and Its Diaspora* (Bloomington: Indiana University Press, 2010) offers a clear window onto the transnational character of the East European diaspora at the time.
8. Jonathan D. Sarna, "The Myth of No Return: Jewish Return Migration to Eastern Europe, 1881–1914," *American Jewish History* 71.2 (1981): 256–268.
9. Gur Alroey, *Imigrantim: ha-hagirah ha-yehudit l'Erets-yisrael be-reshit ha-meah ha-esrim* (Jerusalem: Yad Ben Zvi, 2004), 208–220.

10. *Journal of Jewish Identities* 4.1, special issue on the Russian Diaspora (January 2011); *Israel Affairs* 17.1, "Special Issue: Twenty Years Together: The 'Great Aliya' and Russian Israelis in the Mirror of Social Research" (January 2011). More than ten years earlier, a large edited volume appeared under a similar title. See Noah Lewin-Epstein, Yaacov Ro'i, and Paul Ritterband, eds., *Russian Jews on Three Continents: Migration and Resettlement* (London: Frank Cass, 1997).
11. The Soviet Union could also be considered a potential site of refuge for those on the radical socialist fringe in their respective countries.
12. The most comprehensive, if not entirely scholarly, accounting of these plans can be found in Eliyahu Benyamini, *Medinot le-yehudim: Uganda, Birobidzhan ve-od 34 tochniot* (Tel Aviv: Hakibuts ha-meukhad, 1990).
13. Henry L. Feingold, *Jewish Power in America: Myth and Reality* (New Brunswick, NJ: Transaction, 2008). A firsthand understanding of this power is described by an activist of the time: see "The Reminiscences of Rabbi Israel Miller," in *Ethnic Groups and American Foreign Policy Project*, Oral History Research Office, Columbia University, 1978. Jews are not the only East European diaspora who possess a degree of "soft" political power in the West. For example, the Ukrainian diaspora in North America remains highly networked with its "homeland." See Alexander Motyl, "Deleting the Holodomor: Ukraine Unmakes Itself," *World Affairs: A Journal of Ideas and Debate* (September/October 2010), http://worldaffairsjournal.org/article/deleting-holodomor-ukraine-unmakes-itself; John Paul Himka, "The Holodomor in the Ukrainian Jewish Encounter Initiative, 2009," https://www.academia.edu/499209/The_Holodomor_in_the_Ukrainian-Jewish_Encounter_Initiative; "Open Letter of Academics Addressed to the Ukrainian Canadian Civil Liberties Association, the Ukrainian Canadian Congress, and the Canadian Museum for Human Rights," April 2011.
14. Dariusz Stola, *Migracje z Polski 1949–1989: Kraj bez wyjścia* (Warsaw: Instytut Studiów Politycznych PAN, Instytut Pamięci Narodowej, 2010), 473, 475. At the same time, 76,000 Germans left Poland.
15. Yosef Govrin, *Yahasei Yisrael-Romania be-shilhei idan Ceauşescu* (Jerusalem: Magnes, 2001), 2, 25, 46, 201.
16. See chapter 3 in Jonathan Dekel-Chen, *Farming the Red Land: Jewish Agricultural Colonization and Local Soviet Power, 1923–1941* (New Haven: Yale University Press, 2005).
17. For examples, see Peter Holquist, "To Count, to Extract, and to Exterminate: Population Statistics and Population Politics in Late Imperial and Soviet Russia," in *A State of Nations: Empire and Nation-Making in the Age of Lenin and Stalin*, ed. Ronald Grigor Suny and Terry Martin (Oxford: Oxford University Press, 2001), 111–144; Terry Martin, "The Origins of Soviet Ethnic Cleansing," *Journal of Modern History* 70.4 (December 1998): 813–861.
18. For examples of Jewish forced migration, see François Guesnet, "Textures of Intercession: Rescue Efforts for the Jews of Prague, 1744–1748," *Simon Dubnow Institute Yearbook* 4 (2005): 355–377; Semion Goldin, "Deportation of Jews by the Russian Military Command, 1914–1915," *Jews in Eastern Europe* 41.1 (2000): 40–72.
19. Yaacov Kellner, *Reshitoh shel tichnun khevrati klal-yehudi: ha-hitarvut ha-memusedet bi-mtsukat yehudei Russya be-reshit shnot ha-70 shel ha-meah ha-19* (Jerusalem: Hebrew University, 1975).
20. In the Ottoman diaspora, the *Alliance* worked to remake local communities in its own image (real or contrived) of enlightenment and productivity. See Aron Rodrigue, *French Jews, Turkish Jews: The Alliance Israélite Universelle and the Politics of Jewish Schooling in Turkey, 1860–1925* (Bloomington: Indiana University Press, 1990), 47–120.
21. Yaacov Kellner, "Mered ha-mityashvim be-Rishon letzion be-1887 u-mered ha-mehagrim be-New York be- 1882," in *Ha-aliyot ha-rishonot: mitos u-metsiyut*, ed. Aharon Fein (Jerusalem: Hebrew University, 1982), 70–76.
22. Judith Elkin, "Goodnight, Sweet Gaucho: A Revisionist View of the Jewish Agricultural Experiment in Argentina," *American Jewish Historical Quarterly* 67.3 (1978): 208–223.

23. For example, see Kellner, "Mered," 70–71.
24. For material connected to these efforts from the mid-eighteenth to the early twentieth centuries, see Lucien Wolf, *Notes on the Diplomatic History of the Jewish Question with Texts of Protocols, Treaty Stipulations and Other Public Acts and Official Documents* (London: Jewish Historical Society of England, 1919); Judith Goldstein, *The Politics of Ethnic Pressure: The American Jewish Committee Fight Against Immigration Restriction, 1906–1917* (New York: Garland, 1990).
25. For example, see Fred A. Lazin, "'We Are Not One': American Jews, Israel, and the Struggle for Soviet Jewry," David W. Belin Lecture in American Jewish Affairs (Ann Arbor, MI: The Jean and Samuel Frankel Center for Judaic Studies, University of Michigan, 2009), 17–18, 31; Interview with Seymour Reich, February 2, 1990, *William E. Wiener Oral History Library of the American Jewish Committee*, "Soviet Jewry Movement in America," 20–21.
26. Interview with Rabbi Herschel Schacter, May 30, 1974, *William E. Wiener Oral History Library of the American Jewish Committee*, 38; Interview of David A. Harris, October 7, 1991, *William E. Wiener Oral History Library of the American Jewish Committee*, 12, 14; Interview of Phil Baum, May 24, 1989, *William E. Wiener Oral History Library of the American Jewish Committee*, 24–25; Interview of Theodore Comet, April 4, 1989, *William E. Wiener Oral History Library of the American Jewish Committee*, 16–21.
27. A number of activists of the time that I have spoken with share this view. I am not at liberty at this time to cite them.
28. Myron Berman, *The Attitude of American Jewry towards East European Jewish Immigration, 1881–1914* (New York: Arno Press, 1980), 516–523; Alfred J. Kutzik, "The Social Basis of American Jewish Philanthropy" (PhD diss., Brandeis University, 1967), 984–989.
29. See endnotes 24–25.
30. Benjamin Nathans, *Beyond the Pale: The Jewish Encounter with Late Imperial Russia* (Berkeley: University of California Press, 2002), and Yuri Slezkine, *The Jewish Century* (Princeton: Princeton University Press, 2004) have explored internal migrations in earlier periods.
31. Daniel Boyarin and Jonathan Boyarin, "Diaspora: Generation and the Ground of Jewish Identity," in *Theorizing Diaspora*, ed. Jana Evans Braziel and Anita Mannur (Malden: MA: Blackwell, 2005), 109–110.
32. Ibid., 85–86.
33. Zvi Gitelman, "Thinking about Being Jewish in Russia and Ukraine," in *Jewish Life After the USSR*, ed. Zvi Gitelman, Musya Glants, and Marshall I. Goldman (Bloomington: Indiana University Press, 2003), 49–60.
34. For example, see Zvi Gitelman, *A Century of Ambivalence: The Jews of Russia and the Soviet Union, 1881 to the Present* (Bloomington: Indiana University Press, 2001), 266–270.

5 · DIASPORA FROM THE INSIDE OUT

Litvaks in Lithuania Today

HANNAH POLLIN-GALAY

The Jewish Community of Lithuania has its official headquarters in the center of Vilnius (Vilna), in a building that its constituents refer to variously as "*bendruomenė,*" "*obshchestvo,*" "*di gemeynde*" [all meaning "community"] or, by some of its original members—"*Pylimo Chetyre,*" the address in Russian.[1] Upon walking in, one is likely to be greeted with "*Shalom!*" followed by conversation in another language. Despite the fact that there are only about 5,000 Jews left in all of Lithuania, this building is often abuzz with activity. For children and young people there are a variety of programs and clubs with Hebrew names: "Dubi," "Ilan," "Knafaim." For the aging community members, who constitute a disproportionately high percentage of the population, the center offers Sunday lectures, a veterans' club, a Yiddish reading circle, a Holocaust survivors' club, informal beginners' instruction in English, Hebrew, and Lithuanian, and a clubhouse called "*Abi men zet zikh*" [as long as we see each other]. The community's website explains that the purpose of this club, where Yiddish and Russian mix as seamlessly as the cookies, tea, and chess, is to provide people with "a second—Jewish—home."[2] There is no doubt that this culturally hybrid community center provides a homelike atmosphere for its participants. But does contemporary Jewish Lithuania have any relation to the historic "*heymland,*" the Jewish homeland that once was? Can Jews currently living in Lithuania still think of their location as a home, a center point on the map of the Jewish diaspora? If the Jewish community of Lithuania does provide a *second* home to its participants, what then constitutes their *first* home? Is there another location on the world map that these Jews look to as the primary locus of their cultural identities?

The premise of the conference on the Russian-speaking Jewish diaspora held in November 2011 at Harvard University implicitly challenged the original paradigm of the Jewish Diaspora, once written with a capital "D," which must always be paired with Zion as the homeland—the object of longing and the symbol of cultural origin. Focusing on the perspective of Jews who have left Eastern Europe and Russia in the recent decades, the conference suggested a model in which the contemporary State of Israel, North America, Germany, and other places of current Jewish residence represent sites of "diaspora." The unsettling of the classic paradigm seems apt, given the period and population being studied, and is in keeping with developments of Diaspora Studies and Transnationalism, which arose largely in the 1990s.[3] Accordingly, we may look at Jewish history through a model of "multiple experiences of rediasporization," as Jonathan Boyarin put it.[4] That is, the tension between center and periphery is perhaps a constant in Jewish culture, while the designation of specific places is dynamic. Such an approach need not negate the validity or importance of religious or political Zionism, but can raise important questions about Russian-speaking Jewish immigrants and their relation to the places they have left.

While the conference description appropriately defined Russian-speaking Jewish communities in Israel, America, and Europe as a contemporary diaspora, it seemed hesitant to offer the Former Soviet Union, or Eastern Europe and Russia, the venerated title of "home." Other, more neutral, conceptually humble names appeared in the conference text: "sending country" and "non-diaspora." But these terms will not suffice; we cannot so easily circumvent the idea of "home," since the very notion of a diaspora relies on the existence of its opposite—a point of origin, a source of dispersal, a locus of imaginative material for defining the authentic and the primary. Yet, to call contemporary Eastern Europe and Russia a Jewish "center" does seem awkward, given the dwindling Jewish populations there—or even offensive, given the massive Jewish annihilation that occurred in many of these places. Delineating home and diaspora must be even more perplexing when living in Eastern Europe. While at a distance one may imagine the former home as one likes, piecing together myth, memory, and nostalgia, those living there must integrate their imaginings of home with a daily reality of the place. Furthermore, with more family and community members abroad, it is not clear what point on the worldwide Jewish map they consider home. As Rebecca Golbert writes about Jews in contemporary Ukraine, we are examining "a cultural community that firstly [sic], has not left home [Eastern Europe], secondly has never gone home (Israel), and finally holds the potential to move to a third destination."[5]

Taking all of these complexities into account, I seek to examine how the Jews remaining in Eastern Europe think about home and periphery today. Using contemporary Lithuania as an example of an Eastern European Jewish "home-symbol" that has been nearly emptied of Jews—first violently and then later by choice—I ask how its Jewish inhabitants represent this place when telling about their own lives.[6] Specifically, I pose the following questions: Do Jews still living in

Lithuania consider the place "home"—in the symbolic sense of a place that provides cultural belonging and confidence in identity? How do they view Jews living abroad? Do they portray Jews abroad as residents of a new diaspora who look back at contemporary Lithuania as home? Or, alternatively, have those Jews who have moved abroad created a new home-center, replacing Lithuania?

In posing these questions, we discover an important tension in the diverse life stories studied here: Lithuania *ought* to be home. The capacity of the lived, physical site to meet these Litvaks' symbolic expectations varies at different moments in remembered history and with regard to different topics. One of the main stages in which these narrators convey a sense of belonging in space, of harmony between one's identity and one's physical surroundings, is through stories of return and rehabilitation in Lithuania following World War II. Likewise, in discussing more recent years, they speak of their interactions with Jews from abroad as an affirmation of the continued centrality of Lithuania in the global Jewish identity map; these Litvaks proudly remain in a place that émigrés can only hope to visit. However, at other times, these same informants speak of themselves as having been left behind, pushed outside the main collective Jewish narrative of the past four decades, in which emigration has been the assumed final step. In such discussions, the narrators depict Lithuania as a kind of "failed" home—a place they hoped would remain a Jewish center but did not.

METHODOLOGY AND SOURCES

I begin with a brief demographic and historical overview of the contemporary Lithuanian Jewish community, but my analysis focuses on oral histories given by Jews born in Lithuania before 1935 and who still lived there at the time of their interview, in the late 1990s or in 2004–2005. My pool of informants includes both those who escaped the Holocaust by fleeing to the unoccupied Soviet Union at the beginning of the Second World War, as well as those who were in ghettoes and camps in occupied Lithuania and in Germany. These prewar "Litvaks" were privy to a wide range of historical stages of Lithuanian Jewish life: its flourishing in the interwar years, its violent destruction during the Holocaust, its confined reconstellation in the Soviet years, its vast reduction starting in the late 1970s, and its further reduction coupled with external support in years following Lithuanian independence. On one hand, this generation has the strongest reasons to embrace Lithuania and elevate it to a Jewish-home symbol, since they remember the place as it once was. On the other hand, this prewar generation also has the strongest reasons to revile the place and render it an "anti-home," recalling the downfall of Jewish life there, both during the Holocaust and in subsequent decades.

My analysis draws from two sets of oral histories: a collection of forty-four personal interviews I conducted in Lithuania in 2004 and 2005, as well as filmed testimonies from the USC Shoah Foundation Institute Visual History Archive. All of the interviews I cite were conducted in Yiddish, with frequent idiomatic slips into Russian. I approached the interviews that I conducted as open-ended life stories, allowing interviewees to narrate their biographies as they saw fit. The Shoah Foundation interviews were focused on the Holocaust, but often include much about life before and after the war.

REDIASPORIZATIONS OF LITHUANIA

The history of Jewish Lithuania offers especially interesting material for exploring ideas about diaspora consciousness and the tension between "here" and "there" that characterizes Jewish cultural paradigms. The well-known appellation *Yerushalayim D'Lita* [The Jerusalem of Lithuania] that Vilna (now Vilnius), the capital of Lithuania, carried since before the start of the nineteenth century simultaneously demonstrates the deferred attachment to another, earlier homeland, Jerusalem, as well as the pride and sense of belonging in Jewish Lithuania. The long and impressive list of cultural achievements that Litvaks achieved over the centuries is well documented and need not be rehearsed in this chapter.[7]

It is important to note, however, that there has been an abundance of texts that do rehearse these Litvak achievements, alongside personal memories and a trope of geographical icons, a description of *shtetlekh* [towns] or cities, streets, buildings, courtyards, bridges, or rivers. Anna Lipphardt has documented how such texts blossomed in the interwar years, both in Lithuania and abroad.[8] Following the Holocaust, the motif of "*Lita* as home" continued to thrive in postwar writings where survivors settled, but with an important change, one that the Israeli Litvak writer Avraham Karpinovitch epitomized with the sentence, "Our Vilna no longer exists."[9] Most postwar writings concur with Karpinovitch; Jewish Lithuania ceased to exist in reality after World War II, thriving instead only as a symbol.[10]

What does life look like from this nonexistent yet symbolically still-potent Jewish center? Demographically, of course, it does not look like much, especially when compared to the flourishing prewar Jewish population in Lithuania, which numbered 240,000 following the inclusion of the Vilna region in 1939.[11] In the years immediately following the Holocaust and the Second World War, there were at most 30,000 Jews estimated to live in the country, of whom approximately 20,000 were of Lithuanian origin. This included the 1,700 who had survived the Holocaust on Lithuanian soil, the 8,000 who had been taken to Germany toward the end of the war, and another 12,000 who had survived in the unoccupied Soviet Union.[12]

Of this postwar population, about 6,000 Jews left Lithuania in the first decade after the war, many of them using the Polish citizenship that they were granted according to the Polish-Soviet repatriation agreement of 1946.[13] From the mid-1950s until the early 1970s, the population remained relatively stable. When emigration restrictions were relaxed in the Soviet Union in the early 1970s, almost half of the Jews living in Lithuania emigrated. The majority of these emigrants came from Vilna and moved to Israel. In 1979, there remained only 14,700 Jews in Lithuania. Following Lithuanian independence in 1990, the new state lifted most emigration restrictions, after which approximately half the remaining Jews left Lithuania, reducing the population to 6,500 by 1994.[14] As of 2001, there were around 5,000 Jews living in Lithuania, the majority in Vilna, Kovna [Kaunas], and Klaipeda.[15]

As the numbers above indicate, emigration, when available, has certainly been the most prominent choice for Lithuanian Jews from the immediate postwar years until today. However, those who did remain saw several markedly different stages of Jewish life in Lithuania—both in official policy and community efforts. In the initial postwar years, survivors in Lithuania established a number of welfare and educational institutions, including several Jewish schools, orphanages, and a Jewish museum—all of which were closed by 1950.[16] After Stalin's death in 1953, restrictions on so-called "Jewish nationalist" activity were relaxed somewhat and, in 1958, a Yiddish theater troupe was formed in Lithuania, which toured in different parts of the Soviet Union.[17] In the late 1980s, after the reforms of *perestroika*, the remaining Jewish community established a variety of official organizations, including a cultural center and a Jewish division of the national library.[18] Following the establishment of Lithuanian independence on March 11, 1990, more such institutions were established, most prominently, the official Jewish Community of Lithuania. With its headquarters in Vilna, the JCL also has branches in Kaunas, Klaipeda, and Šiauliai [Shavl]. Additionally, there are functioning synagogues in Vilnius and Kaunas, with very small regular attendance. The Chabad Lubavitch Community, which arrived in Lithuania in 1994, conducts religious and charitable services.[19] In addition to such documented cultural activities, these oral histories tell us about the ongoing existence of unofficial Jewish culture in postwar Lithuania—Jewish friendships, professional contacts, and recreation. It is in large part through the oral reconstruction and evaluation of these past activities that informants offer a portrait of current Jewish identity in Lithuania.

LITHUANIA AS HOME: MYTHS OF RETURN

Central to the original Jewish paradigm of diaspora is the idea of promised, or deferred return to *Eretz Yisrael*. It is well known that the modern Zionist movement translated the biblical idea of *shivat tzion*, return to Zion, into a contemporary political and social philosophy.[20] In the writings and oral histories of Jews who survived the Holocaust, the motif of *failed* return to Eastern Europe appears as a vehicle to express their feelings of alienation and rejection in their former hometowns. As just one of countless examples of a failed return story, Sheina Sachar-Gertner, who wrote an autobiography in 1985, describes her encounter with Kovna/Kaunas after the war as follows: "I would go for walks on the open streets of Kovna. I knew the city before the war. The Germans didn't manage to blow up the city's buildings. I recognized the houses where Jews had lived. It seemed to me that the houses were dressed in black, as if they were mourning the victims."[21]

Instead of finding solace or sanctuary in the buildings she recognizes from her childhood, she sees only signs of death. In the autobiography as a whole, this moment serves to explain why Lithuania cannot serve as Sachar-Gertner's home and why she must immigrate to Israel. Thus, stories of return or non-return are an important, traditional rhetorical method of defining a place as a home-point in the Jewish world map.

How do those Jews who have remained in Eastern Europe incorporate the motif of return, so crucial to the Jewish paradigm of diaspora, into their life stories? Posing this question can help us approach the larger issue of whether they consider Lithuania home. While not without reservations, many of the informants do use the language of homecoming and revival when addressing their return to Lithuania after the war as well as the subsequent decades.

As a vivid example of such a return narrative, Dora P., who grew up in Zhezhmir [Žiežmarai] and lived in Vilna/Vilnius, tells of her return to Kaunas after World War II, where she lived for many years. She first introduces her arrival to Lithuania from the Russian city of Saransk in the following way:

> In '45 when the war just ended, we were among the few who came back from the army, a few who had been partisans, a few who came back from Russia. When we would walk in Kovna on Laisves, we would cry out and grab one another. Anyone who was Jewish, we were amazed to see each other. We gathered together—I, my brother and my husband and a few others who had come from the army. We went on the Laisves and looked for Jews.
>
> (*But, how did you find one another?*) By chance. Walking on Laisves, we would meet by chance. People would appear from the world beyond.[22]

She casts the concrete reality of Laisves Street, a name she repeats three times, as a sanctuary of return for those who had been wandering in the immaterial space of "the world beyond"[23] during the time of the Holocaust. She tells of these chance meetings on the street as a rehabilitation of "we," a group reassembled from the "few" arriving separately from different directions. In her telling, Dora assigns Kovna the elevated role of homeland, a potent agent of restoration and resolution after a period of dispersal.

Meir N., whom I interviewed in 2004, tells of his return to Lithuania as a return to his previous identity, to Jewish culture and to true friends. Having fought in the Red Army during the Second World War, Meir settled in the Ural regions of Russia after the war where he married a non-Jewish Russian woman with whom he lived until 1975. Then, he abruptly says: "In '75, I traveled away from the Urals with two suitcases and came to Vilna. Here, I found work in a factory. . . . I worked there for ten years and got married a second time, in 1980, to a Jewish woman. She was an artist. I started to help her make frames for pictures. These are her pictures [pointing to the walls]."[24] Here, Meir portrays his return to Vilna as a self-corrective act, leaving a bad marriage with someone he considers different from him and returning to his personal center, to a way of life he considers closer to the "original." Compounding the already prominent connection between his second wife, the place of Vilna, and his sense of restored continuity, the paintings that he points to on the walls while speaking are all depictions of the old Jewish quarter of the city. That is, Meir connects all that which he reveres as restorative—his second wife, his return to Jewish culture—to the idea of Lithuania as home.

Even when relating quite difficult postwar experiences, informants often still shape these troubling recollections into the narrative framework of homecoming. Meishe Geguzhinskis, who was interviewed by the Shoah Foundation in 1996, relates that after surviving Dachau and being nursed back to physical health in Germany, he decided to travel to Munich because "from Munich you could travel home, to our fatherland, to Lithuania."[25] Meishe uses this elevated home-rhetoric—going so far as to call the place a "fatherland"—in answer to those who tried to dissuade him from returning, saying, "Where are you going? You're traveling home? What kind of a home is that? You lost your parents and your family there." Meishe underscores that he was aware of other options and that his return to Lithuania was a willful choice, based on a belief about where he belongs. Nonetheless, this journey proved to be quite difficult, according to what he tells. Having been a concentration camp inmate in German-occupied territory, Meishe was suspected by the Soviet authorities of spying for the Germans, making it difficult for him to find work. Later, he recalls anti-Semitism destroying his career. Nonetheless, Meishe continues to speak of Lithuania as the destination of his return, as the symbol of what home ought to be.

In some life stories, the motif of homecoming and restoration extends beyond their narration of the immediate postwar years into memories of cultural life in the 1950s and 1960s. Speaking of this period, Borekh K. enthusiastically describes the Vilna synagogue in the decades after the war.[26] "On Jewish holidays, so many people used to come to *shul* on Rosh Hashanah, Passover, Chanukah, Shvues. So many people came on the holidays that you couldn't get in the door. People would stand outside, it was that packed."[27] Borekh's description of holidays in the 1950s and 1960s echoes his recollections of Jewish religious life before the war, a seeming assertion that Lithuania maintained some element of Jewish continuity.

Aside from this description of religious life on the holidays, Borekh, like a great many others, recounts informal Jewish socializing in Lithuania. Describing a common Jewish vacation spot, Palang [Palanga], he tells: "In Palang there was a special section that they used to call 'the Jewish quarters,' an area where Jews from Kovna, from Vilna and other areas used to come. And they knew that in that area they'd find Jews." Others speak of Jewish dances and riverside meeting spots for Jews in Vilna and Kovna.[28] These depictions of lively informal Jewish culture in Lithuania in the postwar period characterize the place as one of Jewish restoration, of rehabilitation, albeit in a different form than before the war.

One couple, Mendel and Khana G., gave me a series of black-and-white photographs of their (mostly his) postwar life.[29] The photos visually narrate the same story of return and restoration in Lithuania that others shared. First we see a picture of Mendel and other Jewish Red Army soldiers celebrating the liberation of Lithuania, then a picture of Mendel completing the schooling that he missed because of the war. Next are a series of scenes similar to the informal culture that Borekh K. describes—vacationing in Palang with other Jews, as well as celebrating the first of May together, receiving military honors with mostly Jewish veterans, attending a Jewish wedding and participating in Holocaust memorial services, also with other Jews. The pictures Mendel and Khana choose to keep and display tell a story of homecoming and rehabilitation in a secular Jewish social environment.

In these instances, the informants adapt the traditional Jewish model of a return story to speak about their return to Lithuania, designating it as their Jewish home-site. This designation is surprising, given the horrors that they and their communities experienced there during the war, as well as the many challenges and limits on Jewish life afterward. In these narrative moments at least, the informants allow for problems and disappointments with the place while still maintaining that it offered them the feeling of homecoming and restoration that they sought. Thus, even at the late date when they shared these interviews—the late 1990s and 2004–2005—the informants credit the place with having served as a home-center at important junctures of their lives.

INTERACTIONS WITH OUTSIDERS: "ABROAD" AS A SOURCE OF AFFIRMATION

While these informants devote much attention to narrating return to Lithuania, and all the local activities that took place there subsequently, they do not shy away from speaking of Jews in the outside world, recognizing that there is significant Jewish life elsewhere. These reflections on Jews abroad seem to be split in two: sometimes interactions with outsiders serve to affirm Lithuania's importance on the global Jewish map. At other times, speaking of Jews living abroad reminds the informants of their own marginality, of their distance from the contemporary loci of Jewish life. Here I address those interactions with Jews abroad that strengthen informants' understandings of Lithuania as a Jewish center.

Fania B., born in Vilna, a survivor of the Vilna ghetto, a former partisan fighter, and currently one of the most active members of the official Jewish Community, provides historic tours and lectures about Jewish Vilna on a regular basis—mostly in Yiddish, but also in Russian and German.[30] Walking through the streets of Vilna with visitors from all over the world, Fania uses every current parking lot, street corner, and boutique store as a starting point for a story about her childhood, her schooling in the *Real Gimnazie*, life in the Vilna ghetto, or the partisan resistance.

In speaking to me about her contemporary life, she presents these visitors as an integral part of her day-to-day experience. In addition to the frequency of visits, mostly in the summer, she often corresponds through letters and phone calls with those whom she has guided. Thus, it is the interest and knowledge of those abroad that allow Fania the opportunity to remember, reflect, and connect her ideas of historic Vilna to the current reality.

The capacity of Jews from abroad to affirm the importance of Lithuania is also apparent in the life story of Berl G., likely the only observant, Orthodox Litvak in Lithuania at the time of the interview. Born in Kelm [Kelmė] and orphaned at an early age, Berl fought in the Red Army during the war, after which he returned to Lithuania and worked as a taxi driver. He renewed his Orthodox religious practice, as he tells it, in the 1960s. In the 1980s and 1990s, Berl served as an unofficial guide and overseer of the Vilna Gaon's grave. Though he went blind in the late 1990s, he still held keys to the grave when I met him in 2004 and, along with help, escorted visitors to this site. Asked to recount his life, he chose to begin by displaying and reciting a letter he received from Israel from Rabbi Shlomo Goren, the first military chaplain of the Israeli Defense Forces, thanking Berl for his supervision and care of the holy grave in Vilna. After discussing the letter, Berl then went on to speak of his reputation throughout the diaspora: "All Jews used to know, in all of America, in all of Israel that I hold this key. If they come to visit in Vilna, they should come to me and not to anyone else."[31] Like Fania, Berl speaks about his exchanges with Jews from abroad as part of the fabric of daily life. Litvaks visiting from the diaspora create a context in which he can be the provider of symbols, the watch-guard of a sacred cultural center. These outsiders thus enable Berl to envision Lithuania as a Jewish home-symbol.

In addition to actual remembered interaction with Jewish people or communities abroad, some informants speak of expected or potential interactions of this sort in the same manner, as affirmation of the continuing importance of Lithuania as a Jewish home-site. One example of such can be found in the life story of Khatzkel Zak, a native of Shukian [Šaukėnai], who testified for the Shoah Foundation in 1994.[32] Khatzkel spends the last segment of his interview proudly narrating how he used a taxicab from his work to travel around Lithuania, collecting money to renovate and maintain the Kovna synagogue in the 1970s.[33] He speaks of the physical maintenance of the Kovna *shul* as a vehicle for maintaining continuity of identity, declaring, "I was raised to go to *shul* from my childhood on, and this is how I will die." Khatzkel's sense of personal continuity, symbolically housed in the structure of the Kovna synagogue, actually depends on recognition from abroad. "I would like all Jews throughout the world to know what is going on with the Kovna shul. In '72 the Kovna Jews left for Israel and other countries. And only a few of us Jews stayed here. So we formed a Jewish core group who would look out for the *shul*."[34] Khatzkel asserts that the Kovna *shul* is maintained by the efforts of the few remaining locals. But Khatzkel finds increased value in this work when those abroad are aware of his activities. Here, he expands the importance of the diaspora beyond actual or recalled interaction, as in Fania or Berl's case, to include the expectation of support and approval from Jews abroad.

Through actual or expected communication with Jews abroad, these Litvaks living in Lithuania rely on the periphery to construct their idea of Lithuania as home. Cultural, religious, and academic tourism allow for exchanges in which local knowledge, access, and preservation efforts of Litvak sites become a desirable asset to those living elsewhere. Being in the position of cultural suppliers to Jews from abroad allows these Litvaks to think of themselves as maintaining the center. Beyond actual interactions of this sort, the expectation or imagined possibility of such exchanges also allows locals to envision contemporary Lithuania as *Lita*—a continuation of the historic Jewish center.

THE OUTSIDE EMPTIES OUT THE INSIDE: "EVERYONE" HAS LEFT

In contrast to such positive or affirmative uses of "abroad" in these Litvaks' life stories, there is another side to their references regarding the contemporary diaspora, one that expresses a sense of loss, abandonment, or disappointment with their own current situation. This mournful tone regarding the diaspora often arises when discussing later emigration from Lithuania, particularly that of the 1970s.[35] In these moments, the informants speak of a large, collective Jewish decision to move away—a rediasporization that has left them out. They render Lithuania as a failed home, a place that does not meet the expectations of Jewish life that they place upon it.

Borekh K. depicts a general narrative tension between homecoming after the Second World War and emigration in the 1970s. From images of fullness and livelihood in the Vilna Shul and Palang vacation spot, discussed earlier, his tone shifts dramatically moments later: "But now, in the 90s, it's become freer. But there are no Jews left. They all left. There are very few Jews left."[36] Repeating this trope of abandonment with more explicit mention of the diaspora, Borekh says at another point, "There were lots of Jews, very many Jews. They all left. For Israel. For America. Whoever was able, to Canada." Here, Borekh's tone renders the diaspora a force that weakens, depletes the home, rather than the agent of affirmation and support we saw earlier. His emphasis is not on the new life that émigrés have found in large communities abroad, but on the resulting emptiness in Lithuania. This abandonment, as Borekh presents it, impairs Lithuania's ability to function as a "home-site" and thus also his own ability to perform authentic Jewish activities, such as going to synagogue. He repeatedly emphasizes, "They *all* left." This collective notion of what "all" Jews have done leaves no room for him and those like him. Borekh tells a story of rediasporization in which he becomes statistically insignificant.

Similarly, Riva K., whose apartment was decorated with souvenirs from Israel when I visited her in Vilna in 2004, spoke very proudly of her children and family who made *aliyah* to Israel. But, together with this affirmation that she draws from abroad, she also connects it to the death and vacancy around her. She exclaims, for example, "We used to have good friends [here]. Oy, there was a time when we used to visit one another! Now, there's nobody left."³⁷ It is not clear if Riva means that her friends have died or emigrated. She conflates "leaving" in both of these senses to mark the emptying out of what she remembers as a lively Jewish community. Like Borekh, Riva intimates that the diaspora has emptied Lithuania of its "home-like" qualities, weakening her ability to function as a member of a Jewish community. She too ejects herself from the collective narrative; in declaring, "There's nobody left," she excludes herself from the count.

Other informants, like Mendel G., pointed to emigration from Lithuania as the reason they speak Yiddish less frequently today. Mendel relates, along with his wife Chana's help: "With whom will I speak in Yiddish today? There were a lot of Jews here. But, a lot left. [Chana: 'His relatives left!']. My relatives left."³⁸ Ironically, Mendel does have highly regular contact with a Yiddish speaker—his wife. Thus, in saying that he has *no one* with whom he can speak Yiddish, Mendel is perhaps expressing a wish for a community of those like him where he lives. Thus, it is not the criterion of diaspora—a tolerant satellite location—that frames his view of Lithuania, but the criterion of home, of community. As a *home*, the place no longer lives up to his expectations following the waves of emigration that began in the 1970s.

The same series of photographs that Mendel and his wife showed me, depicting happy scenes of Jews socializing in the 1950s and 1960s, ends with a picture of a long table surrounded by people in festive dress and a mix of solemn and pleasant expressions. This, they explained, was a picture of a going-away party, held in honor of friends leaving Lithuania to make *aliyah* to Israel in the 1970s. The very fact that Mendel preserves and displays a picture of this event communicates its centrality in his own life story. As in the comments of others, this picture seems to indicate that Mendel sees that the Jewish collective has moved on without him.

These references to the diaspora as emptying or weakening Lithuania— terminating its role as the "center"—contradict the various affirming roles that the diaspora plays in other moments of the same life stories. In this sense, they show the conflict and indecision that result in occupying a place that is imagined as a Jewish center, but nearly emptied of Jews. Unsure of how to define their own surroundings, these remaining Jews in Lithuania also assign conflicting roles to the Jewish communities abroad.

Relating these observations to the larger context of diaspora studies, the question arises: is the ambivalence and multiplicity of identifications expressed by Jews living in Eastern Europe today unique to their situation or is it typical of diaspora consciousness in general? Steven Vertovec, a scholar of transnationalism, has suggested that what defines "diaspora" is not a specific set of activities or demographics, but instead a structured way of thinking based on the idea of being "home away from home" or simultaneously "here" and "there."[39] Indeed, the deep incorporation of Jewish communities abroad into their way of thinking—as both a source of affirmation as well as a vehicle for expressing loneliness—does resemble Vertovec's model of dual identification. But there is a crucial difference: Instead of feeling "home away from home," these Litvaks in Lithuania express a sense of being "away from home at home." That is, though they use the diaspora as a counterpoint to Lithuania, the place they ultimately long for is Lithuania itself—in another time period.

In analyzing the diaspora, we should bear in mind that its conceptual counterpart, in this case the Former Soviet Union, is neither a static relic of the past, nor a vacant space on the map, but a dynamic social entity that changes and reacts to the diaspora, both through literal as well as imagined interaction. Often, as is the case for Jewish Eastern Europe, the idea of a place as "home" in cultural imaginings seems discordant with our understanding of the place as a contemporary reality. Those still dwelling in this symbolic home-location face the challenge of relating these conflicting interpretations of their surroundings. In my study, a suggestion of what could be done in other such emptied "centers," the informants face this dilemma with great ambivalence. Sometimes they succeed in keeping historical layers of the place alive in the present day. This, as we saw, is often managed with the help of Jews from abroad who visit and take an interest in the Jewish sites there. At other times, they articulate a sense that the collective Jewish narrative, to which they hoped to belong, has moved on without them.

NOTES

1. For geographical names in Lithuania, I use Yiddish transcriptions in order to be consistent with the material I am quoting. At the first appearance of each name, I include the Lithuanian name in parenthesis. For Kovna, Vilna, and Lita, I use the more recognizable English transliterations, rather than the YIVO spelling.
2. "Jewish Community of Lithuania," last accessed August 3, 2011, http://lzb.lt/en.
3. See, for example, Daniel and Jonathan Boyarin, "Diaspora: Generational Ground of Jewish Identity," *Critical Inquiry* 19.4 (1993): 693–725; Avtar Brah, *Cartographies of Diaspora: Contesting Identities* (London: Routledge, 1996); James Clifford, *Routes: Travel and Translation in the Late Twentieth Century* (Cambridge, MA: Harvard University Press, 1997).
4. Clifford, *Routes*, 248.
5. Rebecca Golbert, "Transnational Orientations from Home: Constructions of Israel and Transnational Space among Ukrainian Jewish Youth," *Journal of Ethnic and Migration Studies* 27.4 (2001): 714.
6. Here, I examine life stories of Jews living within the borders of the contemporary Lithuanian state. Historic Jewish Lita extended far beyond the current political borders, stretching approximately from Riga to Pinsk on a north-south axis, and from Bialystok to Smolensk from west to east. These borders correspond roughly to the fourteenth-century territory of the

Grand Duchy of Lithuania, and demarcate the area in which Jews spoke a distinctive dialect of Yiddish, followed specific customs, and internally referred to themselves as *Litvaks*, or Lithuanian Jews. See Dovid Katz, *Lithuanian Jewish Culture* (Vilnius: Baltos Lankos, 2004), 15–17. It would be interesting to examine how Jews currently living in the areas of Poland, Latvia, and Belarus that were once Liteh/Lita relate to traditional Lithuanian Jewish identity and compare it with those studied in this chapter, who live in a place that still goes by the same name, albeit in another language. Such a comparison, however, is beyond the purview of this chapter.

7. For more on the history of Lithuanian Jews in general, see Dov Levin, *The Litvaks: A Short History of the Jews of Lithuania* (Jerusalem: Yad Vashem, 2000) and Dovid Katz, *Lithuanian Jewish Culture* (Vilnius: Baltos Lankos, 2004).

8. Anna Lipphardt, "Post Holocaust Reconstruction of Vilne, 'The Most Yiddish City in the World,' in New York, Israel and Vilnius," *Ab Imperio* 4 (2004): 7.

9. Avraham Karpinovitch, *Af vilner vegn* (Tel Aviv: I. L. Peretz Publishing House, 1987), 149.

10. As examples of such postwar texts from outside of Lithuania: *Liteh* (New York: Jewish Lithuanian Culture Society, 1951); Aba Geffen, *Defying the Holocaust: A Diplomat's Report* (California: Borgo Press, 1993); Avraham Kariv, *Lithuania, Land of My Birth* (New York: Herzl Press, 1967); Musie Landau, *Mit shraybers, bikher un mit vilne* (Tel Aviv: Leyvik House, 2006); Ida Markus-Karabelnik and Bat-Sheva Leviatan-Karabelnik, *Kelm- Etz Karut* (Tel Aviv: Dionon, University of Tel Aviv, 1993); Sheina Sachar-Gertner, *The Trees Stood Still* (Framingham, MA: Holocaust Survivors Publication Co., 1981); *Vilner almanakh* (New York: Moriah Offset Co., 1992). As an interesting example of this type of place-themed literature transported back into Lithuania, see Genrikh Granovskii, *Litovskii Ierusalim: kratkii putevoditel' po pamyatnym mestam evreiskoi istorii i kul'turi v Vil'niusye* (Vilnius: Lituanis, 1992).

11. Sidney and Alice Goldstein, *Lithuanian Jewry 1993: A Demographic and Sociocultural Profile* (Jerusalem: Harman Institute for Contemporary Jewry, 1997), 8.

12. Ibid., 8–9.

13. Ibid., 9.

14. Ibid., 8.

15. Jewish Community of Lithuania, "Our Rebirth," http://www.lzb.lt/en/ (last accessed August 2011). For more information on the current population, see also, Natalija Kasatkina and Tadas Leončikas, *Lietuvos etninių grupių adaptacija: Kontekstas ir eiga* [*The Adaptation of Ethnic Groups in Lithuania: Context and Process*] (Vilnius: Eugrimas, 2003), 239–281.

16. Dov Levin, *Baltic Jews under the Soviets 1940–1946* (Jerusalem: Hebrew University, 1994), 328–334.

17. Milan Chersonskij, *The Fiftieth Anniversary of Jewish Amateur Art Collectives* (Vilnius: Jewish Community of Lithuania, 2006), 19–24.

18. Fira Bramson, "Sredi knig," in *The Jewish Museum*, ed. Yevsey Ceitlin (Vilnius: Lietuvos valstybinis žydų muziejus, 1994), 287–288.

19. Solomon Atamuk, *Juden in Litauen. Ein geschichtlicher Überblick vom 14. bis 20. Jahrhundert*, trans. Zwi Grigori Smoliakov (Konstanz: Hartung-Gorre Verlag, 2000), 223–228.

20. Theodor Herzl's famous book *The Jewish State* is perhaps the most significant example of translating the idea of "return" to Zion into a contemporary political aim. See Theodor Herzl, *The Jewish State*, trans. Silvie d' Avigdor (London: Nutt, 1896).

21. Sachar-Gertner, *The Trees Stood Still*, 36.

22. Dora P., interview by author, January 20, 2005. For the sake of privacy, I list only the first name and first initial of the last name of those I interviewed. The Shoah Foundation Institute lists interviewee's full names.

23. "*Fun yener velt*."

24. Meir N., interview by author, November 8, 2004.

25. Meishe Geguzhinskis, *Shoah Foundation Institute Visual History Archive*, 13698.

26. Known as the Choral Synagogue or "Taharat haKodesh."
27. Borekh K., interview by author, February 15, 2005.
28. Nina K., interview by author, December 13, 2004; Leah Z., April 7, 2005; Hirsh P. March 7, 2005.
29. Mendel and Chana G., interview by author, February 14, 2005.
30. Fania B., interview by author, November 11, 2004.
31. Berl G., interview by author, January 19, 2005.
32. Khatzkel Zak, *Shoah Foundation Institute Visual History Archive*, 12694.
33. Called *Ohel Yaakov*, built in 1871. See *YIVO Encyclopedia*, s.v. "Kaunas," http://www.yivoencyclopedia.org/article.aspx/Kaunas.
34. Khatzkel Zak, interview.
35. In fact, the sorrow expressed in connection to emigration in the 1970s is often so strong that it seems almost exaggerated in scale, especially when compared to their more subdued discussion of the Holocaust. Dori Laub has noted a similar tendency among many Holocaust survivors to deflect their painful memories of the war and postwar years to subsequent events. For further reflection on what he calls "Second Holocausts," see Shoshana Felman and Dori Laub, *Testimony: Crises of Witnessing in Literature, Psychoanalysis and History* (New York: Routledge, 1992), 65–72.
36. Borekh K., interview.
37. Riva K., interview by author, February 23, 2005.
38. Mendel G., interview.
39. Steven Vertovec, "Conceiving and Researching Transnationalism," *Ethnic and Racial Studies* 22.2 (1999): 452.

6 · RUSSIAN-SPEAKING JEWS AND ISRAELI EMIGRANTS IN THE UNITED STATES

A Comparison of Migrant Populations

STEVEN J. GOLD

Since the early 1970s, the two largest groups of Jewish immigrants to the United States have come from the Former Soviet Union [FSU]—more than 600,000, including some non-Jews[1]—and from Israel—175,000 or more.[2] Both groups are well-educated, urbanized, and tend to settle in the same environments, especially in the older Jewish neighborhoods of New York, Los Angeles, and other major cities. Both groups achieve high levels of earnings in the United States and are well-represented among the self-employed and professionals. Both show high rates of naturalization. Of course, both groups belong to the same religion.[3] Particularly since the 1990s, the two groups have become important segments of the American Jewish community, expressing their Jewish and national identities alongside the host population but in ways of their own choosing. They add to the diversity and vitality of American Jewish life and foster contact among American Jews, their countries of origin, and locations where their co-nationals have settled.

Despite these commonalities, their experiences of migration, adaptation to American society, national and Jewish identities, and collective behaviors have been quite different. While continuing to value Russian language and culture, Jews from the former Soviet Union, most of whom entered the United States as refugees, generally see themselves as "New Americans," and few plan to return to the FSU. In contrast, Israelis, who came as voluntary immigrants, retain stronger ties to their country of origin and express significant ambivalence about their presence on American soil.

This chapter compares the experience of Russian-speaking Jews and Israeli immigrants in the United States and considers how their presence is shaping the American Jewish community and affecting relations with migrants' co-national communities in their countries of origin, as well as in alternative points of settlement.

THE EVOLVING STATUS OF CONTEMPORARY JEWISH MIGRANTS

Despite the American Jewish community's long record of assisting recently arrived co-religionists and the presence of sizeable, active, and confident Russian and Israeli migrant populations in the United States, since the 1970s, a fraction of the local and international Jewish establishment objected to these newcomers' presence in the country. They were regarded as "Jewish communal deviants."[4]

Of the two groups, Israelis received the coldest reception. Prior to the 1990s, most Israelis and American Jews considered the existence of Israeli emigrants to be an ideological, demographic, military, and economic threat to the Jewish State. As a consequence, Israeli emigrants were condemned as *yordim*—a stigmatizing Hebrew term which describes those who "descend" from the "higher" place of Israel to the diaspora—as opposed to immigrants, the *olim*, who "ascend" from the diaspora to Israel.[5] In the 1970s and early 1980s, Israeli politicians such as Prime Minister Yitzhak Rabin were especially vitriolic on this issue, calling Israeli emigrants "moral lepers," "the fallen among the weaklings," and "the dregs of the earth."[6] However, by 1992, Rabin had recanted these statements.[7]

During that time, Israeli emigrants largely accepted the *yordim* epithet and, as a result, remained marginal both to Israel and the American Jewish community. Indeed, Drora Kass and Seymour Martin Lipset asserted, "If Jews have been the proverbial marginal people, Israeli emigrants are the marginal Jews."[8]

While these émigrés tended to reside in Jewish neighborhoods and became involved in traditionally Jewish occupations, they seldom utilized communal services or maintained a collective voice in local Jewish life. However, following the lead of the Israeli government, which has increasingly accepted its citizens' migration to gain access to a wide range of globally available social and economic opportunities, American Jewish organizations have recently created outreach programs for Israeli immigrants.

While Russian-speaking Jewish migrants resettled in the United States with the support of local Jewish institutions, their presence also caused considerable consternation because they were rejecting Israel as a homeland. According to journalist J. J. Goldberg: "The first (American) Soviet Jewry activists in the 1960s hardly intended their work to result in Jewish immigration to the United States. The movement was from the start a Zionist enterprise, conceived by Israelis and driven by activists who wanted the world's second largest Jewish community 'repatriated'—brought en masse 'back' to Israel, their ancestral homeland."[9]

From the late 1960s until the mid-1970s, the majority of Soviet Jews granted exit visas did settle in Israel. However, between 1976 and 1989, at least half opted to move to the United States instead, and by the late 1980s, less than 10 percent each year chose the Jewish State.[10] Accompanying the rise in immigration was a growing call to resettle Soviet Jews exclusively in Israel.[11] Soviet Jews who opted for other destinations were labeled *noshrim* [dropouts] and were subject to inferior treatment by resettlement agencies in Europe.

Proponents of settlement in Israel demanded that the United States deny Soviet Jews group-level refugee status in hopes of increasing migration to Israel. They had considerable success. In late 1989, the American administration revoked Soviet Jews' universal refugee status and, instead, provided it only on a case-by-case basis, favoring those with relatives already in the United States.[12] By the 1990s, Israel received far more Soviet Jewish arrivals than the United States, although the numbers entering both countries were substantial through much of the 1990s.[13]

Despite such efforts to condemn the settlement of Israeli and Russian-speaking Jews in the United States, by the mid-1990s a series of political, economic, ideological, and demographic developments had transformed the status and treatment of these populations. The net effect was to enhance the self-determination and autonomy of recently arrived Jewish migrants in the United States.

METHODS

Data for this chapter were collected through several research methods including literature review, survey research, analysis of existing data, in-depth interviews, and fieldwork conducted since 1982 with Russian-speaking and Israeli Jewish communities in California, Michigan, New York, and Florida.

MOTIVES FOR MIGRATION

Most Russian-speaking Jews entered the United States with refugee status shaped by the Cold War context.[14] Blocked mobility, anti-Semitism, and restrictions on travel—as well as the desire for family unification and free religious and cultural expression—motivated their exit. Following the fall of the Soviet Union, Jews continued to leave in record numbers, fleeing a hostile and unstable environment. In contrast, Israelis entered the United States as voluntary immigrants. They came in search of economic and educational opportunities, to broaden their horizons, and because of their disenchantment with the current Israeli society. Few planned to stay permanently.

DEMOGRAPHICS

Russian Jews

Unlike most immigrant and refugee groups who are largely youthful populations, Russian-speaking Jewish families include many elderly individuals. According to the 2000 census, 40.4 percent of persons born in the former Soviet Union living in the United States were over forty-five years of age. Of the 67,458 persons age eighteen and over who were born in Russia and became naturalized in the United States between 2003 and 2010, more than 40 percent were over the age of forty-five. Of these, 66 percent were married. Only 35 percent were male.[15]

Refugee families experience problems because the elderly have difficulties learning English, finding employment, and making their own way in the United States. At the same time, elderly relatives provide social benefits since they assist with childcare and help build stable and interconnected communities since they often interact in parks, communal agencies, and apartment buildings.[16]

Israelis

The number of Israelis living in the United States has been the subject of intense controversy. Estimates drawn from the 2000 U.S. census, the Israeli census, and Israeli Border Police data suggest that approximately 153,000 to 175,000 Israelis, including those born in Israel and elsewhere, reside in the United States.[17] Rebhun and Lev Ari estimate the total population of Israelis, including their U.S.-born children and American spouses, to be 250,000.[18] In contrast to Russian-speaking Jews, Israelis in the United States tend to be relatively young. Of the 21,661 persons born in Israel age eighteen and up who became naturalized in the United States between 2003 and 2010, less than 27 percent were over the age of forty-five.[19] According to the 2000 U.S. census, Israeli immigrants' median age in 2000 was thirty-seven, and only 4.4 percent were age sixty-five and over. In 2000, the population was 55 percent male and 45 percent female. The proportion of married Israelis living in the United States is quite high: about 71 percent in 2000. Of the 21,661 persons born in Israel age eighteen and up who became naturalized in the United States between 2003 and 2010, 74 percent were married and 56 percent were male.[20]

FAMILY AND GENDER PATTERNS

Russians

Patterns of family composition of those that have their roots in the FSU reinforce intimacy and mutual involvement among Russian émigrés in the United States. Because of Soviet housing shortages and the desire to maximize available resources for children's mobility, family size was typically small. Families rarely had more than one or, at the most, two offspring. Soviet grandparents retired early (women at age fifty-five, men at sixty) and were often extensively involved in the lives of their children and grandchildren, with whom they lived. Russian families often brought over their aged members in order to maintain family unity, provide childcare, and guarantee an environment more secure than that of the FSU. Elderly women outnumbered men and were significantly older, indicating their greater life expectancy and the continued demographic impact of the Second World War.[21]

Jews in the former Soviet Union often got married and had children at a much younger age than their counterparts the United States. As a consequence, both in the FSU and in the United States, parents and children tend to be much closer in age than American families with similarly high educational profiles. It is not uncommon to find four generations residing together in one household. The labor force participation of parents and children overlaps for many more years than among the American middle class, allowing employed parents to be actively involved in shaping their children's careers (by offering advice, exercising influence, or working together in family businesses) and facilitating multiple earner households.[22] In the United States, many Russian-speaking Jewish families retain their Soviet-based ideas about marriage. A Moscow-born entrepreneur in Los Angeles told me: "My daughter is seventeen—she goes to Fairfax High. She has her boyfriend and wants to get married and start her own family. I understand her, so we are supporting that. We are not so worried about college now."[23] This continued emphasis on early marriage for women maintains Soviet-based patterns of family closeness, but in the American context, it can thwart a young woman's ability to obtain a higher education and adversely affect her career options as a result. According to the 2000 U.S. census, the pattern of early marriage and childbearing has been maintained in the United States. The fraction of women born in the FSU residing in the United States who are unmarried by age forty (4 percent) is less than one third (14 percent) of that of all U.S. women and substantially lower than that of other migrant populations as well, including women born in China and Latin America.[24]

Jews from the former Soviet Union who have relocated to the United States tend to be satisfied with their decision. Although they retain cultural and linguistic patterns associated with their country of origin and enjoy interacting with their co-ethnics, they are content to fit into the widely accepted pattern of "hyphenated American" ethnic membership. Their white skin, legal immigration status, and high educational profile grant them a privileged position in their new homeland, which contrasts quite favorably with the centuries of oppression their ancestors endured in the country of origin.

Adaptation of Russian Children

Reflecting their access to family and community resources, Russian-speaking Jewish immigrant children who have entered the United States since the 1970s generally have a strong educational background and do well in American schools. For example, in a 1991 comparison of the twelve largest immigrant groups attending

New York City public schools, grades 3–12, who had been in the country three years or less, students from the FSU ranked first in reading scores, second in math, and fifth in English. Their reading and math scores were much higher than the average for all students, including the native born. In addition, their mean increase in score over the previous year was the highest of all groups in both reading and English, and among the highest in math.[25] Russian immigrants' educational accomplishments make sense because many describe America's educational opportunities as a major reason for their families' immigration.[26] They also have high rates of attending college (over 70 percent of a sample of New York residents between age eighteen and thirty-two who had been in the United States at least six years). However, they often choose their college or university on the basis of location rather than prestige. A New York–based study found that only around 10 percent go away to college.[27]

Israeli Emigrants' Patterns of Gender and Family Adaptation

In nearly every study of Israelis in the United States, we find that while migration was a "family decision" and the family as a whole enjoys economic benefits as a result of migration, the decision to migrate was generally made by the men and was explicitly for the expanded educational and occupational opportunities available in the United States.[28] Once in the United States, men often enjoy the benefits of such expanded opportunities, and accordingly, feel more comfortable with the new country. Women, however, especially those with children and established careers, have more negative views of migration. Even when Israeli women work in the States, they have less of a professional identity than men and would prefer to return home.[29] In Rachel's words:

> For most of the people who came here, the men came and the women came after them. Like when I came, my husband came for a job. I had to leave my job and I had to find a new job and it was very painful. I think more and more now there are women coming on their own, but if you look at most cases, it is the men coming after jobs and it means that the women are the ones that have to take care of finding apartment, finding schools for kids—and they get depressed, very badly depressed.[30]

In reflecting on their experience in the United States, Israelis contrast the nation's positive economic and occupational environment to its communal and cultural liabilities: immigrants almost universally regard Israel as a better place for children. At least prior to the start of the Al Aqsa Intifada in 2000 (which involved suicide bombings in public settings), it was seen as safer, with fewer social problems. It also did not impose the manifold generational conflicts Israelis confront when raising children in the United States. Furthermore, in Israel Jews are culturally and religiously dominant. The institutions of the larger society teach children Hebrew and instruct them in a Jewish national, ethnic, and religious identity, as well as Jewish history. In the United States, however, Israelis become a minority group and lose communal networks based upon family, friendship, and neighborhood, which provided a social circle and assistance in raising children.

The presence of young or school-age children in Israeli immigrant families often heightens their ambivalence about being in the United States. Role reversals sometimes occur between parents and children, with the younger generation gaining power over their elders. This is because children generally become Americanized and learn English much faster than their parents.

In sum, while both Russian-speaking Jewish families and Israeli families do relatively well in the United States, Russians tend to be more satisfied, while Israelis continue to express ambivalence regarding their life in the United States. This may be because Israelis have the option of returning to a welcoming and familiar destination—their country of origin—which Russian-speakers generally lack.

ECONOMIC ADJUSTMENT

Russian-Speaking Jews

Russian-speaking Jews who have entered the United States since 1970 have very high levels of education, often in technical and professional fields. Consequently, their economic progress has been impressive, yielding near-universal entry into the American middle class. According to the 2000 census, 59.9 percent of FSU-born persons residing in the United States age 24–65 had a bachelor's degree or greater. Thus, they are much better educated than all foreign-born Americans, of whom only 26 percent have a bachelor's degree or higher. Their educational achievements also outstrip those of the native-born population. Of employed Russian-born persons age eighteen and over who became naturalized between 2006 and 2010, 15 percent are in management, professional, and related occupations (see table 6.1).[31] Reflecting their high levels of education, recent Russian immigrants experience rapid economic mobility. According to the 2000 census, FSU-born men in the labor force, age 25–64, were earning a median income of $38,000 in 1999. For purposes of comparison, the median income for all foreign-born men age 25–64 in the United States who were in the labor force was $27,000 in 1999. According to the 2000 census, FSU-born women in the labor force, age 25–64, were making a median income of $24,500 in 1999, while the median income for all foreign-born women, age 25–64, in the United States labor force was $19,400 in 1999.

According to the 2000 U.S. census, 73 percent of immigrants from Russia/FSU in the labor force, age 25–64, were employed as managers, administrators, sales, professionals, or technical specialists, while 54 percent of all foreign-born persons in the U.S. labor force, age 25–64, were employed in the same categories. Other important occupational categories are gender-based: craft work (frequently in construction and jewelry) for men and service occupations for women.[32]

TABLE 6.1. Persons Naturalized during Fiscal Years 2006–2010 by Region/Country of Birth and Selected Characteristics. Region/Country: Russia

Characteristic	Total	Male	Female	Unknown
Total	44,906	15,623	29,278	5
Occupation				
Management, professional, and related occupations	15.21%	18.20%	13.62%	
Service occupations	3.82%	1.95%	4.82%	
Sales and office occupations	4.40%	2.43%	5.46%	
Farming, fishing, and forestry occupations	0.04%			
Construction, extraction, maintenance, and repair occupations	0.88%	1.40%	0.06%	
Production, transportation, and material moving occupations	2.93%	5.41%	1.61%	
No occupation/not working outside home	17.31%	14.06%	19.05%	
Homemakers	2.12%	0.08%	2.23%	
Students or children	11.80%	10.86%	12.31%	
Retirees	1.25%	0.97%	1.03%	
Unemployed	2.14%	1.73%	2.00%	
Unknown	54.95%	38.91%	55.18%	1

SOURCE: Department of Homeland Security 2011 Profiles on Naturalized Citizens, http://www.dhs.gov/files/statistics/data/dsnat.shtm.

One economic asset of recent Russian immigrants over natives and other immigrant groups is the high proportion of women with professional and technical skills—a product of the FSU's egalitarian educational system. As of 1981, 67 percent of Soviet women in the United States were engineers, technicians, or other kinds of professionals prior to migration, whereas only 16.5 percent of American women worked in these occupations. According to the 2000 census, 31 percent of Soviet-born women in the United States were college graduates. This is more than double the 15.1 percent figure of college graduation for all foreign-born women. As of 2000, 47.1 percent of Soviet women in the United States are employed as managers or professionals in the United States. In contrast, the figure for all foreign-born women is 33.2 percent. A smaller proportion of Russian immigrant men, 45.5 percent, are employed as managers or professionals. The 2000 census reports that 12 percent of Russians/former Soviets (14.9 percent of men and 9.5 percent of women) are self-employed. The rate of self-employment for all foreign-born Americans is 10.8 percent—11.9 percent for foreign-born men and 9.3 percent for foreign-born women. Of the 29,278 Russian women age eighteen and up who became naturalized in the United States between 2006 and 2010, 19 percent had no occupation or were not working outside the home (see table 6.1). Of these, about 12 percent (or 2.2 percent of all recently naturalized Russian women) were homemakers. Fourteen percent of Russian-born men had no occupation or were not working outside of the home.³³ While the average income of Russian migrants suggests a generally successful integration into the American middle class, the economic adjustment of this population ranges widely from poverty to significant wealth.

Israelis

The 2000 census shows that Israelis in the United States are relatively well educated. Forty-three percent have a bachelor's degree or higher. Half of the population age 24–65 are employed as managers or professionals, while 31.4 percent are in technical/sales or administrative occupations. About 6.7 percent are in the service industry and 11.9 percent are operators or laborers.³⁴ Of employed Israel-born individuals age eighteen and up who became naturalized between 2006 and 2010, almost 24 percent are in management, professional, and related occupations. Consequently, they have higher-status occupations than Russians who became naturalized during the same time (see table 6.2).³⁵

Israeli-Americans' rate of self-employment—33.4 percent—is among the highest of all nationality groups recorded in the 2000 U.S. census. The earnings of Israelis in the United States are considerable. The median household income of Israelis in the United States was $81,000 in 2000. However, there are significant gender differences in Israelis' economic activity. The median income of Israeli men was $38,000, exceeding that of all foreign-born men by $15,000. In contrast,

TABLE 6.2. Persons Naturalized during Fiscal Years 2006–2010 by Region/Country of Birth and Selected Characteristics. Region/Country: Israel

Characteristic	Total	Male	Female	Unknown
Total	14,816	8,368	6,440	8
Occupation				
Management, professional, and related occupations	23.61%	26.05%	20.47%	
Service occupations	2.41%	2.26%	2.61%	
Sales and office occupations	6.96%	7.39%	6.41%	
Farming, fishing, and forestry occupations	0.02%	0.04%	0.00%	
Construction, extraction, maintenance, and repair occupations	1.05%	0.51%	0.00%	
Production, transportation, and material moving occupations	2.23%	1.68%	0.47%	
No occupation/not working outside home	13.14%	7.76%	20.16%	
Homemakers	3.52%	0.08%	6.40%	
Students or children	7.28%	5.95%	9.02%	
Retirees	0.55%	0.47%	0.47%	
Unemployed	1.80%	1.15%	2.64%	
Unknown	50.38%	49.44%	49.11%	1

SOURCE: Department of Homeland Security 2011 Profiles on Naturalized Citizens, http://www.dhs.gov/files/statistics/data/dsnat.shtm.

the median income of Israeli women in the United States was little more than half that of men: $20,000, and only about $2,200 more than the median income for all foreign-born women in the United States. As native speakers of Hebrew who are often trained as educators, Israeli women frequently find employment as instructors in American Jewish synagogues and schools. Others work as professionals, managers, and administrators, and in clerical jobs.[36]

While men attain high rates of labor force participation, a surprisingly large fraction of Israeli women are not in the labor market. Despite their relatively elevated educational profiles, their labor force participation rate (about 54 percent) is below that of all foreign-born women in the United States (59 percent).[37] This can be considered an indicator of Israelis' economic advancement over their status in Israel because, in their country of origin, a single income could not support the family, while it can in the United States.

A survey of naturalized Israelis in New York found that only 4 percent of the women indicated "housewife" as their occupation in Israel, while 36 percent did so in the United States. This makes Israelis distinct from many other contemporary immigrant groups, which maintain higher labor force participation rates for women in the United States than in their countries of origin.[38] Of the 6,440 Israeli women age eighteen and up who became naturalized in the United States between 2006 and 2010, 20 percent had no occupation or were not working outside the home. Of these, about a third were homemakers; 7.8 percent of Israel-born men had no occupation or were not working outside of the home (see table 6.2).[39]

RELATIONS WITH AMERICAN JEWS

Russian-Speaking Jews

The majority of American Jews share regional origins with recently arrived Russian-speaking co-religionists. However, most native-born Jews have lived in the United States for several generations. Moreover, their families left Russia and Eastern Europe prior to the establishment of the Soviet Union. Accordingly, their cultural, linguistic, ideological, educational, and religious characteristics are unlike those of the newly arrived.

American Jews often view Russian-speaking Jews as modern-day counterparts of their own grandparents: Jews leaving the oppressive and anti-Semitic lands of Eastern Europe for the freedom and opportunity of America. While far more ultimately settled in Israel, the American Jewish community and U.S. government provided several hundred thousand Soviets with prized refugee status and a generous package of services and benefits for rebuilding their lives.[40]

Russian-speaking Jewish immigrants are grateful for the benefits and services they receive from American Jews, but they have very different outlooks and life experiences than their hosts. Accordingly, Jewish immigrants from the FSU sometimes lock horns with the host community with regard to the nature of group identity, religious involvement, and location of settlement. Admitting that conflicts between migrants and hosts have long characterized the American Jewish population, the sociologist Paul Ritterband argued that current issues of contention are almost completely opposite of those of the past: "The 1880–1914 Russian Jewish immigrants were offered a network of settlement houses and other institutions designed by the earlier wave of German Jewish immigrants as a means of Americanizing their all-too-traditional and exotic co-religionists. By contrast the contemporary American Jewish community, itself composed largely of descendants of earlier waves of East European immigrants, has attempted to Judaize the immigrants."[41] In both periods, conflicts developed as hosts directed new arrivals toward patterns of adaptation that were not of the immigrants' own choosing.

Primed by decades of anti-Soviet/Russian propaganda and having heard numerous tales about Soviet Jewish *refuseniks* from the Soviet Jewry movement seeking religious freedom, American Jews generally assumed that Russian speakers came to the United States to reestablish their religious identities, would graciously accept instructions on how to become American Jews, and would rapidly repudiate their linguistic, cultural, and sentimental attachments to the FSU. Accordingly, American Jews were often taken aback to find that the newcomers were more interested in finding jobs and attending to their children's futures than frequenting synagogues or keeping kosher; had their own ideas about religious and national identity; prized the Russian language, culture, and landscape; took pride in the accomplishments of the FSU; and retained elements of a Russian identity in the United States.[42] According to Fran Markowitz, "As American Jews found some of the ways that Soviet Jews act to be alien, they came to label these behaviors and the individuals associated with them not 'Jewish' but 'Russian.'"[43] As a consequence, during the 1970s and 1980s several articles in the *Journal of Jewish Communal Service* provided resettlement staff with patronizing hints on how to bring Soviet émigrés into the American Jewish community for their own good. For example, one article asserted: "It is absolutely essential to exploit ESL [English as a second language]classes . . . where they are actually a captive audience . . . for inculcating Jewish attitudes and values . . . to foster a positive Jewish self-concept while developing Jewish cognition, Jewish language expression and Jewish life skills."[44]

By the late 1980s, it was widely acknowledged that most Soviet Jews in the United States were not interested in becoming religious in the manner expected by their hosts. Initial hopes for rapid religious assimilation were replaced by a more realistic acknowledgment of Soviet émigrés' secular and ethnic (rather than religious) identification.[45] An American rabbi who worked with Soviet Jews reflected on this realization: "One of the disappointments that many rabbis felt was that most of the Soviet Jews did not find a need to express their Jewishness. We should have understood this, because they come from a secular, atheistic country, but it was difficult to accept."[46]

Most recently, Jewish scholars and community activists have recognized that while Russian-speaking Jews frequently express their Jewishness in ways at variance from the local Jewish population, they often have a stronger Jewish identity and more extensive Jewish social ties than do American Jews.[47]

Israeli Emigrants' Relations with American Jews

While they share a religion, and a sizeable fraction have common ancestral origins in Eastern Europe, Israeli and American-Jewish notions of group membership often contrast because the basic group identities associated with being either Israeli or American Jewish are rooted in distinct cultural and national contexts. For many Israelis, ethnic identity is secular and national. While they are knowledgeable about Jewish holidays and speak Hebrew, they often connect these behaviors to "Israeliness" rather than Jewishness.

A significant fraction of Israelis do not actively participate in organized religious activities and are accustomed to relying on the larger society and public institutions to socialize their children, free of charge. Hence, they often complain about paying fees to join a synagogue or attend holiday services.[48] Moreover, Reform and Conservative Judaism, with which the great majority of American Jews affiliate, are all but unknown in Israel. Finally, while American Jews are accustomed to life as a sub-community in a religiously pluralistic society, Israelis grew up in an environment where religion and nationality were one and the same.

Because of Israelis' lack of familiarity with American forms of Jewish involvement, some pundits decry their assimilation into non-Jewish cultural patterns. They assert that the Israelis' very exit from the Holy Land signifies a traitorous move away from the Jewish ideal, and that their participation in and contribution to Jewish activities is limited and oriented toward secular pursuits with little religious content: meals, parties, Israeli folk dancing, and sports.[49] Other observers argue that Israelis are able to actively participate in American Jewish life while simultaneously maintaining their links to Israel. They note that Israelis speak Hebrew, live in Jewish neighborhoods, are involved in a variety of Jewish institutions, and visit Israel frequently. A growing body of surveys reveals that Israeli immigrants engage in many religious and cultural Jewish behaviors at higher rates than is the case among native-born Jews, and also are more likely to live in neighborhoods characterized by high Jewish population density.[50]

When comparing Israeli immigrants' observance of Jewish religious practices—including lighting candles on Shabbat and Chanukah, attending synagogue on the High Holy Days and Shabbat, and fasting on Yom Kippur—with their patterns in Israel, data collected during both the 1990s and more recently reveal that among naturalized Israelis in New York and Los Angeles, ritual behaviors have actually increased over time and far exceed those of U.S. Jews. Amplified rates of ritual practice may reflect the efforts of these Jewish migrants to retain their religious identity within a predominantly non-Jewish country.[51] Finally, a growing number of Israeli-American parents seek to maintain or reestablish connections with Israeli and/or Jewish behaviors through special family activities of their own creation or involvement in various Israeli-American programs, such as after-school Israeli Hebrew courses and Hebrew-language scouting activities.

COMMUNAL LIVES

Russian-Speaking Jews

Russian and American Jews maintain distinct attitudes and social habits. Because they often feel at odds with American Jews, Soviet emigrants gravitate toward their own enclaves where they can interact in a familiar environment and maintain a measure of control over their adaptation to the United States. This tendency is enhanced by the fact that the population includes many elderly people who are limited in their ability to adjust to American life and speak English and, hence, are highly dependent upon co-ethnic settings.

Because Russian immigrants have relatively high rates of self-employment, their neighborhoods feature numerous ethnically oriented shops, restaurants, service providers, and media industries that present a venue for socializing and identity reconstruction. While these communities have geographic, cultural, religious, and economic links with those of American Jews, the co-national preference often predominates. Furthermore, during the 1990s, such communities were themselves often stratified into subgroups on the basis of class, ideology, region of origin, occupation, religiosity, income, tenure in the United States, and other factors. However, such communities have become more integrated since that time.[52] Russian immigrant enclaves have a strong attraction for the broader nationally defined population, who often commute long distances to and from work in order to live among co-ethnics. As has been the case among various immigrant enclaves during the early twentieth century and more recently, a fairly high level of institutional completeness exists. For example, in West Los Angeles or Brooklyn, a Russian immigrant can interact with neighbors; shop for food, clothes, appliances, or medication; see a doctor or dentist; attend religious services; read a newspaper; watch cable TV; visit a local park to play dominoes; spend an evening in a nightclub; and interact with numerous acquaintances, all without speaking a word of English.

Coming from large cities, accustomed to living in apartment buildings and dependent on public transportation and co-ethnic shops and services that assist the elderly, Russian-speaking Jews are much more attached to urban locations than are native-born Jews and other Jewish immigrants like Israelis, who often gravitate toward suburban communities.[53] Only 10 percent of Russian-speaking Jews in the greater New York City area live in suburban counties.[54]

Russian Jews' shared discomfort with American values and cultural patterns is a reason some avoid their American co-religionists. Even those Russian Jews born in the United States often maintain a preference for fellow Russians as friends and marriage partners. The authors of a New York–based study of émigré youth found that, as they approach adulthood, the children of Russian-speaking Jewish immigrants frequently develop a new appreciation for co-ethnic interaction and make efforts to improve their Russian-language skills to facilitate interactions with fellow émigrés.[55]

The political affiliations, or at least voting preferences, of most American Jews (including American Israelis) tend to be Democratic.[56] In contrast, many Russian-speaking immigrants are politically conservative and when they become naturalized citizens, identify with the Republican Party. Having been admitted to the United States with refugee status from the discredited and now defunct Soviet Union, recent Russian immigrants continue to hold conservative political views. A New York–based survey of Russian-speaking Jews' voting patterns in the election of 2004 found that 77 percent favored George W. Bush.[57]

Some of the greatest differences between American Jews and Russian Jewish immigrants are found in their patterns of religious and ethnic identification—apparent commonalities that would seem to bring these groups together. This is because, for most American Jews, Judaism is a religious identity, rooted in religious knowledge and practice. In contrast, Judaism or Jewishness was regarded as a "nationality" (ethnic group) in the atheist Soviet Union.

Further separating American Jews from Russian immigrants is the fact that they are not very comfortable with the Western denominations with which the vast majority of American Jews associate. Rejecting Reform and Conservative movements, many Russian-speaking Jewish migrants affiliate with Chabad—an ultra-Orthodox, hasidic sect. Although they lack religious training, Russian immigrants are drawn to Chabad's familiar ambiance and make use of its extensive immigrant-oriented programming, including "Russian synagogues" in major areas of settlement. In the following quote, a Russian-speaking Chabad rabbi in Los Angeles described his organization's appeal to Jewish émigrés:

> We never push people, but they feel much better, more comfortable with their own community, with their own tradition, with their own language.
>
> They come to me after being to American services and they say, "Which kind of synagogue is this? What is it? Instead of a cantor [there] is a lady? She sings with a guitar? A cantor has to be with a beard and stand with his back to the people and praying and a nice voice and you start to cry when he singing. [Why] is she standing like that with a guitar and she smiles?"[58]

Finally, as refugees from a society lacking in a tradition of volunteerism, Russian-speaking Jews are highly individualistic and tend to avoid participating in communal organizations—a major feature of the collective lives of American Jews.[59]

Despite Russian immigrants' feelings of distance from American Jews, most see their eventual amalgamation with co-ethnic hosts as both positive and inevitable. Based on his analysis of the New York Jewish Population Study of 1991, Paul Ritterband argued, "In many ways, the new immigrants, despite their lack of religious training and with few exceptions, score as high—or higher—on the religious, secular and affiliational dimensions of Jewishness as do other New York Jews."[60]

As larger numbers of immigrants from different parts of the FSU established themselves in the United States, they built their own communities reflecting regions of origin, educational level, religious orientation, ideological outlook, cultural styles, and other factors. Annalise Orleck contrasted the adaptation of Bukharan and Georgian Jews from non-European regions of the FSU to that of Jews from the European FSU. The former, she found, were far less "Sovietized" than their co-nationals from Moscow, St. Petersburg, or Kiev. Accordingly, they were able to retain entrepreneurial occupations, more traditional gender roles, and a much higher degree of religiosity than the latter. These ethnic resources have been put to use in the development of a prosperous enclave in Queens.[61]

Nevertheless, hailing from what was, prior to 1990, a single state where religious and voluntary collective activities were highly regulated by the government, Russian-speaking Jews in the United States are more uniform and less diverse than Israeli emigrants in the United States, who are characterized by a broad array of religious, subcultural, ideological characteristics, and national origins. They also have ready access—including citizenship—to Israel, as well as many other states.

Israeli Emigrants' Communal Patterns

Most Jews who entered the United States during the last 300 years have been *de jure* or *de facto* refugees, with few opportunities to return to their countries of origin. By contrast, Israelis retain the real possibility of going back to Israel; indeed, American Jews, the Jewish State, and even the immigrants themselves generally agree that they should return. This distinguishes Israelis from most other Jewish immigrants in U.S. history.

While most Jews immigrating to the United States have become staunchly patriotic soon after their arrival, Israelis in the United States often discuss their desire to return home, and many make frequent trips back to Israel, sometimes culminating in permanent repatriation. In the words of a community leader in Los Angeles: "Israelis would always suffer a certain touch of nostalgia because they are missing the things that they grew up with. Psychologically, most Israelis did not come here to be Americans. They did not come here to swear to the flag; to sing the national anthem and to go to Dodgers games. They came here to have the house and the swimming pool and the two cars and the job and the money."[62]

Despite their ambivalence, Israelis have been active in building a life for themselves in the United States and in pursuing U.S. citizenship. In fact, Israeli immigrants have developed many activities and organizations in order to soothe their misgivings about being abroad. Communal activities include socializing with other Israelis, living near co-ethnics and within Jewish communities, consuming Hebrew-language media produced in both the United States and Israel, frequenting Israeli restaurants and nightclubs, attending co-ethnic social events and celebrations, joining Israeli associations, working with other Israelis, consuming goods and services provided by Israeli professionals and entrepreneurs, keeping funds in Israeli banks, sending children to Israeli-oriented activities, raising money for Israeli causes, calling family and friends in Israel on the phone, and hosting Israeli visitors.

In the course of fieldwork in Los Angeles during the early 1990s, we identified some twenty-seven Israeli organizations—ranging from synagogues, Hebrew schools, and political groups, to scouting programs, sports teams, business associations, and even a recreational flying club.[63] This number of organizations exceeds that created by other middle-class immigrant groups in Los Angeles, including Iranians and Soviet Jews. Prior to the late 1980s, American Jewish organizations delivered few, if any, resources to Israeli emigrants. More recently, these organizations have come to see Israelis as providing a vital, new, Jewish-identified population to an otherwise shrinking and aging community. The Israeli presence is especially appreciated in older urban neighborhoods, where large numbers of local Jews have recently left for more family-friendly suburban locations or retirement communities. Accordingly, American Jewish organizations now supply Israeli newcomers with various services. Jewish population studies in New York (1991, 2002, 2011), Los Angeles (1997), and elsewhere enumerate Israelis, and note their presence as one of the few positive tendencies in a general trend of shrinking Jewish demographics.[64]

The Israeli community in the United States reflects much of the social diversity that exists in the country of origin. As such, the population reveals numerous subgroups defined in terms of age, social class, religious outlook, occupation, ethnicity, educational level, ideology, lifestyle, time in the United States, and other factors. While members of these diverse subgroups occasionally interact, they are much more likely to spend time among those with whom they share similar backgrounds, outlooks, and resources.[65]

TRANSNATIONALISM

Russian-speaking Jews are aware of Russian Jewish communities around the world, including in Russia, Ukraine, Israel, the United States, Germany, and Canada, and there are transitional ties among these communities. Some fraction of the population makes regular trips to these locations for business and political activities, as well as for leisure. Nevertheless, if one accepts Alejandro Portes and his colleagues' rigorous definition of transnationalism as "Occupations and activities that require regular and sustained social contacts over time across borders for their implementation,"[66] relatively few Russian-speaking Jews maintain a genuinely transnational lifestyle, especially when compared to the Israeli American population.[67]

By contrast, Israelis are more likely to engage in transnational lifestyles associated with frequent international travel. They often have access to networks in both the United States and Israel that can provide a broad variety of resources ranging from pre-travel information to job opportunities, childcare, housing, and a social life. While some Israelis in the United States lack legal resident status, as a group they are very likely to become naturalized and are among a select few nationalities allowed to have dual citizenship. Despite national, ideological, and religious differences between Israeli and American Jews, Israelis do feel connected to other Jews and see themselves as members of the same ethnic and religious group. It would appear that the whole notion of being an Israeli versus an American is not nearly as clear-cut a distinction as the literature on international migration often suggests. Instead, such factors as flexible notions of ethnic and national identity, access to and participation in social and occupational networks, and the ability to sustain cultural competence and legal status in more than one society allow Israelis to maintain meaningful forms of simultaneous involvement in multiple national settings.

The physical and cultural arrival of these two groups of immigrants to the United States represents a significant moment in American Jewish life. Notable for their high levels of skill and education, "Russians" and Israelis are supplementing an aging American Jewish population and transforming its demographic, ideological, economic, and religious characteristics, while altering relations between Israeli and diaspora Jewish communities. While the settlement of these migrants may reflect a move away from emphasizing Israel as the sole point of settlement for Jewish migrants, the extensive interconnections among various Jewish populations that their migration produces both expands and reinforces the web of links between Jewish people and communities in multiple national settings.

Reflecting a general geographic trend among American Jews, recently naturalized Russians and Israelis appear to favor Western/Sunbelt locations over the Northeast. According to Department of Homeland Security data, for persons age eighteen and up born in Israel who became naturalized in the United States, the numbers settling in California have exceeded those settling in New York—long the home of the largest Israeli population in the United States—in every year from 2003 to 2010. Furthermore, even though New York has by far the largest Russian-speaking Jewish population in the United States, in the years 2007–2010, individuals age eighteen and older who were born in Russia and became naturalized in the United States, the numbers settling in California also exceeded those choosing New York.[68]

CONCLUSION

Israeli Americans appear to be both more diverse and more involved with their country of origin and the host society than Russian-speaking Jews in the United States. They are also younger; have higher rates of management, professional, and related occupational employment; and have a more even sex ratio than Russian speakers. Moreover, while Israel obviously maintains a vibrant Jewish community, the FSU has lost much of its Jewish population. Accordingly, we might expect that Israeli emigrants in the United States will continue to be involved with their country of origin, while Russian speakers will become more focused on their host societies—including the United States, Canada, Germany, and Israel. These two populations, which were treated with more than a little condescension by their host societies during the 1970s, have now become vital parts of American and world Jewry. Their accomplishments, high levels of success, and contributions to their host communities are impressive, especially when we note that large fractions of both groups have been in the United States for only two decades. Credit for their achievements goes to the migrant populations themselves, as well as to the openness, flexibility, and tolerance of American society, generally, and to its Jewish community, in particular.

NOTES

1. Office of Refugee Resettlement [ORR], "Report to Congress Administration for Children and Families" (Washington, DC: U.S. Department of Health and Human Services, 2007), 17.
2. Yinon Cohen, "Migration Patterns to and from Israel," *Contemporary Jewry* 29 (2009): 115–125.
3. Steven J. Gold, *Refugee Communities: A Comparative Field Study* (Newbury Park, CA: Sage, 1992); Steven J. Gold and Bruce A. Phillips, "Israelis in the United States," *American Jewish Yearbook* 96 (1996): 51–101; Steven J Gold, "Israeli and Russian Jews: Gendered Perspectives on Settlement and Return Migration," in *Gender and U.S. Immigration: Contemporary Trends*, ed. Pierrette Hondagneu-Sotelo (Berkeley: University of California Press 2003), 127–147; Uzi Rebhun and Lilach Lev Ari, *American Israelis: Migration, Transnationalism, and Diasporic Identity* (Leiden and Boston: Brill, 2010).
4. Steven M. Cohen, "Israeli Émigrés and the New York Federation: A Case Study in Ambivalent Policymaking for 'Jewish Communal Deviants,'" *Contemporary Jewry* 7 (1986): 159.
5. Sherry Rosen, "The Israeli Corner of the American Jewish Community," Issue Series 3 (New York: Institute on American Jewish-Israeli Relations and the American Jewish Committee, 1993).
6. Shoal Kimhi, "Perceived Change of Self-Concept, Values, Well-Being, and Intention to Return among Kibbutz People Who Migrated from Israel to America" (Ph.D. diss., Pacific Graduate School of Psychology, 1990).
7. Rosen, "The Israeli Corner," 3.
8. Drora Kass and Seymour Martin Lipset, "Jewish Immigration to the United States from 1967 to the Present: Israelis and Others," in *Understanding American Jewry*, ed. Marshall Sklare (New Brunswick, NJ: Transaction Books, 1982), 289.
9. J. J. Goldberg, *Jewish Power: Inside the American Jewish Establishment* (Reading, MA: Addison-Wesley, 1996), 180.
10. For details, see Zvi Gitelman, *Jewish Identities in Postcommunist Russia and Ukraine: An Uncertain Ethnicity* (New York: Cambridge University Press, 2012), 245–247.
11. Steven J. Gold, *From The Workers' State to The Golden State: Jews from the Former Soviet Union in California* (Boston: Allyn and Bacon 1995); Annalise Orleck, *The Soviet Jewish Americans* (Westport, CT: Greenwood Publishing Group, 1999).
12. Sanford J. Ungar, "Freedom's Door Shut in Face of Soviet Jews," *Los Angeles Times*, November 12, 1989, M2, M8; Elaine Woo, "Anticipated Reunion Turns Into a Nightmare for Soviet Émigré," *Los Angeles Times*, November 24, 1989, B12; "Visa Applicants Deluge Embassy in Moscow," *New York Times*, October 3, 1989, 4; Madeleine Tress, "United States Policy toward Soviet Emigration," *Migration* 3/4.11/12 (1996): 93–106.
13. Steven J. Gold, "Israeli Immigrants in the U.S.: The Question of Community," *Qualitative Sociology* 17.4 (1994): 325–363.
14. Steven J. Gold, "After the Cold War: Comparing Soviet Jewish and Vietnamese Youth in the 1980s to Today's Young Refugees," in *How to Help Young Immigrants Succeed*, ed. Gerald Holton and Gerhard Sonnert (New York: Palgrave Macmillan, 2010), 75–88.

15. United States Department of Homeland Security, *Yearbook of Immigration Statistics 2010* (Washington, DC: Department of Homeland Security, Office of Immigration Statistics, 2011).
16. Fran Markowitz, *A Community in Spite of Itself: Soviet Jewish Émigrés in New York* (Washington, DC: Smithsonian, 1993); Steven J. Gold, "Gender and Social Capital among Israeli Immigrants in Los Angeles," *Diaspora* 4 (1995): 267–301.
17. Cohen, "Migration Patterns," 115–125.
18. Rebhun and Lev Ari, *American Israelis*, 15.
19. United States Department of Homeland Security, *Yearbook of Immigration Statistics 2010*.
20. Ibid.
21. Vladimir Shlapentokh, *Love, Marriage, and Friendship in the Soviet Union: Ideals and Practices* (New York: Praeger, 1984).
22. Philip Kasinitz, John H. Mollenkopf, Mary C. Waters, and Jennifer Holdaway, *Inheriting the City* (New York: Russell Sage Foundation, 2009).
23. Gold, *From the Workers' State*, 32.
24. United States Bureau of the Census, "Census of Population, 5% Public Use Microsample" (2000).
25. New York City Public Schools, "Test Scores of Recent Immigrants and Other Students, Grades 3–12" (1991).
26. Kasinitz, Mollenkopf, Waters, and Holdaway, *Inheriting the City*.
27. Aviva Zeltzer-Zubida and Philip Kasinitz, "The Next Generation: Russian Jewish Young Adults," *Contemporary Jewry* 25 (2005): 193–225.
28. Gold, "Gender and Social Capital"; Mira Rosenthal and Charles Auerbach, "Cultural and Social Assimilation of Israeli Immigrants in the United States," *International Migration Review* 99.26 (1992): 982–991; Lilach Lev-Ari, *The American Dream—For Men Only? Gender Immigration and the Assimilation of Israelis in the United States* (El Paso, TX: LFB Scholarly Publishers, 2008).
29. Shoal Kimhi, "Perceived Change," 95.
30. Gold, "Israeli and Russian Jews," 137.
31. United States Department of Homeland Security, *Yearbook of Immigration Statistics 2010*.
32. United States Bureau of the Census, "Census of Population."
33. United States Department of Homeland Security, *Yearbook of Immigration Statistics 2010*.
34. United States Bureau of the Census, "Census of Population."
35. United States Department of Homeland Security, *Yearbook of Immigration Statistics 2010*.
36. Steven J. Gold, *Israeli Diaspora* (London: Routledge, 2002).
37. United States Bureau of the Census, "Census of Population."
38. Gold, "Gender and Social Capital," 267–301.
39. United States Department of Homeland Security, *Yearbook of Immigration Statistics 2010*.
40. Timothy J. Eckles, Lawrence J. Lewin, David S. North, and Dangole J. Spakevicius, "A Portrait in Diversity: Voluntary Agencies and The Office of Refugee Resettlement Matching Grant Program" (Washington, DC: Lewin and Associates, 1982); Gold, "After the Cold War," 75–88.
41. Paul Ritterband, "Jewish Identity among Russian Immigrants in the U.S.," in *Russian Jews on Three Continents: Migration and Resettlement*, ed. Noah Lewin-Epstein, Yaacov Ro'i, and Paul Ritterband (London: Frank Cass, 1997), 333.
42. Dina Siegel, *The Great Immigration: Russian Jews in Israel* (New York: Berghahn Books, 1998); Larissa Remennick, *Russian Jews on Three Continents* (New Brunswick, NJ: Transaction, 2007).
43. Fran Markowitz, "Jewish in the USSR, Russian in the USA," in *Persistence and Flexibility: Anthropological Perspectives on the American Jewish Experience*, ed. Walter P. Zenner (Albany: SUNY Press, 1988), 84.
44. Alvin I. Schiff, "Language, Culture, and the Jewish Acculturation of Soviet Jewish Émigrés," *Journal of Jewish Communal Service* 57.1 (1980): 44–49.

45. Joel M. Carp, "Absorbing Jews Jewishly: Professional Responsibility for Jewishly Absorbing New Immigrants in their New Communities," *Journal of Jewish Communal Service* 66.4 (1990): 366–374.
46. Jennifer Barber, "The Soviet Jews of Washington Heights," *New York Affairs* 10.1 (1987): 41.
47. Steven M. Cohen and Judith Veinstein, "Israeli Jews in Greater New York: Their Numbers, Characteristics and Patterns of Jewish Engagement" (New York: UJA Federation of New York Report, March, 2009).
48. Gold, *Israeli Diaspora*.
49. Moshe Shokeid, *Children of Circumstances: Israeli Immigrants in New York* (Ithaca, NY: Cornell University Press, 1988).
50. Pini Herman, *Los Angeles Jewish Population Survey '97*, Jewish Federation of Los Angeles (1998); Cohen and Veinstein, "Israeli Jews"; Uzi Rebhun, "The Israeli Jewish Diaspora in the United States: Socio-Cultural Mobility and Attachment in the Homeland" (Division of Jewish Demography and Statistics, The Avraham Harman Institute of Contemporary Jewry, The Hebrew University of Jerusalem, 2009), later published as "Israeli Jewish Diaspora in the United States: Socio-cultural Mobility and Attachment to Homeland," in *Transnationalism: Diasporas and the Advent of a New (dis)Order*, ed. Eliezer ben-Rafael and Yitshak Sternberg (Boston, Brill, 2009).
51. Gold and Phillips, "Israelis in the United States," 51–101; Pini Herman, *Los Angeles Jewish Population Survey '97*, Jewish Federation of Los Angeles, 1998; Cohen and Veinstein, "Israeli Jews"; Rebhun, "The Israeli Jewish Diaspora."
52. Gold, *From The Workers' State*.
53. Gold, *Israeli Diaspora*.
54. UJA Federation of New York, "New York Jewish Community Study 2002" (New York: UJA Federation of New York, October 2004).
55. Zeltzer-Zubida and Kasinitz, "The Next Generation," 193–225.
56. Rebhun and Lev Ari, *American Israelis*, 148.
57. Samuel Kliger, "Russian-Jewish Opinion Survey 2004" (New York: Research Institute for New Americans RINA, 2004), hhp://russianprogram@ajc.org.
58. Gold, *Refugee Communities*, 222–223.
59. Calvin Goldscheider and Alan S. Zuckerman, *The Transformation of the Jews* (Chicago: University of Chicago Press, 1984).
60. Ritterband, "Jewish Identity among Russian Immigrants in the U.S.," 333.
61. Orleck, *The Soviet Jewish Americans*.
62. Steven J. Gold, "The Place of Israel in the Identity of Israelis in the Diaspora: An Ethnographic Exploration," in *Israel, the Diaspora and Jewish Identity*, ed. Danny Ben-Moshe and Zohar Segev (Brighton, UK: Sussex Academic Press, 2007), 187.
63. Gold, "Israeli Immigrants in the U.S.," 325–363.
64. Steven M. Cohen, Jacob B. Ukeles, and Ron Miller, *Jewish Community Study of New York: 2011* (New York: UJA Federation of New York, 2012).
65. Gold, *Israeli Diaspora*.
66. Alejandro Portes, Luis E. Guarnizo, and Patricia Landolt, "The Study of Transnationalism: Pitfalls and Promise of an Emergent Research Field," *Ethnic and Racial Studies* 22.2 (1999): 319.
67. Mark Tolts, "The Demography of the Russian-Speaking Jewish Diaspora" (paper presented at Conference on the Contemporary Russian-Speaking Jewish Diaspora, Harvard University, November 14, 2011).
68. United States Department of Homeland Security, *Yearbook of Immigration Statistics 2010*.

PART III POLITICAL AND
ECONOMIC CHANGE

In this section, we ask whether and to what extent migration affects people's attitudes and their political and economic behavior. Many assume that socialization to cultural norms and social and political behavior occurs mainly in childhood, and that our thinking and behavioral patterns are pretty much set for life after that. However, there is considerable evidence for political resocialization in adulthood. Immigrants, especially, may undergo such resocialization as they move from one political system to another. On the other hand, the Soviet system seemed to have socialized its citizens intensely and effectively so that values and behaviors adopted in the USSR and its successor states will survive migration. Some believe the system produced *Homo Sovieticus*, a species distinguished from other humans by its way of thinking and acting, especially in politics. It did so by barring contact with noncommunist systems, controlling all the mass media, using schools, the military, and social organizations as agents of socialization, in a word, controlling thought and behavior to a much greater extent than most regimes.

In chapter 7, Olena Bagno-Moldavski asks whether *Homo Sovieticus* was as distinctive and unchangeable as generally assumed. Do Russian-speaking Jewish immigrants to Israel and Germany, carrying their political baggage, retain their outlooks and behaviors, or do their new political environments affect how they think and act? Bagno-Moldavski addresses this important issue with a methodologically sophisticated analysis of surveys in Israel and Germany, comparing them with Jews in Ukraine. She finds that a change in political and social environment does make a substantial difference in political attitudes and participation. Russian-speaking Jewish immigrants in Israel, "which readily absorbs repatriates by providing immediate access to citizenship, motivates political engagement and has a stronger impact on trust, efficacy, and protest than German politics' effect on immigrants' orientations." Bagno-Moldavski's conclusion, which has implications far beyond the case of RSJs on the move, is that "experiences rooted in respondents' present environments are more influential for their orientations than norms learned in their past."

Yaacov Ro'i asks the same question as Bagno-Moldavski—to what extent do migrants change—but more in the realm of culture than in politics. Also using survey and other data, Ro'i explores whether the "thin" Jewish culture developed in the FSU was retained after immigration to Israel. Were immigrants willing and able to exchange their thin culture for a "thicker" one, or had it become so intrinsic that "any intrusion upon their habits aroused antagonism?"

Ro'i traces the evolution of the Russian speakers' "thin culture" after their arrival in Israel. They learn Hebrew rapidly, while not abandoning their native Russian. Despite having grown up in a militantly atheist environment, many become more curious and positive about Jewish religious traditions. One of the attractions of becoming Israeli is that the immigrants became part of a national majority, one that has its own territory, neither of which applied to them in the FSU. At the same time, they take pride in their original culture and believe that they have brought its best attributes to Israel. How long a distinctive Russian-Israeli culture and identity will be sustained by such convictions remains to be seen.

In the United States there has been a national debate on whether immigrants are a burden or a boon for the economy. In Israel, it is crystal clear that the Russian-speaking immigrants have contributed enormously to the economy. Since nearly half of them arrived in Israel with some form of higher education, they were well positioned to integrate themselves into the developing hi-tech sector. As people who had worked in urban industries, they fit in nicely with the Israeli economy that had moved away from agriculture toward light industry and knowledge-based industries.

Gur Ofer's chapter measures the economic situation of earlier and later waves of Russian-speaking immigrants. Ofer finds that time in Israel is the single most powerful explanatory variable in measuring immigrants' economic trajectory. Comparing the two immigrant waves to the Jewish population of Israel and to the part of the population which originates in Europe and the Americas, Ofer observes that the earning gaps between immigrants and the local population are not very large and are closed over time. As has been widely reported, immigrants experience downward mobility in the prestige of their occupations since their training and skills acquired in the Soviet Union do not always mesh easily with the demands of the Israeli (or European/American) labor markets.

A fascinating comparison of immigrants' consumption patterns with those of veteran Israelis shows that while during the first few years in Israel immigrants' spending on food, entertainment, and transportation differs quite markedly from that of the settled population, in a relatively short period of time this difference disappears. Ofer concludes that because of their cultural and economic ties to the FSU, Russian-speaking immigrants have come to be a diaspora of the "Russian" homeland, thus reversing the traditional Jewish conception of Jews living outside Israel being "the diaspora."

7 · POLITICAL NEWBORNS

Immigrants in Israel and Germany

OLENA BAGNO-MOLDAVSKI

A tolerant attitude to corruption, a passive citizenry, and a lack of trust are among the many flaws ascribed to the former USSR—the historic cradle of Russian-speaking Jewry. The political norms of the populace are often seen as one of the obstacles to reform in the former communist bloc, raising questions about the implications of living under communism for democratic attitudes. Does living in the former USSR, indeed, have a lingering impact on political attitudes? Do these attitudes persist when former Soviet citizens move to established democracies?

Depending on the underlying dynamics of the process, immigrants' conceptual understandings of trust, protest, efficacy, and other basic political terms such as political culture, democracy, electorate, elections, and participation, may differ from those of their host cultures. These questions demand a careful analysis of political socialization. Views of political socialization began to shift in the 1990s from static to more flexible, experiential models, although this shift was not followed by changes in dependent categories such as political attitudes toward culture or democracy. Two hypothetical scenarios clarify the difference between the static, cultural approach to socialization as opposed to an experiential approach.

Scenario A

If political socialization early in life determines attitudes and behaviors, then we would expect individuals to express stable behavioral patterns and attitudes over their lifetimes. For example, according to this model, if the "average citizen" of a liberal democracy moved to Russia as an adult, we would expect him or her to support Russia's marginal, democratic parties, volunteer in Russian civil society, and trust his or her fellow Russian citizens, regardless of his or her actual integrative experiences in the local environment. Similarly, individuals socialized in the

Soviet polity should "remain Soviet" in their attitudes and behaviors, even decades after moving to a democratic country. This expectation presumes that socialization is a finite process in which surroundings mold orientations at early stages of an individual's development but have a negligible impact during adulthood. This view suggests that fundamental political change is impossible within a single generation because citizens would instinctively reject new ideas and practices. It also implies that, in former Soviet countries, democracy may be impossible without generational change because the current majority was socialized by the Soviet system and continues to define the political landscape. Empirical evidence from former communist republics often supports this view.[1]

Scenario B

If we assume that political socialization is a *lifelong* process, we can argue that elements of political culture respond to external events. Researchers could assume that political changes can have a decisive impact on the attitudes of adults. This means that demographic replacement of older age cohorts is not a necessary precondition for democratization. Moreover, this could mean that the return to nondemocratic practices in the post-Soviet context is not due to individuals' inflexibility. In contrast, the suppression of democratic behaviors is a result of relapsing institutional practices, which motivate abstention from politics and create a deficit of democratic attitudes.[2]

This chapter estimates these alternative scenarios based on data gathered from Russian-speaking Jews who were socialized in former communist countries and subsequently moved *en masse* to Germany and Israel. We utilize contemporary Ukraine as a contrast to Israel and Germany because, at their time of emigration to those countries, Soviet Jews resembled Jews in Ukraine. At the time of emigration, these populations shared a country of origin (the USSR); Soviet socialization, history, and education; demographic profiles; family structures; and often, familial connections.

Ukraine has become a major source of emigration to Germany (half of all immigrants) and Israel (39%) since 1989, when an estimated 400,000 Ukrainian Jews, not including their non-Jewish family members, left for the West. Neither Germany nor Israel imposed entrance restrictions on Russian-speaking Jews until 2006, when German policy changed. These countries' "open-door" policy is important because it counters the possible effect of self-selection bias, when political systems "select" immigrants through entrance restrictions. This choice of population and countries neutralizes explanations that result from the initial distinctiveness of the immigrant groups and from the selection bias in immigrants' choice of destinations.

I begin with a theoretical background, then survey Jewish immigration from the FSU to Israel and Germany, and discuss differences in the political contexts of these countries. The next section presents hypotheses, data, and the variables. The presentation of results is followed by concluding remarks.

THEORETICAL BACKGROUND

Socialization

Socialization is the process of internalizing salient political orientations, values, and conduct.[3] The scholarly literature structures socialization processes around four archetypical models that offer divergent views regarding the importance of life stages for political learning.[4] The "persistence" model suggests that pre-adult learning persists throughout life and hardens with time. The "impressionable years" model is a variant of the persistence model; it suggests that people's attitudes are most susceptible to influence when young adults become aware of the world around them. Following this critical period of openness and internalization, political predispositions (such as perceived efficacy, trust, and tolerance) stabilize and become stronger with age.[5] This reduced openness means that the most volatile and influential moment for socialization is people's twenties. By contrast, the "life cycle" model suggests that people form specific types of attitudes at certain periods in their lives. For example, radical views are more prevalent among the young, whereas later in life, people become more conservative. The final model posits "lifelong openness," that is, that individuals remain equally open to changes in attitude at all stages of life[6] and that change is facilitated by institutional settings,[7] which produce different socialization outcomes.

The persistence, impressionable years, and life cycle approaches differ in their argumentation, but they all assume that attitudinal changes take place by replacing older cohorts with younger ones. In contrast, the lifelong openness approach places less emphasis on age cohort and views individuals as being continuously receptive to changes. Specifically, this model suggests that the components of immigrants' political culture are indeed sensitive to the effect of the host environment.

Trust, Efficacy, and Protest

Trust, efficacy, and protest are three distinct elements of political culture, which includes a wide repertoire of attitudes and behaviors related to all spheres of political life. The choice of these elements is by no means arbitrary. Efficacy and protest are components of political culture that signify the presence or absence of an active citizenry. Trust is a liberal component of political culture, intimately related to liberal norms such as tolerance and support for democratic freedoms. Trust in fellow citizens is an attitude that facilitates democracy, contributing to social integration, stability, and development.[8] The norms that substantively produce trust include virtues such as truth-telling, meeting obligations, and reciprocity. Efficacy is a concept that captures individuals' perceived ability to participate in and influence the political processes.[9] It thrives under direct democracy[10] and measures individuals' self-assessment of their skill in political activism. Protest, also termed latent or unconventional political activism, is a multifaceted action intended to challenge elites through public and private expressions of discontent.

It conveys individuals' demands to institutions and exerts influence outside of the electoral process.

Trust, efficacy, and protest are learned in the process of socialization. If the open model of political socialization captures reality better than static models, these elements of immigrants' political culture ought to reflect the influence of their hosts' political cultures.

FSU JEWS IN ISRAEL, GERMANY, AND UKRAINE

Israel and Germany are the nation-states of their Jewish and German citizens, respectively. FSU immigrants in Israel join the dominant national group, while, in Germany, they comprise a very small ethnic minority. In Ukraine, Jews have full citizenship rights and participate in political life on an equal footing with others. Table 7.1 summarizes the political environments in all three countries. The variation in FSU Jews' political environments in Germany and Israel is partially explained by the ethnic concept of citizenship that ascribes a different weight to the political engagement of these immigrants by the two nation-states.

Until very recently, Germany had a *jus sanguinis* basis for citizenship (i.e., citizenship conferred by descent or "blood" rather than by place of birth). Policies based on this model of citizenship push for assimilation to the norms of the national ethno-cultural realm. More than 200,000 Russian speakers with Jewish backgrounds reside in Germany. They were allowed into the country after its unification on October 3, 1990. While they were granted refugee status in accordance with the Geneva Convention definition, they were granted residence permits issued for an indefinite period rather than permanent residency or full citizenship. Germany offers a broad net of welfare support (language courses, unemployment benefits, health coverage, pensions, and subsidized rent), but the electoral rights of the Russian speakers remain restricted until they acquire citizenship.

Israel hosts almost one million former Soviet citizens, most of whom arrived during the early 1990s. Russian speakers now constitute roughly 16 percent of the country's electorate; the largest proportion of them originated from Ukraine. Heterogeneous state-sponsored ethnic immigration produces a societal mixture that is hard to monitor without the common ethno-ideological denominator. In this situation, membership in a nebulous Jewish collective solidifies the borders of a nation, even if the Law of Return admits Russian speakers who are not *halakhically* Jewish.

The last census conducted in the Ukrainian Soviet Socialist Republic in 1989 showed that Ukraine was home to almost half a million self-identified Jews (486,384). By 2001, the Jewish population of Ukraine had shrunk considerably, with slightly more than 100,000 people remaining. An estimated 400,000 Ukrainian Jews had emigrated, mainly to Israel and Germany. Jews in Ukraine, like all Ukrainian residents, acquired citizenship following the proclamation of

TABLE 7.1. Legal and Socio-Political Background in Germany, Israel, and Ukraine

	Germany	Israel	Ukraine
Legal status of FSU Jews	No citizenship (after 6 to 8 years)	Automatic citizenship (*jus sanguinis*)	Automatic citizenship (*jus soli*)
Size of the group	Small (0.2% of population)	Large (16%)*	Small (0.2%)
Declared perception of Jewish migrants' by the host state	Inclusion, massive state support	Inclusion, state support	Not applicable
Political participation as a group	Minimal	Maximal	Minimal
Acceptance of the minority status by the group	Maximal	Minimal	Maximal
Issues for political participation	Not related to Germany, rather to Israel/Jews	Related to Israel	Related to Ukraine and to Israel/Jews
Electoral system	Mixed. 328 electoral districts, proportional representation and single member constituencies (PR and SMC). Threshold 5%	One electoral district (PR). Threshold 2%	Mixed.† 225 electoral districts (PR) and (SMC). Threshold 3%
Type of government	Federal Republic	Parliamentary Democracy	Transitional: Presidential / Parliamentary Republic
Size of parliament	598 + surplus	120	450

*The proportion of all Russian-speaking immigrants in Israeli population.
†The electoral laws of Ukraine were changed several times. The "mixed" system was implemented in 2006 while the survey was conducted in 2005.

independence in 1991 based on their Soviet passports, and thereafter, the children of Ukrainian Jews were entitled to citizenship based on the *jus soli* (birth confers citizenship) principle.

The potential for FSU immigrants to exert political influence in Germany and Ukraine is very different from that in Israel. In Germany and Ukraine, they constitute a small fraction of the society (around 0.2 percent), while in Israel they form an electorate with significant political leverage, reinforced by the rules of the Israeli electoral system, which features a low electoral threshold.

Russian-speaking Jews were socialized initially in the USSR, and if we accept the experientialist approach to socialization, immigrants' political attitudes should reveal a tendency to change in a direction that places their orientations in between those of their country of origin and of their host societies. Thus, if nationals in the host society have high scores for efficacy, trust, or protest, and the control group (Jews of Ukraine) has low scores, then immigrants' scores should be greater than in the home society and lower or equal to the score found in the host society, and vice versa [Hypothesis 1]. Socialization based on experiences implies that social, economic, and political engagement in the host society produces changes in attitudes. Therefore, I expect that the relative contribution of personal characteristics detached from the influence of their host society to the explained variance of trust, protest, and efficacy should be lower than the contribution of social, economic, and political characteristics belonging to the host environment [Hypothesis 2]. Professional and linguistic reeducation, work experience, involvement in civil society and communal and political organizations are all platforms where individuals learn about their new reality, including political attitudes salient in the host country.

The German state facilitates immigrants' incorporation via various state-sponsored humanitarian, social, cultural, and religious organizations that, among other functions, expose newcomers to political attitudes salient in Germany. In Ukraine, Jews interact with nonstate communal agents. They join national parties or run as independent candidates in single-member constituencies. The platforms of Jewish politicians never reflect their ethnic origins and focus, instead, on national and domestic issues (e.g., Efim Zvyagilski in 1990–2002, Viktor Pinchuk in 1998, Alexander Feldman in 2002–2011, Volodymyr Groisman in 2014–2015). In Israel, both political and communal agents, whether supported by the state or by external sources, are engaged with migrants' integration. In that country, national political parties and their municipal proxies are the most relevant forces for integration because, from the day of their arrival, FSU immigrants are allowed to participate actively in politics, forming or joining political parties and movements. Aliyah,[11] Democratic Choice, Yisrael Ba' aliyah, and Yisrael Beiteinu are all parties established and run by Russian-speaking immigrants. These differences in the three settings suggest that the accumulated influence of the political engagement on trust, protest, and efficacy should be stronger in Israel than in Germany [Hypothesis 3].

Data

Primary surveys of democratic values conducted from 2005–2008 in Ukraine, Germany, and Israel by the European Social Survey [2002] provide the necessary data to test our hypotheses.[12] Participants in the primary surveys were adult, first-generation immigrants from the former Soviet Union who moved to either Germany or Israel;[13] in Ukraine, these were Jews and their relatives who were theoretically eligible to emigrate to either Germany or Israel but had chosen to remain in Ukraine. The samples obtained for Israel are probability based, while the Russian-speaking Jews in Germany and Ukraine were surveyed with purposive non-probability samples.

In Germany, Russian-speaking respondents were surveyed in three rounds between November 2005 and October 2006. They were from different localities in the state of Lower Saxony, as well as from Berlin, Potsdam, Hamburg, and Bonn. The data on the socio-demographic characteristics of the general population of FSU immigrants were obtained from interviews with statisticians from the Jewish Benevolent and Education Society (ZWST), which has full statistics on the number of arrivals and their initial place of residence. When compared with data provided by the ZWST, my sample replicates major demographic characteristics of the immigrant Jewish population in Germany. In the sample (N = 200, response rate 57 percent), approximately 30 percent of respondents were not registered with the Jewish community. Thus, the sample also provides some information on unregistered immigrants. Religious community centers register about half of all newcomers, and at the time of the survey, the centers reported 106,000 members, among them 12,000 who had been living in Germany since before 1991. There are no official statistics regarding the remaining 112,000 immigrants who were initially accepted by ZWST.

In Ukraine, the study population was surveyed in October and November 2005. Respondents from Eastern and Central Ukraine were targeted using a snowball method via personal networks, communal organizations, and the media. Of the 400 distributed questionnaires, 238 responses were received (response rate of 60 percent).

The data for Israel were collected in January 2006. The random probability sample was initially pooled from the general registry of all adults from the USSR or former Soviet republics who lived in Israel in 2008 and had immigrated to the country after 1989 (N = 860,756). Six hundred potential respondents were targeted. The response rate was relatively high (55 percent, N = 328). Before being designated as nonresponders, participants were contacted at least twice. Interviews were conducted both during the day and at night. Respondents were targeted via their mobile phones in addition to landline phones.

The impact of selection bias, suggesting that certain "types" of people are attracted to different countries, cannot be ruled out completely, but field research conducted in Israel and Germany indicates that the decision to emigrate was often made by one family member, while the rest followed suit. Respondents often conceded that they had applied to both countries (and often also to Australia, Canada, or the United States at the beginning of the 1990s) and had opted for the first available option. Respondents in Ukraine who were in the process of emigration also said they had applied or intended to apply to the embassies of Israel, Germany, and Canada. This seems to suggest that the problem of self-selection in the study is minimal, although it can never be refuted unless a cross-country panel study is designed. Overall though, the use of an immigrant population with identical initial characteristics, the use of a control group, and a cross-country design creates solid conditions under which to test the open model of political socialization.

Variables and Method

Protest: A latent factor modeled with three variables. The respondents were asked if they have "signed petitions," "taken part in lawful public demonstration," or "contacted a politician or government official."[14]

Trust: A latent factor based on two questions: "Would you say that most people can be trusted, or that you cannot be too careful in dealing with people?" and "Do you think that most people would try to take advantage of you if they got the chance, or would they try to be fair?"

Efficacy: A latent factor comprising two items that describe the respondent's assessment of his political effectiveness. Interviewees were asked, "How difficult is it for you to form an opinion on a specific political issue?" and "Can you take part in a group that deals with political issues?"

Independent Variables

Social engagement [SE]: Social engagement, a latent factor, modeled on the basis of three questions: "Do you belong to/attend sports clubs," "... professional associations?" The response alternatives were dichotomous: "0—I do not belong" or "1—I belong to an organization." The third question reads: "All things considered, how adjusted you feel you are to the host society?" (Score 0–4).

Economic engagement [EE]: Individuals' work environments can influence their political attitudes. Some studies show that being employed full-time constitutes a personal constraint that might increase the costs and risks of political claim making; however, others did not find this dependency. In this study, economic engagement is added to the model to test whether this characteristic has any effect on changing political attitudes among immigrants. It is measured with a variable that indicates respondents' employment status (score 0–2).

Political engagement [PE]: This is a set of three measured variables. The survey items read: "Are you a member of a political party?" (PM, score 0–1), "Do you work/volunteer for a political party?" (PW, score 0–1), and "How often do you follow politics in the news on TV, the radio, or in the daily paper?" (PI, score 0–4).

Individual characteristics: Age (18–95) and level of education (score 0–7) are measured exogenous variables not influenced by the host environment.

Method

The causal effects of economic, political, and social engagement on protest, trust, and efficacy are estimated using structural equation modeling (SEM). This analytical tool permits variable relationships to present a more complete picture of the entire model.[15] It combines both measurement and path relationships between variables in a single model and enables the analysis of indirect relationships between variables.[16]

Results

Overall, trust, efficacy (i.e., feeling that a person can understand politics), and protest scores reported by immigrants follow the predicted logic [Hypothesis 1]. Trust among immigrants in Germany develops in the expected direction:[17] immigrants in Germany are more trustful than Jews in Ukraine and less trustful than German natives (see figure 7.1).[18] In Israel, Russian speakers express lower levels of trust compared to all other groups, including Israeli natives. Trust in Israel is also negatively related to political engagement and age.[19] Hence, encounters with the Israeli political system negatively affect trust, while employment and education have indirect positive and total positive effects on it, respectively. In Germany, political interest reduces trust, while social engagement and education increase it. The indirect effect of age on trust is negative while its total effect loses significance. From the fieldwork conducted in Israel, it follows that the low trust among immigrants can also be explained by negative experiences related to immigration. Newcomers often stated that they were especially hurt when their "fellow Jews in the Jewish country" took advantage of their lack of understanding of the surrounding reality.[20]

Ukrainian Jews have the lowest level of efficacy compared to German and Israeli nationals and FSU immigrants. The nature of political life in Ukraine, particularly its high levels of corruption,[21] as well as lingering tensions between the president and the parliament made it more difficult for citizens to feel that they can influence political processes. In Israel, political interest and membership in political parties help immigrants maintain a sense of efficacy. Higher education also has an indirect positive effect. On the other hand, in Germany, where political life is much less volatile and FSU immigrants are not entitled to citizenship, the sense of efficacy is lower. Younger age, higher education, social engagement, and party membership all have a positive effect on efficacy.

Immigrants in Germany protest more than the majority. This finding is in line with the political process model, which envisages higher levels of activism among minority groups.[22] In Israel, however, Russian speakers and the majority protest to the same extent. Despite their immigrant status and distinct characteristics that assign them to a minority, FSU immigrants in Israel are a part of the national majority of Israeli Jews, in contrast to the situation in Germany and Ukraine where Jews are ethno-religious minorities.

To estimate the importance of integration experiences over individual traits, I constrained the respective sets of variables and calculated a chi-square test statistic for moment structure analysis. The results of the χ^2 test, significant when experience-related traits are constrained, suggest that both in Israel and in Germany, socioeconomic and political engagement in the host societies are more important for explaining levels of trust, efficacy, and protest than individual

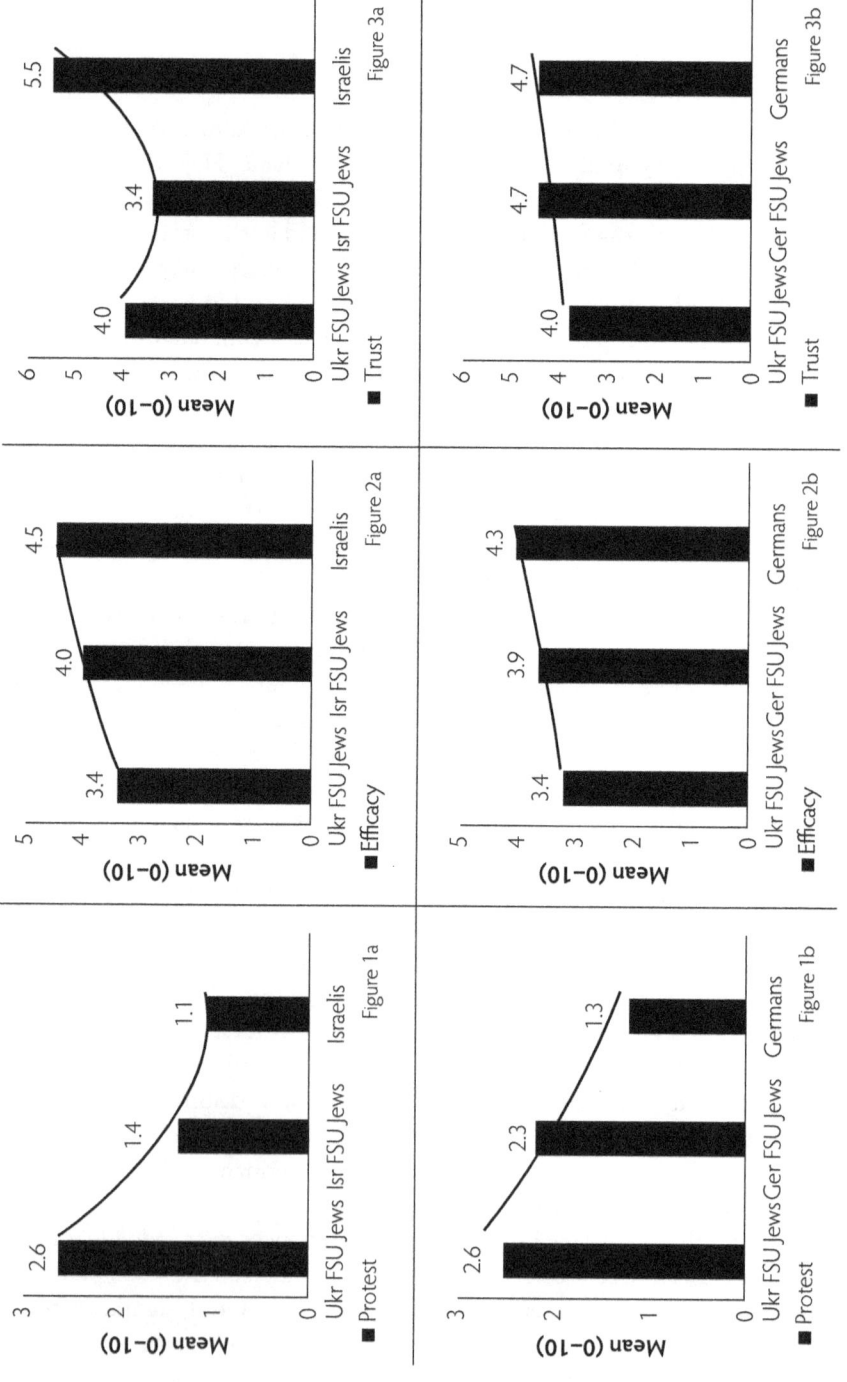

FIGURE 7.1. Trust, Efficacy, and Protest in Germany, Israel, and Ukraine

traits.[23] In all instances, integrative characteristics are more important for predicting political attitudes of the Russian speakers when compared with characteristics not influenced by the host environment.

Furthermore, the relative contribution of political engagement to the explained variance of trust, efficacy, and protest is larger for FSU Jews in Israel compared to their counterparts in Germany. For FSU Jews in Germany, political engagement explains about half the variance in protest, while for Russian speakers in Israel, it explains four-fifths of such variance. Political engagement explains about one-tenth of the variance for both efficacy and trust in Germany, while in Israel, it accounts for one-third of the variance for trust, and one-fifth for efficacy.[24] Overall, the data support the idea that socialization is a dynamic process that continuously affects Russian-speaking Jews and their dependents in Israel and Germany.

CONCLUSIONS

This chapter reveals the importance of ongoing socialization for understanding complex political phenomena. It does not support the thesis that socialization in Soviet political culture has lingering implications for the political integration of first-generation immigrants, suggesting that integration-related experiences affect both liberal and participatory political orientations.

The orientations of Russian-speaking Jews in Israel and Germany suggest that the present, rather than the past, shapes adults' political outlook. This follows from the finding that migrants' orientations vary, to a large extent, in accordance with the political norms prevalent in their new homelands, and that their orientations are more dependent on current socio-political surroundings than on personal characteristics not affected by migration. The Israeli political environment, which readily absorbs "repatriates" by providing immediate access to citizenship, motivates political engagement and has a stronger impact on trust, efficacy, and protest than German politics' effect on immigrants' orientations. Germany does not grant citizenship to the Russian-speaking Jews, but it has an elaborate system of special representation for foreigners at the municipal level. Noncitizen representatives of ethnic and religious minorities can influence governance through Foreigners' Advisory Councils, which have limited powers but can advise local politicians before decisions are made that concern noncitizens. Immigrants cannot elect or be elected on the national or European levels, and communal and municipal organizations become proxies for electoral political activities. Jewish communal organizations incorporate *halakhic* Jews, while the rest integrate and achieve political influence through advisory councils or other civil and communal organizations created to preserve the immigrants' Russian cultural background. The effect of multifaceted social integration is reflected in the models that predict efficacy, protest, and trust among Russian-speaking immigrants in Germany. Overall, my analysis suggests that experiences rooted in respondents' present environments are more influential for their orientations than norms learned in their past.

The next step in research may be a test of the open model, applied to non-immigrant cases. When natives have to adjust to a new political environment (e.g., a nondemocratic system), the open model of political socialization is also at work. For example, the relapse to authoritarianism in contemporary Russia and the wide support for nondemocratic norms among the very populace that brought an end to the USSR about two decades ago can serve as the basis for this future research. The challenge of this chapter was to study immigration-related experiences as catalysts of change and to suggest that "immigration" can be substituted for by any major emotionally loaded event that brings a person to adjust to new circumstances (e.g. revolution, war, civic unrest, regime change, etc.). Moving beyond immigrant populations, the open model of political socialization can provide a basis for better understanding the changing nature of political norms and behaviors.

NOTES

1. Ekaterina Bashkirova, "Russia, Belarus, and Ukraine: Construction of Democratic Communities," in *Democracy and Political Culture in Eastern Europe*, ed. H. D. Klingemann, D. Fuchs, and J. Zielonka (London and New York: Routledge, 2006), 123–145. For an opposing view, see William Mishler and Richard Rose, "Generation, Age, and Time: The Dynamics of Learning during Russia's Transformation," *American Journal of Political Science* 51 (2007): 822–834.
2. Vladimir Gelman, "State Power, Governance, and Local Regimes in Russia: A Framework for Analysis," *Russian Politics and Law* 49.4 (2011): 42–52.
3. Gabriel Almond, "Introduction: A Functional Approach to Comparative Politics," in *The Politics of Developing Areas*, ed. Almond and James Coleman (Princeton: Princeton University Press, 1960), 3–64. Gabriel Almond and Sidney Verba, *The Civic Culture: Political Attitudes and Democracy in Five Nations* (Princeton: Princeton University Press, 1965). David Easton, *A Systems Analysis of Political Life* (New York: John Wiley and Son, 1965).
4. David Sears and Sheri Levy, "Childhood and Adult Political Development," in *Oxford Handbook of Political Psychology*, ed. David Sears, Leonie Huddy, and Robert Jervis (Oxford: Oxford University Press, 2003), 60–109.
5. Ronald Inglehart, *Culture Shift in Advanced Industrial Societies* (Princeton: Princeton University Press, 1990).
6. Mary Douglas and Aaron Wildavsky, *Risk and Culture: An Essay on the Selection of Technological and Environmental Dangers* (Berkeley: University of California Press, 1982). Michael Thompson, Richard Ellis, and Aaron Wildavsky, *Cultural Theory* (Boulder, CO: Westview, 1990). Charles Lockhart, "Political Culture and Political Change," in *Culture Matters: Essay in Honour of Aaron Wildavsky*, ed. Michael Thompson and Richard Ellis (Boulder, CO: Westview, 1997), 91–105.
7. Ruud Koopmans and Paul Statham, "How National Citizenship Shapes Transnationalism: A Comparative of Migrant and Minority Claims-Making in Germany, Great Britain, and the Netherlands," in *Toward Assimilation and Citizenship: Immigrants in Liberal Nation-States*, ed. Christian Joppke and Ewa Morawska (London: Palgrave, 2003), 195–238. Marco Giugni and Florence Passy, "Migrant Mobilization between Political Institutions and Citizenship Regimes:

A Comparison of France and Switzerland," *European Journal of Political Research* 43 (2003): 51–82.
8. Susan J. Pharr and Robert D. Putnam, *Disaffected Democracies: What's Troubling Trilateral Countries?* (Princeton: Princeton University Press; 2000). Pippa Norris, ed., *Critical Citizens: Global Support for Democratic Government* (Oxford: Oxford University Press, 1999).
9. Paul R. Abramson, *Political Attitudes in America* (San Francisco: W. H. Freeman, 1983); F.L.F Lee, "Collective Efficacy, Support for Democratization, and Political Participation in Hong Kong," *International Journal of Public Research* 18.3 (2006): 297–317.
10. Shaun Bowler and Todd Donovan, "Democracy, Institutions and Attitudes about Citizen Influence on Government," *British Journal of Political Science* 32 (2002): 371–390.
11. Aliyah was the party created by Misha Nudel'man (professor of economics from Lviv), vice speaker of the Knesset. It has never been popular but he claimed that it was a predecessor of all the "Russian" parties.
12. Norwegian Social Science Data Services, "ESS Round 1: European Social Survey Round 1, 2002 Data," data file ed. 6.2 (Norway, 2002).
13. I assume here that all migrants departing the FSU 1989 or later left voluntarily, in the sense that the individuals were not expelled from their homeland, but rather driven away by a mixture of socioeconomic and security "push" factors.
14. Details available in author's online appendix, tables 4–5, http://www.inss.org.il/index.aspx?id=4300&researcherid=6654.
15. H. E. Bullock, L. L. Harlow, and S. A. Mulaik, "Causation Issues in Structural Equation Modeling Research," *Structured Equation Modeling* 1.3 (1994): 253–267; Eric Hanushek and John Jackson, *Statistical Methods for Social Scientists* (New York: Academic Press, 1977).
16. The full pass model is presented below. Dependent variables are influenced by a full set of integrative and personal characteristics (first equation), when social, political, and economic integrative characteristics are also directly affected by age and education.

$$\text{Trust} \mid \text{Efficacy} \mid \text{Protest} = \Upsilon_0 + \Upsilon_1 SE + \Upsilon_2 EE + \Upsilon_3 PW + \Upsilon_4 PI + \Upsilon_6 Age + \Upsilon_7 Edu + \zeta_1$$
$$SE = \Upsilon_{01} + \Upsilon_{11} EE + \Upsilon_{21} Age + \Upsilon_{31} Edu + \zeta_2$$
$$PI = \Upsilon_{02} + \Upsilon_{12} Age + \Upsilon_{22} Edu + \zeta_3$$
$$EE = \Upsilon_{03} + \Upsilon_{13} Age + \Upsilon_{23} Edu + \zeta_4$$

Models are estimated using a maximum likelihood procedure. To meet the assumption of homoscedasticity, all variables were standardized (z-scores). The relative importance of parameters is assessed by constraining the respective sets of variables, calculating a chi-square test statistic for moment structure analysis and examining unstandardized values of the coefficients across the models.
17. Statistical analysis was performed using two-way analysis of variance, followed by Turkey's HSD test and the Waller–Duncan test. A difference with two-tail 95 percent confidence level was considered significant. Insignificant differences between the following groups were found: trust—groups of FSU Jews in Israel and Ukraine, FSU Jews in Germany, and Germans; protests—FSU Jews in Germany and Ukraine, FSU Jews in Israel, and Israelis; efficacy—the groups of FSU Jews in Israel, Germany, and Ukraine.
18. Germans/Israelis—majority population in Germany/Israel (Source: the ESS 2002); Ger/Isr FSU Jewish-immigrant populations in Germany/Israel; Ukr FSU Jews-Ukrainian Jews/family members.
19. Author's online appendix, table 1, http://www.inss.org.il/index.aspx?id=4300&researcher id=6654.
20. For example, in 2002 in a language school for adults in the suburbs of Tel Aviv, two different families became victims of fraud when Russian-speaking salespersons came to their homes, sold books in Hebrew in one case, and "medical" equipment in the other, received "security

checks," and left the families with two-thirds of their state-granted allowance for the following nine months. The police did not deal with the cases. This happened thirteen years after massive FSU immigration to Israel had begun; in these early years, fraud was frequent and larger in scope.

21. Transparency International reported that Ukraine's score varied around 2.4 out of 10 in 2005. See http://transparency.org/regional_pages/europe_central_asia.

22. Doug McAdam, "The Biographical Impact of Activism," in *How Movements Matter: Theoretical and Comparative Studies on the Consequences of Social Movements*, ed. Marco Giugni, Doug McAdam, and Charles Tilly (Minneapolis: University of Minnesota Press, 1999), 119–146.

23. Author's online appendix, table 2, http://transparency.org/regional_pages/europe _central_asia.

24. Author's online appendix, table 3, http://transparency.org/regional_pages/europe_central _asia.

8 · THE MOVE FROM RUSSIA/THE SOVIET UNION TO ISRAEL

A Transformation of Jewish Culture and Identity?

YAACOV RO'I

It is widely accepted that Soviet citizens who remained in the Former Soviet Union [FSU], with the possible exception of the Baltic States, have retained elements of their Soviet mindset, personality traits, and upbringing. This chapter explores one aspect of that residue among former Soviet Jewish *olim* [immigrants to Israel]. In a previous essay, I suggested, as others have done, that Soviet Jews developed a "thin" Jewish culture in the post-Stalin years,[1] meaning that their Jewish identity and culture became extremely amorphous since they lacked a language of their own, a religious tradition, a distinct habitat, or dress.

The wide variety of norms used to denote collective identity include a primordial attachment, a natural affinity, sensed, in the words of Clifford Geertz, "by virtue of some unaccountable absolute import attributed to the very tie itself."[2] The "givens" that help shape an individual's nonrational notion of who he is and "with whom, indissolubly, he belongs," include, according to Geertz, blood, looks, and way of life.[3] "Thin culture" is the term used to denote a diluted form of culture, compared to the traditional perception of what is now called "thick culture"—a distinct language, religion, dress, or even cuisine. Thin culture comprises "a common and distinct system of understandings and interpretations that constitute a normative order and world view and provide strategic and stylistic guides to action."[4] One scholar has suggested that thin culture should not be perceived as being in contradistinction to thick culture but, instead, as a point somewhere on the continuum between thick culture and no culture at all, attained by the dilution or discarding of such aspects of thick culture that are incompatible with theory or inconsistent with observation.[5] In the same vein, he stresses that thin culture is empirical, individualist, relatively unbounded and diverse, dynamic, and labile.[6]

Although they possessed only a thin Jewish culture, Soviet Jews seemed to be manifestly different from their non-Jewish neighbors. Indeed, this thin culture became an integral part of Soviet Jewish existence. My purpose is to examine how this thin culture was retained when FSU Jews immigrated to Israel. Were the immigrants willing and mentally able to exchange their thin culture for a "thicker" one, or had it become so intrinsic to their mentality that any intrusion upon their habits aroused antagonism? Did the change in their physical surroundings as a result of emigration bring about, or even necessitate, a transformation in their behavior? Can we assume that the differences in the Jewish aspects of the immigrants' behavior, identity, and culture—as compared to other sectors of the Israeli population—relate to their Soviet background, or should they be attributed to their absorption or integration in Israel?

These questions require compound answers. To begin, Soviet Jewish immigration to Israel cannot be seen as an integral whole; instead, we must take into consideration a large conglomerate of approximately one million souls.[7] Therefore, every generalization we make must have its exceptions. In addition, research has shown unequivocally that a person's cultural and collective identities consist of a number of composite parts. Furthermore, Jewish identity both in Israel and in the diaspora has undergone major transformations in the last two centuries. Research also shows that the Soviet Jewish community has manifested both a tendency toward separatism and, simultaneously, toward integration.

THE COMPONENTS OF SOVIET JEWISH THIN CULTURE

Soviet Jewish "thin culture" is related less to content than to mentality. Indeed, Soviet Jews had little to no knowledge of Jewish culture or history, let alone tradition, and most of them had minimal interest in acquiring such knowledge. Nevertheless, they felt themselves to be Jewish.[8] The very fact of being born Jewish made them different in their own eyes and in the eyes of those around them. This was not solely due to a series of subjective experiences; instead, it was a part of their inner psyche. Being Jewish was "a central parameter of their existence."[9] While they were disparaged and excluded as "different" in the Soviet Union, many Jews developed self-esteem that emanated largely from their educational and professional achievements and relatively high social status. They therefore attributed positive attainments to their Jewishness, and, whenever possible, endowed it with propitious content.[10] For instance, they believed that their values, beliefs, and attitudes made them culturally and morally superior to their non-Jewish neighbors.

In Moscow, Leningrad, and other large cities such as Kiev, Kharkiv, Odessa, and other republic capitals with considerable Jewish populations, Jews credited themselves with being the carriers of *kul'turnost'*—the prototype of the late nineteenth-century Russian intelligentsia. The idea of belonging to the intelligentsia, both individually and collectively, was central to Soviet Jewish ethnic identity and the manner in which Soviet Jews socialized their children. This reflected the way they defined their behavior, intellectual experiences, cultural tastes, and preferences. Soviet Jews' attitudes included a sense of being somehow Russian: their language and "thick" culture were Russian, and the landscapes to which they were attached were those of Russia (or Ukraine, etc.). They did, however, have an existential feeling of Jewish solidarity, emanating, at least in part, from sharing a common fate and an evolving common past, in which the Holocaust played a major role. To some, both within the community and beyond, the belief in a distinct Jewish fate seemed nothing less than mystical. Soviet Jews were naturally drawn to, and sensed kinship with, fellow Jews—first and foremost with other Soviet Jews. Their close friends were mostly Jews, and they were attracted to the cultural production of Soviet Jews. They were proud of the achievements of Jews both within and beyond the Soviet Union. In some cases, their conscious realization of belonging to the Jewish collective began when they suddenly realized the excitement they felt when the subject of Jews cropped up in a book or movie.[11] Many had Jewish books in their homes, often a Russian translation of the works of Yiddish writer Sholem Aleichem.

In the Soviet Union, interethnic marriage was quite common. In the 1920s and 1930s this was often ideologically motivated. While this phenomenon was less common after the Second World War, it became increasingly acceptable, especially in metropolitan centers where young Jews mixed freely with the surrounding society and in small towns with few Jews. In mid-sized cities, where the population was divided by ethnic belonging, it was probably less frequent. Yet ethnic boundaries remained—Jewish partners tended to retain Jewish images and folklore, oftentimes transmitting them to their children.[12]

Two basic conclusions emanate from the above: the first is that Soviet Jewish thin culture was very much a product of upbringing and of the environment in which Soviet Jews' personae was created. Second, the thin culture of which we speak relates not so much to the content of Soviet Jews' culture (in the classical sense of the word) as to their attitudes, perception of their identity, and everyday conduct. It was not a remnant of an age-old tradition that the Jews carried with them as they modernized, but, instead, a new, thin culture that they generated themselves.

THE MODIFICATION OF SOVIET JEWISH THIN CULTURE IN THE 1980S

Soviet Jewish thin culture began to undergo a transformation prior to the great exodus of the early 1990s. There were several reasons for this:

A. With the visible rise of nationalism in the early 1980s among Russians and non-Russians, it was no longer sufficient for Jews to belong to Russian culture. They, along with other urban ethnic minorities, found that they had also to somehow affiliate with their ethnic group. Yuri Slezkine speaks of the "unique antagonism" that emerged between Russians and Jews "over two competing and incommensurate nationalisms."[13]

B. The opportunities for emigration created in the 1970s led hundreds of thousands of Jews to apply for invitations [*vyzovy*] from authentic or pseudo-relatives in Israel as a prerequisite of applying for emigration. Many of them did not actually wish to move to Israel but intended to immigrate to the United States or other Western countries. Many others did not wish to emigrate immediately but wanted to have the preliminary document in case their situation began to deteriorate. Both these groups had taken a step that indicated a readiness to act as Jews and give open expression to a collective identity that had hitherto existed solely in their private world. Even those who went to countries other than Israel received assistance from Jewish organizations to resettle abroad. The mere thought of emigration revealed a measure of commitment to their Jewishness even if some did hope to shake off their Jewish identity and its historical consequences after their immigration to an open society—something they had been unable to do in the Soviet Union.

C. The appearance of the Russian chauvinist organization, Pamyat', in 1983 and its invigoration under conditions of *glasnost* in the Gorbachev years meant that anti-Semitism threatened to become more prominent and aggressive as the domestic situation worsened. This frightened some people, especially those with young children, adolescents, or young adults who had not yet embarked on their careers. The option of concealing their Jewishness no longer existed, especially for the "core" Jewish population—those with two Jewish parents. Many Jews had deluded themselves for years into thinking that they could eventually blend unnoticed into the surrounding society, as they became *Homo Sovieticus* in the great melting pot of the "new Soviet people." However, with the growth of Russian nationalism, they realized that this was no longer possible, and in response, Jews began to look for alternatives that would enable them to react effectively to the dangers ahead.

D. Although only a few individuals were sufficiently attracted by Judaism to take up a traditional Jewish way of life, many began studying Jewish topics—history, language, literature—on their own and, more often, in groups. Gorbachev's reforms enabled the establishment of "informal societies," most of which functioned as cultural associations. Indeed, in the last two or three years before the Soviet Union's final collapse, a plethora of opportunities for Jewish study existed, and a growing number of Jews, especially those who were resolved to immigrate to Israel, made use of them.

THE EMIGRATION

Approximately 150,000 Soviet Jews arrived in Israel in the 1970s. Emigration slowed in the early 1980s and began in earnest again in 1988. Between 1989 and 1991, some 400,000 immigrants reached Israel; another 300,000–400,000 did so in the course of the nineties, bringing the total to one million (including some 300,000 non-Jews—children of non-Jewish mothers, partners of Jews, and first-degree relatives of people married to Jews—entitled to immigration under the Law of Return).[14]

Here, I address the cultural changes that occurred among Ashkenazi Jews from areas of the Soviet Union in its pre-1939 borders, who arrived in Israel as adults. Those who came from the "Western territories" annexed to the Soviet Union in 1939–40 (as well as Georgian and Bukharan Jews) generally had "thicker" Jewish cultures. I conducted my study with the help of questionnaires distributed to a small group of *olim* from a variety of Soviet cities and regions.[15] I must stress that my discussion relates to the way the *olim* perceive themselves, not to how they are seen by veteran Israelis, even though their self-perception certainly includes their reflection or understanding of the way Israelis see them.[16]

THE ISRAELI REALITY

In order to comprehend what has happened to the mindset of Soviet Jewish immigrants in Israel, it behooves us to examine the structural characteristics both of the absorbing society and of the immigrant group. In particular, we must examine how much of a role ethnicity plays as a mobilizing force. Indisputably, there is a mutual influence between those who "absorb" and those who become "absorbed."

Since its inception, Israel has been a society of immigrants. It came into being primarily in order to implement the "ingathering of the exiles." Though over the years the proportion of Israelis born abroad has decreased, the older generation of Israelis perceives Israel as a land of immigration. At least in theory, in the early twenty-first century, many Israelis still perceived immigration as essential in fashioning the Israeli nation.

Despite the consensus regarding the centrality of immigration, Israeli values have changed in the last generation or so—following, though not necessarily due to, the Great Exodus of Soviet Jews (1990–1991). Israel is no longer a society based on absolute, consensus values; the nation-state has eroded as has the country's fundamental organizational context. A new dialectic has come into being between modern national identity and the process of globalization. At the same time, Israeli society has become increasingly multicultural. Whereas in the first decades of Israel's existence, it was generally accepted that the ultimate objective was achieving a "melting pot," more recently, the emphasis has been on retaining the heritage, traditions, and distinctive features of each community. This shift makes it more difficult to analyze and pinpoint the transformations that former Soviet citizens have experienced since their immigration.

Similarly, as a result of globalization and technology, immigrants around the world are less enclosed by geographic boundaries and political frameworks. To an extent at least, the barrier between immigrants and veterans has worn down. Ethnic and communal isolation are becoming increasingly impossible.

At the same time, Israel has remained primarily a Jewish state. Its first official language is Hebrew, its calendar centers around Jewish holidays, and its school curricula present Jewish history as its national history. While the greater part of its population is secular, a majority sees the Jewish religion as the national faith and relates positively to Jewish traditions.

THE CULTURAL AND PSYCHOLOGICAL BAGGAGE OF THE SOVIET/FORMER SOVIET JEWISH *OLIM*

It may well be argued that, in the Soviet Union, the Jews' "Russian" culture nevertheless possessed distinct Jewish features. While their language was "high" Russian and the writers among them wrote impeccable prose and poetry, some claimed that there was something manifestly Jewish about their language. Several questionnaire respondents maintained that they invariably found a Jewish component to literary works authored by their fellow Soviet Jews.[17]

Larissa Remennick, an Israeli sociologist who is herself a "repatriate" from the Soviet Union, has discussed the complexity and dynamism of the Russian-speaking *olim*'s collective and individual identity.[18] She maintains that Soviet Jewish identity was characterized by ambivalence as a result of "the constant need for adjustment and social mimicry." According to Remennick, the

> composition of the Israeli Russian-speaking community is a virtual blueprint of the enlarged Jewish population of the FSU.
>
> The identity of this group was shaped along three main axes—Russian, Soviet, and Jewish, with dramatic individual differences in the manifestation of each component of this ideological mix.... If they had any deities at all, these were Pushkin and Chekhov, Pasternak and Bulgakov (as the icons of the Russian high culture), on the one hand, and social mobility (expressed in the cult of education and professionalism), on the other.

Other features included the paramountcy of familial ties and "far-reaching informal social webs ... their main survival and advancement resource in the face of the hostile outside world. Their collective identity was mainly based on the common past, which left a painful historic dent in almost every Jewish family, and on a difficult present ... or, in other words, on the sense of common destiny. They also shared their peculiar mental and social duality as a 'discriminated elite.'" While many of their "Soviet-type qualifications and skills proved to be as unconvertible a currency as were Soviet rubles," they took with them into emigration "their real treasure of social networks with each other (or social capital, in current sociological parlance)."[19]

In the Soviet Union, Jews perceived their Jewishness as ethnicity, just as members of other ethnic groups around them did. By law, every Soviet citizen belonged to an officially recognized nationality.[20] Since, however, none needed to identify with or belong to any religion, a Jew in the Soviet Union could not be ethnically Russian but could be a Christian.[21] Soviet Jews, therefore, were fully cognizant of their Jewish ethnicity although they were cut off from "the locus of their homeland and their culture for generations." The determinist nature of the individual's nationality—his/her parentage—was a non-variable according to Soviet nationalities theory. This meant that sons of Jewish fathers and non-Jewish mothers who frequently had Jewish-sounding surnames and patronymics saw themselves and were identified by others as Jews.

THE "RUSSIAN-SPEAKING" COMMUNITY IN ISRAEL

Inevitably, the "return" to the historical national home implied far-reaching changes in the socio-political environment of former Soviet Jews.[22] Among others, it prompted a need to find a common denominator between the old Jewish identity and the new Israeli one. Despite their self-perception as Jews, little could be pinpointed in the Soviet Union as visible Jewish behavior, either because there were no facilities for national expression by exterritorial ethnicities or because such expressions were socially unacceptable and/or politically undesirable. This began to change with the decision to go to Israel, culminating in actual immigration to Israel where society expected "Jewish" behaviors. Most former Soviet *olim* learned to speak Hebrew and celebrate (or at least commemorate) Jewish holidays. At the same time, though, most immigrants continued to perceive themselves as Jewish,[23] fewer than 60 percent of respondents (N = 800+) in a 1993 survey by Zvi Gitelman saw being Jewish as important in their lives; the proportion was lower among younger people.[24] For many, even though they celebrated Jewish holidays and identified Jewish history as their national history, their Israeli nationality superseded their Jewishness; being Jewish simply became part of being Israeli. Interestingly, some *olim* testified that from adolescence or early adulthood onward they had seen Jewish history as their history, although their sole acquaintance with it was through literature—particularly the memoirs of Ilya Ehrenburg and the works of Leon Feuchtwanger, which were considered legitimate reading in the Soviet Union.

Possibly the most salient change was the acquisition of the Hebrew language. Most former Soviet *olim*, except some in the oldest age cohort, took great pains to learn Hebrew. For those who found jobs, Hebrew became their primary language at work. For those in their twenties and thirties who immigrated with school-aged children or younger, Hebrew has often become the primary language in the home. The change in language brought about by emigration, especially among the younger generation, implies a cultural transfer—a process of learning and forgetting involving a transfer of "ideas, conceptions, and habits" from one reality to another. Through language we create our "social and cultural, public, and individual space."[25] The more fluent their Hebrew, the more the *olim* exchanged their Jewish identity for an Israeli one.[26] Many of the subjects in a study on the "Russian" immigration reacted to this transformation by comparing the role of Hebrew and Yiddish, and in the eyes of some who left the FSU at the age of forty and above, Yiddish retained its role as a "vehicle" for transmitting Jewish tradition and culture and as "a primary indicator of Jewish identity."[27]

Another change is in immigrants' attitudes toward Judaism and its practice. Unquestionably, the adoption of Jewish rites is part of adapting to the social norms of their new surroundings. Besides celebrating, or somehow commemorating, Jewish holidays, the Russian-speaking *olim* circumcise their sons,[28] many grown men also underwent circumcision after arriving in Israel, and many give their children a bar or bat mitzvah. Many of them show "greater respect [for] spiritual and behavioral aspects" of Judaism even though they remain non-observant in their daily conduct. In Dina Rubina's short story "Poster," Tanya contributes 180 shekels to a philanthropic organization and gives 18 shekels to a beggar in gratitude for her son's life being saved from a suicide bombing because it was the traditional sum given in charity when God saves someone's life.[29] Many manifestly retain the Soviet Marxist perception that to be a modern person means, among other things, to be an atheist. Yet, a large number of respondents in a recent survey admitted to "spiritual inclinations that often amounted to 'diffuse' or implicit religiosity, a loosely defined faith in the Supernatural and the Sacred." Moreover, most Russian Israelis "seem to have become part of the national consensus on the controversial matter of state-religion merger." They have completed, after two decades, admittedly with only "partial success ... their transfer from State Socialism to State Judaism."[30]

Remennick finds that, in addition to material difficulties and the struggle to survive in the unknown, murky waters of market capitalism, "many immigrants experienced cultural shock in the face of ethno-racial diversity of all receiving societies" (Israel, the United States, Canada, and Germany). Entering the "host social structure from its bottom, living in poorer neighborhoods and working in unskilled jobs," they crossed paths in Israel with Arabs and Moroccan Jews and developed negative attitudes that were a carry-over of their sense of being *kul'turnyi* and of their feelings of moral and cultural superiority vis-à-vis their non-Jewish neighbors in the Soviet Union.[31] These sentiments changed only gradually (if at all) as Russian-speaking Israelis worked their way up the social ladder and encountered their professional peers.[32] It was only at this point that they became "more willing to adopt elements of the new lifestyle and everyday culture." Even then, the process of cultural transition occurred, especially in "more external and instrumental domains," while the immigrants have tended to retain their core cultural values. These are "the preservation of the Russian language and cultural consumption, and attempts to transfer it to their children; the indisputable value of education, hard effort, and social mobility; close-knit families with life-long exchange of intergenerational support; reliance on informal social networks rather than formal institutions; and clear in-group preference in personal relationships."[33] In similar ways, the Russian-speaking *olim* retain transnational ties with former friends, neighbors, and work colleagues who immigrated elsewhere or remained behind in the FSU.

However, one major transformation occurred that underscored the transition from a Jewish to an Israeli self-identification. One of the most fundamental traits of the ethnos in Soviet thinking was that of common territory—the link between indigenous nation and national homeland, a postulate given concrete expression in the administrative division of the Soviet state into national union and autonomous republics. The Jews felt themselves spurned and excluded as an extra-territorial ethnic group. They were denied the primordial ethnic awareness that the Soviet regime invoked among the over fifty titular ethnic groups who could boast their own union and autonomous republics.[34] The establishment of Israel as a Jewish state gave Soviet Jews, for the first time in modern history, a national state to which they felt they belonged. Upon arrival in Israel, Soviet Jews quite naturally reverted to the political concepts they had internalized in the Soviet Union, such as the primogeniture of the titular ethnic group and the expectation of accompanying rights and greater privileges. Soviet Jews in Israel felt, for the first time in their lives, that they enjoyed the superior status to which they had always aspired and had known that, as an extra-territorial minority, they could never achieve in the Soviet Union.[35] They therefore were quick to adopt a sense of "Israeliness" and identified easily as Israelis, frequently adopting hawkish positions in Israeli politics and relating to the Arab population much as they felt they had been treated in the Soviet Union.

At the same time, Soviet immigrants comprised a sufficiently large contingent in the Israeli population to establish a community life of their own with a Russian infrastructure including media, libraries, community centers, and other facilities. One study has dubbed this "a structured system within which they forge[d] a new identity" grounded in their Israeli present and Russian-Soviet past, with its environment and culture. Moreover, seeing themselves as highly cultured [*kul'turnyie*] and having in their ranks a large proportion of talented cultural producers, their community created many cultural artifacts that enabled them to preserve their identity and remain within an almost wholly Russian cultural environment.[36] The Russian speakers are the only wave of immigration since Israel's inception to "openly [refuse] to suppress the language and culture of their country of origin." Although their Russian is peppered with Hebrew words and inflections, Russian "scores better than Hebrew [among the *olim*] for its aesthetic value and as a vehicle of culture."[37]

In the mid- and late-1990s, the Russians' effort to maintain a separatist or particularistic cultural space was given expression in the "Russian Party," Yisrael

Ba'aliyah [literally, "Israel on the Rise," but also "Israel in Immigration"]. However, just before the turn of the twenty-first century, with the creation of a second Russian party, Yisrael Beiteinu [Israel Is Our Home], this separatist orientation was replaced by what Dimitry Shumsky terms a "general-national Jewish foundation." This was not similar in any way to their Jewish identity in the Soviet Union, but was posited on their status as Israeli citizens and their concern that Israel remain an ethnically Jewish state.[38]

The desire to be Israeli did not, then, necessarily involve enhancing their Jewish culture, except perhaps in the realm of cuisine; for example, many female *olim* boast of their adoption of traditional Jewish, as well as specifically Israeli, dishes. For the most part, the thick culture of the immigrants remained Russian. Since Soviet Jews historically understood their Jewishness within ethnic rather than religious parameters, they saw no contradiction in retaining Russian culture as their thick culture. Just as their Jewishness set them apart from their surroundings previously in the Soviet Union, in Israel, their Russian qualities created some sort of barrier between the immigrants and their neighbors. Some *olim* felt that after five or more years in Israel, they had exchanged their Jewish identity for a "Russian" one.[39] Whereas in the Soviet Union they were considered Jews by the surrounding society, in Israel, they were seen as "Russians," and so, as it were, ceased being Jews. It has been suggested that, living within their own ethnic group, they could permit themselves to push their "complex rapport to their Jewishness" into the background.[40]

The considerable amount of institutional autonomy that former Soviet *olim* established included opening stores that sold pork and other "Russian" foods. In the mid-1990s, there were said to be between twenty and forty such stores in every large city with a considerable proportion of Russian-speaking *olim*.[41] This is just one of the features of their life in the Soviet Union that they had been unwilling to surrender. Although it became a bone of contention with the Israeli establishment—together with the issue of *giyur* [conversion] and rites of passage (e.g., marriage and burial)—former Soviet *olim* do not accept that they are less Jewish or not good Jews because they do not follow the precepts of traditional Judaism.[42] Those who celebrate Jewish holidays—which seems to be the majority—do so because they perceive them as national holidays and/or because they see the Jewish tradition as part of their national heritage. These *olim* believe that it is incumbent upon Israel to reflect its Jewishness, either directly by religious content or by rendering it as national content.[43]

Many of those who are not *halakhically* Jewish nevertheless identify as Jews, just as they did in the Soviet Union, based on their status as the children of Jewish fathers, or occasionally, simply because they had a Jewish grandparent. In the words of one such person, who emigrated from Moscow at the age of twenty-three, "At one point I thought of converting, but today [nine years after *aliyah*] I feel no need to. Jewishness is not genetics but a definition of a common fate and common goals."[44]

Not all observers interpreted the Russian-speaking *olim*'s institutional autonomy as signifying that they had distanced themselves from the Israeli reality and Jewish identity. Rather, they contributed a new momentum to the secularization and pluralization of Israeli society, having brought with them the Soviet ethnic definition of Jewishness. Indeed, this can surely be interpreted as a larger trend representative of a certain segment within Israel's veteran population. Moreover, some prominent intellectuals among the "Russian" *olim* have proposed that former Soviet Jews could serve as a consolidating force in Israeli society, which, they argue, is otherwise threatened with disintegration. They viewed these immigrants as the only community in Israeli society with the aggregate of primordial attributes to constitute a nation. Soviet Jews, they contend, had borrowed Russian culture's best spiritual attributes—a universalist understanding of religion, an incessant striving for absolute truth, and a tendency toward philosophical thinking—and, in the process, had imparted their own ethnic character to these attributes—a specifically Jewish intellectual flair and Jewish creative openness. This made them a community with immense spiritual strength whose Jewishness derives not from rational factors but "from the heart."

Certainly, among some of the immigrants, including *halakhic* non-Jews, their Jewish ethnicity becomes a point of pride, and they acquire a new consciousness of their distinctive Jewish identity within Israeli society.[45] Indeed, many of them are said to deplore the flimsy nature of many Israelis' Jewish culture. Having been deprived of an identity with content, they came to Israel—in the words of Natan Sharansky—hoping to find precisely that and "could not accept" the Israeli "model" of "the new Jew, a creation that lacked history or cultural ties to the past." Sharansky quotes one *oleh* telling him, "I thought in coming to Israel that I would add three thousand years of history. Instead, I lost thirty. The Soviets began history in 1917. In Israel, it begins in 1948."[46]

In the Soviet Union, ideology was supranational; in its early years, it spoke of proletarian internationalism and later, of the creation of a supranational "Soviet nation." Yet, in practice, the Soviet Union was structured nationally, within the realm of social interaction as well as regime policy. Ideology preached universalism; reality upheld particularism, and the Soviet people gradually lost their faith in the former. Not surprisingly, then, the Israeli identity of Soviet Jewish immigrants is accommodative. According to Sharansky, however, Soviet Jewish immigrants have not simply adapted to Israeli identity—they have helped to transform it, in keeping with the abovementioned analysis.

The dimensions of the "Russian" *aliyah*, combined with its participants' high level of education, enabled it to have an immediate effect on Israeli attitudes. Indeed, it contributed to Israeli society, enabling it to become what Theodore Herzl termed a mosaic of "cultural attachments and interests . . . while [remaining] committed to a Jewish identity that would connect everyone." Thanks to the Russian *aliyah*, a "public space" has been created in Israel "for different groups to express fully their unique identities." Russian-language media, theater, and so on have actually "helped connect new arrivals to their new culture." The result has been that the "hyphenation" of identity—as Russian-Jewish-Israeli—has been enhanced rather than erased.[47]

As time passes, the immigrants' Russian culture is in danger of becoming increasingly shallow and anachronistic, and may gradually become a thin Russian culture. Their language is not only interspersed with Hebraisms, but they are increasingly out of touch with the changes occurring in the colloquial Russian of the post-Soviet Russian Federation. This applies particularly to the younger generation, who are not as convinced as their parents regarding the superiority of the Great Power culture as opposed to that of a small Middle Eastern state. For them, Israeli culture is Western, modern, and technologically oriented. At the same time, young "Russian" families tend to send their children to "Russian" preschools, sometimes just because the children remain there more hours than in other preschools. Some also continue to send school-age children to extracurricular Russian programs in order to give them what the parents feel is a richer classical culture.[48] Even among the young, and certainly among their parents, the immigrants' social milieu is composed primarily of "Russian" Jewish *olim* like themselves. One study found that although the majority of young immigrants learned Hebrew and "the new cultural codes," they, too, "prefer their Russian-speaking circle of friends and have not abandoned their Russian roots." They rely largely on Russian-language media (whether imported from the FSU or produced in Israel) as a source of information and entertainment. These newspapers, TV channels, radio broadcasts, and Internet serve as a "vessel of cultural continuity."[49]

A book dedicated to the "Russian" *aliyah*, written by a "Russian" repatriate, speaks of the cultural chasm that separates "Russians" and Israelis and notes that, rather than diminishing over time, it only seems to grow. In the author's view, the Russian-speaking *olim* have a split, hyphenated Russian-Israeli identity that is the inevitable consequence of postmodern global mobility. She insists that, after being exposed to Hebrew culture, "most Russians abandon it mockingly as narrow-minded, shallow, and dull."[50] Although she underscores the diverse backgrounds of her subjects, who came from various Soviet republics, her attempt to reach conclusions and generalizations based on the homogeneity of the Soviet experience and mentality serves only to highlight the obstacles that stand in the path of any such study. Each immigrant underwent different trials and encounters with Israeli society and reacted accordingly, in conformity with his or her own specific character, education, and/or profession.

CONCLUSION

While the substance of Soviet Jewish thin culture has inevitably changed with immigration to Israel,[51] many of its social and conceptual features have been retained. Former Soviet Jews in Israel continue to associate most intimately with their fellow immigrants from the Soviet Union. They still tend to perceive themselves—particularly the older generation—as an oppressed elite, unable to capitalize on their professional and educational capabilities. The reasons are no longer political, but subjectively they have a similar impact, causing rancor and frustration. Soviet immigrants are also prone to perceive their values, attitudes, and even traits as singular, setting them apart from their surroundings. They have their own social and cultural frameworks, specific ways of spending leisure time, and "Russian"-centered topics of conversation. Indeed, Soviet Jews internalized many of the characteristics of the Russian intelligentsia. Yet, notwithstanding their Soviet background, all of their singularities in thought processes and education, and the ensuing difficulties in their socio-cultural absorption, former Soviet *olim* have imbued their collective identity with positive content and "thickened" its Jewish aspects. It has been said that cultural heritage is learned and is therefore extrinsic to the individual—it can be relinquished or not learned or unlearned (at least, it can be after a generation or more). But cultural heritage is also the product of early socialization and constant reinforcement in the group, where it is often highly valued and therefore tenacious. As a defining characteristic of ethnic group membership it becomes "an intrinsic feature" thereof.[52]

The "Russian" *aliyah* is numerically greater than any previous wave of immigration to Israel—a fact that endows it with a sense of self-importance. In addition, its cultural heritage, certainly in its participants' eyes, is far superior to that of any other significant immigrant group in Israeli society. Moreover, whereas previous immigrant groups were subjected to a melting-pot ethos, in which the ultimate objective was "to become Israeli," the "Russians" arrived in a period of multiculturalism that legitimized the retention of their group specificity and helped preserve boundaries within society.[53] At the same time, the influence of the surrounding society, on the one hand, and the sense of being in their own state precisely because it is Jewish, on the other, mean that those who arrived in Israel as adults and remember the "Soviet Pharaoh" have adopted "thick" elements of Jewishness, even if *à la* Israeli. This is all the more true for those who arrived as children or adolescents, even if they were born to two "Russian" parents and grew up in a typical close-knit multigenerational Russian-Jewish family with Russian-speaking grandparents. Soviet Jewish thin culture will thus become a testament to the resilience of what was, even after the destruction of the Holocaust, the second largest Jewish community in the world.

NOTES

I wish to thank Dimitry Shumsky and Dima Adamsky for reading a draft of this chapter and providing me with valuable insights. I also wish to thank Dina Moyal for helping me with the questionnaires.

1. See Julia Lerner and Rivka Feldhay, eds., *Russians in Israel: The Pragmatics of Culture in Migration* (Tel-Aviv: Van Leer Jerusalem Institute and Hakibbutz Hameuchad, 2012). Our

discussion addresses culture and identity together on the understanding that culture is, in fact, an expression of the identity both of the individual and of the collective.

2. Clifford Geertz, "The Integrative Revolution: Primordial Sentiments and Civil Politics in the New States," in *Old Societies and New States*, ed. Clifford Geertz (New York: The Free Press, 1963), 109–110. Geertz's main concern—the formation of distinct groups demanding recognition as a collective whose differentiation must bring with it political rights in new states—is not relevant to our debate. I will not discuss the political implications of this attachment either in the wider context or in relation to Soviet Jewry. I hope to return to an analysis of these implications elsewhere as they are clearly pertinent to understanding Soviet Jewish identity.

3. Ibid., 128.

4. Stephen Cornell, "The Various Ties that Bind: Content and Circumstances in Ethnic Processes," *Ethnic and Racial Studies* 19:2 (1996): 271.

5. Personally, I would avoid implying that there can, in fact, be a condition of "no culture at all."

6. William Mishler, "On Culture, Thick and Thin: Toward a Neo-Cultural Synthesis," in *Political Culture in Post-Communist Europe*, ed. Detlef Pollack, Jorg Jacobs, Olaf Muller, and Gert Pickel (Burlington, VT: Ashgate, 2003), 237–256.

7. Similarly, I would hesitate to state that it is possible to categorize all Soviet Jews under a single rubric at any time, even in their country of origin.

8. Responding to our question of whether they felt more Russian since coming to Israel, many stated that they had never felt Russian. They, like Jews the world over and people of other nationalities as well, entertained a deep, inner sense of connection to the ethnic group to which they belonged, especially after the Holocaust. For a discussion of some of the complexities of modern Jewish identity, see Mordecai Nisan, *Emotion and Cognition in the Development of Jewish Identity: A Psychological Inquiry* (Jerusalem: Mandel Foundation, 2010).

9. Dimitry Shumsky, "Ethnicity and Citizenship in the Perception of Russian Israelis," in *Challenging Ethnic Citizenship: German and Israeli Perspectives on Immigration*, ed. Daniel Levy and Yfaat Weiss (New York: Berghahn Books, 2002), 59.

10. This was not always the case but became more common with the passing of time, particularly after the mid-1960s.

11. Nisan, *Emotion and Cognition*, 35.

12. For the Jewish self-identity of children of mixed marriages, see Elena Nosenko, *Byt' ili chustvovat'?* [*To Be or to Feel?*] (Moscow: Kraft, 2004).

13. Yuri Slezkine, *The Jewish Century* (Princeton: Princeton University Press, 2004), 330.

14. From the point of view of Jewish identity and culture, these *halakhic* non-Jews fall into three categories. First, people who were born to a non-Jewish mother and a Jewish father who were considered Jews by Soviet society and perceived themselves as Jews and continued to do so in Israel. Paradoxically, in the Soviet Union they tended to identify as Jews more frequently than children of Jewish mothers and non-Jewish fathers who had a Russian patronymic. Second, people who were born to non-Jewish parents but with a Jewish grandparent. They were not considered Jewish in the Soviet Union and developed a much weaker attachment to Judaism, which is reflected in their conduct and perceptions in Israel. Finally, there are partners of Jewish immigrants who themselves have no formal connection to Judaism or Jewishness.

15. I distributed questionnaires to approximately eighty *olim* who left the FSU after the age of eighteen (working on the assumption that younger people had not had the opportunity to contemplate their collective identity and associate consciously with any group culture). My original assumption was that by discerning a number of variables—age at emigration (20–35, 36–50, 51 and above); period of emigration; and place of birth and of residence at time of emigration—I would be able to identify the determinants of the retention of thin Jewish culture within different groups and to reach meaningful conclusions. Some questionnaires were filled out in face-to-face interviews; others were mailed to respondents.

16. For instance, to questions on whether they feel more Russian in Israel than in the FSU, and whether their Russianness in Israel somehow replaced their Jewishness in the Soviet Union in setting them apart from the surrounding population, I received sixteen positive replies that specifically attributed this to the way that veteran Israelis perceived them.
17. Altogether, 31 percent of respondents said they felt largely or partly that the cultural production of Soviet Jews had a Jewish flavor.
18. Larissa Remennick, *Russian Jews on Three Continents: Identity, Integration and Conflict* (New Brunswick, NJ: Transaction, 2007), 23–27. I have opted for the description "Russian-speaking" in accordance with the terminology used by Russian sociologists rather than calling them "Russian," as is common in Israel, both because they are not ethnic Russians and because many came from parts of the FSU outside Russia.
19. Ibid., 48–51.
20. Famously, they were designated Jewish in Article 5 of their internal passports which defined every citizen's "nationality."
21. For the Jewish self-identification of Jews who converted to Christianity in the Soviet Union, see Judith D. Kornblatt, *Doubly Chosen: Jewish Identity, the Soviet Intelligentsia, and the Russian Orthodox Church* (Madison: University of Wisconsin Press, 2004).
22. This also applied to *olim* for whom Israel was not primarily the Jewish home. One study speaks of those who perceived Israel primarily as a country that was the opposite of Russia—Larisa Fialkova and Maria N. Yelenevskaya, *Ex-Soviets in Israel* (Detroit: Wayne State University Press, 2007), 106.
23. See Elazar Leshem, "The Immigration from the Former Soviet Union and the Religious–Secular Cleavage in Israeli Society," in *Mirusiyya leyisrael: zehut vetarbut bema'avar* [From Russia to Israel: Identity and Culture in Transition], ed. Moshe Lissak and Elazar Leshem (Tel-Aviv: Hakibbutz Hameuchad, 2001), 131.
24. Gitelman, *Immigration and Identity: The Resettlement and Impact of Soviet Immigrants on Israeli Politics and Society* (Los Angeles: Wilstein Institute Research Report, 1995), 29, 36, 41. One immigrant who arrived at the age of thirty-five with two small children told me, "Everywhere else I'd send my children to a Jewish school. In Israel, I could choose a school for its merits. Israel is the only place where my Jewish nationality is unimportant."
25. Olaf Terpitz, "'Here' and 'There': The Aspect of Cultural Transfer in the Literary Discourse of the 1990s," in *Jewish Emigration from Russia. 1881–2005*, ed. Oleg Budnitskii (Moscow: Rosspen, 2008), 348–349.
26. Leshem, "The Immigration from the Former Soviet Union."
27. Fialkova and Yelenevskaya, *Ex-Soviets in Israel*, 251. Many of them did not have any or much Yiddish but had nostalgic memories of the language used by their parents and grandparents, which they, like the Soviet regime, identified as the Jewish national tongue.
28. Those who circumcised their newborn sons included mixed families, even when the infant was not *halakhically* Jewish—*Haaretz*, May 3, 1995.
29. Dina Rubina, "Moda'ah," in *Ruhot harefa'im shel Yisrael* [*Israel's Ghosts*] (Tel-Aviv: Yedioth Ahronoth and Chemed, 2003), 436. Rubin was frequently mentioned by respondents as the most popular Russian-speaking Israeli writer.
30. Larissa Remennick and Anna Prashizky, "Evolving Attitudes and Practices in the Religious Field among Former Soviet Immigrants in Israel," *Sociological Papers* 15 (2010): 47–52. In their survey, 9 percent defined themselves as Orthodox; this is probably above the proportion of religious Jews among Russian-speaking *olim*. At the same time, there are former Soviet *olim* who feel anger, revulsion, or aversion toward what they see as the forceful imposition of religious norms on Israeli society and, especially, toward the behavior of the ultra-Orthodox [*haredim*] and the fact that they do not perform military service.
31. For the "Russian" *olim*'s disdain of Ethiopian Jews, see the documentary film *Yidishe Mama*, directed by Gennady Kochuk and Fima Shlik, 2008.

32. Thirty-eight percent of our respondents in 2011 said they felt superior or partly superior to veteran Israelis, and 54 percent felt superior or partly superior specifically to *mizrahim* [Israelis originating from countries in the Middle East and North Africa].

33. Remennick, *Russian Jews on Three Continents*, 372–375. Fialkova and Yelenevskaya, *Ex-Soviets in Israel*, 112. Note that in class, university students group together with coethnics. Just two of their interviewees stressed that they had Israeli friends, and they were not close, intimate ones.

34. The number of Jews who lived in the Jewish Autonomous Oblast of Birobidzhan in the Soviet Far East was negligible.

35. Soviet nationalities policy made national rights contingent on territorial belonging—that is, an ethnic group inhabiting the administrative unit that bore its name, e.g., Ukrainians in Ukraine, Georgians in Georgia, and so on, enjoyed certain privileges, such as education, media, or literature in their national tongue. Dimitry Shumsky has written a brilliant analysis of the Soviet *olim*'s attitude to the Arabs as an ethnic minority in a polity in which they, the "Russians," have become part of the dominant titular majority. He suggests that they have internalized the imperial Russian-Soviet orientalist discourse and compare the Israeli-Palestinian conflict to the Russian-Chechen one. Shumsky, "Ethnicity and Citizenship," 154–178.

36. Anne de Tinguy, "Les Russes d'Israël, une minorité très influente," *Les Etudes du CERI* 48 (December 1998): 8.

37. Fialkova and Yelenenvskaya, *Ex-Soviets in Israel*, 243. One study demonstrates the significance for the "Russian" *olim* of their cultural capital, their affiliation to a rich universal culture that is a source of pride and inspiration. It maintains that while economically and often socially integrated, they continue to contrast "our" to "their" (the veteran Israelis') culture. Sabina Lissitsa, "'Russian Israelis'—The Emergence of a Transnational Diaspora," in *Every Seventh Israeli: The Jews of the Former Soviet Union—Patterns of Social and Cultural Integration*, ed. Alek D. Epstein and Vladimir (Ze'ev) Khanin (Ramat Gan: Bar-Ilan University, 2007), 231–256.

38. Shumsky, "Ethnicity and Citizenship," 164–165, 168.

39. Eleven percent of our respondents said they felt more culturally Russian since coming to Israel, and 16 percent claimed they felt more Russian because they are perceived as such by their surroundings (see endnote 9).

40. Tinguy, "Les Russes d'Israël," 13.

41. *Haaretz*, May 3, 1995.

42. Leshem, "The Immigration from the Former Soviet Union," 134–146. Leshem provides details regarding the secular attitudes and conduct of the mass of the Russian-speaking *olim*, not merely those from mixed families.

43. Ibid., 146.

44. *Haaretz*, April 14, 2008.

45. Asked whether their perception of Jewishness as a whole and of their own Jewishness specifically had changed since arriving in Israel, 45 percent of respondents said there had been no change; 40 percent said their Jewish identity had been enhanced; and 15 percent claimed it had been weakened.

46. Natan Sharansky, *Defending Identity: Its Indispensable Role in Defending Democracy* (Washington, DC: PublicAffairs, 2008), 157–158.

47. Ibid., 159–162.

48. For secondary school children who learn Russian, see *Haaretz*, February 19, 2008.

49. Michael Philippov and Anna Knafelman, "Old Values in the New Homeland: Political Attitudes of FSU Immigrants in Israel," *Israel Affairs* 17.1 (2011): 39. For the self-"ghettoization" of the children of Russian-speaking *olim* and their distancing from Jewish and Israeli customs and culture, see *Haaretz*, June 29, 2007.

50. Elana Gomel, *The Pilgrim Soul: Being a Russian in Israel* (Or Yehuda: Kinneret, Zmora—Bitan, Dvir, 2006), 18, 26.
51. It has also been transformed among Jews who remained in the FSU, but this point is not germane to this chapter.
52. Gerald D. Berreman, "Social Inequality: A Cross-Cultural Analysis," in *Social Inequality: Comparative and Developmental Approaches*, ed. Gerald D. Berreman (New York: Academic Press, 1981), 16.
53. These boundaries will therefore be preserved, despite continuous renegotiation in the sense laid down by Fredrik Barth in the introduction to his edited volume, *Ethnic Groups and Boundaries. The Social Organization of Cultural Difference* (Oslo: Universitetforlaget, 1969), 9–10: "categorical ethnic distinctions do not depend on an absence of mobility, contact and information, but do entail social processes of exclusion and incorporation whereby discrete categories are maintained *despite* changing participation and membership in the course of individual life histories." Barth emphasizes that group categories, i.e., ethnic labels, will most often endure even when individual members move across boundaries or share an identity with people in more than one group.

9 · THE ECONOMIC INTEGRATION OF SOVIET JEWISH IMMIGRANTS IN ISRAEL

GUR OFER

Two major waves of immigrants from the Soviet Union and the FSU arrived in Israel after the late 1960s. The first wave, coming primarily in 1968–1979, numbered approximately 160,000 people. The second, much larger wave of nearly 850,000 came between 1989 and 1999, growing to more than 950,000 by 2010.[1] The majority of the first-wave immigrants arrived during the early 1970s, and the majority of second-wave immigrants between 1989 and the early 1990s. The first wave became roughly 5 percent of the population of Israel, and the second added approximately 18 percent to it. Aside from the significant difference in volume between the two waves, they also differed in several other key respects. In the first wave individuals who chose to immigrate to Israel out of national Jewish aspirations predominated. They also formed a kind of social and economic elite within the Soviet Jewish community. The second wave was motivated primarily by a desire to escape the troubled and collapsing Soviet Union and included a more representative cross-section of the Soviet Jewish community. Both waves consisted mostly of families rather than individuals. Their motivations for immigration ranged from economic betterment to political dissidence.

The first wave arrived in Israel following the 1967 Arab-Israeli war but largely prior to the next such war (October 1973)—a period of economic stagnation and instability with high inflation. The second wave arrived in Israel during a period of economic stability and moderate growth. The second wave also benefited from the presence of a large group of Russian-speaking veteran immigrants from the first wave. Finally, there was a significant difference in the absorption policies of the Israeli government between the two waves. During the 1970s, the predominant policy was to direct immigrants to "absorption centers" in locations determined by the Ministry of Absorption. However, the absorption centers strained to accommodate large numbers of immigrants, and the Israeli government shifted to a policy of "direct absorption."[2] Beginning in 1987, immigrants were allowed to choose their initial place of residence and were entitled to financial support to rent an apartment in the location of their choice. This was part of a comprehensive "absorption basket" that covered the immigrants' basic needs. The Israeli government also encouraged immigrants with higher education and professional training or experience to enroll in Hebrew languages courses through *ulpanim* at no cost. These "direct absorption" policies were preferred by the immigrants and were deemed more effective by the state.

Building on the literature on economic aspects of absorbing and assimilating Russian-speaking immigrants in Israel, especially during the 1990s,[3] in this chapter I offer a comparative analysis of the economic outcomes of absorption of the two migration waves (M70 and M90) as of 2009. Despite the aforementioned differences between the two waves, we hypothesize that the differences in absorption outcomes between the two waves can be attributed primarily to their disparate lengths of stay in Israel.

The relatively long time elapsed between the date of immigration and the point of observation in this study (2009) brings into the analysis immigrants who were relatively young at the time of migration—children of migrant families too young to have ever engaged in the Soviet labor market. Depending on their age at the time of immigration, they also likely completed some or all of their schooling in Israel rather than in the FSU. They also had more time to master Hebrew and to acclimate to other institutional and cultural aspects of life in Israel. Clearly, the process of assimilation for these younger immigrants has been different, and presumably easier and quicker than that of their parents. For this reason, we have divided the migrants who came during each of the two waves into "young" and "old" age cohorts: "M70y" and "M70o," and "M90y" and "M90o." The dividing age is twenty years at the time of migration. By and large the people belonging to M70o were in their fifties or older in 2009, and those belonging to M90o were, on average, twenty years younger.[4] The two migration cohorts or the four migration-age cohorts are distinguished in the analysis. We compare these migrant groups with the veteran Jewish population denoted as JP. We also draw comparisons with the segment of the veteran, Israeli Jewish population originating in Europe and America, excluding the *haredi* community, designated as JP*.[5] This last group, JP*, is more similar to the FSU immigrants than the JP group in terms of cultural traditions and socioeconomic status. The main data sources used in this study, all from the Israeli Central Bureau of Statistics [CBS], are the Social Survey [SS], the labor force surveys [LFS], income surveys [IS], and the expenditure survey [ES], for the period around 2009.

In the next section of this chapter, I survey the primary economic characteristics of the various immigrant groups as well as other, related characteristics. Next, in the main section of the chapter, I examine the integration of these immigrants into the Israeli labor force: the extent of their participation in the labor force, their income levels and relevant determinants, and their occupational distribution. The final section focuses on immigrants' consumption patterns.[6]

GENERAL CHARACTERISTICS OF THE TWO IMMIGRATION WAVES IN COMPARATIVE PERSPECTIVE

The main characteristics of the two immigration waves from the FSU and of various segments of the Israeli population are assembled in table 9.1. The table reflects data from 2009 and covers all adults twenty years of age and older. The data are from the Social Survey published by the CBS. As can be observed, both groups of immigrants include a lower proportion of males, but the gender gap in the 1970s wave ($M70$) is smaller. The average ages and proportion of people fifty-five and older are higher in the $M70$ group. The average household size (HH) of the $M90$ group is significantly smaller than in the two veteran Israeli groups. The HH of $M70$—3.3 persons per household—lies between the HH sizes of JP (3.6) and that of JP^* (3.1). The levels of education among the $M70$ and $M90$ groups are higher than those of JP (veteran Jewish population), especially the proportion that graduated from university. However, the gap virtually disappears in comparisons with the JP^* group (veteran Jewish population of European/American origin). A much higher proportion of the immigrants reported that their health status was "not so good" or "not good." This is explained, at least partly, by their higher age relative to the veteran groups. A much smaller proportion of the immigrants reports being "*haredi*" or even "religious," and a much higher proportion identifies as secular. Again, somewhat smaller differences from JP and JP^* are recorded for $M70$. Finally, proficiency in Hebrew is much lower among the M groups, but here too, the gap is significantly smaller for $M70$.[7]

Two general observations may be made: 1) differences in a number of demographic and economic characteristics for the M groups are typically smaller when compared with the JP^* group than with that of JP; 2) whenever relevant, the early wave of migrants, $M70$, is closer to the veteran populations in characteristics that are behaviorally determined. I hypothesize that this fact represents a more general pattern of assimilation over time that will be replicated in the other major components of this analysis.

ASSIMILATION INTO THE LABOR MARKET

How long does it take for immigrants to join the labor market? To what extent does the quality of their job(s) reflect the immigrants' labor qualifications (particularly those brought from abroad, such as occupation and rank) and additional attributes acquired through training, whether on or off the job, formal or informal (including mastery of Hebrew)? To what extent do immigrants' patterns of

TABLE 9.1. General Characteristics: The Jewish Population and Immigration Waves

Variable		M90	M70	JP	JP*
Obs. 2009		1,071	142	5,123	2,603
1	Gender				
1.1	(M%)	43.00%	47.24%	49.35%	49.01%
2	Age				
2.1	Average	48.25	53.00	44.46	43.18
2.2	25–54	52.31%	49.40%	58.13%	54.99%
2.3	55 +	38.14%	48.96%	29.70%	29.05%
3	Education				
3.1	Years average	14.14	13.70	13.82	14.55
3.2	Academic (13 +)	74.10%	64.98%	69.12%	76.43%
3.3	No certificate	13.49%	29.66%	35.15%	20.74%
3.4	Matriculation	15.90%	9.35%	20.63%	25.57%
3.5	Michlala (Junior College)	31.98%	22.53%	19.09%	18.88%
3.6	University	38.63%	38.46%	25.07%	34.78%
4	Health				
4.1	Not so good + not good	34.77%	37.47%	15.81%	11.43%
4.2	Have a problem	47.05%	55.17%	34.99%	31.95%
4.3	"Disturbing" problem	69.20%	77.24%	62.87%	54.71%
5	Hebrew (Speaking)				
5.1	"Good" + "very good"	46.35%	78.20%	96.14%	97.16%
6	Religiosity (Jewish)				
6.1	"Haredim" + "religious"	2.46%	11.71%	22.73%	12.72%
6.2	"Secular"	51.67%	49.78%	36.59%	54.99%
7	Participation in LF	65.53%	63.60%	67.94%	71.01%
8	Unemployed (% of LF)	5.55%	5.69%	7.59%	7.06%
9	Independent (% of empl.)	6.39%	9.39%	14.60%	13.69%
10	Part time (% of empl.)	78.51%	87.70%	79.75%	80.01%
11	Work related to study (% of relevant)	39.32%	62.58%	62.00%	61.26%
12	Years of work experience	19.46	18.71	26.79	23.20
14	Weekly hours	41.84	44.75	41.73	42.42
15	Gross monthly wages	6,288.31	9,672.57	8,694.71	9,339.95
16	Gross household income	9,031.16	11,518.01	11,952.75	13,502.28
17	Persons per household	3.02	3.45	3.71	3.36
18	HH income per person	2,989.42	3,334.37	3,222.66	4,022.72
19	Satisfaction from wages	44.49%	54.53%	61.94%	62.80%
21	Satisfaction from econ. position	38.64%	56.73%	62.25%	64.21%
22	Satisfaction from life	74.29%	89.52%	89.61%	90.70%

SOURCE: Social Survey 2009.

employment correspond to those in their country of origin and/or to general patterns of labor force participation in Israel? How many became financially independent of government support? Did women from the FSU preserve their high level of labor force participation and their relatively higher representation in so-called "male" occupations such as medicine, engineering, economics, and education? Finally, how do all these elements of employment converge to determine the incomes of the immigrants compared with that of the veteran population? Partial answers to some of these questions will be offered through my own analysis, while other explanations will be sought in other studies and in secondary sources.

LABOR FORCE PARTICIPATION

According to the 2009 Social Survey (SS), the average labor force participation rates among individuals twenty and older in the two immigrant waves are marginally lower than those of the two veteran Jewish groups (see table 9.1). However, these average rates for $M70$ and $M90$ can be attributed to the significantly lower participation rates among $M70o$ and $M90o$. Participation rates among the young cohorts of both waves are even higher than among the two veteran populations. Clearly, the different age compositions of the groups are responsible for some of these discrepancies. The participation rate of immigrants is marginally lower than among the veteran groups. The number of part-time workers is similar among JP, JP^*, and $M90$ but lower among $M70$ immigrants, and the number of weekly hours worked is virtually the same among all four groups. This underemployment deviates from patterns of employment in the FSU where part-time employment was quite rare. However, the legacy of Soviet economics is reflected in the very low number of self-employed workers, which is less than half the veteran Israeli rate of 13.3 percent among $M90$ (6.3 percent), with slightly higher rates among $M70$ (9.3 percent), which indicates a trend toward convergence, albeit at a gradual pace. Note, however, that the rate of independent workers among $M70y$ is higher than those of the veteran groups.

The levels and patterns of labor force participation of the FSU immigrants in the Israeli labor force are estimated using dichotomic (0,1) equations, in which the participation rates, the dependent variables, are explained by a number of independent variables that affect participation. There are separate equations for women and men. The participation equations are:

Participation (0, 1) = F(Age, AgeSQ, Education, WorkYrs, Hebrew, BadHealth, HHsize, Childreno–5, $M70o$, $M70y$, $M90o$, $M90y$)

Where:

Participation = Participation in the labor force, "1" if yes and "0" if no, as the dependent variable:

Education = Number of school years (anywhere)[8]
WorkYrs = Number of working years (anywhere)
Hebrew = Proficiency in Hebrew: Average score of speaking, reading, and writing as reported by the people.
BadHealth = Health status "not so good" and "not good" according to self-evaluation.
HHsize = Household size
Children0–5 = Number of children 0–5
Four "dummy" variables for the four migrant groups

We ran separate equations for men and women for each of the two veteran Israeli Jewish populations (*JP* and *JP**). A separate equation is estimated for each of the four groups of immigrants.

All of the estimated equations produce high adjusted Rsq values. Among the independent variables, age, health status, household size, the presence of young children (in the female equations only), all variables have the expected signs and are always statistically significant. The number of years in school has the expected signs but is statistically significant only in the female equations. Surprisingly, proficiency in Hebrew is not significant throughout. There are no significant differences in the results for the two veteran populations.[9]

Estimates of the coefficients of the four dummy variables are slightly negative or positive but are entirely statistically insignificant. That indicates that migrant groups have a labor force participation rate similar to that of the veteran Jewish populations. In other words, there is virtually full assimilation regarding labor force participation. The only exceptions are a statistically significant positive coefficient among men of the *M90y* cohort and a near-significant, positive participation coefficient among women of *M900*. Yet, in the *JP** equations, all migrant coefficients are statistically insignificant. These findings are consistent with our main hypothesis that the second immigration wave is progressing in the footsteps of the earlier one and that full assimilation will likely be achieved soon.

Somewhat surprising is the absence (with only the weak exception mentioned above) of high work force participation rates among immigrant women in the 1990s in contrast to their high participation rates both in the FSU and in Israel in the 1970s. This may reflect the trend of declining workforce participation rates by women, which is explained in part by a shift to part-time work in Russia and other FSU states following the transition from communism. In both cases, this trend reflects the response of women to the end of Soviet authorities' heavy pressure to participate in the labor force using, among other strategies, wage policies as a stick and postsecondary education as a carrot.[10]

EARNINGS

We include two sets of earning equations, one based on the 2009 Social Survey and the other on the 2009 Income Survey. There are some differences between the two surveys, including sampling methods, questionnaire designs, research questions, and populations studied.[11] The equations follow the customary standard used in the literature for wage functions, in which *LnWage*, the dependent variable, is explained by a vector of independent variables reflecting different earning capacities (see below). The key finding in all of the estimates is that the earnings of $M700$, $M70y$, and $M90y$ are, in most cases, not statistically different from the earnings of the two veteran Jewish populations. Per contra, all estimates for the $M900$ population still show significantly lower earnings as of 2009. The two income functions are as follows:

The SS function:
LnWagess = F(LnHours, Age, AgeSQ, Education, Hebrew, Tenure, BadHealth, WorkStudy, M900, M90y, M700, M70y, [OCs])
Where:

LnWagess = LN of monthly gross earnings
LnHoursss = LN of monthly hours worked
Education = Years of schooling
Hebrew = Good Hebrew—Simple average of the levels of speaking, reading, and writing
Tenure = Years worked
BadHealth = Bad health, where health problem affects the ability to work
Work&Study = Relevance of schooling to the content and requirements of the job (0–1)
Four dummy variables, one for each of the migrant groups
OCs = Occupations, added as a series of dummy variables at a second stage.[12]
   Dum1 (high academic professions) is omitted from the estimations.

The *Income Survey (IS)* function:
LnWagesis = F(LnHours, Age, AgeSQ, Education, Disability, M900, M90y, M700, M70y, [OCs])

Where all variables are defined as above except for *Disability*, which obtains the value 1 when a person receives an allowance from the Israeli Institute of National Insurance, and 0 if not.[13]

Examining the earning differences between the four migrant groups and the two veteran Israeli Jewish populations, we find that $M900$ is the only group with consistent negative earning gaps, all statistically significant. The negative earning gaps of this population range from 25 to 35 percent in the SS equations, about 5 points less when the OCs dummy variables are included. In the IS equations, the negative gaps are somewhat higher. The income gaps for women are somewhat higher than for men. All of the earning coefficients in the equations of the other three migrant groups in the SS equations and in the JP equations of the IS are not statistically significant (tables 9.3 and 9.4, not shown here). Statistically significant negative earning gaps appear only in the JP* comparisons of the IS: for men, in the $M70y$ and $M70o$ equations, and for women, only in the $M70o$ equation. Relatively speaking, these gaps are quite modest, hovering around 25 percent (table 9.3).

The estimated earning gaps by the coefficients of the dummy variables are actually *under*estimates. This is because at least three of the control variables in the SS and the IS equations reflect only a partial picture of the earning gaps. In addition to these variables, the migrants are less proficient in Hebrew, they report a greater mismatch between their education and training and the content of their current jobs, and many are employed in occupations ranked below those they were trained for and worked in while living in the FSU. The coefficients for proficiency in Hebrew are positive and significant and, hence, improvements in the use of Hebrew at work can help immigrants obtain higher-paying jobs, which have the potential to close the income gap and overcome the mismatch between the immigrants' job positions and their education and training. This potential can be observed by comparing the earning gaps between the two estimates when the relevant control variable is either included in or excluded from the equation. In the case of the occupational dummy variables, the differences can be observed in tables 9.3 and 9.4 (not shown) where the equations that include occupations show smaller earning gaps. The difference is hidden in the low occupational profiles of the immigrants relative to their former occupations in the FSU. Some of the earning gaps can be narrowed or even closed over time by climbing down this ladder. This phenomenon of offering lower occupational positions to immigrants became a central issue in the scholarly literature on absorption and in policy discussions during the 1970s, 1990s, and beyond.

THE OCCUPATIONAL RETREAT

As shown above, part of the earning gaps for the FSU immigrants to Israel is "hidden" in their lower occupational status compared to the two veteran Jewish Israeli populations. This constitutes an assimilation gap only if the occupational composition of the immigrants was higher in their country of origin and if this higher composition reflected more or less equivalent quality of the occupational levels to the composition in Israel. Even so, the occupational downgrading of the immigrants is probably due to the lack of specific human capital necessary to perform effectively in Israel and to complement their imported, general human capital. Proficiency in Hebrew is probably the most important element of specific human capital, but is not the only factor. The downgrading of the immigrants' occupational composition might have been caused also by the large gap between the occupational demands of the Israeli economy and the occupational composition of the immigrant groups. For example, there is a much higher proportion of academics among the immigrants, including a large number of physicians (about 10,000) compared with about 15,000 practicing medical doctors in Israel during the 1990s. Compared to the FSU, Israel had a much larger service sector, which was ready to hire many immigrants, especially women, including many with very high educational attainment and prestigious occupations in the FSU.

When we compare the occupational structure of the Jewish population in Israel with those of the four immigrant groups (all in 2009) and then compare the occupational structure of the immigrants in Israel with that of the FSU in earlier years (tables 9.5 and 9.6, not shown here),[14] we see several interesting findings. In the top white-collar occupations (academics, professionals, and managers, categories 0–2), the $M700$ group had acquired the occupational composition of the veteran Jewish population in Israel by 2009, while the $M900$ group, men and women alike, still lagged behind on this score. Both migration waves lag behind the occupational composition of the JP^* population—the segment most similar in labor force preparedness and characteristics to the FSU migrants. Second, while still living in the FSU, the two migrant groups had a much "higher" occupational profile than they have in Israel (as of 2009). The differences in the occupational compositions of immigrants between the Soviet Union and Israel during the 1970s are assembled in table 9.6 (not shown). These gaps imply that many people—a third or more of all men and nearly 60 percent of women—were forced to shift their occupations downward upon migration.[15] Several studies show engineers moving downward to positions as technicians, and of technicians to positions as skilled industrial workers. Among women, there is a shift from academic and professional positions in the Soviet Union to clerical and service positions in Israel. The figures in tables 9.5a and 9.5b (not shown) may hint at a dynamic process, in which the initial downward shift in occupational composition is quite dramatic but recovers gradually over time. Sarit Cohen-Goldner and Zvi Eckstein (2008) and Zvi Eckstein, Sarit Cohen-Goldner, and Tali Larom (2006) constructed a dynamic model that demonstrates how improvement in Hebrew proficiency and specific professional training helped immigrants reclaim white-collar positions after working for a few years as blue-color workers.[16] Part of this recovery was due to the high-tech sector that emerged in Israel during the 1990s, creating high demand for engineers, technicians, and other academic professionals. Similar dynamic trends appear in a paper by Efrat Averbach and Aviad Tur-Sinai (2010) that is based on the Israeli censuses of 1995 and 2008.[17] They explore differences between the human capital of native-born Israelis and immigrants in the context of the Jorgenson and Fraumeni (1989) model. The paper shows that immigrants, during their first years in Israel, worked in occupations below those that fit their education; hence, their human capital contribution is lower than that of the native Israelis.

However, with the passage of time, some immigrants managed to move up the occupation ladder to levels that matched their education and, in this manner, to increase their human capital and narrow, though not close the gap with the Israeli natives. Furthermore, Ofer et al. (1983) show that the more qualified immigrants in every occupational group had a better chance of keeping their occupations, while those less qualified had to move downward. Finally, studies also show that downward occupational mobility was accompanied by a parallel decline in rank within each occupational group, as suggested by the small number of immigrants assuming positions as managers.

As explained above, $M70y$ and $M90y$ are composed of people who immigrated to Israel with little or no work experience in the Soviet Union and, in many cases, with little to no occupational education. In 2009, up to a third of these two younger cohorts had an occupation in the top academic groups of 0–2, compared with 40 percent or more in these occupations among the two veteran Jewish populations. The difference is mostly concentrated in the top academic professions (group "0") and in the managerial group. It is not clear what explains these gaps for the young migrants.

CONSUMPTION PATTERNS

Israel's population is composed of people who came from dozens of countries, each with its own consumption patterns and priorities, cuisines and tastes. As a result, Israel is highly pluralistic while featuring an intensive process of mutual influences—a "melting pot." Immigrants from the FSU are full participants in this dynamic social setting. Here we follow the process of assimilation in their consumption habits. There could be many causes of changes in consumption patterns upon immigration to a different country: climate, composition of supply and of relative prices, and, as mentioned, the consumption patterns of others. Among the distinctive features of consumption patterns in the FSU were: food occupied a higher percentage of total consumption than "normal"; high consumption of bread, potatoes, meat, and alcohol; high spending on smoking and tobacco products, on culture and entertainment (due to high demand and low prices), on public transportation (due to the limited supply of private cars), and recently, on computers and the Internet. On the other hand, there were lower expenditure shares on housing (due to limited supply as well as low rent and utility costs) and on health care, which was supplied primarily by the state at little to no cost.[18]

Analysis of the immigrants' varied consumption patterns is done by estimating the Engel functions for Israel for each consumption item or group. Two functions are estimated. The share of consumption of a given item in total consumption (SHxx) serves as the dependent variable and is explained by the level of household income per "standard adult."[19] We also utilize the basic "Engel curve" and a more elaborated function as follows:

$SHxx = F[LnIncome, Age, Children_{0-18}, Periphery, Education, M_{70}, M_{90}]$
Where:
Age and *Education* are the age and years of education of the head of the *HH*.
Children 0–18 is the number of children 0–18 in the *HH*.
Periphery measures "distance" from the center, both geographically and in socioeconomic terms—an index compiled by the *CBS*.[20] Living in remote or poor regions may delay assimilation. Because questions on consumption were directed to the head of the households rather than to individuals, we estimate expenditure equations using two migration groups, M_{70} and M_{90}, as our dummy variables rather than with the four age cohorts.[21] The estimates via the long equations "purify" the dummy coefficients of M_{70} and M_{90} by taking into account differences in consumption habits not related to immigration.

At this stage, consumption patterns of the immigrants are compared only with those of the Jewish population, *JP*, in Israel. The income variable *LnIncome* is always highly statistically significant while the other independent variables are significant most of the time. Our main focus, however, is directed at the estimation of the dummy variables.[22] It turns out that the M_{70} group is almost fully assimilated to the *JP* patterns, while the M_{90} group preserved some features of either "old" or distinctive consumption patterns. For a given level of income, M_{90} immigrants spend proportionally more than *JP* on food, and within food, more on meat, fruit, and potatoes (though not more on bread). They dine out at restaurants less often, consume more alcohol, but don't smoke more than *JP*! The M_{90} group spends more on health and computers but less on books and newspapers. Understandably, they spend less on "culture," perhaps since there is a limited supply of "culture" available in Russian in Israel and, in many cases, prices are high. M_{90} immigrants also spend even less on education, possibly due to, among other factors, having fewer children (though only to a marginally significant degree). Finally, M_{90} immigrants spend more on public transportation since they still have fewer cars than *JP* (though more than they had in the Soviet Union). However, this extra spending on public transportation disappears in the long equation.

The coefficients of the M_{90} dummy variable in the long equations produce very similar results to those of the short ones.[23] By contrast, almost all of the coefficients of the M_{70} dummy variables are not statistically significant—an indication of near-complete assimilation to Israeli consumption patterns and of the road still to be traveled by the M_{90} group.

CONCLUDING NOTES

One way to summarize the various elements of economic assimilation by the two waves of immigration from the FSU to Israel is to look at the economic status of immigrant households compared with the two veteran Jewish populations. We look at income levels per person and subjective satisfaction levels regarding heads of households' economic status. The data are presented in the lower part of table 9.1. The monthly income per person of $M70$ is higher than that of JP but lower than that of JP^*. Income per person of $M90$ has reached the level of JP but trails behind $M70$ and JP^*. This further supports our hypothesis on the dynamics of assimilation.[24] Data on ownership of apartments, their value, and owner satisfaction, on ownership of a private car, and on pension arrangements all follow the same pattern (bottom of table 9.1). Subjective satisfaction regarding wages and "from life" are all significantly lower among the $M90$ group, while the evaluations of heads of $M70$ households fall just below those of the veteran Jewish groups regarding satisfaction from wages and economic position. With regard to general satisfaction with life, the $M70$ HH fall between those of the two veteran groups. While $M70$ seems to have almost fully assimilated economically in Israel, those in $M90$, twenty years after this group's major wave of immigration, still have some distance to travel in this direction.

In addition to the primary aspects of economic absorption and assimilation described above, one can identify more specific economic phenomena and behaviors that add color and detail to our more general picture. For example, one could discuss the development of semi-isolated enclaves—partly self-supported communities preserving a "Russian" way of life and patterns of consumption. These generally include ethnic grocery stores and other commercial enterprises (including some chain stores), restaurants and bars, Russian bookstores, services of various kinds, and, sometimes, even schools in which Russian is the dominant language. In the Israeli economy at large, there are concentrations of a "Russian" presence and activities in the high-tech sector, in healthcare and nursing, in music, and in tourism. It is also worth examining the role of immigrants in the sphere of economic relations, investments, and trade with Russia and other FSU economies. Here, the "Russian" community in Israel functions as a diaspora vis-à-vis Russia and the FSU—specifically, a diaspora in a developed economy with higher productivity and technological levels than the FSU. In this way, the Jewish immigration from the FSU has established a new model of Jewish diaspora—one in which the FSU has replaced Israel as the diasporic "center." In this sense, the community of immigrants from the FSU has joined the many Jewish communities in Israel that function as diasporas of many countries around the world.

NOTES

Thanks to Beata Shwartz who collected and organized the data and made the econometric estimations.

1. Central Bureau of Statistics (*CBS*), SP No. 1365, 2009. With other *CBS* data for the 2000s (Social Survey, 2008, 2009, other years; Income Survey, HH Expenditure Survey, Labor force Survey, all 2009 and various years).
2. Elazar Leshem, "The Policies of Immigration Absorption and the System of Absorption Services to Immigrants: The Early Absorption Stage," in *Profile of an Immigration Wave: The*

Absorption Process of Immigrants from the Former Soviet Union, 1990–1995, ed. Moshe Sicron and Leshem (Jerusalem: Magnes Press, 1999), 44–45.

3. See, for example, Reuben Gronau and Zvi Eckstein, "Absorption of Mass Migration in the 1990s," *Economic Quarterly* 42.148 (April 1991); Sicron and Leshem, eds., *Profile of an Immigration Wave*; Elazar Leshem, *Integration of Immigrants from FSU, 1990–2005* (Jerusalem: Massad Klita, 2009); Zvi Eckstein, Sarit Cohen-Goldner, and Tali Larom, "A Decade of the Integration of Immigrants from the Former Soviet Union in the Israeli Labor Market" (Mimeo, 2006); Cohen-Goldner and Eckstein, "Labor Mobility of Immigrants: Training, Experience Language and Opportunities," *International Economic Review* 49.3 (2008): 837–872. The reference lists in these studies are very long and also include references to the immigration wave of the 1970s. Gur Ofer, Aaron Vinokur, and Yarom Ariav, *Absorption in Work of Soviet Immigrants: A Comparative Analysis* (Jerusalem: Falk Institute, 1983) is a study of the earlier wave. To some extent, the present study follows in its footsteps. An English version is included in D. Schwartz, ed., *Studies in Absorption* (Stockholm, 1987).

4. In what follows, we use $M_{70} = M_{70y} + M_{70o}$, and similarly for M_{90}. The M_{70} group is relatively small, only 142,000, and any subdivision thereof is even smaller, which serves to limit their statistical significance.

5. The continental origin of Jews in Israel is defined by the CBS by being born on (or, sometimes, having immigrated from) a given continent, plus those born in Israel to a father who was born on (or immigrated from) that continent.

6. Due to space limitations, this version of my larger work concentrates on a fuller description and analysis in the text and does not include tables except table 9.1, which presents the relevant dimensions and characteristics of the population groups included in my analysis. A version of the chapter that includes additional tables and an appendix can be obtained from the author.

7. Note that JP* also excludes the *haredi* population, which is characterized by very low labor force participation and a high incidence of poverty.

8. A continuous variable created from interval data provided to us by the SS database.

9. A sample of the estimated equations is provided in the appendix to the full version of this chapter.

10. Ofer, Vinokur, and Ariav, *Absorption in Work of Soviet Immigrants*; Ofer and Vinokur, *The Soviet Household under the Old Regime: Economic Conditions and Behavior in the 1970s* (Cambridge: Cambridge University Press, 1992), 271–318.

11. The former surveys those twenty years of age and older; the latter surveys those fifteen years and older.

12. Dum 1, OCs. 0–2 in the CBS classification indicates academic, professional employees, and managers. Dum 2, OCs. 3–4 indicates employees in clerical and other white-collar services. Dum 3: OCs. 5–8 indicates skilled workers in agriculture and industry. Dum 4, OCs. 9 indicates unskilled workers. Dum 5, OCs. X indicates "profession unknown."

13. The equations are estimated in linear form with OLS. Separate equations are estimated for men and women and for the two veteran populations. Within these groups, separate equations are estimated for each of the four immigrant subgroups. All equations are estimated with and without the occupational dummies.

14. See Sicron and Leshem, eds., *Profile of an Immigration Wave*; Leshem, *Integration of Immigrants from FSU*; Cohen-Goldner and Eckstein, "Labor Mobility of Immigrants"; Eckstein, Cohen-Goldner, and Larom, "A Decade of the Integration"; Ofer, Vinokur, and Ariav, *Absorption in Work of Soviet Immigrants*; Ofer, Vinokur, and Bar-Chaim, "Absorption and Economic Contribution of Immigrants from the Soviet Union," in *Studies in Absorption*, ed. D. Schwartz (Stockholm, 1987); Ofer, Karnit Flug, and Nitsa Kassir, "Absorption in Work of Soviet Immigrants to Israel in the 1990s: Aspects of Preservation of Original Occupations," *Economic Quarterly* 42.148 (April 1991): 135–171.

15. Leshem, *Integration of Immigrants from FSU, 1990–2005*, 98–103; Sicron and Leshem, *Profile of an Immigration Wave*; Ofer, Vinokur, and Ariav, "Absorption in Work of Soviet Immigrants"; Ofer, Flug, and Kassir, "Absorption in Work of Soviet Immigrants to Israel in the 1990s."
16. Sarit Cohen-Goldner and Zvi Eckstein, "Labor Mobility of Immigrants: Training, Experience, Language, and Opportunities," *International Economic Review* 49.3 (2008); Zvi Eckstein, Sarit Cohen-Goldner, and Tali Larom, "A Decade of the Integration of Immigrants from the Former Soviet Union in the Israeli Market" (mimeo, in Hebrew, 2006).
17. Efrat Auerbach and Aviad Tur-Sinai, "Immigration, Occupation, Education, and Their Influence on Human Capital in Israel" (mimeo, in Hebrew, 2010).
18. Ofer and Vinokur, *The Soviet Household under the Old Regime*.
19. The measure of "standard adult" (SA) endows every consecutive member of a family or HH a declining weight. This is justified on the grounds of increasing returns to scale in consumption. Accordingly, a family of one person receives a weight of 1.25 SA, a family of two receives 2 SAs, an HH of three persons receives 2.65 SAs, etc. (*CBS*, Introduction to the HH Expenditure Survey, 2009).
20. The *CBS* compiled an index of being on the periphery (representing socioeconomic status and geographic distance from the center of Israel), in which 1 indicates residence far from the center and 5 indicates residence in the center.
21. Also, there is no separation between men and women.
22. This information is provided in tables 9.7a and 9.7b (not shown), in which we present the values and statistical significance of the two dummy variables (as measured by the T statistic).
23. The long equations put expenditures on education in negative territory. This seems to be due to the variables for the age and number of children. It also eliminates the significance of the (negative) coefficient for bread.
24. Notice also that the same is true with respect to household size: the smallest for $M90$ (2.88), followed by $M70$ (3.33) that surpasses JP^* (3.12) but trailing behind JP (3.58).

PART IV RESOCIALIZATION
AND THE MALLEABILITY
OF ETHNICITY

It has long been established that ethnicity is malleable in different ways. In the nineteenth and twentieth centuries, "ethnic entrepreneurs" mobilized groups of people to take on, be conscious of, and act upon new ethnic categories. Some were successful, others not, and the issue is still very much alive. Attempts were made to create political, state-connected identities that would supersede regional ones. Thus, Germans and Italians were united politically; Norwegians were split off from Sweden; and Palestinians and Jews demanded states of their own. After nearly half a century of the regime's attempts to create a Yugoslav state and identity that would take precedence over all others, the Serbs, Croats, Slovenes, Bosnians, and Macedonians of Yugoslavia rejected them in a series of wars that broke the country apart in the early 1990s.

Movements to create or strengthen ethnicity achieved varying degrees of success. "Ruthenians" were refashioned as "Ukrainians," while parallel attempts among Belarusians were less successful. Attempts to create a sense of being Nigerian among 250 ethnic groups and languages have been marginally more successful. Today Catalans insist on being differentiated from Spaniards, Moldovans from Romanians, and some Scots, Welsh, and others in the "United" Kingdom treasure their identities and cultures.

Obviously, the issue of political and even cultural identity is more complicated for those who migrate from one country to another. They have to reconsider their identities. Some change their political allegiance but not their self-defined ethnicity; others change both. A small minority changes neither.

It is rarely acknowledged that over time, the same ethnic group may change the cultural content and nexus of its identity. Since the late eighteenth century, Jews and their neighbors have debated the category into which Jews fit best—religion or ethnicity? In the USSR, where religion had no official recognition, Jews were classified as a *natsional'nost'* [ethnic group] after 1918 and thus, occupied the same niche as Russians, Belorussians, Tajiks, Uzbeks, and over 100 other ethnic groups. Over the course of four or five generations raised in the Soviet Union, most Jews accepted this categorization, rejecting the idea that they were a nation or a group defined by religion. However, when they migrated in large numbers to Israel, they became part of a Jewish nation and a Jewish state. When they immigrated to Germany or the United States, they entered societies that had traditionally viewed Jews as a religious group (with the exception of Nazi Germany where they were considered a sub-human "race"). Since the great majority are secular, what does being "Jewish" mean in states that do not recognize them officially as a "nationality?"

This section explores the ways in which Russian-speaking Jewish immigrants adjusted their self-conceptions in Germany and even in Russia itself. Because post-Soviet Russia and other FSU states lifted restrictions on Jews and permitted them to express themselves ethnically and religiously as they chose, and those states also no longer required their citizens to be identified officially by ethnicity, even in the FSU Jews are free to redefine themselves.

Eliezer Ben-Rafael and Sveta Roberman study Russian-speaking Jews in Germany, albeit using quite different methods. Ben-Rafael's sociological study, based on "large N" surveys, finds that RSJs in Germany, especially the younger ones, incorporate certain elements of Judaism (religion) in their self-conceptions, cling to Russian culture as their own, and do not easily amalgamate into German society. Instead, they strengthen their Jewish identities and attach themselves to the State of Israel and to RSJs in other lands.

Roberman's ethnographic study finds that at least some of the RSJs in Germany use their Jewishness instrumentally. That is, they are highly aware that other Jews may not regard them as "genuine Jews," but they find their Jewishness useful in extracting material benefits both from the German state and the Jewish community. Aside from the young immigrants, few actively participate in the social life of Germany. They "perform" their Jewishness because that is what Germans and non-German Jews expect of them, and they are materially rewarded for doing so. Yet, Roberman's informants are aware that they "live at the expense of the memory of the victims of the Holocaust," and many are discomfited by the thought.

Even in Russia itself, Jewish identity has changed since the end of communism, though not in a uniform direction. Elena Nosenko-Stein has studied Russian Jews who live in the "provinces" (not in Moscow or St. Petersburg). The hundreds of interviews that she conducted lead Nosenko-Stein to describe five archetypes of Jewish identity in present-day Russia. She warns that these categories are in flux, and that a stable, common Russian-Jewish identity has not emerged yet, if it ever will. In this regard, Russian-speaking Jews will be no different from Jews elsewhere—there are and will be different understandings of what it means to be a Jew, with different attitudes and behaviors flowing from these understandings.

10 · RUSSIAN-SPEAKING JEWS IN GERMANY

ELIEZER BEN-RAFAEL

A significant portion of the Jewish exodus from the Former Soviet Union [FSU] settled in Germany in the 1990s.[1] Unlike the Russian-speaking Jews [RSJs] who immigrated to a Jewish national society—Israel—and formed a new ethno-cultural entity there, or those in the United States who joined an existing minority, in Germany RSJs came to constitute the overwhelming majority (90%) of the Jewish population. On the ashes of the Nazi destruction, they built a renewed Jewish community even though they themselves had largely lost their Jewish heritage during decades of a Marxist-Leninist regime. Although they had no experience of community life, they nevertheless clung to Jewishness by virtue of identification more than by identity.[2]

MIGRATION, TRANSNATIONALISM, AND RSJS

Present-day globalization[3] compels us to study migration in relation to the formation of transnational diasporas.[4] One speaks of "insertion" instead of "integration," meaning that groups enter new societies without abandoning their allegiance to their original cultures and motherlands. Such developments question how people come to define their collective allegiances, which are not necessarily uniform among members and do not appeal to everyone to the same degree.[5] The contemporary pluralism of Jewishness is a good example of such divergences in identity formation. What seems to still hold most versions together is that Jews worldwide generally refer, *grosso modo*, to the same people when speaking of Jews, and their formulations of Jewishness draw many of their symbols from the same sources, notwithstanding varying interpretations.

Contemporary Jews live in very diverse social and cultural contexts and under a variety of influences. In many Western societies, Jews evolve in environments marked by individualism and a weak density of community life. Jewish identity is grounded primarily in self-understandings that may fluctuate from milieu to milieu or from individual to individual. This is especially true of RSJs in Germany because of their history; they experience a Jewishness that offers few landmarks to which to cling.

What they found in Germany could not fully structure their new existence as a Jewish community. Fewer than 15,000 Jews remained in the country after 1945.[6] A few had settled in East Germany (the German Democratic Republic) in the name of political conviction, while in West Germany, governmental efforts restored physically damaged Jewish institutions. In 1950, a Central Council of Jews was established as an umbrella organization for several organizations that experienced only a slow increase in membership until the 1970s.[7] The sudden collapse of the USSR and Germany's reunification set off an unexpected mass immigration of RSJs in the 1990s, encouraged by special legislation. The number of Jewish communities jumped to 130 with 107,000 members (though there were many more unregistered immigrants). Germany's Jewish population of about 200,000 became one of Europe's largest, and many foreign institutions provided a fresh stimulus to communal growth. Today, Berlin has seven synagogues—Chabad, the Lauder Foundation, the Union of Progressive Jews, and others, in addition to newly created religious and secular organizations active in the city.[8] The research presented here investigates how RSJs react to these externally generated efforts.

THE RESEARCH PROJECT: THE SAMPLE

This research was conducted in 2008–2009 with a questionnaire intended for a representative sample of Jews living in Germany. We reached 1,200 subjects, including 10 percent "veteran" German Jews and 90 percent RSJs (1,018 individuals). In this chapter, we focus on RSJs who were contacted through Jewish schools, clubs, and student organizations, and through snowballing, starting from initial interviewees. This latter procedure weakens the random quality of the samples, but the large number of respondents maintains the credibility of the results.[9] Each interview lasted twenty to twenty-five minutes. The interview questionnaire was available in both German and Russian, and respondents chose the language. During the analysis, we correlated sociological variables with attitudes toward significant issues. Here, we examine selected findings.

The demographics of the RSJs in Germany are instructive. Sixty percent immigrated after the age of eight and have resided in Germany for less than ten years; 29 percent arrived after the age of eight and have resided in Germany for eleven to fifteen years; 11 percent immigrated after the age of eight and have resided in Germany for over fifteen years. On the other hand, this population is relatively aged: 32 percent are under forty years old, 26 percent are between forty-one and sixty, and 42 percent are over sixty. In our survey, 45.5 percent of our respondents were male. In addition, 60 percent of respondents live with a spouse or a partner;

two-thirds of them (66.3%) have children. Finally, 63 percent have a postsecondary education.

INSERTION IN SOCIETY

Nearly a fifth (18.6%) of the respondents are students, a smaller contingent (12.6%) consists of workers or employees, and another contingent (9.7%) are professionals or business people. The salient trait is that over a third (34.1%) are unemployed and live on social welfare, and another quarter are retired. This proportion of nearly 60 percent falling outside the labor market tends to locate this population at the margins of German society. It signals the difficulties of converting human capital acquired elsewhere into locally relevant qualifications. Hence, a majority (59%) evaluate their income as below the national average—a highly exceptional situation for a Jewish diaspora. As a result, this population is not entirely enamored with its new society. Less than half (45.3%) describe their "insertion" in society as (very) satisfactory and only a half "feel at home."

Only a small minority (13.2%) feel close to religious Orthodoxy, while a fifth are closer to liberal Jewish movements. One in every three defines him- or herself as somehow traditional, and another third as secular. One quarter of respondents stem from families where one parent is not Jewish, and 38 percent of those who have a family of their own live with a spouse or partner who is not *halakhically* Jewish.

All in all, this population is still taking its initial steps toward integrating into German society. Characteristically of such a group, differences among respondents fall according to age and length of residence. Age makes a difference on a variety of counts, especially regarding language (see table 10.1). For example, three quarters of the subjects under forty years of age evaluate their German as good or quite good, while the figure for the elderly (sixty-one plus) is much lower. In the family and among friends, who are often RSJs themselves, Russian remains the prevailing language. But the use of German has gained ground among the young in all areas of activity investigated. Those under forty are also more attached to German society and describe insertion into society as more satisfactory than the elderly; unlike the latter, they reject the idea that the memory of the Shoah seriously impedes their progress in German society. Length of stay has a similar impact, but in a contrary direction—German is used more extensively among the more veteran immigrants in a variety of areas, and nearly 60 percent evaluate their command of it as good or quite good; the figure for the less veteran is 25 percent. Moreover, longer residence is also linked to more positive attitudes toward society, greater social integration, and a feeling of being at home. All of the above illustrate the hardships of settling in a new society and the processes of progressive insertion.

Since degrees and types of religiosity can create divisions among Jews, an additional question that arises is the extent to which this factor is relevant for social

TABLE 10.1. The Age Factor

	Under 40 years of age	40–60 years of age	61 years of age and more
1.1 Languages used for reading (N = 935)			
German	14.7	2.5	1.5
Russian	28.4	56.7	70.1
German and Russian	54.8	40.8	28.0
Other	2.0	0.0	0.4
Total	100.0	100.0	100.0
1.2 Watching television (N = 922)			
German	42.3	22.2	15.3
Russian	17.5	31.6	52.6
German and Russian	38.6	45.8	31.7
Other	1.6	0.4	0.4
Total	100.0	100.0	100.0
1.3 Language spoken with partner (N = 748)			
German	14.1	3.8	0.5
Russian	69.6	92.4	95.7
German and Russian	11.0	3.8	3.2
Other	3.0	0.0	0.5
Total	100.0	100.0	100.0
1.4 Language spoken with children (N = 706)			
German	4.3	1.3	1.5
Russian	70.0	89.0	92.5
German & Russian	21.4	9.3	5.8
Other	4.3	0.4	0.3
Total	100.0	100.0	100.0
1.5 Integration in German society (N = 930)			
Not satisfactory	8.6	15.2	21.7
Somewhat satisfactory	28.4	39.9	42.2
Satisfactory	31.0	33.7	33.5
Very satisfactory	32.0	11.2	2.6
Total	100.0	100.0	100.0
1.6 Unpleasant aspects in Germany: Memory of the Shoah (N = 892)			
Not at all	16.1	9.7	9.7
A little	33.9	14.1	6.7
Moderately	30.2	32.0	23.7
Very much so	19.8	44.2	59.9
Total	100.0	100.0	100.0

integration (see table 10.2). Table 10.2 shows that command of German should denote respondents' readiness to invest efforts into social integration.

The degree that memories of the Shoah represent a difficulty for living in Germany as Jews should be indicative of respondents' motivation to fully integrate into the society. On the other hand, appreciation of German culture should point to a readiness to absorb the prevailing culture. Therefore, we asked about respondents' aspirations for their children. Finally, perceptions of the opportunities children have for achievement should show the extent to which the larger society is viewed as open and fair. The data indicate that command of German is still problematic among respondents, that they have mixed feelings toward living as Jews in post-Shoah Germany, and that the objective of learning German culture is only moderately endorsed. Yet, a large majority is convinced that growing up in Germany holds promise for their children. Hence, we discern instrumental, though not overly enthusiastic, attitudes toward German society, but high hopes for the next generation.

TABLE 10.2. RSJs' Integration into German Society

	Orthodox	Liberal	Traditional	Secular
2.1 Knowledge of German (N=861)				
Poor	18.3	30.1	29.6	36.9
Somewhat	29.8	37.7	36.5	32.2
Quite good	32.7	21.3	19.6	14.3
Good	19.2	10.9	14.2	16.6
Total	100.0	100.0	100.0	100.0
2.2 In the context of the past, is living as a Jew in Germany (N = 878)				
Very problematic	9.1	5.9	3.4	10.5
Problematic	50.0	39.4	44.5	31.4
Not problematic	40.9	54.8	52.1	58.1
Total	100.0	100.0	100.0	100.0
2.3 Importance of children's adopting German culture (N = 718; %; Chi sq = 0)				
Not at all	27.9	11.5	10.2	11.5
A little	20.9	9.1	14.4	6.7
Moderately	27.9	46.1	49.3	49.6
Very much so	23.3	33.3	26.0	32.1
Total	100.0	100.0	100.0	100.0
2.4 Positive aspects in Germany: Perceptions of promise for children (N = 660; %; Chi sq = 0)				
Not at all	4.9	7.8	0.5	2.6
A little	4.9	1.3	0.5	0.4
Moderately	24.4	10.4	14.5	13.4
Very much so	65.9	80.5	84.5	83.5
Total	100.0	100.0	100.0	100.0

Considering the relationship of religiosity to these attitudes, we find that Orthodox respondents' self-rated control of German is higher than that of secular respondents, with intermediary religiosity categories falling in between. One possible explanation for this may be, as shown by additional data, that Orthodox RSJs tend to be younger than secular RSJs. This also probably explains the fact that half of the Orthodox respondents' friends are not Russian speaking, while the corresponding figure for the secular is around one quarter. Thus, it appears that religiosity has no direct effect on language learning or integration. At the same time, the secular appear to attach less importance to the memory of the Shoah with regard to integration into society and more strongly insist that children should learn German culture. They are also more appreciative of the social possibilities that Germany offers their children. In brief, religiosity or secularism has no consistent impact on individuals' aspirations regarding social integration. Younger age and length of stay seem to be more important factors.

One might expect endogamy or exogamy in respondents' families of origin and in their own families to influence their degree of integration into society, but we did not find that this factor made much difference. The main finding concerns the social relations of mixed couples: 41 percent of those whose partner is Jewish have close friends who are exclusively Jewish, but that is true of only 25 percent of those living with a non-Jewish partner. Hence, exogamy points to more openness to non-Jews, even though it is still impossible to speak of qualitatively different patterns. All in all, we may conclude here that RSJs do involve themselves in German society but without assimilating to it, at least not at this early stage.

COMMUNITY BUILDING

To what extent are the newcomers joining the Jewish community in Germany and participating in its (re)building? Religiosity, to be sure, should enter into this question, so we found it useful to divide our sample along a four-category continuum: Orthodox religiosity (e.g., modern Orthodox and ultra-Orthodox); non-Orthodox religiosity or liberal Judaism (e.g., Reform or Conservative approaches); traditional orientation (i.e., observance of some customs out of collective solidarity and respect for the Jewish heritage); and secular Jewishness (i.e., absence of any religious or traditional obligation).

Most respondents are members of local Jewish communities, but only a quarter describe contacts with these communities as continuous. The vast majority attends synagogue services only from time to time and has little exposure to Jewish media. Yet, many respondents have either only Jewish friends (as a rule, RSJs). The largest group has both Jewish and non-Jewish friends. Only a few have only non-Jewish friends. Hence, one may speak of Jewish and mixed Jewish–non-Jewish milieus.

Unsurprisingly, Orthodox respondents show stronger attachment to the synagogue than other groups. They are also more exposed to Jewish media and socialize more with Jews in general, and with RSJs, in particular. Hence, Orthodox Jews who are a small minority among RSJs are actually the most active segment of the Jewish community. The liberal and the traditional are less involved, and the secular appear to be the least engaged. On the other hand, it is the youngest age group (under forty) that shows the strongest involvement in the community: three quarters attend synagogue at least several times a year, while the figure for those over sixty is also relatively high—nearly 60 percent. Similarly, length of stay in Germany is significant: respondents who have been in Germany for a longer time show stronger attachment to Jews and Jewry. This means that many RSJs who did not have any Jewish communal experience in their countries of origin have found that their present home-countries are favorable to the building of, and participation in, a Jewish setting.

However, degree of religiosity, age, and length of residence cannot tell the whole story of community building. An additional factor is endogamy versus exogamy. As expected, Jews of mixed ethnic ancestry show weaker attachment to the Jewish community, are less often affiliated with Jewish organizations, and attend synagogue in smaller numbers. Hence, while three-fourths of the respondents who stem from homogeneous families are affiliated with Jewish organizations, the corresponding figure for respondents from mixed parentage is just over half (52%). Similarly, RSJs who live with a non-Jewish partner are less attached on several counts (contacts with Jewish institutions, patterns of socialization, etc.) than those living with a Jewish partner. Yet, it also appears that mixed descent or mixed family life does not necessarily cause a rupture with Jewish life.

In conclusion, we found that the communities that RSJs have greatly contributed to or have revived in recent years still revolve around the synagogue—a religious institution *par excellence*. At the same time, RSJs also form Jewish milieus that include religious and nonreligious people as well as *halakhically* and non-*halakhically* Jewish individuals. This is a community that is by no means an enclave, let alone a ghetto, but is still a distinct entity composed of structures and networks.

COLLECTIVE IDENTITIES

These considerations lead to the central question of collective identity that legitimizes community building. In this respect, RSJs find themselves confronted with many options. Jewishness was RSJs' marker under the Soviet Union, and they could see solidarity with Israel as symbolizing a Jewishness liberated from a dominating regime. RSJs could also see themselves in an identity that combines Jewishness and Russian culture and language. They also could see themselves as "Jews in Germany," combining their allegiance to Jewishness with their presence in Germany. "German Jewishness" would express an aspiration to constitute a "normal" ethnic group in their new society. On the other hand, to consider oneself mainly as Russian speakers would express their solidarity with the ethnic Germans from the former Soviet Union who resettled in Germany in large numbers and who, like the RSJs, carry Russian language and culture with them. Table 10.3 shows how far respondents relate to these various stances. It appears that "feeling part of the Jewish people" is undeniably the strongest allegiance among RSJs. It is closely followed by solidarity with Israel. The third allegiance goes to the RSJs themselves as a focus of commitment, demonstrating the existence of a self-awareness as a collective. On the other hand, feelings of solidarity with Russian speakers in Germany rank only in fourth place, while feelings of belonging to the former country's nation—Russia, Ukraine, or another component of the former Soviet Union—and to the German nation, have only weak appeal.

Seeing the importance of Jewishness, one may ask what RSJs mean by this term. Our data show the following: religion is the primary axis of Jewishness for a slight majority (51.3%); culture comes in second, for a large minority (42.7%); ethnicity reaches the third place, obtaining almost 30 percent; and group solidarity stands fourth with a support of more than a quarter (27.4%). Religious affiliation thus remains the primary motivator, in spite of the fact that only a minority feels close to Orthodox Judaism and another minority follows non-*halakhic* denominations. These findings are supported by the fact that Orthodox respondents show stronger attachment to Judaism and the Jewish people than do the secular. This is further confirmed by the aspiration to give children a Jewish education and to expose them to Jewish media. A majority of the secular have no objections to their child's marrying a non-Jew. Surprisingly, a substantial minority of the Orthodox shares the same attitude. This is probably due to the influence of the open and liberal atmosphere that prevails in German society.

On the other hand, and as expected, many Orthodox respondents conceive of Judaism and the Jewish people in *halakhic* terms, whereas the secular emphasize cultural and educational practices. In accordance with these data, membership of the Orthodox in Zionist or pro-Israel organizations (17%) is substantially higher

TABLE 10.3. Feeling Part of/Solidarity with Given Collectives (%)

Feeling part of/solidarity	Very much	Moderately	A little	Not at all	Index*	Total	N
The Jewish people	47	35	14	4	0.37	100	867
Israel	62	23	10	5	0.36	100	957
The RSJ community	29	39	24	8	0.32	100	930
RS community	17	40	23	20	0.30	100	854
Nation of origin	12	32	28	28	0.25	100	932
German nation†	3	20	31	46	0.16	100	946

*Index calculated by giving numerical increasing values to each answer, multiplying by the number of respondents who choose this value and dividing the sum obtained by the general number of respondents in the given category: (A*4+B*3+C*2+D)/ N.
†On this count, we probably have findings that exaggerate the positive since we did not differentiate RSJs and the veteran non-RS Jews of our original sample.

than that of the secular (5.6%), even though it is still quite low. Also noteworthy is the impact of age. Those under forty express a stronger desire to offer their children a Jewish education while those over sixty, who probably do not have school-aged children, report stronger feelings of belonging to the Jewish people, higher rates of membership in Jewish organizations and RSJ frameworks. Respondents under forty conceive of Judaism and the Jewish people in more *halakhic* terms than those over sixty, and, as mentioned, Orthodoxy is also more popular among this age cohort than among the elderly.

While RSJs are nearly unanimous in their attachment to Jewishness and solidarity with Israel, despite the fluctuations correlating with age, length of stay or religiosity, less unanimity is observed regarding attitudes toward the country of origin and, even more so, the new homeland. Here, age again plays a role. Respondents over sixty maintain stronger contacts than younger respondents with their former country and visit family and friends more frequently. In the same vein, RSJs who have resided in Germany for sixteen years or more also retain fewer contacts with their former country than those who came later. Half of those who have lived in Germany ten years or less visit their former country twice as frequently as those who have lived there sixteen or more years (i.e., at least once every two years).

One should also underscore here that respondents from heterogeneous families refrain from cutting cut off relations with relatives or friends who remained in the original homeland and continue to share feelings for the latter. This complements the finding that RSJs feel themselves to be a distinct group. This supports the thesis that RSJs constitute a transnational diaspora that pertains to the Jewish world, yet, at the same time, is not alienated from other cross-cutting allegiances.

The behavior and feelings of individuals originating from mixed, Jewish–non-Jewish families is especially interesting. Where do they stand in this intermingling of collective identities when compared with Jews who grew up in homogeneous Jewish families?

Individuals from ethnically mixed families feel less a part of the Jewish people, exhibit less solidarity with Israel, and relate more strongly to their country of origin. Yet, heterogeneous family origin does not necessarily cut off individuals from Jewishness and solidarity with Israel. Only a small minority is insensitive to Jewishness or Israel, and the difference from respondents from homogeneous families is by no means drastic. Yet, it is undeniable that these individuals are more attached to their former homelands though, again, without too sharply contrasting with respondents of homogeneous origin who also may retain some feelings for the "old" country.

We wanted to look at the deeper differences in significance of Jewishness according to respondents' endogamy versus exogamy. Table 10.4 shows that both homogeneous Jewish origin and the practice of endogamy are strongly associated with considering Jewish education as at least moderately important; this is clearly less characteristic of respondents who are of heterogeneous origin or who have

TABLE 10.4. Exogamy and Jewishness—Selected Items

	Respondent's family of origin resp.		Respondent's partner	
	Heterogeneous (N = 267)	Homogeneous (N = 683)	Non-Jewish (N = 259)	Jewish (N = 670)
4.1 Importance that children get Jewish education (%)				
Not at all	39.3	26.9	42.6	24.1
A little	22.2	26.4	24.3	25.4
Moderately	20.9	25.2	18.7	28.5
Much so	17.6	21.6	14.5	22.0
Total	100.0	100.0	100.0	100.0
4.2 Feeling about child marrying a non-Jew (%)				
Opposed	10.4	17.5	6.1	21.1
Unenthusiastic support	25.7	43.0	31.7	43.5
No opposition	63.9	39.6	62.2	35.4
Total	100	100	100	100
4.3 Synagogue attendance (%)				
Never	23.5	8.0	19.5	8.6
Rarely	35.1	41.3	41.4	40.6
Several times a year	21.6	27.3	22.6	28.6
Frequently	19.8	23.5	16.5	22.2
Total	100	100	100	100

non-Jewish partners. Nevertheless, a good third of the two latter categories still endorse the importance of a Jewish education, and a majority among them supports it at least "a little." A similar distribution appears with respect to the feelings of respondents toward the possibility that their child might marry a non-Jew. Here, wide majorities accept this possibility in the two exogamous categories. These majorities contrast with the attitudes of the other two categories of respondents. Yet, as with the previous data, we find important minorities that do not easily endorse this possibility.

Moreover, differences between categories tend to fade away on the issue of synagogue attendance. In all categories, those who "never" or "rarely" attend are a majority or near majority. However, the data show that "never" is outnumbered by the sum of the three other categories. This by no means negates the fact that the two homogeneous categories do, as a whole, attend synagogue more frequently that the two heterogeneous ones.

In brief, we find large proportions (though still minorities) of mixed-descent individuals and of those who live with non-Jewish partners who contribute to a fluidity of the meanings of attachment to Judaism among RSJs. Even so, they by no means create a clear boundary beyond which Jewishness is totally lost.

When widening the most important of those three criteria, namely, attitudes toward Jewish education for children, by taking into consideration religiosity, age, and length of residence, we unearth quite unexpected findings. As a general rule, for a majority of our respondents, this kind of education is important. This attitude holds a smaller majority among the secular, but it increases substantially in the other religiosity categories. On the other hand, besides the Orthodox, the strongest support for Jewish education is voiced by both the younger and the more veteran RSJ residents. Hence, notwithstanding the differences of opinion over what constitutes Jewishness, and despite the fact (or perhaps because of it) that respondents themselves were often deprived in this respect in the FSU, they are now anxious to provide a Jewish education for their children.

Table 10.5 shows that settling in Germany strengthens allegiance to Judaism and the feeling that Jewish education for children is a "must." Second, it means that younger RSJs who received at least a part of their education in Germany are more sensitive than their parents or elder siblings to the importance of Jewishness for their children. This, we may deduce, indicates that they also value Jewish education for themselves as well.

These attitudes seem to counter the fluidity of allegiances to Jewishness that we see throughout the RSJ population, stemming from the large number of individuals of mixed descent or who are exogamous and from the hesitancies of many others, for whom the meaning of Jewishness is ambiguous.

TABLE 10.5. The Importance of Giving Children a Jewish Education

	Not at all	A little	Important	Total
1. Religiosity (N = 760) (X^2 = 0)				
Orthodox	7.5	20.4	72.1	100.0
Liberal Judaism	22.3	24.6	53.2	100.0
Somewhat traditional	19.7	23.1	57.2	100.0
Secular	44.9	30.8	24.3	100.0
2. Age groups (N = 795; %) (X^2 = 0)				
40	19.4	23.9	56.7	100.0
41–60	33.5	30.6	35.9	100.0
61 +	35.7	22.9	41.4	100.0
3. Length of stay (N = 831; %) (X^2 = 0)				
10	33.2	22.7	44.1	100.0
11–15	30.9	32.4	36.7	100.0
16 +	13.3	18.9	67.7	100.0

CONCLUSION

We have seen that RSJs insert themselves into German society with undeniable difficulties but that this process becomes smoother with the passage of time and the emergence of younger generations. At the same time, RSJs are also attached to the projects of building communities and forming milieus that correspond to their sensibilities. What moves this dynamism is the feeling of belonging to the Jewish people and solidarity with Israel—the two most prominent allegiances among our respondents. Allegiance to Jewishness is related primarily to religion, despite the fact that most respondents do not identify with Orthodox Judaism and many define themselves as "secular." Though a majority do attend synagogue from time to time, the general attitude among them mixes *halakhic* and educational criteria in their definition of Jewish identity and displays quite liberal attitudes toward exogamy.

In Germany, many RSJs find the necessary conditions to reattach themselves to Jewishness after decades of alienation, though the sons and daughters of mixed families or those who live with non-Jewish partners have more ambiguous commitments to Jewishness. However, our research reveals additional features that mark the singularity of RSJs. It reveals a population that has entered the Jewish world without abandoning its distinctive language and culture. In this respect, RSJs in Germany constitute a segment of a wider and dispersed entity—a transnational diaspora of Russian-speaking Jews—that is now one of the major subgroups of global Jewry. On the other hand, and this is particularly relevant to the case of Germany, RSJs may also see themselves a part of a Russian-speaking population, that is, the "*aussiedler*"—German ethnics who lived in the FSU.

These multiple influences and loyalties raise questions about the future of this population. Michal Bodemann forecasts RSJs' assimilation into the German society on the basis of their "empty Judaism" (my words, not Bodemann's). This assumption, however, is not sustained by our findings that show that RSJs have tended to adopt markers of Jewishness and strengthen their Jewish affiliation. Bodemann also contends that RSJs experienced Nazism less dramatically than other Jewish populations and, therefore, are less reluctant to integrate into German society.[10] This too is not supported by our data, which show an awareness of the respondents to the *problématique* of Jewish life in Germany.

Diana Pinto predicted in 1996 that RSJs in Germany and elsewhere in Europe would be able to contribute to a European Jewry that would serve as an axis of the Jewish world, in addition to Israeli and American Jewries.[11] Several factors cast doubt on this projection—in particular, the absence of a common European language and the numerical weakness of the total Jewish population in comparison with Israel and the United States. Such a project might have to wait for the further "Jewish maturation" of RSJs, which, however, seems well on its way when one considers RSJs' present-day activism. Numerous RSJ figures are already playing prominent roles as rabbis and community leaders, heads of clubs and cultural centers, and RSJ journalists have set up a new press.

RSJs in Germany also participate in transnational-diaspora structures that bind them to their counterparts in Jerusalem, Moscow, and New York. Germany's RSJs who now constitute the bulk of the country's Jewry, are neither a continuation of past German Jewry, nor its transformation or metamorphosis. They are a transplant that is anchoring itself in new soil and developing new roots. It is one more chapter in the history of Jewish migrations.[12] In keeping with this legacy, RSJs, whatever their hesitancies regarding what Jewishness means to them, nevertheless attribute to Jewish education the ability to transmit to the young that which makes Jewish life meaningful.

NOTES

1. Eliezer Ben-Rafael, M. Lyubansky, O. Glockner, P. Harris, Y. Israel, W. Jasper, and J. Schoeps, *Building a Diaspora: Russian Jews in Israel, Germany and the USA* (Leyden and Boston: Brill, 2006); Larissa Remennick, "'Idealists Headed to Israel, Pragmatics Chose Europe': Identity Dilemmas and Social Incorporation among Former Soviet Jews Who Migrated to Germany," *Immigrants & Minorities* 23.1 (March 2005): 30–58.
2. Zvi Gitelman et al., eds., *Jewish Life after the USSR* (Bloomington: Indiana University Press, 2003).
3. Stephen Castles, "Migration and Community Formation under Conditions of Globalization," *International Migration Review* 36.4 (2002): 1143–1168.
4. Yasemin Nuhoglu Soysal, "Citizenship and Identity: Living in Diasporas in Post-War Europe?" *Ethnic and Racial Studies* 23.1 (2000): 1–2.
5. Eliezar Ben-Rafael, "Ethnicity, Sociology of," in Vol. 7 of *International Encyclopedia of the Social and Behavioral Sciences* (London: Elsevier, 2002), 483842.
6. Nachum Tim Gidal, *Jews in Germany: From Roman Times to the Weimar Republic* (Cologne: Konemann, 1998).
7. Julius Schoeps, ed., *Neues Lexikon des Judentums* (Munich: Wissenschaftler aus 14 Ländern, 1998).
8. R. Bachmann and I. Runge, *WIR—Der jüdische Kulturverein e.V. 1989–2009*. (Berlin: Mannheim, 2009).
9. In social science research, snowball sampling is a non-probability sampling technique in which given subjects ("seeds," in the jargon of the method) yield names from among their acquaintances. Thus, the sample grows to a sufficient number of respondents able to provide useful data for research. This technique is often used for populations that cannot be accessed from lists that would make random selection possible. Such a sample might be subject to biases but using many "seeds" from various milieus and places may allow researchers to make quite accurate estimates about the features and attitudes of the population investigated. See Jan Brace-Govan, "Issues in Snowball Sampling: The Lawyer, the Model, and Ethics," *Qualitative Research Journal* 4.1 (2004): 52–60. For a recent example, see the large-scale research by the European Union Agency for Fundamental Rights (FRA), *Discrimination and Hate Crime Against Jews in EU Member States: Experiences and Perceptions of Antisemitism* (Luxembourg: Publications Office of the European Union, 2013).
10. Michal Y. Bodemann, *The New German Jewry and the European Context: The Return of the European Jewish Diaspora* (New York: Palgrave Macmillan, 2008).
11. Diana Pinto, *A New Jewish Identity for Post-1989 Europe*, Policy Paper 1 (London: Institute for Jewish Policy Research, June 1996).
12. Steven M. Cohen and Arnold Eisen, *The Jew Within* (Bloomington: Indiana University Press, 2000).

11 · PERFORMING JEWISHNESS AND QUESTIONING THE CIVIC SUBJECT AMONG RUSSIAN-JEWISH MIGRANTS IN GERMANY

SVETA ROBERMAN

THE CHILDREN OF LIEUTENANT SCHMIDT

"I would call all the people who came here with the Jewish migration to Germany the 'children of Lieutenant Schmidt,' and I am one of them, neither better nor worse than the others," observed Volodia, a man in his late fifties who immigrated to Germany from Ukraine in the late 1990s. Lieutenant Schmidt was a hero of the 1905 Russian Revolution and was incorporated into the post-revolutionary Soviet pantheon. Though Lieutenant Schmidt had only one child, when Volodia alludes to the "children of Lieutenant Schmidt," he refers us to the story of imposture described in the very popular Soviet satirical novel, by Ilya Ilf and Evgeny Petrov, *The Little Golden Calf* (1931). The main character in the story is Ostap Bender, a masterful con artist who, in one of his most famous ruses, passes himself off as a son of the revolutionary hero, Schmidt.

In post-revolutionary Russia, the status of revolutionary hero entitled one to special privileges, including monetary benefits. Pretending to be a hero or, more commonly, the relative of a hero, in order to qualify for special privileges was a widespread practice in Soviet Union.[1] Presenting himself as the son of Lieutenant Schmidt, Bender's character extracts undeserved privileges and material benefits in the Russian provinces, abusing and exploiting the naiveté, ignorance, and dutiful loyalty of local party functionaries. Drawing an analogy between the "children of Lieutenant Schmidt" and Jewish migrants to Germany, Volodia suggests that the immigrants, like Ostap Bender, are impersonating someone else for monetary gain and privileges they do not really deserve. While Bender capitalized on his purported kinship to a revolutionary hero, these immigrants use their Jewishness. Just as Bender was an impostor, Volodia suggests that the migrants are not "real" Jews but impostors.

Volodia, who is himself *halakhically* Jewish, exposes the precarious situation of the migrants' life: even when they are Jews, people doubt that they really are. The phrase that I consistently heard from my interviewees and acquaintances—*my igraem v evreev* [we are pretending to be Jews]—was the strongest reflection of this precarious position. People emerged as "impostors of themselves," to use Laura Nesbitt's terminology.[2] Or, drawing on Erving Goffman's theatrical metaphor, they fail to play the Jewish role successfully, even though they are actually Jewish.

One inspiration for Goffman's analysis of social realities was the philosopher William James, who, instead of asking what constitutes reality, focused on this question: "Under what circumstances do we think things are real?"[3] In this chapter, I explore a situation in which role-playing or passing as Jewish loses its "realness," and the behavior of the individual, as well as that of the group, is not perceived as true. Instead, it is interpreted as "deceit" and "imposture."

I bring together different "theaters" for the performance of Jewishness—artistic and mundane, individual and communal. I examine actual behavior and explore how Jewishness is imagined and narrated with the aim of understanding how and why the project of reinventing Jewishness is so challenging. My objective, however, is to move beyond descriptions of the failure to reinvent tradition. In my larger project, I approach the reconstruction of Jewish tradition by Russian immigrants in Germany as just one arena in the immigrants' larger civil performance. The reinvention of Jewishness is the arena that determines the framing, questioning, and negotiating of immigrants' encounter with the German host state and society and their relationship to the Holocaust.

THE RULES OF THE GAME

For Germany, the acceptance of Russian-speaking Jewish immigrants was another step in repentance and restitution for the Holocaust. As a whole, the arrival of Russian Jews was seen as an opportunity to strengthen the country's aging and shrinking Jewish community and to resurrect German Jewish life.[4] As for the immigrants, most of whom were struggling in the harsh post-Soviet environment, migration to Germany was akin to winning a lottery ticket to the Western world of affluence.

Opening its doors to these immigrants and offering them generous welfare support (particularly during the 1990s), the German state made no particular demands on the newcomers, with one exception: Germany expected them to be Jewish. In other words, Jewishness was the identity that the newcomers were expected to present and perform.⁵ In this sense, Jewishness emerged not as an ethnic, cultural, and religious identity but as an identity by which to cultivate migrants' civic belonging in the host country.⁶ This expectation remained largely implicit in the early stages of migration. For many immigrants, the realization that their "being Jewish" was an essential factor in the migration contract surfaced only after their arrival in Germany.

For Mila, a middle-aged woman from St. Petersburg, immigration to Germany was her opportunity "to leave Russia and live in Europe." After she arrived in the country, she began to realize that she was now expected to perform the content of Jewish identity and practice, which emerged as "the rules of the game":

> This whole project of Jewish migration to Germany.... What was actually its ultimate goal? The creation and re-creation of the Jewish community in Germany. That's why this migration was accepted into the country and allowed to live here, and was provided for and given a lot, by the way.... The people, on their part, have to fulfill the expected terms.... If those are the rules of the game, one has to fulfill them, otherwise it is unacceptable, it is not decent [Russian: *neprilichno, neporiadochno*].

Norms of mutuality and reciprocity, social contribution and obligation, moral responsibility and commitment stood at the core of the Soviet code of civic ethics. Although frequently broken in everyday practice, these norms were well known, presenting an ideal of social life. Thus, in order to establish their civic position in the new country as "moral and decent," Russian Jewish immigrants had to transform themselves into Jews. However, embodying Jewishness was difficult for the migrants.⁷ A wide gap existed between who they were and who they were expected to be. Many jokes reflected this. For instance: "They thought that Nobel laureates in *taleisim* [prayer shawls] would come, and who came? Instead, *we* came [Russian: *a priehali my*]!" The feeling of not really being what they ought to be infiltrated the migrants' consciousness. It surfaced in recurring questions and a sense of puzzlement about their own identity and it created a specific structure of embarrassment and discontent about unfulfilled expectations.

"IT IS EASIER FOR ME TO PLAY THE ROLE OF A NON-JEW"

By the end of the Soviet era, what was left of Jewish identity and Jewishness had been emptied of content and meaning.⁸ Jewishness had become an "empty" or "floating" signifier. "An 'empty' or 'floating signifier' is [something] that can mean different things to different people," writes Daniel Chandler.⁹ Who is a Jew? What is it to be Jewish? Is it possible for a Jew not to be Jewish? These questions have not disappeared from everyday conversations and interactions; they emerge in Internet forums and are frequently discussed in the immigrant media, and there are no definitive answers.

Denis, a man in his mid-forties, has been performing for a number of years in a Jewish theater that was founded by a group of immigrants. Not a professional actor, Denis is cast mostly in minor roles. Contemplating the roles he usually plays, he discovered, to his own astonishment, that they are mostly Germans or anti-Semites. Actually, there is only one role in his current repertoire in which he plays a Jew—a rabbi, at that. Although the part is small, it occupies a rather prominent position in the play. But, "to tell the truth," Denis doesn't like it. He doesn't understand the role; he does not know how to shape the character and present it to the public. He feels he is not suited to the role personally or professionally. Despite the make-up and beard on his face, and despite the fact that he has learned how to walk like an old man, he fails to embody the part of a rabbi.

In the same production, Denis plays another minor role: that of Boris, an alcoholic. The public's reaction to this character is completely different; the audience connects emotionally with him, understanding the character, and laughing at the right moments. It is easy for Denis to play this role. He understands the alcoholic Boris and succeeds in capturing him on stage despite the fact that, as Denis remarks, "Personally, I have never had any inclinations to alcoholism." But, he adds, with a hint of irony, "Despite my Semitic looks, the roles of non-Jews and the roles of anti-Semites are much easier for me than Jewish characters. It is easier for me to play the role of a non-Jew."

Denis was born in a Ukrainian town after the Second World War. On of the eve of the war, Jews comprised a significant portion of the population, and some survivors returned to the town after the war. Denis did not like the Jews of his childhood, though he was one himself. For him—the son of a retired army officer who held a rather prominent position in the town's leadership—the Jews of the older generation, including his grandparents, looked like *mestechkovie liudi* [shtetl people], and the *mestechkovost'* [shtetl manner] disgusted him. He did not like the way that "shtetl people" used to speak: "They spoke awkward, incorrect Russian. They lived in constant fear of their neighbors; and the latter definitely had reason to hate them. There was definitely something about those Jews." Denis pauses. His eyes flick away to the side, and he avoids looking at me. He seems to be embarrassed by what he is saying. For Denis, the world of the *mestechkovost'* remained an appalling place, and for him, it epitomized Jewishness. All his life Denis has been trying to flee from that world of *mestechkovost'*, from the embarrassing "cloak of Otherness" in which he had been "enclosed"[10] by virtue of being born Jewish. However, Denis wonders, "Is it possible to escape it completely, to transform oneself totally?" Denis, to cite Sartre, is "haunted" by his Jewishness.[11] For many of the immigrants I met, Jewishness is repulsive, a heavy burden they must bear. The image of the shtetl presented above is only one of the images that haunt the migrants' microcosm.[12]

Today, the revulsion that Denis feels toward Jewishness and his desire to escape from it—tendencies that dominated Denis's feelings for many years—have weakened. He tries not to speak negatively about the "old world," though he has not yet learned to speak about it positively. Recently, he has begun to develop sentimental feelings toward shtetl Jews. "Maybe it comes with age," he says. "Today, I see them as having kept and preserved Jewish tradition over the centuries... they were really religious people, they did not pretend to be religious, like people do here." Denis concludes, "All in all, it's still a complicated issue for me; today, I can say that I love *evreistvo* [Jewishness], but I have problems with Jews. I feel closer to the Russians. They seem more sincere to me."

IDENTITY DEVOURED BY ITSELF

The motifs of insincerity, pretense, and imposture reappear over and over in migrants' perceptions of Jews and Jewishness in Germany. Why are immigrants' Jewish identity and the Jewish practices they pursue so persistently presented as not really "genuine" or "sincere," but as a kind of pretense? Generations of alienation from Jewish tradition have turned the practice of Judaism into a novelty for many. Thus, the behavior of those newly engaged in Jewish practice is hard for many to understand or to fit into existing cognitive schemas. They manage their inability to understand and accept through skepticism, disbelief, and mockery. "Look at them... the Orthodox!" said someone who had once held a high-status position at the Jewish community center about a group of immigrants who had started to follow an Orthodox Jewish lifestyle. "They know as much about Orthodox Judaism as they know how to build a satellite! They are only putting on a show of being Orthodox...!" But illiteracy in matters of tradition can provide only a partial explanation. To understand better the quotation above, we must look into additional contexts into which the immigrants' Jewishness has been embedded.

"Being of Jewish descent is not a luxury but a means of transportation," according to the well-known, late-Soviet joke.[13] This articulated the realities of the period of late socialism when a rare opportunity to emigrate from the Soviet Union was opened up for the Jews, while remaining unachievable for most others. That opportunity became particularly valuable with the collapse of the Soviet Union and the economic and social crises of the post-*perestroika* era. Jewish origins became a "ticket" to a better life elsewhere. A common saying that had already been formulated in Germany went, "Hardly anybody came to the country to be Jewish," explicitly uncovering the use of Jewishness as a ticket into an affluent Western country. German policies not only created an immigrant group for many whose Jewishness did not mean much, but it also brought in a number of immigrants with fake Jewish documents. In general, the situation devalued Jewishness and raised doubts regarding its authenticity.

Another crucial factor undermining Jewishness was the particular choice of Germany as the country of immigration. Almost every interview I conducted and almost every casual conversation I had with immigrants would either begin with or contain self-legitimating explanations of why they were in Germany and not elsewhere. This pattern reveals the enduring tension and ambivalence of living in the country of the Holocaust, one that had accompanied earlier Jewish immigrants as well. Take, for example, the vivid ambivalence and tension in the two following contrasting claims. Luda, a twenty-five-year-old law student, assertively posited: "Germany is a comfortable country to live in, and I like it, and I should not be ashamed of the fact that I want to live in this country when it gives me such a comfortable life." Another woman in her forties whispered to me: "Here, we are nothing but traitors. We are the betrayers of our grandparents. Many of us feel that way, but few of us would dare to say it. What's for sure is that my grandparents are turning in their graves." Torn from tradition and deprived of its content, haunted by multiple, internalized anti-Jewish images, and further undermined and devalued when used as a ticket for migration to the country responsible for the Holocaust, Jewish identity has been devoured from the inside out.

THE TROPE OF INSTRUMENTALIZATION

If not perceived as genuine, how then is Jewishness imagined and talked about by these immigrants? Jewishness is presented through the trope of instrumentalization, which means that people turn Jewishness into a tool for profitmaking [*kardom lakhpor bo*, in rabbinic terms], just as the "instrumental" concept of ethnicity would predict. Germany, where Jewish life is institutionalized and state financial support of Jewish organizations and communities is an important component of that institutionalization,¹⁴ is fertile ground for the development of this trope. Let us listen to some narratives regarding the instrumentalization of Jewishness and identify the contexts, scripts, and images that nourish and sustain the instrumentalization trope.

After migrating, Dima, today a medical doctor, found himself in a small, formerly East German town. Before the arrival of Russian Jews, there had been no Jewish community in the town. Dima's encounter with the community left him with unpleasant memories: "The leadership of the community . . . it looked like they elected themselves. All of them seemed to be former communists . . . those people who stood at the head of the leadership were not religious at all. But when the 'important' people from the *Land* [state] government came and the media was present and all that, the community leadership demonstratively put on yarmulkes and posed with the Torah scroll." The specific interpretive paradigm of presenting the community leadership as former "party members" who are now playing the role of "devout Jews" emerges as the organizing interpretive scheme in many other immigrants' accounts and descriptions of Jewish communal settings.

As many have observed, behaving "as if" is a salient feature of totalitarian and socialist societies.¹⁵ From the birth of the Soviet state and throughout its existence, the subject's relationship with the collective and the state had to be built on practices of imposture and was governed by the practice of "putting on the masks," as Sheila Fitzpatrick has called it.¹⁶ In order to survive and successfully promote oneself through Soviet hierarchies, particularly in the postwar period, Jews—who were suspected of disloyalty to the regime—had, "more than any other group[,] to adapt themselves to the regime," as one of the immigrants noted.[17] Becoming a "devout communist" was a primary tactic of adaption to the system. These Soviet realities advanced the particular self-imagery of the chameleonic Jew: quick to change identities and match himself to new realities and contexts. According to this image, someone who had once played the role of the "devout communist," and who, upon arriving in Germany, sensing the local context, and realizing that Jewishness has the potential to open doors, took off the mask of the "devout communist" and became "a devout Jew" instead.

As Fitzpatrick notes, the practice of putting on masks has always existed in parallel with the practice of tearing off masks—exposing the imposture. My informants were invested in tearing off the mask of fake Jewishness. The "Jewish tradesman" is one of four prototypical Russian-Jewish archetypes described by Felix Dreizin ("the clever Jew," "the rabbi," and the "family man" are the others).[18] The image of the tradesman is the best developed of the four and is the most common in Russian-Jewish imagery. The tradesman looms, not as a professional category, but as the prototypical national character type. It signifies a particular universe of traits and modes of behavior. Dreizin's description of the tradesman's features notes that "he is of low human caliber." His occupation is a "dishonest business [and] he never hesitates to cheat both Jews and non-Jews. To this end he is willing to humiliate himself [and] to make a clown of himself" to get ahead and make money.[19]

The image of the Jewish tradesman ruling the community has captured the immigrants' imagination. A young immigrant woman who works as a secretary at the community center remarks to a group of visitors that she is guiding around the community building, "They [the leadership] are doing some *gesheftn* [dubious business]. You know, Jews! Jews can't do without making some *gesheftn*," she said. Everything can be turned into a *gesheft*. Among the practices often ascribed to community functionaries was *pripiski*—falsely over-representing the number of community members. *Pripiski* was an everyday, accepted strategy in Soviet life and was used at all levels of the Soviet apparatus. Fraudulent numbers in economic reports, references to nonexistent activities, and so on, comprised an integral part of the creation of the "as if" worlds of affluence, progress, and development in the Soviet Union. In the German context, the practice of *pripiski* was the strategy employed to obtain greater financial support.

For those educated in the Soviet Union, the practice of *pripiski* brings to mind the *mertvye dushi* [dead souls], a manipulative game played by Chichikov—the hero of Nikolai Gogol's masterpiece, *Dead Souls* (1842). During the period of serfdom, Chichikov purchases the "souls" of the dead serfs in order to establish himself as a member of the landed gentry. Soviet-era realities, which were saturated with simulative practices and performances, turned the idiom of "dead souls" into a popular metaphor for various "absent presences" and "present absences." When it resurfaces in Germany, the *pripiski* practice takes on a particularly macabre meaning. Restituting for the Holocaust and trying to restore the world destroyed, the German state supports Jewish organizations and communities. By misusing the allotted funds via *pripiski* (or any other practice of financial fraud), not only do community functionaries violate the German civic order, but their "dead-souls" manipulation of numbers exploits the Holocaust dead as well. This improper use of the past is captured by immigrant discourse in a powerful and sharp metaphor, *doit' Holocaust* [to milk the Holocaust]. "For how long and to what extent is it possible to milk the Holocaust?" someone asked pointedly. Of all forms of the instrumentalization of Jewishness, "milking the Holocaust" is the gravest sin.

Russian Jewish immigrants are said by some to use Jewishness to gain different material benefits while failing to fill it with any content—religious, traditional, or ritualistic—in return. Jewishness is used for free. To use a popular term in the immigrants' discourse, one that is widespread in contemporary Russian slang, immigrants turn Jewishness into a freebie [*halyava*][20] to be exploited. The *halyava* may be an object, service, or privilege that exists outside of circles of reciprocity—a "freebie" often received at someone else's expense. This image of Jewishness becomes tangible in some migrants' perception of the *obshchina*—the Jewish community, which is not presented as a place of collectivity or ritual, but imagined primarily as place to extract *halyava*. "Many come to the *obshchina* for nothing else but to get some *halyava*" was a refrain I heard repeatedly. A free meal at holiday celebrations, a subsidized trip to a children's summer camp, even gossip about a sale overheard at the community premises are examples of the *halyava* that can be received at community centers. "People come to the community just to eat, to eat *na halyavu*. The moment they don't get the food for free in the community, they stop coming, they go to another place," said Ira, an immigrant in her mid-forties, emphasizing the lack of commitment, involvement, and mutual contribution that runs through people's attitudes toward the community and symbolizes attitudes toward Jewishness in general.

"Look! Here they are. Here they are, our *krestonostsi* [Crusaders] are coming," roars Tolia, the security guard in one of the community centers when his security-camera screen showed a group of people approaching the center's doors. He continues: "The Red Cross is situated on this same street, some five hundred meters from here. They go there, fetch food and clothes there, and on their way back, they come to the *obshchina* [Jewish community center] to receive some more *halyava*.... That's why they are coming here, those *krestonostsi!*" Tolia paints the community as a place where people come to get *halyava*, but he also incorporates the term *krestonostsi* to describe the situation. The Russian word *krestonostsi* has two parts: a noun, *krest* [cross] and a verb, *nosit'* [to carry]. Literally, the word means "bearers of the cross." While the expeditions of the medieval crusaders were for the salvation and protection of the cross, Tolia's *krestonostsi* seek *halyava* things. In playing with the word *krestonostsi*, Tolia turns the "bearers of the cross" into bearers of freebie products and benefits. By instrumentalizing Jewishness, using it *na halyavu*, the immigrants turn Jewishness into imposture and appear to be people "playing" at being Jewish, even when they are, in fact, Jewish.

Emptied of content, haunted by interwoven negative Jewish and Soviet imageries, and undermined by factual and imagined practices of instrumentalization, Jewishness struggles to serve as a meaningful frame of identity. Indeed, the entire project of reinventing Jewishness remains far from successful. More than twenty years after the outset of the Russian-Jewish migration, the future of the Jewish project in Germany appears vague and unclear to many, though not all, immigrants as well as to those working and connected with the communities. Among many, the project of resurrecting Jewish life among Russian-Jewish immigrants is seen as an unrealized goal and has been declared a failure.

But what does this problem of reinventing the tradition mean for the migrants' group position vis-à-vis the German host state? Commenting on the situation, one interviewee remarked ironically, "The Germans thought that they were bringing Jews, but it turned out that they brought *goyim* [Gentiles, non-Jews]." Another reflective voice remarked that the situation as a whole looks like "a deception of the German state." The latter statement, though, is too harsh to say aloud, and most immigrants would prefer that such words be left unspoken. The migrant group as a whole is not inclined to open discussion. Tensions and ambivalences are managed through ironic remarks, jokes, and occasional barbed or critical comments. Under the surface lies the immigrants' difficulty to create a recognizably Jewish persona, and, consequently, to position themselves as acceptable civic subjects in their host country. The failure to frame civic German-Russian-Jewish identity in the present complicates immigrants' relations with the Holocaust. The lack of active social and civic participation in the host country (performed via Jewishness, in this case) puts the immigrants in the position of living at the expense of the memory of the victims of the Holocaust. The tension is manifest in the aforementioned phrase, "milking the Holocaust" and is articulated in such phrases as "we are trading our ancestors' ashes" or "we are living on our ancestors' ashes."

NOTES

1. See Sheila Fitzpatrick, *Tear off the Masks: Identity and Imposture in Twentieth-Century Russia* (Princeton: Princeton University Press, 2005).
2. Laura Nesbitt, "Creating Identity Out of the Postcolonial Void," *Journal of African Literature and Culture* 3 (2006): 117–133.
3. Erving Goffman, *Frame Analysis: An Essay on the Organization of Experience* (Cambridge, MA: Harvard University Press, 1974), 2.
4. Franziska Becker, "Migration and Recognition: Russian Jews in Germany," *East European Jewish Affairs* 33.2 (2003): 20–34; Robin Ostow, "From Victims of Antisemitism to Postmodern Hybrids: Representations of (Post) Soviet Jews," *European Judaism* 36.2 (2003), 110–117.

5. See Franziska Becker, *Ankommen in Deutschland: Einwanderungspolitik als Biographische Erfahrung im Migrationsprozeß Russischer Juden* (Berlin: Dietrich Reimer Verlag, 2001); Becker, "Migration and Recognition," 20–34.
6. See Sveta Roberman, *Sweet Burdens: Welfare and Communality among Russian Jews in Germany* (Albany: SUNY Press, 2015), introduction.
7. For an extended discussion see ibid., chapter 7.
8. Zvi Gitelman, *A Century of Ambivalence: The Jews of Russia and the Soviet Union, 1881 to the Present* (Bloomington: Indiana University Press, 2001); Gitelman, "Thinking About Being Jewish in Russia and Ukraine," in *Jewish Life after the USSR*, ed. Zvi Gitelman, with Musya Glants and Marshall Goldman (Bloomington: Indiana University Press, 2003), 49–61; Rosalina Ryvkina, *Kak zhivut Evrei v Rossii? sotsiologicheskii analiz peremen* (Moscow. Paralleli: Dom evreiskoi knigi, 2005).
9. Daniel Chandler, *Semiotics: The Basics* (London: Routledge, 2002), 74.
10. Sander L. Gilman, *Jewish Self-Hatred* (Baltimore: Johns Hopkins University Press, 1986), 3.
11. Jean-Paul Sartre, *Anti-Semite and Jew* (New York: Schocken Books, 1974).
12. For review and further discussion of these images see Sveta Roberman, "Haunting Images: Stereotypes of Jewishness among Russian Jewish Immigrants in Germany," *East European Jewish Affairs* 42.3 (2012): 325–341.
13. Because only Jews, ethnic Germans, Armenians, and some Evangelical Christians were permitted—selectively—to emigrate from the USSR from 1971 to 1989, Soviet wags observed that "A Jewish spouse is not a luxury but a means of transportation."
14. See Y. Michal Bodemann, "'How One Stands to Live There as a Jew . . .': Paradoxes of Jewish Experience in Germany," in *Jews, Germans, Memory: Reconstructions of Jewish Life in Germany*, ed. Y. Michal Bodemann (Ann Arbor: University of Michigan Press, 1996), 19–49.
15. See Alexey Yurchak, *Everything Was Forever, Until It Was No More: The Last Soviet Generation* (Princeton: Princeton University Press, 2005); Slavoj Zizek, *The Sublime Object of Ideology* (London: Verso, 1991).
16. Fitzpatrick, *Tear off the Masks*.
17. Readers' Letters Column, *Evrejskaia Gazeta* [Jewish Newspaper], July 2008, 17.
18. Felix Dreizin, *The Russian Soul and the Jew* (Lanham, MD: University Press of America, 1990).
19. Ibid., 6.
20. There is no consensus regarding the etymology of the word *halyava*. One explanation, proposed in Dal's classic lexicon of the Russian language *Tolkovij slovar' zhivogo velikorusskogo yazyka* (Moskva: Diamant, 1998), connects the word's origin to a Polish word referring to the top of a boot; during visits to others' homes, people used to take food from their hosts and conceal it inside the top of their boots, thus receiving an extra portion that was not their due. Another etymology sees it a derivative of the Hebrew word *halav* [milk] and traces its use back to nineteenth-century Odessa where, every Friday, milk was distributed to the Jewish poor. With this connotation of a "freebie," *halyava* entered the slang of criminals, spreading from there to everyday speech. For more on the concept and practices of *halyava* in the Soviet Union and contemporary Russia, see Roberman, *Sweet Burdens*, chapter 2.

12 · INVENTING A "NEW JEW"

The Transformation of Jewish Identity in Post-Soviet Russia

ELENA NOSENKO-STEIN

Russian Jewry today is a very heterogeneous ethnic and cultural minority that has no common cultural self-identification. In the Soviet era, Jewish self-identification was almost totally separated from Judaism; its Soviet secular variant was based mainly on ethnicity. In post-Soviet Russia, people of Jewish origin began choosing their self-identification amid new challenges—globalization on one hand, and attempts at ethnic and religious revival on the other. What is a "new Jewish" self-identification in today's Russia? How does it differ from other types of self-identification among people of Jewish origin? I propose to describe and analyze the mechanism of constructing a "new Jewish" self-identification in post-Soviet Russia.

In the twentieth century, Russian Jewry underwent profound changes. After being discriminated against as a religious minority in the Russian Empire and subsequently becoming a privileged ethnic group in the early Soviet era, it became an ethnic and cultural minority in the late Soviet period. Currently, Jews in the Russian Federation are a culturally heterogeneous minority, and we can observe several cultural self-identifications among people of Jewish origin. My previous research showed that different types of cultural self-identification among contemporary Russia's Jews are based on various "sets" of symbols and values. Moreover, during the last decade a "new Jewish" self-identification based on the Russian variant of "civil" or "civic" Judaism—a specific set of symbols and practices—became popular among some young people of Jewish origin. It is important to clarify the mechanism of forming this identification as well as to demonstrate the ambivalent role of Jewish organizations in constructing a "new

Jew" in Russia. By "Jews" in Russia, we usually mean people of Jewish origin or an "enlarged" Jewish population that includes both *halakhic* and non-*halakhic* Jews.

SOURCES AND METHODS

This chapter is based on my research conducted since 1999 in several urban Russian centers. Initially, I studied the cultural identities of the offspring of Russian-Jewish intermarriage in Moscow and St. Petersburg, Russia's two largest cities, where the majority of Russia's Jewish population lives. However, almost half of Russia's contemporary Jewish population inhabits small and middle-sized urban centers. Therefore, since 2006, I conducted research in other cities and towns: Smolensk, Penza, Velikyi Novgorod, Krasnodar, and others. All these urban centers, with the exception of Roslavl' (Smolensk region), were located "beyond the Pale" (of Settlement), so these Jewish communities were relatively small. In this research, I continued to study persons of partly Jewish origins ("half-Jews," "quadroons"), but also included individuals who had two Jewish parents ("full Jews") (see table 12.1).

I used qualitative methods, such as oral and life history, since they are particularly useful for studying problems of cultural identity. I gathered 250 in-depth interviews, as well as eighteen "expert" interviews with communal leaders, rabbis, Jewish activists, and the like. Interviews were informal and indirect, but I utilized a special interview guide that included several groups of topics. Interviews lasted from thirty minutes to six hours, depending on the wishes of the informants. While there is no representative sample in qualitative research, I took into account the principle of "theoretical fulfillment."[1] As a result, the texts of the interviews are the main source for this study. Informants told me about many events and their role in forming their self-identification. Informants were aged between seventeen and eighty-eight; 137 of them were women. Of all the informants, 221 had higher education or were students of universities and colleges at the time of the interview. I found informants through my contacts with Jewish organizations, using snowball sampling.

TABLE 12.1.   What Can You Say About Your Jewish Roots?

I am fully Jewish	44.9%
I am three-quarters Jewish	2.9
I am half-Jewish (matrilineal)	17.4
I am half-Jewish (patrilineal)	18.8
I am one-quarter Jewish (each of my parents)	2.9
I am one-quarter Jewish (one of my parents)	8.7
I have more remote Jewish roots	4.4
Total	100

NOTE: N = 320.

In addition, I carried out a quantitative survey to verify the results of my qualitative research. The general sample includes 320 respondents whom I found primarily through Jewish organizations. Most informants were between sixteen and thirty years old or older than sixty. These age cohorts represent the age structure of the visitors and clients of Jewish organizations. The data of this survey are an additional and important source. In some cases I used the data of sociological polls conducted by other scholars.[2]

An additional, very important source was participant observation in the Russian "periphery" during my relatively brief field trips. I also used a number of Russian web resources where problems of Jewish life have been discussed.

DIFFERENT JEWS AND THEIR SELF-IDENTIFICATION(S) IN CONTEMPORARY RUSSIA

Most Jewish communities in Russian urban centers remain quite small due to seven decades of Soviet rule, the catastrophic losses of the Second World War and the Holocaust, mass Jewish emigration in the early 1990s, and low birth rates. There are no truly reliable statistics regarding the total Jewish population in contemporary Russia, and it is therefore an issue for debate.[3] According to the 2002 census, for example, there were about 230,000 Jews in Russia.[4] But these numbers included only persons who described themselves as Jews in the census. Those who had one Jewish parent very often called themselves non-Jews and were not included in these numbers. Demographers and Jewish communal leaders argue as to whether the data are accurate; indeed, the last census's procedure as a whole has been criticized. Nevertheless, these results appear to more or less reflect the demographic reality—most people of Jewish origin, those born both in monoethnic families and in families with one Jewish spouse, who identify themselves as Jews, seem to have been included among these 230,000.[5] We do not know, however, the exact numbers of "half-Jews," *halakhic* or non-*halakhic*. According to some leading Russian demographers, they number more than those with two Jewish parents (700,000 and 550,000, respectively, in 1989).[6] At the same time, scholars point out that the number of Russia's "half-Jews" is constantly increasing. For this reason, there are no reliable statistics regarding the Jewish population of many urban centers. Consequently, scholars must rely on lists relating to community membership, such as the recipients of assistance from philanthropic organizations and even visitors to communal centers. At the same time, it must be noted that many of Russia's Jews do not identify themselves at all with any Jewish community. Ethnic self-identification(s) prevailed in the USSR and still prevail in post-Soviet Russia.

We must note the variability in different countries of Jewish identity and self-identification. Many stress that there is no such thing as a single Jewish identity in the modern world but, rather, different Jewish identities, which can coexist, even in the same country.[7] Indeed, this is even more true of the offspring of Russian-Jewish marriages that are prevalent in Russia today. In many cases, it would be incorrect to describe these people as Jews, because they often declare themselves non-Jews and were brought up in the Russian cultural tradition. Besides, Jewish self-identification evolved rapidly during the twentieth century, becoming ever more diversified.

From the beginning of the Soviet era, the effort to separate Jews from Judaism was very vigorous; a "new Jew" emerged based on new secular symbols and values.[8] However, it was relatively straightforward to construct the Soviet variant of secular Jewish identity and culture since it was derived from the deep crisis of traditional Jewish culture in the late nineteenth and early twentieth century.[9] Overall, after the Second World War, antireligious rhetoric in the USSR diminished somewhat. At the same time, the creation of the Soviet "empire" and its accompanying Russification led to certain preferences in the religious sphere. As a result, there were sources of information about Christianity, such as popular books and scholarly research. In contrast, the anti-Semitic politics of the Soviet authorities resulted in an information vacuum regarding Judaism and Jewish traditions.[10]

After perestroika and the collapse of the USSR, a religious renaissance, real or imagined, began in Russia. Russia's Jews, like non-Jews, were involved in this process.[11] There has been some discussion of the patterns of Jewish religious revival in the 1990s.[12] The revival of interest in Judaism and Jewish culture led to a sudden transformation of Jewish self-identification among at least some people of Jewish origin.

As noted, Jewish identities vary within the same country; this is certainly true in Russia where Jews do not have a common ethnic, national, or religious identity. There is no single common Jewish self-identification but several cultural self-identifications based on different symbols and values. Moreover, when studying them in Russia, we have to consider two different cohorts of informants—those born in mixed marriages and those having both Jewish parents. These "half" Jews and "full" Jews often have different self-identifications and patterns of behavior. I have already suggested a typology of cultural self-identifications for those born in Russian-Jewish families based on the analysis of my interviews.[13] This typology likely applies to the children of ethnic intermarriage in many countries. Here, I propose a typology of cultural self-identifications for both cohorts. It is important to remember that individuals, especially those of mixed origin, can change self-identifications and often do so several times during their lifetime.

1. *"Eastern Ashkenazi" self-identification.* People of this type are mostly elderly (seventy and over). Their early childhood took place in a *shtetl* or in a traditional, Eastern Ashkenazi Jewish cultural environment. Many of them speak or understand Yiddish (48% of respondents in this group); some of them graduated from Yiddish schools in the Soviet Union (a possibility until the mid-1930s). The events of the Second World War and Holocaust are, however, central to their

self-identification.[14] I call them "Guardians" since they preserve some elements of traditional Jewish culture [*yiddishkeit*] except Judaism. Only 4 percent of respondents in this group say that they observe Jewish religious rituals; 18 percent state that they observe some of them. Sometimes they attend a synagogue as part of traditional way of life, but most of them prefer implicit rather than explicit faith. As Yakov B., a seventy-three-year-old pensioner (Veliky Novgorod, 2007), said:

> Of course I am a Jew! All my relatives were Jews, my mother and father were Jews, they lived in Belarus. [...] They spoke Yiddish, me too, I studied in a Jewish school and would like for young people to speak Yiddish now. [. . . .] I don't believe in God and don't visit a synagogue because there is no synagogue here. If there were a synagogue I wouldn't go there; besides I don't like our rabbi. [. . . .] But sometimes I think that it is worth going to a synagogue in order to remember my parents and grandparents. They believed in God and observed everything.

About a third of the informants in this group do not speak Yiddish but have a secular, Soviet variant of Jewish self-identification that became prevalent in the FSU after the Holocaust and the destruction of *yiddishkeit*.[15] For these informants, religion is of little importance. Abram P., an eighty-two-year-old journalist, both of whose parents were Jewish, told me (Penza, 2007): "I always felt that I was Jewish. But I was an atheist and I am an atheist now. I think that one has to adopt a religion with mother's milk. Then it will be a real religiosity, not demonstrative like we can often see now. What is important for being Jewish? Genes, genes, genes! Mother's and father's genes."

Nearly nine of ten respondents consider ethnicity—a belief in common origins ("Jewish blood," "Jewish genes")—most important for being Jewish. These results correlate with the data of other sociological surveys. For example, in St. Petersburg, 81 percent of respondents age seventy and over also gave a positive answer to a similar question about the fundamental essence of Jewishness.[16]

2. *"Russian" (or non-Jewish) self-identification.* These informants usually declare that they are Russians and have never considered themselves Jews, although do not deny their Jewish origin. "Full" Jews, in particular, usually do not reject their Jewishness, although they, like "half-Jews," affirm that they "feel Russian." Both prefer Russian values and often declare that they are Russian Orthodox Christians. They always consider Jews an out-group. This is a positive type of cultural identification with the dominant cultural group. At the same time, informants believe that their Jewish origins are enough in order to be Jewish. Igor L., a sixty-two-year-old journalist, whose parents were both Jewish, told me (Moscow, 2006):

> I know that this is a problem. I am a Jew because my parents and grandparents were Jews. But I was raised in Moscow, Russian is my native language, I love Russian

literature. My mother was a Christian, even in the Soviet period. She never insisted that I be a Christian too. But when I was a student I began reading theological writings of Russian Orthodox philosophers and many of my friends were Russian Orthodox.... Now I know many Jews—they are Christians like me.

Sometimes informants identify themselves with Russians and Russian culture through the prism of Russian Orthodox experience, as Natalia A., a nineteen-year-old student (Moscow, 2000), explained: "I am Russian because I am Russian Orthodox. All my family is Russian Orthodox, we celebrate Russian Orthodox holidays. We never observed any Jewish holidays." She also said that she often went to a church with her mother and Jewish father.

From 1960 through the 1980s, some Soviet Jews converted to Christianity, primarily Russian Orthodoxy. In many cases this did not weaken their Jewish self-identification but, on the contrary, strengthened it. Judith Deutch Kornblatt, who analyzed these late baptisms of some Soviet Jews, interpreted them as a Soviet rather than religious phenomenon (whether Jewish or Christian).[17] Many baptized informants claim they are Jews and have a paradoxical Jewish-Christian self-identification.[18] According to various surveys, between 14 and 24 percent of Russia's Jews are Christians.[19] My research shows that about 17 percent of respondents, both "full" and "half Jews," affirm that they have been baptized, though conversion to Christianity was especially widespread among the children of Russian-Jewish intermarriages.

3. *The "negative" type* (informants declare their self-identification as "internationalist" or "cosmopolitan"). These informants are strongly assimilated and do not differ much from the "Russian" group. However, they associate Jewishness with a negative personal experience. Their negative Jewish self-identification was formed mainly in the context of anti-Semitism. This type of self-identification is widespread in both cohorts of informants (29 percent of the general sample). Most of them are non-believers. For example, Vladimir K., a sixty-six-year-old pensioner (Penza, 2007), said: "Of course, I am a Jew. Who else? My parents were Jews and I have been registered as a Jew in my passport. But there wasn't anything specifically Jewish in our family. Everything was common, like in all Soviet families.... However, sometimes in different periods of my life I experienced negative attitudes to Jews. And I never was silent and didn't keep my Jewishness secret, although some people did so."

Informants also perceive Jews as an out-group except in situations of anti-Semitism when their "dormant Jewishness" immediately awakens. In some cases, informants claim they are Russian Orthodox, and it is a surprise for them to hear that simultaneously held Jewish and Christian identities are incompatible. This realization is a result of the almost total detachment from Judaism and the lack of information available in the Soviet era. For instance, Irina N., a forty-nine-year-old librarian (Moscow, 2000), was astonished: "Why not? This is his or her [the individual Jew's] right to choose a faith. Are there any prohibitions for them? Why can't they be Christians?" However, in the last two decades, even some informants with this type of self-identification have become interested in Jewish culture and traditions and sometimes attend Jewish cultural, youth, or other organizations.

4. *"Ambivalent" or "transitional" self-identification* (29 percent of the general sample). People in this group often say that, in some situations, they are Russians, and in others, they are Jews. They were brought up in a Russian environment, but in recent years some have become interested in Jewish culture and traditions. Informants often call themselves "Russian Jews." Igor B., a forty-three-year-old journalist (Velikyi Novgorod, 2007), ironically observed: "I know that I am a Jew. Why, it would be silly to deny that with such a face. But I am not crazy about my Jewishness.... I am not religious although it is fashionable now to be Russian Orthodox. But I don't go either to a church or synagogue. That is not for me." Informants perceive Jews and Russians either as an out-group or as an in-group depending on their individual situation. Their unstable self-identification is much influenced by their involvement in Jewish life and by anti-Semitism. This type can be considered either positive or negative, with a perception of belonging to either the dominant group or the minority according to the situation. Many informants of this type are unbelievers or agnostic, though some declare they are Russian Orthodox. Most believe in something—a higher power, fate, karma, etc. Sometimes they are interested in Judaism and its history, but they never convert. Alexander S., a thirty-seven-year-old artist who also attended some courses at the Jewish University (St. Petersburg, 1999), said about his family: "My grandparents in both [the Russian and Jewish sides of my family] prayed and observed religious rites. But we were not brought up in any religion because our childhood coincided with the militant anti-religious period in our state." Then he asked me to switch the tape recorder off and said that he was Russian Orthodox but not observant.

5. *"New Jewish" self-identification.* I call it "new" because it differs from pre-Revolutionary Jewish identity, as well as from Jewish identities in the United States, Western Europe, and Israel. These informants had no traditional Jewish education. Nevertheless, they knew something about Jewish values and traditions from older relatives. In recent years, they have often tried to find their Jewish roots by studying Jewish culture, history, Hebrew, and by taking part in Jewish public life. They perform some Jewish rituals and perceive Jews as an in-group. This is a positive identification with an ethnic or religious minority. Few of them become observant Jews. As Denis O., thirty-two, a businessman (Krasnodar, 2007), explained:

I always felt Jewish. It would be ridiculous to deny it—with my face [laughing]. But I was brought up in a very Soviet family. All of us were nonbelievers, never visited a church or synagogue. [....] Several years ago, I became acquainted with a very good rabbi; I had a difficult period, and he helped me a lot, explained many things to me. And I understood that a Jew must be an observant Jew. [....] Since then, my father and brother distanced themselves from me. My father has more or less made up with me now. But my brother cannot accept my choice even now; his brother had been Russian for a long time and suddenly he became an ardent Jew—why? He doesn't want to speak to me.

Some informants were baptized in their childhood or converted to Christianity in an attempt to resolve some internal issues. Esther Ch., a nineteen-year-old student at the Jewish university whose mother is Jewish (St. Petersburg, 1999), said: "I feel awkward, but I was baptized when I was a baby. My mother didn't know that it was not the right thing to do; she was quite ignorant about that and didn't know what was correct and what was not, how to believe and what to observe. But I never believed in all these Trinities, or in Christ."

CONSTRUCTING SELF-IDENTIFICATION

How is this "new Jewish" self-identification constructed? The informants are mainly youth and young adults (up to thirty-five years old). Most attend public Jewish events, and some are even Jewish activists. As mentioned before, the percentage of persons observing Jewish law [*halakhah*] or Jewish rituals in Russia is low—between 1 and 4 percent, depending on social group. Moreover, sociological polls demonstrate the very low significance of Judaism for most Russia's Jews. Thus, less than 1 percent of Russian and Ukrainian Jews believe that knowledge of the basic principles of Judaism is necessary for being Jewish.[20] In 2004, less than 1 percent of respondents in St. Petersburg, age seventy and over, thought that Judaism is the main element in being Jewish.[21] Moreover, my survey shows that even some informants with the "new Jewish" self-identification (about 13 percent) have been baptized (see table 12.2). These results are quite similar to my own (see table 12.3).

Except for a few intellectuals who live primarily in large urban centers, those we classify as "new Jews" are not interested in Yiddish culture; they do not speak Yiddish and do not want to learn it or listen to Yiddish songs and music. They do not hope their children (current or future) will learn Yiddish either. At the same time, 16 percent of our respondents believe that knowledge of Hebrew is important for being Jewish; 4 percent speak Hebrew, and 14 percent would like to study it. According to a survey carried out by Vladimir Shapiro and his assistants in St. Petersburg, about a third of respondents ages 16–19 and 20–29 claim to speak Hebrew poorly or fairly; 5 percent speak fluently or well.[22]

TABLE 12.2. Religiosity among Russian Jews

Nonbelievers	27%
Agnostics	11
Believe in God (Higher Essence, etc., but do not adhere any religion)	25
Judaism	13
Russian Orthodoxy	13
Christianity (do not consider themselves either Russian Orthodox or Catholics or Protestants)	4
Buddhists	4
Traditional cults, worship of nature and its gods	3

SOURCE: Data from a survey conducted by the Sociological Service of Sreda in 2013, http://sreda.org/arena.

TABLE 12.3. If You Believe in God What Religion Do You Choose?

Confession	Percent
Judaism	22.0
Christianity	10.0
Russian Orthodoxy	10.0
Buddhism	2.0
Islam	0
I cannot choose a concrete confession	16.0
I do not answer	2.0
No answer	38.0
Total	100.0

NOTE: N = 320.

"New Jews" are not familiar with East Ashkenazic cuisine but usually mention *matzah* and gefilte fish, which they usually refer to simply as *"ryba"* [fish], as "real Jewish food" (69 percent of respondents in this group). At the same time they believe that *hatsilim*[23] and *humus*[24] are traditional Jewish dishes, though they are technically Israeli. During my research trips to various cities and towns in Russia, no one under the age of fifty could say what *tsimmes*[25] is.

The real shock is ignorance about the Holocaust. My previous research demonstrated that the memory of this tragedy was not transmitted at the familial level in Russia.[26] Sociological surveys conducted among Jewish youth in Russia and Ukraine confirm my conclusions. This survey shows that Jewish students of Jewish schools and colleges have little knowledge of these events: "All respondents said that they had been told about the Holocaust in school, but only 54 percent of respondents . . . said that they knew something about that from home." I agree with authors who claim that "despite a widespread impression, we cannot suppose, at least a priori, that memory of the Holocaust is carefully transmitted from generation to generation in post-Soviet states."[27] Young and middle-aged persons of Jewish origin know little about the tragedy of the Holocaust and do not want to have information about it. They read almost no books (even fiction) about the Holocaust, watch few Holocaust movies (if they do so, they prefer American ones), and rarely listen to stories about it. Even among young informants living in Moscow and St. Petersburg, where Jewish life is rather active, not many know how many Jews were murdered by the Nazis.

What explains this ignorance and indifference? Of course, these tragic events are receding into the past, especially for the youth. Indifference can also be a result of the dramatic attenuation of Jewish collective memory in Russia—the absence of cultural transmission from generation to generation. As far as we can see, lectures and other events in Jewish youth centers cannot fill the vacuum. The absence of a Holocaust museum in Russia (with the exception of small, local museums) or an electronic alternative is also striking.

It should be noted that a "new Jewish" self-identification does not depend on anti-Semitism. Most young informants (68 percent) do not fear anti-Semitism, in contrast to the attitude of informants with "negative" types of cultural self-identification. The survey conducted by Shapiro supports my results: only one-sixth of respondents between sixteen and nineteen years old said that fear of anti-Semitism had influenced their Jewish consciousness.[28] This could be explained by the limited social experience of informants. In any case, their "new Jewishness" is based on other symbols and values. One of them is religiosity. We can observe a tendency toward religious revival among people of Jewish origin, which sometimes results in observance of Jewish ceremonial laws. Some informants who have the "new Jewish" self-identification (4 percent) become Orthodox Jews.

Few "new Jews"—less than one percent—identify with Reform Judaism, the largest of the American Jewish denominations.[29] As we have already seen, some of them prefer Christianity. For those who pursue conversion to Judaism, it is a result of personal choice—a kind of "experiment" or attempt to locate "pillars" for their unstable Jewish self-identification. Some leaders of Jewish organizations claim that 5–10 percent of young informants are both Orthodox and Reform Jews. They pretend to be observant Jews, attend Orthodox (mainly hasidic) or Reform services, and sometimes they attend both. The percentage of observant Jews is higher in large urban centers where Jewish life includes an active synagogue and rabbis. According to some surveys, 13 percent of respondents in the late 1990s identified Judaism as the "most attractive religion."[30] A poll conducted in Moscow's Jewish organizations in 2004 shows that about a third of respondents preferred Judaism.[31] My research reveals that only two to three percent of respondents in Russia's small and medium-sized urban centers are observant Jews.

In spite of all outreach efforts by the Chabad Lubavitch movement and its sponsors, most young people of Jewish origin prefer Reform and Conservative Judaism (table 12.4), although most of them blend the Reform and Conservative movements.

TABLE 12.4. What Movement in Judaism Do You Prefer?

Movement	Age					
	16–19	20–24	25–34	35–54	55–69	70+
Orthodox Judaism	0.0%	0.0%	33.3%	0.0%	27.8%	15.8%
Hasidism	0.0	16.7	0.0	7.7	5.6	0.0
Conservative Judaism	25.0	0.0	11.1	7.7	5.6	10.5
Reform Judaism	25.0	16.7	11.1	23.1	11.1	15.8
It does not matter	0.0	0.0	11.1	7.7	5.6	0.0
Another answer	0.0	16.7	0.0	7.7	16.7	10.5
I do not know the differences among them	50.0	50.0	33.3	38.5	22.2	36.8
No answer	0.0	0.0	0.0	7.7	5.6	10.5
Total	100.0	100.0	100.0	100.0	100.0	100.0

NOTE: N=320.

People with the "new Jewish" self-identification prefer ceremonial laws and rites that they consider important. This is a kind of so-called "civil religion"—a set of symbols and values, both religious and secular, highly esteemed by members of the community and of great importance for a particular individual—that can be observed in many countries.[32] This civil religion includes respect for some religious and nonreligious symbols and values that are widespread in a particular community or state. It is typical for people who choose a "civil religion." Some also speak of a "civil Judaism," which is widespread in some countries as a kind of quasi-religion that includes various symbols and practices,[33] including: Judaism, Torah, the Sabbath, Jewish festivals (especially Passover and Chanukah), the Holocaust, support for the State of Israel, and Jewish names. Some also include anti-Semitism, Jewish social circles, and Jewish education.

The so-called "Jewish renaissance" in Russia is only fifteen to twenty years old, so a Russian variant of "civil Judaism" is just beginning to form. It often imitates Israeli or American models. My research allowed me to define some patterns of "civil Judaism" in Russia.[34] Thus, Russians with the "new Jewish" self-identification tend to prefer:

1. The Sabbath (informants usually refer to it as *shabbat* and sometimes use the Russian word *subbota* but never say *shabes*). Usually informants just light candles and occasionally "welcome the Sabbath" at communal or youth centers. Slightly more than half the respondents in this group think that the Sabbath is the main Jewish ritual.
2. About a third of the respondents in this group said they observe some elements of kashrut. They "try not to eat pork," at least at youth centers. The head of one of these centers told me (Moscow, 2009) that members of the Jewish youth club fast during Yom Kippur but eat pork at home on other days. Some

"new Jews" (12 percent) try not to mix milk and meat but purchase food in non-kosher stores.

Matvey R., a twenty-year-old student whose father is Jewish, told me (St. Petersburg, 1999): "My religious principles largely coincide with Judaism but I am not observant. [I am] partly observant."—"What do you observe?"—"Mostly the Sabbath, sometimes festivals and kashrut—in a specific manner—I try not to eat pork and mix milk and meat." Jewish festivals (especially Chanukah and Purim) are the most popular holidays—34 percent and 26 percent, respectively are observed in this group—as they are joyous. Many informants, not only those with the "new Jewish" self-identification, consider Passover "boring." Other surveys show that the most popular holidays are Rosh Hashanah (the Jewish New Year), Chanukah, Purim, and Passover.[35]

3. The State of Israel is important to about a third of this group. For informants with the "new Jewish" self-identification, this means an interest in the country, expressed through youth programs, trips to Israel, lectures, movies, and educational programs in Israel. At the same time, immigration to Israel is no longer attractive to most young respondents. Only three percent of young people from small and middle-sized urban centers say they will move to Israel; most prefer to relocate to large Russian cities, especially Moscow.
4. Preference for marrying a fellow Jew or at least a person of Jewish origin (14% of respondents). Anna S., who is twenty-six years old and works at the Jewish cultural center, commented (Moscow, 2004): "When I got married [her husband is Jewish], his origin didn't matter, I even didn't know about it. But now, after I started working at our center, I see that this was good luck. I feel Jewish and try to observe what I can. So, I can live only with a Jew. There are some unmarried girls at our Center, they say: 'I'd marry a Jew. Whom else?' Otherwise it would be impossible. Besides, Jewish husbands are better."
5. Jewish names. A few respondents (6 percent) want to use Jewish names, at least when socializing at Jewish youth centers. At home, they usually use their former, non-Jewish names. Stas K., a twenty-one-year-old student whose father is Jewish, said (Penza, 2007): "I ask everybody here [at the youth center] to call me David. Why David? You see, my name is not Jewish and I want to have a Jewish one. Besides, I am red haired like King David."
6. Studying sacred texts (4% of respondents in this group). This ranks lowest, confirming that Judaism is not of great importance for those we have termed "new Jews."

As mentioned, only some young respondents believe that these rituals and practices—the Russian variant of "civil Judaism"—are important for being Jewish. However, many young people of Jewish origin after "being Jews" for some time, stop being so. Many of them perceive these symbols and rituals as a kind of game or youth fashion. Most of them come to prefer a secular Jewish self-identification or even a non-Jewish one, not thinking anymore about their "Jewish roots."

CONCLUSIONS

The "new Jewish self-identification" is uncertain and unstable; it is still in the process of formation. Because the Jewish family plays a very minimal role in the transmission of Jewish cultural heritage, the East Ashkenazic self-identification has little impact on "new Jews." At the same time, the significance of various Jewish organizations and youth programs that are constructing a new Jewish identity in Russia is only growing.

NOTES

1. Martin Hummersley, *The Dilemma of Qualitative Method: Herbert Blumer and the Chicago Tradition* (London and New York: Routledge, 1989); Daniel Bertaux, "From the Life History Approach to the Transformation of the Sociological Heritage," in *Biography and Society: The Life History Approach in the Social Sciences*, ed. Daniel Bertaux (Berkeley: University of California Press, 1981).
2. Valery Chervyakov, Zvi Gitelman, and Vladimir Shapiro, "Thinking about Being Jewish in Russia and Ukraine," in *Jewish Life after the USSR*, ed. Zvi Gitelman with Musya Glants and Marshall I. Goldman (Bloomington: University of Indiana Press, 2003), 49–60; Zvi Gitelman, Valery Chervyakov, and Vladimir Shapiro, "Natsional'noe samosoznanie rossiiskikh evreev. Rezultaty sotsiologicheskogo issledovaniya 1997–1998," *Diaspory* [*Diasporas*] 3 (2000): 52–86; Rosalina Ryvkina, *Kak zhivut evrei v Rossii? Sotsiologicheski analiz peremen* (Moscow: Parallely, 2005); Vladimir Shapiro, Maria Gerasimova, Irina Nizovtseva, and Natalia Sianova, "Evrei Sankt-Peterburga: uchastie v obshchinnoi zhizni," *Diaspory* 3 (2006): 95–149.
3. Mark Kupovetsky, "Yehudei brit ha-moatsot le-she'avar: misparim ve-hitiashvut ba-olam," in *Yehudei brit ha-moatsot be-me'avar*, ed. Liudmila Dymerskaya-Tsigelman (Jerusalem: Hebrew University in Jerusalem, Centre for Research and Documentation of East European Jewry, 2002) 4.19: 132.
4. *Osnovniye itogi Vserossiiskoi perepisi naseleniya 2002 goda* (Moscow: Goskomstat, 2003), 13.
5. Note that in the 2010 census, the number of self-identified Jews declined to about 156,000.
6. Alexandr Sinelnikov, "Nekotoriye demograficheskiye posledstviya assimilyatsii evreev v SSSR," *Vestnik evreiskogo universiteta v Moskve* 1.15, 85.
7. Jonathan Webber, "Modern Jewish Identities," in *Jewish Identities in the New Europe*, ed. Jonathan Webber (London: Oxford Centre for Hebrew and Jewish Studies, Littman Library of Jewish Civilization, 1994), 76–80; Bernard Wasserstein, *Vanishing Diaspora: The Jews in Europe since 1945* (London: Penguin Books, 1997).
8. This process in the first two decades of the Soviet era has been described by Anna Shternshis, *Soviet and Kosher: Jewish Popular Culture in the Soviet Union, 1923–1939* (Bloomington: Indiana University Press, 2006); see also Zvi Gitelman, *Jewish Nationality and Soviet Politics* (Princeton: Princeton University Press, 1972) and David Shneer, *Yiddish and the Creation of Soviet Jewish Culture* (New York: Cambridge University Press, 1994).
9. Jonathan Frankel, *Prophecy and Politics: Socialism, Nationalism and Russian Jews, 1862–1917* (New York: Cambridge University Press, 1981); Zvi Gitelman, *A Century of Ambivalence: The Jews of Russia and the Soviet Union, 1881 to the Present* (Bloomington: Indiana University Press, 2001); Steven Zipperstein, *Imagining Russian Jewry: Memory, History, Identity* (Seattle: University of Washington Press, 1999); Benjamin Nathans, *Beyond the Pale: The Jewish Encounter and Late Imperial Russia* (Berkeley: University of California Press, 2002).

10. Gennady V. Kostyrchenko, *Gosudarstvenny antisemitizm v SSSR: Ot nachala do kulminatsii, 1938–1953* (Moscow: Materik, 2005).
11. Semyon V. Kozlov, *Evrei v Moskve v 90-e gody XX veka: Deistvitel'no li proiskhodit religiozny renesans?* (Moscow: Institut etnologii i antropoligii RAN, 1999); Elena Nosenko, *Byt' ili chuvstvovat'? Osnovnye aspekty samoidentifikatsii s potomkov smeshannykh brakov v sovremennoi Rossii* (Moskva: Kraft+—Institut vostokovedenia RAN, 2004).
12. Yuri Tabak, "Relations between Russian Orthodoxy and Judaism," in *Proselytism and Orthodoxy in Russia: The New War for Souls*, ed. J. Witte and M. Bourdeaux (New York: Orbis, 1999), 141–150; Anna Shternshis, "Kaddish in a Church: Perceptions of Orthodox Christianity among Moscow Jews in the Early Twenty-First Century," *Russian Review* 66 (April 2007): 273–294.
13. Nosenko, *Byt' ili chuvstvovat?*, 52–53.
14. I have written about the role of the Holocaust and Jewish resistance in Elena Nosenko-Stein, "Nevstrecha pokoleniy? Puti formirovaniya evreiskoi samoidentifikatsii v sovremennoi Rossii," in *Dialog pokoleniy v slavianskoi i evreiskoi kulturnoy traditsii*, ed. Olga Belova (Moscow: Institut slavianovedenia RAN; Tsentr 'Sefer,' 2010), 207–221.
15. See, for example: Mordechai Altshuler, *Soviet Jewry Since the Second World War* (New York: Greenwood Press, 1987); Yaacov Ro'i and Avi Becker, eds., *Jewish Culture and Identity in the Soviet Union* (New York: New York University Press, 1991); Zvi Gitelman, *A Century of Ambivalence: Revolution, Repression, and Revival: The Soviet Jewish Experience* (Lanham, MD: Rowman & Littlefield, 2007).
16. Shapiro et al., "Evrei Sankt-Peterburga," 116.
17. Judith Deutsch Kornblatt, "Jewish Converts to Orthodoxy in Russia in Recent Decades," in *Jewish Life after the USSR*, ed. Zvi Gitelman, with Musya Glants and Marshall I. Goldman (Bloomington: Indiana University Press, 2003), 220.
18. See about this phenomenon: Elena Nosenko-Stein, "Aliens in an Alien World: Paradoxes of Jewish Christian Identity in Contemporary Russia," *East European Jewish Affairs* 40.1 (April 2010): 19–41.
19. According to a poll conducted by Zvi Gitelman et al., 13.7 percent of Russia's Jews "prefer Christianity." See Zvi Gitelman, Valery Chervyakov, and Vladimir Shapiro, "Natsional'noe samosoznanie rossiiskikh evreev. Materialy sotsiologicheskogo issledovania, 1997–1998 gg. Zavershenie temy," *Diaspory* [*Diasporas*] 3 (2001): 72. According to a survey by Rozalia Ryvkina, the percentage of baptized Jews who attend different Jewish organizations, is extremely high—24 percent. See Ryvkina, *Kak zhivut evrei v Rossii?*, 120.
20. Chervyakov et al., "Thinking about Being Jewish," 52.
21. Shapiro et al., "Evrei Sankt-Peterburga," 117.
22. Ibid., 107.
23. Eggplant dish.
24. Ground up chickpeas.
25. A traditional East European Jewish stew, usually made with carrots, fruit, and meat.
26. Elena Nosenko-Stein, "'Lost Jews,' 'Chimeras,' or 'The Hope of the Nation?' Jews, Russia, Mixed Marriages, and Historical Memory Revisited," *Anthropology and Archaeology of Eurasia* 48.1 (Summer 2009): 39–66.
27. Zeev Khanin, Alek Epstein, and Viacheslav Likhachev, "Proiekt 'MASA Shorashim': soderzhatel'nye i pedagogicheskie aspekty (sotsiologicheskiy analiz)" (manuscript).
28. Vladimir Shapiro, Maria Gerasimova, Irina Nizovtseva, and Natalia Sianova, "Evrei Sankt-Peterburga: uchastie v obshchinnoi zhizni," *Diaspory* 4 (2006): 175.
29. See Alexandr B. Sinelnikov, "Evrei 'po otsu' i 'oti dedu': nekotorye rezultaty sotsiologichesk ogo oprosa v letnykh evreiskikh lageriakh NETSER," in vol. 2 of *Nauchnye trudy po iudaike*:

Materialy XVII Mezhdunarodnoi ezhegodnoi konferentsii po iudaike' (Moskva: Sefer, 2010), 280–293.

30. Gitelman et al., "Natsional'noie samosoznane," 72.
31. Ryvkina, *Kak zhivut evrei v Rossii?*, 120.
32. Robert N. Bellah, "Civil Religion in America," *Daedalus* (Winter 1967); Robert N. Bellah, *Beyond Belief: Essays on Religion in a Post-Traditional World* (New York: Harper and Row, 1991); Charles S. Liebman and Eliezer Don Yehiya, *Civil Religion in Israel: Traditional Judaism and Political Culture in the Jewish State* (Berkeley: University of California Press, 1983).
33. Jonathan S. Woocher, *Sacred Survival: Religion of American Jews* (Bloomington: Indiana University Press, 1986).
34. Elena Nosenko-Stein, "Iudaizm, khristianstvo ili 'svetskaia religia'?: Vybor rossiyskikh evreev," *Diaspory* 2 (2009): 6–40.
35. Shapiro et al., *Evrei Sankt-Peterburga*, 112.

PART V MIGRATION AND RELIGIOUS CHANGE

For Marxists, religion is a fantasy, used to divert the attention of the exploited from their misery to delusions of a better life after the earthly one. According to this worldview, religion was craftily exploited by the ruling classes as a defense against a revolt by the downtrodden. Once the proletariat seized power, religion would no longer be needed as an instrument of rule, nor could it withstand the challenges of science. Especially in Russia, where, as a nineteenth-century official put it, the system rested on three pillars—autocracy, the Russian nationality, and Russian Orthodoxy—once the tsarist system was overthrown, those pillars would either collapse by themselves or would have to be destroyed.

Immediately after the Revolutions of 1917, with revolutionary fervor, the Bolsheviks set out to destroy religious institutions, challenge religious beliefs, and drive religious functionaries into "productive" work. Organizations of militant atheists and the agitation-propaganda department of the Communist Party mounted campaigns to inspire the "toiling masses" to seize religious institutions and turn them into workers' clubs, schools, libraries, museums, and workshops. Atheism was a required course in institutions of higher learning and was promoted by the mass media and public programs. Although campaigns against religion abated during the Second World War, they were relaunched in 1957–1964. Atheism remained a central tenet of Communist ideology until the collapse of the Soviet system.

Judaism was certainly not one of the historical "pillars" of the tsarist regime, but, in the Bolsheviks' eyes, it had the same pernicious effects as other religions and had to be eliminated from Soviet society. Hundreds of synagogues were closed or assigned to other purposes, as were thousands of churches and mosques. The law forbade teaching religion to anyone under eighteen; no religious texts were published; and no contact was permitted with Jewish religious institutions or leaders abroad. The result was at least two or three generations who were ignorant of the beliefs and practices of Judaism. Remnants of traditional religion survived in people's memories until the pre-revolutionary generation had passed away, but their meaning and significance were unknown. Only with *glasnost* and *perestroika* in the late 1980s was religious teaching resumed, most often by people coming from abroad, and public religious life revived.

Therefore, it is no surprise that some who left the USSR for places less hostile to religion chose to investigate Judaism and found meaning in it. A far smaller group has found Christianity more appealing. Since the Soviet system distinguished sharply between religion and ethnicity, claiming to be simultaneously Jewish and Christian poses less of a problem for Russian-speaking Jews than it does for Westerners and Israelis, who see such an identity as an oxymoron.

Nelly Elias and Julia Lerner, both FSU immigrants to Israel, sensitively investigate an immigrant church in southern Israel and the "Christian spiritual quest of immigrant youngsters who are of non-Jewish or mixed ethnic origin." The authors suggest that immigrants look to religion as a source for personal identity formation, a supportive community, and a means to assert a transnational identity shared with fellow believers in the FSU and elsewhere. Ironically, for some, religion—even if Christian—is "a way to belong to the Israeli national collective." This is so because "the national religion in Israel that links nationality with religion also accentuates religious affiliation as the most legitimate mechanism for social and political belonging. By contrast, the post-Soviet universalistic character of spiritual beliefs provides grounds for adopting alternative ways of belonging that extend beyond the boundaries of Israeli national religion."

Of course, for most who turn to religion, Judaism is their faith of choice. "Return" [*teshuvah*] is often a tortuous path, strewn with false starts, retreats, deviations, and even turning back. The *ba'al teshuvah* has a long history in Judaism, but Anna Shternshis shows how contemporary technology is used to create and subsequently reinforce self-conscious, transnational communities of Russian-speaking returnees to Judaism. Today, people who originate from the same state but now live in different countries are connected more intensely and frequently by the Internet than earlier waves of migrants could be. The subset that seeks religious affiliation also enjoys these increased opportunities for connection. Shternshis examines blogs to gain insight into the subculture of Russian *ba'alei teshuvah* and the dilemmas they face. She focuses on a blog that ran in 2004–2008 "and was devoted to criticism of the Jewish Orthodox lifestyle from the point of view of a person who experienced a 'return to Judaism' and then regretted it." The narrative resembles *maskilic* [Jewish "Enlightenment"] autobiographies of the early nineteenth century and, perhaps ironically, Soviet antireligious propaganda. Shternshis suggests that her analysis of the popular site Livejournal, which "combines the intimacy of a diary with the public openness of a town hall and becomes a virtual home for subgroups in the Russian Jewish diaspora," reveals the potential of the blogosphere as a source for ethnographic research.

The chapters make clear that just as migration brings about social, cultural, and political change, it can lead to migrants changing their religious beliefs and behavior, or lack thereof.

13 · POST-SOVIET IMMIGRANT RELIGIOSITY

Beyond the Israeli National Religion

NELLY ELIAS AND JULIA LERNER

This chapter presents some preliminary insights from our ongoing research that seeks to cast light on immigrants' religiosity by examining the construction of religious identity and consciousness among post-Soviet immigrants in Israel. This immigrant group is especially interesting, not only with regard to recent religious trends in Israeli society, but also in connection with global interest in immigrant religiosity. We first explore the theoretical and contextual complexity of the content and context of Russian-speaking immigrant religiosity in Israel and suggest three possible explanations for the global and local nature of this emerging religiosity. Then, we apply our approach to the analysis of two cases that represent different manifestations of religious choice among Russian-speaking immigrants in Israel that fall outside the boundaries of the Jewish "national religion"—the immigrant church in southern Israel and the Christian spiritual quest of immigrant youngsters who are of non-Jewish or mixed ethnic origin.[1] Bringing these cases together, we consider the Russian-speaking immigrants' religious transformation at the crossroads of two cultural and ideological contexts: the Israeli national context, which emphasizes Judaism as path to belonging, and the Russian-Soviet context, which is ambivalent toward religion and provides multiple options for spiritual seeking.

RUSSIAN-SPEAKING IMMIGRANTS IN ISRAEL VIS-À-VIS RELIGION: THE CONTEXT OF THE STUDY

The massive wave of immigration in the 1990s, followed by a smaller stream that continues until today, have brought about one million immigrants to Israel from the former Soviet Union. This highly heterogeneous collective was welcomed in Israel according to the Law of Return and was considered a mass Jewish homecoming. Israel officially encouraged and welcomed this arrival of immigrants from the FSU because of its potential contribution to the "demographic wars" taking place within Israeli society between Jews and Arabs, *Ashkenazim* and *Mizrahim*.[2] The expected contribution of the ex-Soviet immigrants to the demographic tension and "culture war" between secular Jewish Israelis and the religious ones is extremely important for our subject.

However, some unexpected dynamics have appeared. First, state institutions soon discovered that a high percentage of the Russian-speaking immigrants belong to "ethnically mixed" families, and many of them cannot be considered Jewish according to *halakhah*.[3] Thus, for example, because of the inseparability of religion and state in Israel, these immigrants cannot marry in Israel or be buried according to Jewish rituals. Furthermore, if they wish to "correct" their "incomplete" Jewishness, they must convert to Judaism, a process that includes the theoretical and practical study of Judaism, and, more importantly, requires proof that the potential convert is actually practicing a religious way of life.[4]

Another reason to question the Jewishness of the post-Soviet immigrants is their cultural distance from Jewish religious traditions, sometimes accompanied by complete ignorance of the Jewish calendar, holidays, and religious codes. Indeed, it is well documented that Jews in the USSR defined their Jewishness mostly in ethnic terms, while their affiliation with Judaism was not seen as an important ingredient in their collective and personal identities.[5] This "ethnic," nonreligious Jewish identity is directly linked to the Soviet background of these immigrants and their participation in the Soviet modernization and secularization project.[6]

Why is it, then, that almost twenty years after immigration, a rather different picture has emerged? According to surveys conducted in the last decade, 30 percent of Russian-speaking Israelis define themselves as "religious,"[7] whereas Larissa Remennick and Anna Prashizky report that only about 30 percent define themselves as nonbelievers,[8] making the rate of FSU immigrants affiliated with some sort of faith even higher than previously thought.[9] Similarly, there is some visible evidence of Russian-speaking immigrants' active participation in local religious communities, both Jewish and Christian.[10] In this chapter, we suggest three possible explanations for the increasing religiosity of the Russian-speaking immigrants in Israel.

Immigrants and Religion

Immigrant religiosity often intensifies during the transition period after arrival.[11] This tendency is hardly surprising in light of the many resources (cultural, social, psychological, etc.) that religion in general, along with participation in the religious community, offers to immigrants during the relocation process. These resources fall into three categories: those pertaining to identity, to community, and to transnational identity.

First, immigrants employ religion as a source of identity. Indeed, religion provides symbols, rituals, and practices that immigrants can use to affirm, pass on, or reinvent who they are vis-à-vis their host and the home countries. Through particular religious choices and practices, immigrants may seek assimilation into the host country's religious models[12] and adoption of a new identity and self,[13] or, alternatively, they may seek to preserve important aspects of their homeland identities.[14]

Second, soon after arrival, immigrants establish their own religious communities that fulfill important functions transcending the traditional role of religious communal life for non-migrant populations. Newly founded religious communities offer immigrants a familiar setting in an unfamiliar world; many even function as extended families for their members, symbolically replacing distant relatives.[15] In addition, these communities may effectively respond to the immigrants' instrumental needs, offering the newcomers material and financial support and improving their access to social and cultural capital, thereby facilitating their personal and collective empowerment.[16]

Third, religious affiliation can connect immigrants to transnational and diasporic institutions, facilitating their relocation from beyond the national borders. The literature shows that immigrants' religious ideas, rituals, and practices are often linked to religious institutions in their country of origin, as well as to ethno-religious communities in other countries where their diaspora resides. That is, the immigrants may use religion to assert a transnational identity through active membership in religious organizations with which they were affiliated prior to emigration.[17]

Scholars of immigrant religiosity have explored religion as a relocation device, but they have less to say about religious transformation among predominantly irreligious immigrants who become religious as a result of their migration.[18] Possible explanations for neophyte immigrant religiosity have been examined mostly in studies on the psychology of religion and focused on its therapeutic features. The insights of these studies correspond to the dominant assumptions in psychology of immigration that consider migration traumatic, accompanied by loss and disorientation.[19] As such, this explanation excessively "psychologizes" both phenomena, limiting them to trauma and immigrants' psychological needs and neglecting their political and cultural meanings. There is another possible explanation for Russian-speaking religiosity in Israel: religion as a way to belong to the Israeli national collective.

Israeli "National Religion"

The centrality of Judaism to the definition of the dominant collective identity in Israel, its articulation as a right to national belonging, and the incorporation of religious affiliation into the foundations of Israeli citizenship certainly influences newcomers.[20] In their study of FSU immigrants' attitudes toward religion, Remennick and Prashizky conclude that just as their counterparts in Russia lean toward Russian Orthodoxy—reflecting the predominant religious milieu—FSU immigrants in Israel drift toward mainstream Israeli norms shaped by the Jewish calendar, holidays, and customs.[21]

Therefore, it appears that the new arrivals gradually adopt or imitate some of the surrounding religious patterns. However, this "integration" thesis fails to explain the adoption of religious choices distinct from the dominant religion in Israel, since some Russian-speaking immigrants join not only mainstream religious congregations, but also become members of ultra-Orthodox and marginalized Jewish religious frameworks, or turn to various forms of Christianity.[22] These religious choices cannot be explained simply by the thesis of integration and belonging but are grounded in the cultural and (ir)religious background of the post-Soviet immigrants.

Post-Soviet Subjects, Post-Soviet Religiosity

FSU immigrants' multivariant religiosity should also be understood through the prism of post-Soviet studies[23] and in the context of a transnational, post-Soviet religious revival. The rapid reconstitution and institutionalization of religious life in the post-Soviet states has combined with a flourishing popular religiosity. In this regard, our informants told us that in today's Moscow "to admit to your coworkers that you don't believe in God is just inappropriate."

Indeed, while Soviet ideology did strive to create a "New Man" inspired by materialist and scientific worldviews, a careful examination of the Soviet ideological and cultural system casts doubts on this process and its results. As suggested by scholars and historians of communist ideology, the dogmas and beliefs of Marxist-Leninist ideology operated rather like theological and eschatological religious systems.[24] The precise ritualistic implementation of these beliefs in the everyday life of the Soviet people reflects the highly ritualistic and performative nature of cultural conditions during the late Soviet period.[25]

Moreover, Marxism-Leninism did not directly or exclusively determine all domains of Soviet life. This allowed a peculiar translation of Soviet ideas into a prevalent spirituality [*dukhovnost'*] and encouraged a permanent quest for "the meaning of life" rather than for material prosperity. In this way, the "religious unconscious" was preserved within the Soviet discourse and experience.[26] Finally, the religious arenas existing at the margins of Soviet ideology and society acquired political and cultural meaning as an opposition to Soviet collectivistic values. Religion came to be associated with the private sphere and was perceived as embodying resistance to the regime and its indoctrination. This perception was especially characteristic of the intelligentsia where the tendency to convert to Russian Orthodoxy became visible.[27]

THE STUDY: MANIFESTATIONS OF RUSSIAN-SPEAKING IMMIGRANT RELIGIOSITY IN ISRAEL

The question of how an alumnus of the Soviet school system could become a practicing Jew or Christian in Israel can be answered in various ways. The transformation of Soviet worldviews into religious ones could be viewed, simultaneously, as resistance to Soviet atheist indoctrination, as a smooth adaptation, or even as fulfillment of the exported Soviet ideological and cultural repertoire, and as adopting the national religion of the host country. In our examination of the different trajectories of Russian-speaking religiosity in Israel, we explore the distinctions between exported and adopted cultural repertoires, religion and ideology, conformity and resistance, assimilation and ethnic preservation, and provide a new perspective on immigrants' religious identity and practice as a way "to belong."

Our study comprises two stages: mapping the emerging field of religious beliefs, practices, and institutions of Russian-speaking Israelis, and a deep ethnographic study in several religious communities selected for focused analysis because they reflect two different religious choices (Jewish and Christian). Preliminary data collected during the mapping stage of the study challenge prevailing assumptions regarding the Russian-speaking immigrants' nonreligiosity. Despite their seemingly secular cultural background, we found that these immigrants are extremely heterogeneous in their religious affiliation and practices within the frameworks of Judaism and Christianity. We also found that FSU immigrants tend to create communal forms of religiosity that were unfamiliar to them in their home country. This may reflect the pattern of adopting local forms of religious life, as can be seen among immigrants in the United States.[28] Another important insight is that Russian-speaking immigrants tend not only to join existing religious frameworks oriented toward local believers, but also to establish their own religious communities and organizations. These immigrant churches and study groups offer us an especially intriguing site for inquiry since they simultaneously reflect both the adoption of the dominant local patterns and autonomous immigrant agency.

We are particularly interested in non-Jewish religious trajectories. As early as the mapping stage of our study, we identified roughly a dozen groups and communities affiliated with various Christian evangelical and messianic groups and denominations. In addition to institutionalized communal activities, the immigrants initiate home groups and informal educational programs to promote Christian doctrine among Russian speakers. These trends in immigrant religious life, which Russian-speaking immigrants consider marginal and insignificant, have been ignored, not only by scholars of contemporary Israeli society, but also by officials of the Ministry of Absorption and the Jewish Agency with whom we conducted a series of in-depth interviews at the first stage of data collection. As such, the personal and cultural meaning of this pattern of immigrant religiosity and its possible impact on Israeli cultural citizenship[29] requires empirical examination.

In our broader study we examine various trajectories of immigrants' religious transformation in Israel, including the two major religious affiliations with Judaism and Christianity. In this chapter, however, we present two empirical cases, each shedding light on different aspects of immigrant religiosity situated outside the boundaries of the Israeli national religion. First, we examine a noncongregational immigrant church in the Beer-Sheva area that aims to unite those Russian speakers who are seeking a new meaning for their "defective" or "incomplete" Jewishness and a network for communal support. Second, we examine immigrant youngsters of non-Jewish or mixed ethnic origin, who are searching for spirituality in the context of an identity crisis and the liminal status forced upon them by the hegemonic cultural and religious attitudes of the host society.

An Immigrant Church

A Christian religious community was established in 2000 in Beer-Sheva[30] at the initiative of FSU immigrants. The church pastor is a young man about thirty-five years old, the son of a Jewish father and a Russian mother. He had professed Christianity while still living in the FSU and belonged to one of the evangelical movements that became very prominent in the post-Soviet sphere.[31] The church is inclusive of any Christian denomination and welcomes any immigrant who professes a belief in Jesus Christ. It has some 200 members and is supported by their monthly dues. Religious services are conducted on Saturdays and combine Jewish and Christian religious motifs. Similarly, on its website, the community presents itself as incorporating three cultural, ethnic, and religious identities—Jewish, Soviet, and Christian: "We are Israelis believing in Jesus Christ. Most of us are immigrants from the former Soviet Union. We have experienced the faithfulness of God in our own lives. He has conferred upon us the Spirit of Life and has returned us to the land of our fathers. . . . As Jewish believers, we appreciate our friendship with our Arab brothers and sisters in Israel."

What are the specific meanings of this conscious attempt by these Russian immigrants in Israel to constitute a Jewish-Christian identity? And what are the cultural resources that allow them to maintain such a complex identity in the Israeli context? To answer these questions, we conducted a series of participant observations during a Saturday service, together with twenty-nine in-depth interviews with church members.

Most of the service consists of performing spiritual songs with the pastor playing drums accompanied by a band. There are no icons, no cross, and no other traditional Christian symbols in the church. As the pastor explains, "Symbols divide in faith, while our goal is to unite!" The pastor also told us that the church has brought together immigrants belonging to different congregations (Russian Orthodox, Roman Catholic, Seventh Day Adventist, and Jehovah's Witnesses): "At first, we belonged to the Charismatic denomination, but later we eschewed all labels. These things [different denominations] divide in faith, whereas we wanted to maintain a good relationship with other churches, so we began accepting everybody. This made us more open. Many people have first found God through us."

Accordingly, the church accepts people of all nationalities, baptized or not. In accepting everybody, the church differs not only from Jewish religious organizations, but also from many immigrant associations, whose members usually must have some specific characteristic, such as place of origin or profession.

An analysis of the interviews conducted with members of the church indicates that more than half are immigrants born to a Jewish father and a non-Jewish mother. These immigrants have recognizably Jewish surnames and patronymics, which made them the object of anti-Semitism in the FSU, but in Israel, they are not considered Jewish since Jewish identity is transmitted matrilineally. In the interviews, they expressed feelings of humiliation, confusion, alienation, anger, and, finally, a desire to restore the lost right to define themselves as they used to do in the past. The pastor (the son of a Jewish father) says: "The members of our congregation are Jewish, of course. Whoever invented that *halakhah*, those were dark people. Nationality is transmitted from father to son. The *halakhah* is a later interpretation. One should see what's written in the original. The Bible says: 'Abraham begat Isaac, Isaac begat Jacob. . . .' This means it's the father that counts. My father is a Jew, and so am I." Anna (thirty-three years old, nine years in Israel) refers to the same biblical citation: "I don't give a damn about what people would tell me. Nobody has the right to define me and my place [in Israel]. I observe it all: kosher food, the Sabbath, the Jewish holidays. Some Jews have only a Jewish father, but they are Jews nevertheless. Today, they [Israeli officials] say that being Jewish is determined by one's mother, but in the past the father was more important. It is written in the Bible itself that Abraham begat Isaac."

In a way, Christian doctrine legitimizes the national identity of non-Jewish immigrants, and also allows all immigrants, including Jews according to the *halakhah*, to embrace the "non-Jewish" part of their identity. It should be noted that the identity of most immigrants has always included both "Jewish" and "Russian-Christian" components, the latter being, for many, no less important than the former. While for Israeli Jews it would be unthinkable to accept the title of "Christian Jew" (since Christianity and Judaism are considered to be mutually exclusive), for our interviewees, this contradiction simply does not exist. The ability to maintain Jewishness as an ethnic and cultural category separate from Jewish religion is anchored in the Soviet perception of Jewishness as an ethno-national identity. At the same time, this perception is supported by Christian doctrine, and they both merge in the articulation of the Russian Jewish-Christian self-definition of the church members. Alexander, age thirty-five, has spent nine years in Israel and is *halakhically* Jewish. He explains:

> Without Israel, our own faith would not have existed. Our faith is completely grounded in the laws of the *Tanakh*.[32] No one denies them. All of the first Christians were Jews. They came to be called Christians only because they followed

Christ. But all this happened inside Judaism. When a person, a Jew, starts believing in Jesus, he does not cease to be Jewish. But the Jews think that he is a *mitnatser*[33] who separates himself from the Jewish people. But we don't think so. You can remain a Jew when you become Christian.

In this regard, Christian doctrine not only legitimizes the national identity of non-Jewish immigrants but also allows all immigrants, including *halakhic* Jews, to realize the "non-Jewish" part of their identity. Hence, the choice of Christianity as a spiritual persuasion helps immigrants overcome the identity crisis they face and, paradoxically, eases their search for a new home.

Alongside the identity crisis forced on them by the host society, a major difficulty that facilitated the interviewees' turn to Christianity was the hardships of integration into the surroundings under conditions of social isolation and a lack of communal and family support. The moment of becoming Christian divides their immigrant narratives in two—life before joining the church and God (hard, meaningless, and hopeless) and life after discovering God through the church (full of substance, joy, confidence, and meaning). Olga, age thirty-three, has spent four years in Israel and says:

> After immigration, I became more religious. I arrived when I was pregnant. Then Aniuta was born, and for the first time in my life I experienced depression. I wanted the grandmas and grandpas to be there, but we were on our own. And it's difficult when you're on your own in Israel. Neither my husband nor I had anybody there. It was scary. [....] Then I visited Mom in Russia, and he [my husband] told me not to come back, but I did anyway. And then he didn't allow us to enter the house; he was drunk. Aniuta was ten months old. I didn't know where to go.... I called the pastor and they took me. We lived in the church hall. They had a bed put there for me, they brought sheets and dishes and all the necessary stuff.... I started reading more, paying more attention to the works of God. I needed God the most when I came back to Israel. I had no one else to rely on.

The word "scary" appears several times in Olga's narrative. She feels vulnerable and lonely in the new country. Moreover, Olga had no one else to turn for help in a moment of crisis but the pastor, and the only shelter she found was the church hall. It is precisely a combination of loneliness and helplessness that compels immigrants like Olga to look for support in religion and in the religious community.

Many interviews, while recounting the difficult conditions of integration into a new society, tell how the immigrant, deprived of support from family, community, or the state, is lost in the face of these difficulties and moves the responsibility for his or her life into the hands of a more capable "leader." While helplessness leads the immigrant to seek support in faith ("You start believing in God when you no longer believe in yourself. And God returns this faith to you"), loneliness brings them into the immigrant church. Marina (twenty-seven years old, eight years in

Israel), a *halakhic* Jew, came to Israel alone as part of a project bringing young people to Israel to study in university. However, she did not manage to enter the university and today she works as a cleaner:

> I was renting a flat together with a friend and her boyfriend. It was a wrong decision. We didn't get along. I had nowhere to go. I felt lonely. It's very difficult to make it on your own. I worked as a cleaner in a shop. There was a lady there. She treated me well, and invited me to church. God has shown me that I am not alone. He said: "You will never be alone again." First of all, He is with me. And there are people with me now, too. You come to the church and everybody is happy to see you. They love you and accept you as you are. This is liberating. You are not alone and you are a free person. Once God is with me, I will never be alone again. Everybody abandoned me here—the state, my family, my friends. But the church abandons no one.

Church members spend a lot of time together, traveling to resorts, having family celebrations, and celebrating holidays. This strengthens the church's role as a "surrogate family." Especially important is the church's function of educating children and adolescents. It offers free afternoon classes for children and conducts "children's services," with songs, games, and conversations on biblical and moral themes. Moreover, the church supports its members not only morally, but also materially; church members give clothes and furniture to each other, rent houses and flats to community members, help each other in moving and renovating apartments, finding jobs, and lending money. It appears that immigrants' active participation in the life of the church is an important psychological and social resource, easing their adjustment, even if it happens on the margins of Israeli society.

The Spiritual Search of Immigrant Youth

This section is based on thirty-eight in-depth interviews with immigrant youth aged 12–18 who are not recognized as Jewish according to *halakhah*. Interviewees were divided equally between the urban center of Israel and the periphery (smaller towns in the southern part of the country) and between two age cohorts (12–14 and 15–18 years old). We found that most of these young people experienced significant difficulties stemming from the ongoing adaptation to their new social and cultural surroundings. One of the most painful experiences was being labeled as outsiders who do not belong to the national majority in Israel. This alienation is frequently reinforced by the Israeli media and by informal contacts with native-born, *halakhically* Jewish peers, thus fostering a sense of alienation from the host society among interviewees: "Once I read an interview with a very important religious person in Israel. He said that immigrants from Russia are not Jewish and that we should not be accepted. I try not to pay attention. But who gives him the right to determine who is a real Jew and who is not? [....] I don't understand this. It bothers me very much and makes me feel like a guest" (female, twelve years old, two years in Israel). In this situation, when the host society did not provide interviewees with meaningful tools for belonging, many found refuge in Christianity even though they did not affiliate themselves with it before immigration. Most interviewees who now define themselves as Christians were born and raised in secular families and, throughout their formative years in the FSU, did not take part in any religious activity. Only eight were baptized in early childhood, but even they did not consider themselves to be religious before arriving in Israel.

Hence, as we will show below, their turn to God and to the Christian faith should be seen as a response to the identity crisis they experienced after the immigration, as well as to loneliness, helplessness, and anxiety stemming from migration to a new country, exacerbated by adolescence. That said, interviewees differed notably in the salience of their religious identity and the centrality of the religious way of life in their adaptation process. For example, twenty-two of them hid their religious affiliation and were not involved in any organized religious activity. These "undeclared" Christians defined themselves as Christians, but were not identified with any particular Christian denomination, had minimal to no knowledge of Christian doctrine, and were not affiliated with organized religious community. In Mikhail Epstein's terms, such a religious worldview can be defined as "minimal" religion, since it is made up of faith alone—belief in God as a guiding and protecting power—but is disconnected from any particular religious doctrine.[34]

Such a weak religious basis is not surprising in light of the post-Soviet immigrants' secular background and lack of intergenerational religious transmission.[35] Indeed, most interviewees described their parents as atheists or as people without any consistent religious identity who vacillated between popular Christian and Jewish rituals (and viewed the latter as a cultural demand expected by the host society). Hence, these interviewees' faith has developed independently, without any parental influence or other agents of religious socialization. Moreover, most of them claimed that, in the past, they did not believe in God, and that they had turned to God only in Israel, in search of emotional support at times of loneliness and helplessness: "In Israel I've started thinking about God. There were many moments when I felt very lonely. When there was nobody around me to ask for help, I turned to God, and I think it helped. It's good to know that God exists. It's nice to feel that you're not alone" (male, fifteen, two years in Israel).

A deep longing for a homeland usually reinforced a feeling of loneliness. In this sense, rare church visits played another important role in the interviewees' lives, since the church (regardless of denomination) was perceived as a piece of one's homeland. Moreover, the interviewees described their feelings during church visits in terms of security and serenity, emphasizing that in the FSU they never experienced such feelings while visiting a church: "Today I feel that I am mostly identified with Christianity. Because it is mine. Even though I wasn't a Christian in Ukraine, nevertheless I am familiar with it: the architecture [of the church], beautiful icons, music, colored eggs. This is part of me, of what I've read, of the films

I've seen. When I visit a church, I feel like I am at home" (male, thirteen, two years in Israel).

From the interviews it is also evident that these interviewees' religious knowledge was limited to a few of the most popular Christian rituals and symbols, rooted in Russian classical literature. Similarly, being disconnected from the traditional sources of religious education, the interviewees were inspired mostly by Hollywood films that include Christian motifs and rituals, which they constantly compared with the Jewish ones. Rather than searching for the guidelines of a religious way of life, the interviewees were looking to Christianity for a substitute for holidays and ceremonies such as Rosh Hashanah, bar mitzvah celebrations, and weddings, which were not open to them in Judaism. This was especially important for the female interviewees who complained about the fact that they could not have a religious wedding in Israel, unlike their Jewish peers, and who were thus planning a Christian wedding ceremony abroad: "I cannot have a Jewish wedding because my mother is not Jewish. But my cousin could, even though her father is not Jewish too! Because in Judaism it is according to your mother's line. But I can have a Christian wedding. I'm planning to go abroad and have a wedding ceremony like a normal person; you know, like in the movies, with candles, flowers, organ music. This way it will be even more beautiful!" (female, fourteen, two years in Israel).

Furthermore, none of these interviewees was affiliated with an organized religious community or shared their religious beliefs with family or friends. In this situation of spiritual isolation and lack of communal support, the interviewees felt very insecure about the legitimacy of their religious affiliation and avoided any visible attributes that might expose their religious identity. It appears, therefore, that lack of affiliation with an organized religious community allows these adolescents to continue their spiritual search without being limited to a strict religious doctrine; on the other hand, lack of communal support places significant limits on their ability to openly lead a Christian way of life.

CONCLUSION

The question of how and why individuals become religious is crucial to understanding the contemporary post-nationalist and post-secular quest for belonging, be it pragmatic, symbolic, or emotional. In the context of migration, belonging is commonly perceived as a search for inclusion within the national collective and affiliation with an ethnic group. Belonging through religious affiliation and practice in the context of migration brings the meaning of modern religiosity into focus and presents the topic for analytical consideration. Our study explores this issue by examining the religious transformation of Russian-speaking immigrants in Israel, thus stressing the power of newly developed religiosity as a device for belonging and for the reinvention of immigrants' individual and communal identities.

Our findings are related to several trends already identified by scholars of religion and migration. First, they should be seen as part of a broader religious awakening in the post-Soviet space, which is defined as a "supermarket of religions" (i.e., a rapid change of religious identities and affiliations). Second, the recent proliferation of evangelical churches in Israel (including the church discussed in this chapter) is directly influenced by the international evangelical movement, which has been "imported" from the United States to the post-Soviet republics and to Israel. Third, it is possible to see our findings in light of research in other countries that points to the strengthening of religious identities after immigration as part of immigrants' adaptation strategies. Finally, these findings also highlight the particular situation of FSU immigrants of mixed-ethnic origin who are looking for a new home in Israel while situating themselves vis-à-vis a variety of social, cultural, religious, and ideological frameworks in Israeli society that emphasize Judaism as a major determinant of belonging.

In this chapter, we chose to present two religious trajectories that fall outside the Israeli national religion. Our case studies shed light on those immigrants who are not considered Jews according to *halakhah*, thus challenging the presumed ethno-national boundaries that have been generally accepted in previous research on religious groups in Israel. As Timothy L. Smith poignantly observed, immigration itself is often a theologizing experience and immigrants frequently react to the alienation and confusion resulting from their arrival in a new country by strengthening their religiosity.[36] Yet, unlike previous studies, which focused primarily on immigrants with a religious background,[37] the present study reveals that irreligious immigrants may also turn to religion and reinvent themselves in religious terms as a reaction to marginalization and exclusion. While a general quest for belonging through religion is clearly articulated in the literature on immigrant religiosity, the cases presented here illustrate the non-obvious idea that nonhegemonic religious choices (aside or even against the national mainstream) can also promote immigrant belonging.

Notwithstanding these observations, we found a significant difference between the intensity and consolidation of religious identity among interviewees affiliated with the church and nonprofessing youngsters. The church simultaneously served as a primary source of social support and of religious knowledge for those who found their way to it. In contrast, the nonprofessing had no encounter whatsoever with the established religious community. Accordingly, they defined themselves as Christians at home, but had only a vague understanding of what this means. Their religious identity was based primarily on belief in God. Moreover, they were profoundly insecure regarding the legitimacy of their religious identity that was kept secret from the outside world. As such, although religious belief does exert a positive psychological effect, it is unable to solve the principal problems immigrant youth face in Israel—social isolation and lack of belonging, and communal support.

Finally, the findings of our broader study support the paradoxical proposition that the development of a Christian identity allows the articulation of a national citizenship that is at times accompanied by a reinforced connection to Israel, relations with Jewish Israelis, and a positive perception of immigrants' belonging to Israeli society. The national religion in Israel that links nationality with religion also accentuates religious affiliation as the most legitimate mechanism for social and political belonging. By contrast, the post-Soviet universalistic character of spiritual beliefs provides grounds for adopting alternative ways of belonging that extend beyond the boundaries of Israeli national religion.

NOTES

1. A considerable number of Russian-speaking immigrants in Israel are of mixed ethnicity. This is particularly significant because the only criterion for recognition as a Jew by Israeli state institutions is the matrilineal principle, in accordance with Jewish religious law. Thus, many immigrants of partly Jewish origin are not considered Jewish in Israel.
2. Yossi Yonah, "Israel's Immigration Policies: The Twofold Face of the 'Demographic Threat,'" *Social Identities* 10.2 (2004): 195–218.
3. Jewish religious law.
4. Yehuda Goodman, "The Giyur of Immigrants: Citizenship, State and Religion in Israel of 2000," in *Citizenship Gaps: Critical Discussion of Migration, Population Management and Fertility* [in Hebrew], ed. Yossi Yona and Adriana Kemp (Jerusalem: Van Leer Jerusalem Institute, 2008).
5. Mordechai Altshuler, *Judaism in the Soviet Vise: Religion and Jewish Identity in Soviet Union between 1941–1964* [in Hebrew] (Jerusalem: Merkaz Shazar Center, 2007); Valeriy Chervyakov, Zvi Gitelman, and Vladimir Shapiro, "Religion and Ethnicity: Judaism in the Ethnic Consciousness of Contemporary Russian Jews," *Ethnic and Racial Studies* 20.2 (1997): 280–305; Mikhail Chlenov, "The Characteristics of the Ethnic and Religious Identity of the Russian Jews," *Jews of the Former Soviet Union in Israel and Diaspora* 20–21 (2003): 254–273; Zvi Gitelman, *A Century of Ambivalence: The Jews of Russia and the Soviet Union, 1881 to the Present* (Bloomington: Indiana University Press, 2001); Zvi Gitelman, "Thinking about Being Jewish in Russia and Ukraine," in *Jewish Life after the USSR*, ed. Gitelman, Musya Glants, and Marshall Goldman (Bloomington: Indiana University Press, 2003), 49–60; Natalia Iukhneva, "Russian Jews as a New Sub-Ethnos," *Ab Imperio* 4 (2003): 475–496; Yaacov Ro'i and Avi Beker, *Jewish Culture and Identity in the Soviet Union* (New York: New York University Press, 1999); Yaacov Ro'i, "Religion, Israel, and the Development of Soviet Jewry's National Consciousness, 1967–91," in *Jewish Life after the USSR*, 13–26; Yuri Slezkine, *The Jewish Century* (Princeton: Princeton University Press, 2005); and, most recently, Zvi Gitelman, *Jewish Identities in Postcommunist Russia and Ukraine: An Uncertain Ethnicity* (New York: Cambridge University Press, 2012).
6. Gitelman, *Jewish Identities*; Tamar Horowitz, *The Soviet Man in an Open Society* (Lanham, MD: University Press of America, 1989); Slezkine, *The Jewish Century*.
7. Central Bureau of Statistics, *Social Survey 2002–2004* (Jerusalem: CBS, 2009); Asher Arian and Ayala Keissar-Sugarmen, *A Portrait of Israeli Jewry: Beliefs, Observances, and Values among Israeli Jews 2000* (Jerusalem: Israel Democracy Institute, 2012); Shulamit Levy, Hanna Levinsohn, and Elihu Katz, "The Many Faces of Jewishness in Israel," in *Jews in Israel: Contemporary Social and Cultural Patterns*, ed. Uzi Rebhun and Chaim Waxman (Hanover, NH: Brandeis University Press, 2004), 265–284.

8. Larissa Remennick and Anna Prashizky, *From State Socialism to State Judaism: "Russian" Immigrants in Israel and Their Attitudes towards Religion*, Special issue of *Sociological Papers* 5 (2010).

9. Ibid.

10. Chen Bram, *From the Caucasus to Israel: The Immigration of the Mountain Jews—Anthropological Perspective on the Communities in the Caucasus and Issues in their Integration into Israel* (Jerusalem: JDC-Brookdale Institute, 1999); Elena Neiterman and Tamar Rapoport, "Converting to Belong: Immigration, Education, and Nationalization among Young 'Russian' Immigrant Women," *Gender and Education* 2.2 (2009): 173–189; Janna Pinsky, "Christian Immigrants in the Jewish State: The Identity of Non-Jewish Repatriates from the FSU in the 90's Immigrant Wave" [in Hebrew] (Master's thesis, Haifa University, 2006); Rivka Raijman and Janna Pinsky, "'Non-Jewish and Christian': Perceived Discrimination and Social Distance among FSU Immigrants in Israel," *Israel Affairs* 17.1 (2011): 126–142; Remennick and Prashizky, *From State Socialism to State Judaism*.

11. Wendy Cadge and Elaine Howard Ecklund, "Immigration and Religion," *Annual Review of Sociology* 33 (2007): 359–379; Carolyn Chen, *Getting Saved in America: Taiwanese Immigration and Religious Experience* (Princeton: Princeton University Press, 2008); Michael W. Foley and Dean R. Hoge, *Religion and the New Immigrants: How Faith Communities Form our Newest Citizens* (Oxford: Oxford University Press, 2007); Peggy Levitt, "Following the Migrants: Religious Pluralism in Transnational Perspective," in *Religion in Modern Lives*, ed. Nancy T. Ammerman (New York: Oxford University Press, 2006); Peggy Levitt, "Immigration," in *Handbook of Religion and Social Institutions*, ed. Helen Rose Ebaugh (New York: Springer, 2006), 391–410; Fenggang Yang and Helen Rose Ebaugh, "Transformations in New Immigrant Religions and their Global Implication," *American Sociological Review* 66.2 (2001): 269–288.

12. Helen Rose Ebaugh and Janet Saltzman Chafetz, "Structural Adaptations in Immigrant Congregations," *Sociology of Religion* 61.2 (2000): 135–153.

13. Chen, *Getting Saved in America*; Brian Hall, "Social and Cultural Contexts in Conversion to Christianity among Chinese American College Students," *Sociology of Religion* 67.2 (2006): 131–148; Kwai Hang Ng, "Seeking the Christian Tutelage: Agency and Culture in Chinese Immigrants' Conversion to Christianity," *Sociology of Religion* 63.2 (2002): 195–214; Fenggang Yang and Joseph B. Tamney, "Exploring Mass Conversion to Christianity among the Chinese: An Introduction," *Sociology of Religion* 67.2 (2006): 125–129.

14. Helen Rose Ebaugh and Janet Saltzman Chafetz, *Religion Across Borders: Transnational Immigrant Networks* (Walnut Creek, CA: AltaMira, 2002); Daniele Hervieu-Leger, *Religion as a Chain of Memory* (Cambridge: Polity Press, 2000); Peter Kivisto, "Rethinking the Relationship between Ethnicity and Religion," in *The Sage Handbook of the Sociology of Religion*, ed. James A. Beckford and N. Jay Demerath III (London: Sage Publications, 2007), 490–510; Jonathan V. Laurence, *Integrating Islam: Political and Religious Challenges in Contemporary France* (Washington, DC: Brookings Institute, 2006); R. Stephen Warner, "Immigration and Religious Communities in the United States," in *Gatherings in Diaspora: Religious Communities and the New Immigration*, ed. R. Stephen Warner and Judith G. Wittner (Philadelphia: Temple University Press, 1998).

15. Cadge and Ecklund, "Immigration and Religion"; Chen, *Getting Saved in America*; Ebaugh and Saltzman Chafetz, *Religion Across Borders*; Adriana Kemp and Rivka Raijman, "Christian Zionists in the Holy Land: Evangelical Churches, Labor Migrants, and the Jewish State," *Identities: Global Studies in Culture and Power* 10 (2003): 295–318; Prema A. Kurien, "Christian by Birth or Rebirth? Generation and Difference in an Indian American Christian Church," in *Asian American Religions: The Making and Remaking of Borders and Boundaries*, ed. Tony Carnes and Fenggang Yang (New York: New York University Press, 2004), 160–181.

16. Peggy Levitt, "Two Nations under God? Latino Religious Life in the US," in *Latinos: Remaking America*, ed. Marcelo Suarez-Orozco and Mariela M. Paez (Berkeley: University

of California Press, 2002); Peggy Levitt, *God Needs No Passport: Immigrants and the Changing American Religious Landscape* (New York: New Press, 2007); Cecilia Menjívar, "Religious Institutions and Transnationalism: A Case Study of Catholic and Evangelical Salvadoran Immigrants," *International Journal of Politics, Culture, and Society* 12 (1999): 589–611; Margarita Mooney, *Faith Makes Us Live: Surviving and Thriving in the Haitian Diaspora* (Berkeley: University of California Press, 2009).

17. Karen Fog Olwig, "A Wedding in the Family: Home Making in a Global Kin Network," *Global Networks* 2 (2002): 205–218; Kivisto, "Rethinking the Relationship"; Levitt, "Following the Migrants: Religious Pluralism in Transnational Perspective"; Levitt, "Immigration"; Fenggang Yang, "Chinese Christian Transnationalism: Diverse Networks of a Houston Church," in *Religion Across Borders*, ed. Ebaugh and Saltzman Chafetz, 175–204.

18. But see Chen, *Getting Save in America*; Yang, "Chinese Christian Transnationalism."

19. Benjamin Beit-Halahmi, *Despair and Deliverance: Private Salvation in Contemporary Israel* (Albany: SUNY Press, 1992); Massimo Leone, *Religious Conversion and Identity—The Semiotic Analysis of Texts* (London and New York: Routledge, 2004); Lewis R. Rambo, *Understanding Religious Conversion* (New Haven: Yale University Press, 1993).

20. M. Herbert Danzger, "The 'Return' to Traditional Judaism in the US, Russia, and Israel: The Impact of Dominant versus Minority Status on Religious Conversion Process," in *Religion, Mobilization and Social Action*, ed. Anson Shup and Bronislaw Misztal (Westport, CT: Praeger, 1998), 174–196; Baruch Kimmerling, *Immigrants, Settlers, Natives: Israeli Society between Cultural Pluralism and Cultural Wars* (Tel-Aviv: Am Oved, 2004) [in Hebrew]; Alexander Yacobson, "Joining the Jewish People: Non-Jewish Immigrants from the Former USSR, Israeli Identity, and Jewish Peoplehood," *Israel Law Review* 43.1 (2010): 218–239.

21. Remennick and Prashizky, *From State Socialism to State Judaism*.

22. Nelly Elias and Natalia Khvorostianov, "Religious Identity Construction of the Non-Jewish Immigrant Youngsters in Israel," in *Jewish Migrants from the Former Soviet Union: The Case of Israel, Germany and the USA*, ed. Christian Wiese (Leiden: Brill, forthcoming); Pinsky, "Christian Immigrants in a Jewish State"; Raijman and Pinsky, "'Non-Jewish and Christian.'"

23. For this approach see also Julia Lerner, "Russians in Israel as Post-Soviet Subjects: Implementing Civilizational Repertoire," *Israel Affairs* 17.1 (2011): 21–37.

24. Paul Frouse, *The Plot to Kill God: Findings from the Soviet Experiment in Secularization* (Berkeley: University of California Press, 2008); Igal Halfin, *From Darkness to Light: Class, Consciousness and Salvation in Revolutionary Russia* (Pittsburgh: Pittsburgh University Press, 2000); Jules Monnerot, *Sociology of Communism* (London: G. Allen & Unwin, 1953); James Thrower, *Marxism-Leninism as the Civil Religion of Soviet Society: God's Commissar* (Lewiston, NY: Edwin Mellen Press 1992); Robert C. Tucker, *Philosophy and Myth in Karl Marx* (Cambridge: Cambridge University Press, 1961); David. B. Zilberman, "Orthodox Ethics and the Matter of Communism," *Studies in Soviet Thought* 17 (1977): 341–419.

25. Alexei Yurchak, *Everything Was Forever until It Was No More: The Last Soviet Generation* (Princeton: Princeton University Press, 2005).

26. Mikhail Epstein, *The New Sectarianism* (Holyoke, MA: New England Publishing Co., 1993); Mikhail Epstein, *Faith and Image: The Religious Unconscious in 20th Century Russian Culture* (Tenafly, NJ: Hermitage Publishers, 1994) [in Russian].

27. Chlenov, "The Characteristics"; Judith. D. Kornblatt, *Doubly Chosen: Jewish Identity, the Soviet Intelligentsia, and the Russian Orthodox Church* (Madison: University of Wisconsin Press, 2004); Larissa Remennick, *Russian Jews on Three Continents* (New Brunswick, NJ: Transaction Publishers, 2007); Sergei Ruzer, "Jewish Christianity as a Form of Jewish Revival: A New Perspective," in *Jews and Slavs*, vol. 21, ed. Wolf Moskovich and I. Fijalkowska-Janiak (Jerusalem, 2008), 371–380; Ruzer, "Jewish Christianity in Russia after the Six-Day War: Israeli Factor, Eschatology, and Nostra Aetate," *Revue des Études Juives* 168.3–4 (2009): 547–561.

28. Chen, *Getting Saved in America*; Ebaugh and Saltzman Chafetz, "Structural Adaptations in Immigrant Congregations"; Yang and Ebaugh, "Transformations in New Immigrant Religions and Their Global Implication."

29. Edna Lomsky-Feder and Tamar Rapoport, "Cultural Citizenship and Performing Homecoming: Russian Jewish Immigrants Decipher the Zionist National Ethos," *Citizenship Studies* 12.3 (2008): 321–334.

30. A mid-sized city in the south of Israel.

31. Mathijs Pelkmans, "Introduction: Post-Soviet Space and the Unexpected Turns of Religious Life," in *Conversion after Socialism: Disruptions, Modernisms and Technologies of Faith in the Former Soviet Union*, ed. Mathijs Pelkmans (Oxford: Berghahn Books, 2009), 1–16; Catherine Wanner, "Advocating New Moralities: Conversion to Evangelicalism in Ukraine," *Religion, State and Society* 31.3 (2003): 87–273; Wanner, "Missionaries of Faith and Culture: Evangelical Encounters in Ukraine," *Slavic Review* 63.4 (2004): 732–755; Wanner, "Evanhelysm, Identychnist' ta Kul'turni Zminy v Ukraini [Evangelicalism, Identity, and Cultural Change in Ukraine]," *Ahora* 5 (2007): 29–39.

32. The Hebrew Bible.

33. Convert to Christianity.

34. Mikhail Epstein, "Minimal Religion and Post-Atheism," in *Russian Postmodernism: New Perspectives on Post-Soviet Culture*, ed. Mikhail Epstein, Alexander Genis, and Slobodanka Vladiv-Glover (New York: Berghahn Books, 1999), 345–393.

35. Epstein, *Faith and Image*.

36. Timothy L. Smith, "Religion and Ethnicity in America," *American Historical Review* 83 (1978): 85–155.

37. Cadge and Ecklund, "Immigration and Religion"; Kivisto, "Rethinking the Relationship."

14 · VIRTUAL VILLAGE IN A REAL WORLD

The Russian Jewish Diaspora Online

ANNA SHTERNSHIS

Immigrants have been intensive users and catalysts in the development of communications technology. Mass migrations catalyzed the development of voice-over-IP [VoIP] programs, which enabled inexpensive phone calls, satellite television, and, above all, computer-enabled communication.[1] Studies have shown that immigrants use the Internet differently from non-immigrants, and also, differently based on how recently they left their country of origin.[2] Recent migrants use the Internet both to obtain detailed information about their new community and to search for news from home. Doing so creates ties within their new community and retains links to the old one. Settled migrants (five or more years since immigration) tend to use the Internet to cultivate connections with people of similar backgrounds and to establish an individual pattern of connecting with home, in order to rebuild familial and communal connections. Their search for shared background, both in terms of their physical location and within virtual chats and advice given to newcomers, functions as a building block of a diasporic identity.

In this chapter, I focus on an aspect of Internet use by settled migrants of the Russian Jewish Diaspora. I discuss communities intentionally constructed as transnational and that focus on issues of identity as opposed to physical survival. The chapter deals with the first decade of the twenty-first century, a period of rapid expansion in the Russian-language Internet, and a time of minimal censorship of Internet usage in the Russian Federation.

THE INTERNET AND RUSSIAN JEWISH DIASPORA

Yandex, the Russian equivalent of Google, reported that in June 2010, over 18 million Russian-language blogs existed (weblogs, online diaries, columns, or other narratives) with 80 million posts. Over 2 million Russian-language blogs were updated daily, with an estimated 250 new blogs appearing online every hour. Almost 13 percent of all Internet content produced in the Russian language originates from the United States, Israel, Germany, and Canada.[3]

Virtual "Russian villages" developed in almost all American cites and function as an information source for newcomers, a meeting point for settled migrants, and a forum for discussion on a wide range of issues relevant to the daily lives and identities of post-migrants.[4] In Israel, where Russian speakers constitute a significant proportion of the population (numbering over a million), Internet-based communication serves as one of the primary means of discussing identity formation and integration for almost all groups of Russian immigrants, both new and established.[5] Similar developments can be seen in Germany, Canada, and Australia. For a growing category of "secondary migrants" (tens of thousands of Russian speakers who first immigrated to Israel, then to Canada or Australia, or back to Russia), Russian-language websites, blog-hosts, and chat groups become a "virtual home" and serve as a point of reference where they can share their experiences and discuss their identities.

Undeniably important, virtual villages are not the only hubs in the Russian diasporic virtual world. During the period under examination, the most popular site among Russian-speaking users, both in Russia and abroad, was LiveJournal (livejournal.com)—a blogging service with a well-developed discussion platform. Each blogging entry has a debating space of its own that is structured like a bulletin board, allows for an unlimited number of comments, and can be organized into threads. The debating feature is particularly popular among Russian-language users; most English-language entries gather only a handful of comments, whereas those in Russian often have dozens, hundreds, and sometimes over a thousand comments. The Russian-language blogosphere on LiveJournal is also a vibrant social space of communication, interactions, opinions, and passionate exchanges.[6]

LiveJournal also allows readers to form communities in which members can post and interact with each other.[7] The communities formed on LiveJournal often structure themselves as "virtual villages." Self-descriptive "rusam,"[8] "rusisrael," "ru_de," and "ru_toronto" communities discuss issues relevant to living in specific regions and offer advice for newcomers, potential migrants, and tourists. Other communities on LiveJournal are intentionally transnational. For example, a community called *"inostranki"* [foreign women], whose members live in over 100 countries, discusses the cultural challenges that Russian-speaking women face in their various places of residence.

Jewish issues frequently come up in community discussions, either in the context of searching for ethnic identity, combating anti-Semitism, or exploring family histories. Often, virtual communities are designed specifically for Russian speakers interested in Jewish topics such as Yiddish, Jewish food, Soviet Jewish culture, Russians in Israel, and more. My study does not claim to cover all topics related to Jews on the Russian Internet. In 2011, when this chapter was drafted, the list of sites solely devoted to Judaism and Israel included over sixty titles, which did not even include sites such as LiveJournal, which hosted thousands of bloggers focusing on Jewish topics.[9] To the contrary, this chapter points out that "there is more we do not know than what we do." In lieu of "starting somewhere," I propose focusing on one, relatively small segment of the Russian blogosphere—the discussion of issues relevant to one particular branch of Jewish culture, namely, ultra-Orthodox Judaism. I will focus on bloggers who claim to live as Orthodox Jews, thus representing the Russian-speaking *ba'alei teshuvah* ["returners to the faith"]—Jews who started practicing Orthodox Judaism as adults.

An analysis of this subculture can lead to many discoveries in our understanding of transformations from one identity to another, including the mechanisms of combining a Soviet upbringing with a Jewish lifestyle, building relationships with parents and with a community of both religious and secular friends, just to name a few issues. In-depth interviews with a statistically significant number of such people located in Israel, Russia, the United States, Canada, Germany, and Australia would have been an ideal way to conduct such a study. However, in the absence of such data, I suggest that reading blogs as a window into the subculture of Russian *ba'alei teshuvah* and the dilemmas that they face can be a productive method of conducting preliminary research. In addition, it can answer questions about the role of the Internet in creating, articulating, and supporting a post-Soviet Jewish Orthodox identity and maintaining the global nature of this subset of the Russian Jewish Diaspora.

Most research on Russian-speaking immigrants online examines how blogs and Internet use highlight the tensions between "ghettoization" and "integration."[10] I follow the lead of Adi Kunstman, who studies the Russian Internet as a post-Soviet "diaspora space," which allows both "people who stayed" and "people who left" to form communities and to develop attachments and conflicts within those communities. He argues that such an approach "addresses complex notions of belonging, otherness and difference as they are negotiated online."[11] I suggest analyzing blogs as literary texts, where writers create their alter egos, public identities, and collective images. To narrow the focus of this chapter, I chose to begin the discussion with an analysis of the blog by "antidos" (antidos.livejournal.com), which ran in 2004–2008 and was devoted to criticism of the Jewish Orthodox lifestyle from the point of view of a person who experienced a "return to Judaism" and then regretted it.

Antidos frequently quoted ultra-Orthodox Jewish bloggers, was predominantly public, and received a large number of comments, both supportive and negative (typically dozens per thread), from other users who understand the issues he raised. I started reading this blog because I was fascinated by the sharp, insider criticism of Orthodox Jews, which touched upon problems in the laws of family purity, the methods of outreach by Lubavitch organizations, false religiosity, and pretentious modesty. I had just finished writing a book on Soviet Jewish culture in the 1920s–1930s with a chapter on state-sponsored antireligious propaganda in Yiddish, so I was curious about contemporary, non-state-supported criticism of Judaism by Russian speakers who were exposed to Judaism in adulthood.

RUSSIAN JEWISH ULTRA-ORTHODOXY: A BRIEF DESCRIPTION

There is little information on the number of Russian Jews who turned to Jewish Orthodoxy in the 1990s and adopted a religious lifestyle. Some preliminary data on Russian Jewish *ba'alei teshuvah* in Israel refers to them as "a very small minority among Russian immigrants" and does not give any numbers.[12] In approaching this new topic, I hypothesize that Russian-speaking Jewish people born in the late 1970s and 1980s represent a transitional generation. Their parents grew up in the Soviet Union and usually maintained a specifically Soviet understanding of Jewish identity, which, in essence, fully divorced Judaism from Jewish ethnicity.[13] In addition, being Jewish was associated with state discrimination and popular anti-Semitism.[14] Exposed to Jewish summer camps, schools, cultural centers, and free trips to Israel, this younger generation has developed a very different sense of ethnicity. In the 1990s, being Jewish came to be associated with the privilege of emigration. In the 2000s, one could observe the growth of a positive sense of Jewish community. Some people began to associate being Jewish with practicing the laws of Judaism. While no quantitative research is available, we do know that by now a community of Russian-speaking Jews who consistently practice ultra-Orthodox Judaism has emerged. Many of them live in Israel, the rest in Russia, the United States, and other countries of the Russian-speaking Jewish diaspora.

RUSSIAN LIVEJOURNAL AND JEWISH ORTHODOXY: A VERY BRIEF OVERVIEW

In 2010, at least twenty Russian-language LiveJournal communities were devoted to Orthodox Judaism. Readers and writers of these communities asked questions about *halakhic* issues and sought practical advice, such as where to buy kosher food and whether certain brands are kosher. These communities included "ru_judaism," "machanaim," "shalom_bait," "parashavua_ru," "chinuch_ru," and "shabbes_koidesh," among many others. "Ru_Judaism" had 648 subscribers, "machanaim" around 600, and "shabbes_koidesh" had 348 in 2010. Many of the subscriptions overlapped, since many people had more than one blogger account, but others did not have accounts on LiveJournal and read the entries only anonymously. Thus, it is impossible to know the exact number of Russian Jewish Orthodox users even within LiveJournal. Based on my multi-year observation of these blogs, I estimate there are at least a few hundred individual users on Russian LiveJournal who positioned themselves as ultra-Orthodox.

Many bloggers who wrote about leading an ultra-Orthodox (*haredi*) lifestyle had considerable followings. Shaul Andruschak, an ordained rabbi who wrote a blog under his own name, attracted 594 registered readers.[15] Uri Superfin, another rabbi known for his uncompromising views on *halakhah* [rabbinic law] and Orthodoxy, who lived in Beitar (an ultra-Orthodox settlement on the West Bank) before moving to Moscow to teach at a yeshiva, had 265 registered readers.[16] Ierakhmiel Kittner ("rabbi_kittner"), born in Dnepropetrovsk, Ukraine, and currently living in Milwaukee, had 490 followers. Rabbi Reuven Piatigorsky ("r5gor"), famous for his outreach in the mainstream media, had a blog with 336 followers. Sharp critics of Judaism also write about the positive aspects of *halakhah* and cover some secular Jewish topics: Evgenii Levin ("o.aronius") attracted an even larger readership of 817 registered subscribers.[17] Finally, the decidedly provocative and emotionally charged nature of the "antidos" blog, with its 206 subscribers, provoked heated, emotional responses, providing much raw data for an analysis of the dilemmas and sore spots of the milieu in question.

ANTIDOS AND THE CRITIQUE OF JUDAISM

Many entries in "antidos" speak about inconsistencies in biblical interpretations, the irrelevance of superstitions, and contradictions in the Holy Scriptures and Midrash. The blog also exposes dishonest rabbis and criticizes religious holidays that require considerable expense and sacrifice on the part of believers. Many of the materials come from the website *Da'at Emet* (http://daatemet.co), supported and likely run by a group of science and humanities professors based in Israeli universities. In one of his posts, "antidos" confirms that reading the *Da'at Emet* website sparked his own doubts about Orthodox tradition on an intellectual, rather than instinctual, level.[18]

The strongest attack is aimed at the Russian-speaking *ba'alei teshuvah*, who, according to the author of the blog, idealize the ultra-Orthodox way of life, take on religious obligations without thinking, and, most importantly, start treating their family members inappropriately in the name of the Divine. In addition, "antidos" argues, they put up with discrimination and abuse in the Orthodox community. The short introduction to the blog of "antidos" explains the rationale of such criticisms: "What is the goal of my journal? *Kiruvniks*, those who return others to the loins of religion, like to prettify Judaism, trying to turn as many secular Jews as possible to *teshuvah*. My goal is to show the other side of the coin, something that kiruvniks don't want to speak about."[19] The language of the disclaimer, which includes the mixture of Hebrew words *teshuvah* [repentance] and Hebrew-derived constructions *hilonimnyi* [secular, *hilonim*, plus the Russian suffix *yi*] and *kiruvnik* [literally, an Orthodox Jewish outreach worker, from the Hebrew *kiruv*, bringing close] hints at the background of the target audience. The use of these terms suggests the author's familiarity with the insider culture of the group and narrows the potential audience of the blog. Though most of the posts are open to all readers, only those "on the inside" will understand, appreciate, or take issue with the writer's assertions.

A typical posting on "antidos" includes a quote from another Russian-language blog, usually ultra-Orthodox, or a citation from a Chabad or another ultra-Orthodox rabbi, or a general statement on the ridiculous nature of some Jewish practices. The posts that discuss the methods of personal transformation, the search for identity, and the relationship to secular (Soviet) values seem to come from the heart and provoke the largest number of comments and cross-referencing. The sorest issue is how newly "converted" *ba'alei teshuvah* reject the world in which they grew up, including their parents. Many posts on "antidos" speak to this, including this one:

> Yesterday and today, I read the letters that I had written when I studied in yeshiva, about 10 years ago. To be precise, I tried to read them. I could manage only part of the page where I explained to my parents the meaning of the letters *bet*, *samekh* and *dalet* in the upper right corner.[20] And I tried to persuade them that if one prays, everything will be good, and that they need to observe the Sabbath and eat kosher, and come to Israel, where jobs will be found for them at a yeshiva. Thank heavens they saved those letters. *God, I used to be such an idiot!!!*[21] (Emphasis in original.)

The relationship between secular, urban parents and their youngsters, newly "returned to Judaism" and overwhelmed by their yeshiva instruction and instructors, is a frequent topic of discussion in many Russian ultra-Orthodox blogs. Core values in Judaism, such as honoring one's parents, are frequently discussed with regard to respecting parents who openly eat pork, desecrate the Sabbath, or worse, encourage grandchildren to try "a little bit of *kolbasa* [sausage]." When the newly religious children start their own families, online debates about allowing grandchildren to see their grandparents and using grandparents as babysitters or caregivers elicit hundreds of comments.

The "antidos" audience, aware of these dilemmas and the public discourse surrounding them, is more likely to support the secular parents than in a blog written for and by ultra-Orthodox readers. However, even here, ambiguities are apparent. For example, one commentator, known for his own ambivalent writings about Judaism, yet not nearly as radical as "antidos," writes: "You used to be young and naïve. Being an idiot has nothing to do with that."[22] Another commentator, who writes his own blog from an ultra-Orthodox point of view agrees: "We all used to be idiots. Respect for parents, however, is a great mitzvah."[23] Because the commenter is an open and unapologetic observer of Jewish tradition, his remarks provoke a deeper discussion (presented here in translation and greatly abbreviated):[24]

ANTIDOS: I know so many cases, when newly minted *"bokhurim"*[25] gave so much sorrow to their parents when they became religious! One person left for yeshiva in Israel, in secret, at night. His escape was organized and planned together with local rabbis. Another one, upon arrival home, read *birkat hamazon* [grace after meals] for thirty minutes, in order to show his parents how serious he was. . . . I don't even mention that all these people did not eat what their parents cooked.

ELI_ME [WHO POSITIONS HIMSELF AS A CHABAD JEW LIVING IN GERMANY]: I used to be the same way. I told my parents that those who worked on Saturday spend everything they earned on doctors and lawyers. Now, I am a lot calmer. Yet, my parents respect my needs; they provide me with a separate fridge, dishes, pots, and so on. When they realized I was serious, they did not create problems.

ANTIDOS: Do you still believe it? [about spending the money earned on Sabbath on lawyers and doctors]. And why did you need your own separate fridge?

ELI_ME: Now I *know* [author's italics] it is true! I needed the fridge because I could take out the bulb out and open it on *Shabbes*. Not my parents' fridge.

ZLATA_GL (WHO POSITIONS HERSELF AS A CRITIC OF THE ORTHODOX LIFESTYLE): Did you buy the fridge with your own money, or did you demand that your parents buy it?

ELI_ME: My parents got tired of looking at how my food, bought with my own money, went rotten because it was in my room without a fridge all Shabbes. They bought me a little fridge, with which I can do what I want. I come home only once a month for Shabbes; thus my parents use the fridge the rest of the time. Everyone is happy.

ANTIDOS: I did not doubt that you would answer the way you answered.

ELI_ME: Can I ask why?

ANTIDOS: Because *haredim* like to *humra* [lit., stringency or over-fulfilling the law] at someone else's expense. I have noticed it many times.

ELI_ME: But you must notice that I did not demand anything from them. Everything I did was required by minimal halakhic rules, not *humras*.

ANTIDOS: Of course you did not demand anything. It is just that your parents worried about your health (and that you will eat rotten food) and thus bought you the fridge. Let me give you another example. Your religion demands that you dip yourself into a *mikvah* [ritual bath]. But your parents are worried that you would get a cold, and so they pay for the furnace in the mikvah building. What you really did was to create a problem for your parents, and then made them resolve it.

The style, tone, and content of this exchange reflect, to a degree, an amalgam of practices, folkloric beliefs, and traditions popular among Russian *ba'alei teshuvah*. Some of those beliefs, like being punished for not observing religious laws, derive from lectures by yeshiva instructors and perhaps informal conversations with authoritative figures, such as rabbis or more knowledgeable acquaintances. In the parts of this exchange that were omitted, discussants relate anecdotes about people they know of who were killed in car crashes while driving on the Sabbath and other stories about righteous people who did nothing wrong and yet were also killed on the Sabbath. The level of the discussion suggests that all participants are familiar with the milieu in which such stories circulate, and have thought to some extent about their relevance and meanings.

The knowledge of—or, rather, the expectation that participants know and understand—terms such as *humra, halakhah, mikvah*, is presumed by all participants in the exchange and hints at their background in the Orthodox Jewish milieu. Moreover, it seems that the basic practices associated with the observance of the Sabbath, such as not turning on the light during the day (thus the fridge story), do not require clarification or explanation. The argument is not even about whether such a prohibition makes sense from a logical point of view (a common subject of discussion among secular Russian Jews), but rather, about how the fulfillment of *halakhic* obligations affects people close to them, especially if the effect is negative.

It is noteworthy that even "eli_me" does not suggest that his goal is to bring his parents closer to the laws of Judaism. Instead, he boasts that he "became calmer" after his parents began to "respect his needs." In effect, parents are seen not only as "a lost cause" for Judaism, but also as lacking authority, whether moral and intellectual, for their grown children. "Antidos" and his supporters do not question this status quo either. Rather, they suggest that the newly religious children are exploiting their parents financially by manipulating them with guilt, all in the name of religion. Religious behavior, therefore, is portrayed as parasitic. Through the dialogue, "antidos" and "zlata_gl" reveal the exploitative nature of the behavior described by "eli_me" by pointing out that his parents actually paid real money for the religious beliefs of their son, which they themselves do not share, and that they have to do this in order to maintain their relationship with their son.

I also believe that the exchange adds to our understanding of the structural transformation of the family that occurred during the collapse of the Soviet Union and the subsequent mass migration of Jews from Russia. In the eyes of many *ba'alei teshuvah*, this change took place by the hand of God. In other words, their return to Judaism—a system of belief known to be centered on the family—now requires the destruction of that family. The collapse of a special, close-knit Jewish family, which was an oasis of resistance to the Soviet regime, is a locus of post-Soviet Jewish nostalgia.[26] For immigrants, the collapse of the family is associated with leaving Russia. For *ba'alei teshuvah*, their embrace of Judaism and an Orthodox lifestyle is the breaking point for their families—even if the families themselves are not dispersed around the globe.

ANTIRELIGIOUS PROPAGANDA OF THE 1920S AND 1930S AND "ANTIDOS"

The arguments used in the exchange quoted above, as well as the rest of the "antidos" blog, strongly resemble the arguments of Soviet Yiddish antireligious propaganda in the 1920s, which emphasized the dishonesty of clerics, the parasitic nature of religious people, and the expense associated with the observance of the laws of Judaism.²⁷ While "antidos" does not seem to share the fundamental argument of Soviet antireligious ideology (i.e., God does not exist, therefore, religion makes no sense), he certainly employs Soviet arguments that explained who "really benefits" from religion and its followers and why. Soviet propaganda explained religion as: a) a lie spread to the masses so that they do not rebel against the existing regime; b) antiscientific (the achievements of archeology, physics, chemistry, and aerodynamics were presented as counter-arguments to religion); c) a mechanism to exploit believers financially (by paying for religious items, clergy salaries, church buildings, etc.); d) a system allowing dishonest clerics to hide their immoral or simply criminal deeds behind the mask of religion; e) a system of beliefs that is harmful to one's health; and f) a way to create ethnic hostility. In addition, specifically anti-Jewish materials asserted that the belief in Jews as the chosen people was false.

Almost all these assertions can be found in the "antidos" blog. The blog is rich with examples of how *haredim* and *"kiruvniks"* force observant Jews to overspend on kosher meat and other kosher products.²⁸ The blog places special emphasis on the immoral behavior of *haredim*, who allegedly lie, steal, and exploit women, all in the name of Judaism and its God.²⁹ "Antidos" asserts similarities between the "false" beliefs of Orthodox Jews and Orthodox Christians.³⁰ "Antidos" even suggests creating an Antidos synagogue, complete with rituals that advocate the abandonment of the religious lifestyle and nonkosher food.³¹ The parallels with the "Living Synagogue" created in the Soviet Union in 1924, with similar rituals and similar goals, are so obvious as to not require elaboration, except that an interview with the author of "antidos" revealed that he was not aware of the Soviet arguments against religion used in the 1920s and 1930s, and he was certainly not aware of the existence of the Living Synagogue.

Perhaps the blog's arguments against Judaism are based on the Soviet antireligious model since the author was exposed to it while growing up in the 1980s in Leningrad. However, many of the postulates of Soviet antireligious propaganda were no longer in operation by that time, certainly not in such detail and not directed toward Judaism specifically. Most authors of Soviet antireligious propaganda geared toward Jews had received a yeshiva education. This background gave them enough information to fight the religious tradition from within. The difference between them and "antidos" is that the latter learned about Judaism later in life and did not associate it with his childhood, but rather with coming of age and being separated from his family.

Antidos has an ambivalent relationship with the Soviet past in general. Whenever he criticizes the world of Jewish Orthodoxy, he compares it to the Communist Party system, with its overbearing control, senseless rituals, and corruption. He is not alone in this criticism. Even openly Orthodox bloggers criticize the structure of the community; in this criticism they often evoke parallels with the

Soviet system.[32] In general, the internal criticism employed by many Russian-language immigrant bloggers, not only Orthodox Jewish ones, evokes accusations that they follow Soviet patterns of behavior, which is seen as a negative thing (though for Russian-language bloggers based in Russia, the Soviet past is not universally viewed negatively). On the other hand, "antidos" wrote frequently about the benefits of secular education (including Soviet education) as opposed to religious education. Though the negativity of Orthodox society is closely associated with the negativity of the Soviet system, the positive attributes of Soviet education are, in his view, unmatched in the world of Jewish Orthodoxy.

ANTIDOS AND THE CONTEMPORARY CRITIQUE OF HAREDI SOCIETY

A numerical analysis of the entries in "antidos," that is, counting how many entries are devoted to particular subjects and estimating the popularity of each entry (as revealed by the number of comments and cross-referencing), reveals that the most popular topic for both the writer and the readers is the position of Russian *ba'alei teshuvah* in *haredi* society. For "antidos," this seems to be one of the sorest issues; thus, it is not surprising that it is the reason he gives for writing the blog.

The critique consists of a few components. *Haredim* do not value secular education and knowledge (e.g., they do not value the prior knowledge of the *ba'alei teshuvah*). *Haredim* believe in *segulot* [magical tricks, often based on Kabbalah], denying the power of science and medicine and relying on tricks instead.[33] Most importantly, *haredim* see Russian Jews as objects for performing commandments or good deeds, rather than recognizing them as equal human beings. A typical post on the topic: "In the past two days, twice someone offered me to shake a *lulav* [palm tree branch used on Sukkot]. Of course, they were Chabadniks. I am a kind person and did not say no. But I was amazed with the absolutely similar behavior *after* I completed the commandment. They *instantly* lost interest in me, and they would disappear ... although I really wanted to talk"[34] (emphases in original). The author refers to the holiday of Sukkot, when the streets of Jewish neighborhoods in Toronto become populated with "mitzvah vans" and individuals who encourage passersby (whom they identify as Jews) to perform the commandment of shaking the *lulav*. According to "antidos," Russian Jews are reduced to objects, even somewhat dehumanized. In response to the post, readers expressed a variety of opinions on the topic:

ONEFINEJEW: It seems that you are egocentric. They need to help so many lost Jews to fulfill this commandment, and they have no time to speak to antidos.[35]
MASHKANY: You should have asked to talk before you shook, and for a long time![36]
ONIONSOUPMIX:[37] It is about quantity. So they can brag to their friends, "I got 45 Jews to shake the lulav today." Don't take it personally.[38]

KOL_MISHAMAYIM: Are you not surprised when a doctor, after he gives you the prescription, loses his interest in you and calls on a new patient? Or, when a seller, who sold you something, turns his attention to another customer? Or, are you trying to talk to them too?[39]

The range of reaction requires little elaboration, except to note that the four comments present typical reactions to posts in "antidos." Some users agree fully, yet most argue, trying either to point out the flawed logic of the author, his unjustified expectations, or his misunderstanding of the situation. Others agree with his assertion and think of additional ways to support the argument. While none of the commentators doubts that Russian Jews are seen as objects for improvement, not all see anything wrong with this situation. In other words, they too feel that Russian Jews need additional education in order to be considered "real" Jews.

The second of the blog's criticisms of the relationship between *haredi* and Russian *ba'alei teshuvah* is that no matter how much a *ba'al teshuvah* succeeds in his religious education, including Talmudic learning, he will never be granted a teaching position in a prestigious non-*ba'alei teshuvah* yeshiva. Moreover, he will never be allowed to marry a woman from a *haredi* family who is not a *ba'alat teshuvah* herself (the same goes for women, though "antidos" does speak about many cases when Russian *ba'alei teshuvah* were tricked into marrying *haredi* men who had mental problems by attracting them to the improved social standing represented by marriage to a non-*ba'al teshuvah*).[40] It is not clear to what extent the author's accusations are true, but the fact that such stories circulate in blogs and as rumors is significant enough to reveal the anxieties associated with being a newcomer in the world of Jewish Orthodoxy.

The claim of "being a second-class citizen" deserves elaboration. Orthodox society, with its perceived elitism—placing Russian *ba'alei teshuvah* on the lowest rung of the social ladder—is subjected to strong criticism.[41] The argument provokes heated discussion among readers of "antidos," who suggest that either the *ba'alei teshuvah* will be treated equally if they are deserving or that they do not deserve to be treated equally (due to their lack of knowledge and important pedigree). Some even assert that they stand a rung higher than non-*ba'alei teshuvah* because they actually understand why they are observing the *mitzvot* [commandments], unlike those who have been observant from birth and perform rituals, prayers, and *mitzvot* automatically, without thinking about their significance or even believing in God. A typical exchange on this topic is represented below:

ANTIDOS: [...] Shaul himself, for some people, is a second-class person because it is unlikely that his mamma went to the mikvah before Mr. Shaul was born.

SHAULREZNIK: [the object of the satire, a user who positions himself as ultra-Orthodox with public pictures of himself with beard, kippah, and sidelocks]: But also for me, some people are second class—those who do not read books, for example. Or those, who blow their noses into curtains. Every society consists of classes and sub-classes, from people who, according to Orwell, consider themselves more equal than others.

ANTIDOS: Welcome to the society of second-class people, Shaul.[42]

It is noteworthy how "shaulreznik" defines a "second-class person." For Soviet-raised bloggers, religious limitations on secular books are problematic. *Haredi* society looks down on reading secular books, and most books are defined as secular. Russian *ba'alei teshuvah* usually have a hard time justifying the prohibition. Many Orthodox bloggers post about the secular books they read during the Sabbath. Discussions about letting children read Russian literature occur on almost every blog from this milieu.

In-depth interviews would have helped reveal whether Russian *ba'alei teshuvah* actually believe that the lack of knowledge of world culture places *haredim* on a comparatively lower intellectual level. The blogs, as a manifestation of "the public private" sphere, reveal that this sentiment is certainly present and somewhat accepted. In this context, "antidos'" complaints can also reflect the expectation that the *haredi* community should feel *flattered* that intellectual Jews like the Russian *ba'alei teshuvah* have joined their society, whereas the *haredim* consider them "second-class" people.

ANTIDOS'S PERSONA: DRAMA IN THE INTERNET AND REAL LIFE

Looking at entries from the inception of the blog in 2004 until its conclusion in 2008—when the author announced, in a private message to his subscribers, that he was going to write under another, less antagonizing name—the story told is essentially the transformation of an ultra-Orthodox young man, a former *ba'al teshuvah*, into a "free" secular Jew who no longer subscribes to Judaism. Periodically, "antidos" informed the readers of his difficulties coping with his wife's lack of desire to leave Judaism, his own doubts about his decision, and his anger toward those who "deceived" him about the Jewish way of life.

As is clear from the first section of this chapter, the story belongs to the genres of fantasy and fictional autobiography. When I met "antidos" in 2007, he was leading an Orthodox Jewish way of life, which included sending his children to Orthodox day schools and observing Sabbath, the laws of kashrut, and family purity. His wife, aware of his online writing, understood it as a form of fiction, which only partially portrayed the "real" views of her husband.

In fact, the first meeting with the author of "antidos" was in the context of the United Jewish Appeal's Russian Jewish community-building initiative. We were scheduled to talk about ways to interest Russian speakers in Judaism and Jewish culture. When he asked me about my research, I mentioned my research on the blog with the name "antidos." He revealed himself as the author (speaking of miracles in real life and breakthroughs in research!). He later wrote about this meeting on his blog, verifying the connection.

The visit described earlier occurred as a follow-up to our initial meeting, when he suggested that I meet his family. During lunch, he spoke about growing up in Leningrad, studying in a yeshiva in Israel, and about his teachers and classmates there. Many of them were readers of his blogs, and he revealed to me that he knew who they were, but he still did not tell them that he had been writing under the pseudonym of "antidos," since he was not ready to be seen as "antidos" in real life.

I think the success of the blog lay precisely in the guarded anonymity of its author and the dramatic tension he built. Readers were attracted by the enigma of his personality, virtual and real. In the first years of the blog's existence, readers speculated on who he was, why he knew their way of life so well, and what had driven him away from Judaism. Some suggested that he could not find his niche in the community, others that living a non-Orthodox lifestyle was easier. Other, less benign commenters insisted that he preferred being rich to being Orthodox. Sometimes, the discussions were more frivolous and analyzed whether "antidos" was a man or a woman, whether he was really Jewish, Orthodox, or even a KGB spy. One speculation posited him as an alter ego of a respected ultra-Orthodox blogger who decided to have some fun and write forbidden things. In reality, this is the closest to the real situation, but none of the suspected bloggers was the author of "antidos."

Another means of building drama was that "antidos" positioned himself as an insider- outsider who was being rejected by the virtual community. For example, he diligently documented all users who "banned" him from commenting on their blogs. "Banning" is a LiveJournal function that allows bloggers to block certain users from posting comments. Usually, the function is used against spam and bullies. However, "antidos" presents the bans against him as his Orthodox readers closing their eyes to uncomfortable truths about Judaism.

In 2008, about a year after our conversation, a year filled with very heated discussion within and outside the blog, "antidos" revealed his name and picture to his subscribers, suggesting that he wished to end the suspense and enter an open discussion in which his opponents knew his background and education, and understood that his doubts were not solely provocative remarks but rather stemmed from the desire to maintain an honest and open dialogue. The end of the suspense meant the end of the critical nature of the blog and the transformation of the "antidos" persona—no longer an ambivalent, uncompromising critic of Judaism.

This narrative of personal transformation bears a strong resemblance to the genre of *maskilic* [Jewish "Enlightenment"] autobiographies of the early nineteenth century. It is accompanied by a critique of superstitions and misunderstandings of Judaism and of the mistreatment of believers, nonbelievers, and non-Jews. It is filled with moments of revelation that become turning points in one's identity. Typically, it is written with a pen name. One can find as many similarities between the antidos blog and *maskilic* writing as with Soviet antireligious propaganda from the 1920s. The notion of *Haskalah* [Enlightenment] as a progressive system of thought as opposed to Judaism as a backward-looking system of life intrigues "antidos." It creates a legitimate intellectual heritage for his thinking (unlike the Soviet antireligious tradition, which is discredited both in his view and that of his opponents). The name of the avatar of his new blog implies an association with the *maskilim* and offers a deeper, more multifaceted examination of Judaism—one that is not purely antagonistic.[43]

The change in blog page and the loss of anonymity or, rather, the loss of secrecy, led to a decline both in readership and the author's effort in writing it. The posts on the new blog are rare and lack the wit and controversy of "antidos'" entries.

CONCLUSIONS

The culture of speaking about private matters in public, familiar to Russian speakers, finds a wide reception among bloggers, who often complain of constraints in their adopted societies, which privilege privacy (especially the United States, Canada, and Germany, and to a lesser degree, Israel). The social space created by *ba'alei teshuvah* bloggers, therefore, becomes a transnational village where leaving Russia is assumed as a part of one's biography and where place of residence is less important than the observance of Jewish religious laws.

The cultural practices that allow in-depth discussions of traditionally private issues and dilemmas make the Russian virtual space a richer ground for research in identity than similar English language resources. LiveJournal, with its large communities of blogs and its transnational nature, combines the intimacy of a diary with the public openness of a town hall and becomes a virtual home for subgroups in the Russian Jewish diaspora. The content analysis of these blogs can provide complex data on numerous transnational groups, including single women in immigration, mothers, computer programmers, cancer patients, children of Russian parents, Russian Israelis living in Canada, and many, many others. Utilizing linguistic, cultural, literary, sociological, and historical methods of analysis, and studying the content of immigrants' blogs, can take us far beyond the concept of computer-mediated communication among non-Russians.

The analysis of the rise, peak, and end of the "antidos" blog on LiveJournal provides not only a glimpse into the world of the Ultra-Orthodox Russian Jewish community, but also reveals the structure and the culture of a segment of Russian Jewish diasporic blogging. "Antidos" wrote about issues that are common to his readers, who live all over the world and who struggle to define themselves and their families through the prism of both Orthodox Judaism and the cultures of their adopted societies. Blogging helps many cope with dilemmas and provides an outlet for frustrations and unresolved issues while serving as sheer entertainment, which often replaces reading, television watching, or even spending time with family (according to many discussions of bloggers). "Antidos'" tendency to provoke, overdramatize, and ridicule catered to his audience, and the discussions that his posts provoked can be analyzed as displays of the Russian Jewish Orthodox "public private" sphere, which otherwise is rarely accessible.

This chapter aims to start a discussion about the richness of the blogosphere material for ethnographic research on Russian Jewish Orthodox Internet users. My analysis of "antidos'" blog opens new dimensions in our understanding of post-Soviet Jewish culture, transitional Russian Jewish identity outside of Russia, aspects of the identity and culture of the generation born in the 1970s and 1980s, and debates within the Russian Jewish religious community. One can only imagine what a more systematic and large-scale study will uncover.

NOTES

1. M. Alstyne and E. Brynjolfsson, "Electronic Communities: Global Village or Cyberbalkans?" September 20, 1996, http://web.mit.edu/marshall/www/Abstracts.html. N. K. Baym, "The Emergence of Community in Computer Mediated Communication," in *Cybersociety: Computer-Mediated Communication and Community*, ed. Steve Jones (Thousand Oaks, CA: Sage Publications, 1995), 138–163; Sage Castles, *Citizenship and Migration: Globalization and the Politics of Belonging* (New York: Routledge, 2000); Paul Dimaggio, Eszter Hargittai, W. Russell Neuman, and John P. Robinson, "Social Implications of the Internet," *Annual Review of Sociology* 27.1 (2001): 307–336; Anada Mitra, "Diasporic Web Sites: Ingroup and Outgroup Discourse," *Critical Studies in Mass Communication* 14.2 (1997): 158–181; Howard Rheingold, *The Virtual Community: Homesteading on the Electronic Frontier* (Reading, MA: Addison-Wesley, 1993).
2. Harry Hiller and Tara Franz, "New Ties, Old Ties, and Lost Ties: The Use of the Internet in Diaspora," *New Media and Society* 6.6 (2004): 731–752, 739.
3. Larissa Remennick, "The Russian-Jewish Transnational Social Space: An Overview," *Journal of Jewish Identities* 4.1 (2011): 1–11.
4. For an in-depth analysis of the Russian websites in San Antonio, Texas, see Filipp Sapienza, "Communal Ethos on a Russian Émigré Web Site," in *Proceedings, Cultural Attitudes towards Communication and Technology, 1998*, ed. C. Ess and F. Sudweeks (University of Sydney, Australia), 116–134.
5. Nelly Elias and Dafna Lemish, "Media Uses in Immigrant Families: Torn between 'Inward' and 'Outward' Paths of Integration," *International Communication Gazette* 70.1 (2008): 21–40. Nelly Elias and Dafna Lemish, "Spinning the Web of Identity: The Role of Internet Use in the Lives of Immigrant Adolescents," *New Media Society* 11 (2009): 533.
6. Adi Kuntsman, "Webs of Hate in Diasporic Cyberspaces: The Gaza War in the Russian-Language Blogosphere," *Media, War & Conflict* 3.3 (December 2010): 299–313. Available at http://mwc.sagepub.com/content/3/3/299.
7. Eugene Gorny, "A Creative History of the Russian Internet" (PhD diss., University College London, 2006).
8. Here is the partial list of Russian communities on LiveJournal that speak about living in American cities: arizona_ru, boston_ru, chicago_ru, florida_ru, lacrus, okla_home_ru, ru_atlanta, ru_austin, ru_dc, ru_dfw, ru_houston, ru_midwest, and many others.
9. A well-organized, albeit heavily abbreviated list of the most important websites devoted to Jewish life and culture can be found here: http://www.jafi.org.il/JewishAgency/Russian/, last accessed on February 10, 2015.
10. Elias and Lemish, "Media Uses in Immigrant Families." Elias and Lemish, "Spinning the Web of Identity." Remennick, "The Russian-Jewish Transnational Social Space." Larisa Fialkova,

"Emigrants from the FSU and the Russian-Language Internet," *Toronto Slavic Review—Academic Electronic Journal in Slavic Studies* 12 (2005), www.utoronto.ca/tsq/12.
11. Kuntsman, "Webs of Hate in Diasporic Cyberspaces," 303.
12. Larissa Remennick, "Religious Russian Jewish Immigrants: Features of the Portrait," *Bar Ilan Sociological Papers* 15 (2010), http://socpapers.org/.
13. Zvi Gitelman, with Valeriy Chervyakov and Vladimir Shapiro, "Thinking about Being Jewish in Russia and Ukraine," in *Jewish Life after the USSR*, ed. Zvi Gitelman (Bloomington: Indiana University Press, 2003), 49–60; and Zvi Gitelman, "E Pluribus Unum? Post-Soviet Jewish Identities and Their Implications for Communal Reconstruction," in ibid., 61–75.
14. While I base this assertion on my own research (*Soviet and Kosher*, etc.), Larissa Remennick notes that her subjects also speak of these same phenomena. See Remennick and Anna Prashizky, "Religious Russian-Jewish Immigrants: Features of the Portrait," *Sociological Papers* 15 (2010), http://www.socpapers.org/sp2010/sp2010-2.pdf.
15. http://andrutchak.livejournal.com/profile.
16. http://uri-superfin.livejournal.com/profile.
17. http://o-aronius.livejournal.com/profile.
18. http://uri-superfin.livejournal.com/26258.html, accessed on June 3, 2011.
19. http://antidos.livejournal.com/, accessed on June 1, 2011.
20. The letters stand for the Aramaic phrase *b'siyata de'shmaya* [with the help of Heaven]. The acronym is written at the top of documents as a reminder to the writer and reader that without God's help we can do nothing of eternal value.
21. http://antidos.livejournal.com/56767.html, accessed on June 6, 2011.
22. http://antidos.livejournal.com/56767.html?thread=557247#t557247, accessed on June 7, 2011.
23. http://antidos.livejournal.com/56767.html?thread=558783#t558783, accessed on June 7, 2011.
24. The full discussion can be found here: http://antidos.livejournal.com/56767.html?thread=560575#t560575, accessed on June 7, 2011.
25. Yeshiva students.
26. Anna Shternshis, "Russian Militia Singing in Yiddish: Jewish Nostalgia in Soviet and Post-Soviet Popular Culture," in *Choosing Yiddish: New Frontiers of Language and Culture*, ed. Lara Rabinovitch, Shiri Goren, and Hannah Pressman (Detroit: Wayne State University Press, 2013), 179–194.
27. Anna Shternshis, *Soviet and Kosher: Jewish Popular Culture in the Soviet Union, 1923–1939* (Bloomington: Indiana University Press, 2006).
28. See, for example, http://antidos.livejournal.com/2006/02/14/, accessed on June 14, 2011, and http://antidos.livejournal.com/2005/10/30/, accessed on June 14, 2011.
29. http://antidos.livejournal.com/230733.html, http://antidos.livejournal.com/225905.html, http://antidos.livejournal.com/2006/10/09/, http://antidos.livejournal.com/173286.html, http://antidos.livejournal.com/2347.html, http://antidos.livejournal.com/8334.html, http://antidos.livejournal.com/65306.html, http://antidos.livejournal.com/2006/09/21/, http://antidos.livejournal.com/2006/10/29/, all accessed on June 14, 2011.
30. http://antidos.livejournal.com/2005/09/28/, http://antidos.livejournal.com/2005/04/08/, accessed on June 15, 2011.
31. http://antidos.livejournal.com/2005/05/29/, accessed on June 15, 2011.
32. http://antidos.livejournal.com/181168.html, accessed on June 15, 2011.
33. http://antidos.livejournal.com/204861.html, http://antidos.livejournal.com/160984.html, http://antidos.livejournal.com/2007/04/13/, http://antidos.livejournal.com/2006/04/23/, http://antidos.livejournal.com/2005/12/20/, http://antidos.livejournal.com/2347.html, all accessed on June 15, 2011.
34. http://antidos.livejournal.com/114894.html, accessed on June 17, 2011.

35. http://antidos.livejournal.com/114894.html?thread=1432526#t1432526, accessed on June 17, 2011.
36. http://antidos.livejournal.com/114894.html?thread=1432782#t1432782, accessed on June 17, 2011.
37. This blogger is an ultra-Orthodox Jewish woman, a Russian-born *ba'alat teshuvah*, who writes in English. Her blog has already been partially studied in Andrea Lieber, "A Virtual Veibershul: Blogging and the Blurring of Public and Private among Orthodox Jewish Women," *College English* 72.6 (July 2010): 621–637. Accessed at http://www.jofa.org/pdf/uploaded/1737-UJFP8603.pdf.
38. http://antidos.livejournal.com/114894.html?thread=1434830#t1434830, accessed on June 17, 2011.
39. http://antidos.livejournal.com/114894.html?thread=1435086#t1435086, accessed on June 17, 2011.
40. http://antidos.livejournal.com/37548.html, accessed on June 15, 2011.
41. Israeli sociologists studying local Russian *ba'alei teshuvah* recorded similar observations. See Remennick and Prashizky, "Religious Russian Jewish Immigrants."
42. http://antidos.livejournal.com/37548.html, accessed on June 15, 2011.
43. I cannot mention the name of his next blog, as the transition to the new blog was announced only to subscribers.

PART VI DIASPORA RUSSIAN LITERATURE

In line with the growing interest in diasporas, more attention has been paid to "diaspora writers" in college curricula and trends in literary criticism. There are exiled writers—Adam Mickiewicz living in France, Thomas Mann in the United States, Breyten Breytenbach in France—and there are émigré writers, some of whom choose to write in a new language (for example, Joseph Conrad and Vladimir Nabokov). Still others continue to write in their original language, such as Sholem Aleichem and Ivan Bunin. The Russian-speaking Jewish diaspora, whose "homeland" is not as clearly defined as those of the aforementioned authors, includes some who write in their original language and others who write in the language of their new country. David Bezmozgis, Gary Shteyngart, Larisa Vapnyar, Anya Ulinich, Yelena Akhtiorskaya, Boris Fishman, among others, have gained wide recognition as Russian-speaking Jews writing in English. The three chapters that follow deal mainly with those who continue to write in Russian and remain part of Russian literature, in most cases, part of "Russian-Jewish literature."

Mikhail Krutikov examines the work of four writers working in Russian, some of whom are well known and acclaimed in Russia itself. According to Krutikov, they are seen as having a common "mind-set," one that is "high-brow, elitist, snobby, pretentious, serious, uncompromising, high-cultural, or complex." Thus, the writers openly proclaim their disdain for mass culture and commercial success. While they are largely unknown in the English-speaking world, they are taken seriously by literary critics in the Russian-speaking milieu. This is to be expected, given the increasing decentralization of Russian-language literature, which is now being published in several countries. In Krutikov's assessment, "Russian Jewish culture remains diverse, complex, and fluid. Rooted in the Soviet past, it undergoes constant revision and re-imagining in accordance with varying aesthetic patterns, ideological commitments, political goals, and commercial interests."

In Stephanie Sandler's view, "Poets whose attitude toward Jewish identity fluctuates provide the most piercing articulations of diasporic dislocation and constitute the vast majority of contemporary Jewish poets. The Nazis would have exterminated these poets, to use a crude description; the writers acknowledge this terrible connection of blood and birth, but they barely register that recognition in the vast bulk of their writing." Sandler analyzes the works of four poets who are "marginally Jewish," one of whom has even converted to Christianity and another who writes in English. She carefully traces Jewish motifs and references in their work, thereby elucidating the complex, often ambivalent attitudes of émigrés toward Jews and Judaism. Sandler shows clearly how differently the poets relate to their Jewishness. "Kaminsky . . . whose work has moved us from prayer, often uttered in despair in Khersonskii's work, to words of praise; from burnished silver ritual objects sold off in desperation or confiscated, through the curious museum exhibits of Temkina, past the burned out words of Gronas, toward the dancing exhilaration and determination of Kaminsky's English. . . . At this moment, early in the twenty-first century, when Russian poetry flourishes in many places around the world, poets of Jewish descent play a strong role in giving to Russian poetry its distinctive, border-crossing, wall-tumbling, boundary-shifting identity."

There are important Russian-Jewish writers in Germany and Austria, not only in Israel and North America. Adrian Wanner addresses several of them, including Wladimir Kaminer—one of Germany's most popular writers who writes in German, a language he did not know when he immigrated at age twenty-three. As Wanner shows, Kaminer and another author, Lena Gorelik (who immigrated as a child), seem unperturbed by living in the land where Nazism reigned, and they are not terribly concerned about their Jewishness. In contrast, the literary persona of Vladimir Vertlib, who has lived in several countries and lately in Austria, "is that of the alienated outsider rather than the happily integrated immigrant."

Wanner writes that "there are important differences between Russian-German and Russian-American writers, which stem from the different nature of their respective host societies. In the United States, the immigrant experience lies at the core of the nation's self-image and cultural mythology, allowing Russian newcomers to insert themselves into a long tradition of immigrant and Jewish writing in America. . . . The situation is very different in Germany, a country that has defined itself traditionally as an ethnically homogenous *Volk* and that only recently (and reluctantly) has begun to grapple with the fact that it has become a destination for immigrants." Thus, for example, "Kaminer's benevolent depiction of Germany has a greater appeal to the German public than the more subversive writings of Vertlib, who continues to raise uncomfortable questions about German xenophobia and anti-Semitism. Kaminer's performance of the 'cool' yet ultimately harmless Russian, and Gorelik's persona of the female 'immigrant overachiever' fit neatly into the utopian projection of the New Germany as a happy, multicultural community." Adverting briefly to RSJ writers in Israel, Wanner finds that many immigrant writers in all of the receiving countries use their "Russianness" to make themselves distinctive, and he wonders how long they can continue to play this card.

For the time being, literature plays a significant role in connecting Russian readers across countries and Russian writers to them as well as to their former country and its culture.

15 · FOUR VOICES FROM THE LAST SOVIET GENERATION

Evgeny Steiner, Alexander Goldshtein, Oleg Yuryev, and Alexander Ilichevsky

MIKHAIL KRUTIKOV

The two post-Soviet decades have been difficult for the Russian intelligentsia, economically and socially. The collapse of the unloved but stable and familiar Soviet system forced many in intellectual occupations to reinvent themselves by looking for alternatives in business, media, religion, and politics. The "death of the Russian intelligentsia" has become a common trope in academic and journalistic discourse.[1] The intelligentsia has lost its social and economic status but retained some influence (though, perhaps, merely symbolic) and has felt increasingly frustrated and redundant during Vladimir Putin's rule. A great number of intellectuals, writers, artists, and scientists have left Russia or found themselves in the newly independent states where their previous status as members of the intelligentsia is no longer valid or recognized. Katerina Clark believes that the roots of the crisis of the Russian intelligentsia "has come less from local factors, such as a shortage of funds, than from broader changes in the world at large which also contributed to the demise of the Soviet state itself." In the "global intellectual economy, their sense of unique identity was even further challenged."[2]

I would argue that, contrary to Clark's sweeping and categorical statement, at least for some members of the Russian intelligentsia, the post-Soviet situation has been beneficial. I will consider four Russian Jews who left the Soviet Union/Russia at the critical moment of the turn of the 1990s and managed to find their place in a global intellectual economy by articulating their unique identity as Russian writers and intellectuals. Each in his own way achieved recognition in Russia (some also found fame abroad) thanks to their ability to translate their experience of social, cultural, and geographical dislocation into the idiom of Russian high culture, which resonated with the interests and concerns of their audiences both inside and outside Russia.

Different in their artistic tastes and ideological outlooks, coming from different regions and backgrounds, and residing in different countries, the four writers nevertheless share certain features. They belong to the same generation, are male, Jewish, and unabashedly elitist in their cultural attitude. As I will try to demonstrate, they use similar imagery and metaphors in their works, otherwise quite different in genre and style, to convey their vision of the world after the collapse of the Soviet Union by engaging with the tradition of Russian and international modernism and the avant-garde, in particular, with the legacy of Joseph Brodsky. Of course, these authors are neither the only émigré writers in contemporary Russian literature nor the most popular ones.[3] Yet, by focusing on these four, I wish to demonstrate the resilience of a certain cultural mindset, which can alternatively be described as high-brow, elitist, snobby, pretentious, serious, uncompromising, high-cultural, or complex. The writers openly proclaim their disdain for mass culture, commercial success, and "readability." Yet all of them have acquired significant "symbolic capital"; in other words, their works provoke debate and are recognized by critics as influential and trend-setting. Some have won prestigious literary awards. However, so far their writing remains practically unknown in the English-speaking world; I hope that this chapter will spark interest in their writing.

THE *ZASTOY* GENERATION

Born between 1955 and 1970, Evgeny Steiner, Alexander Goldshtein, Oleg Yuryev, and Alexander Ilichevsky belong to "the last Soviet generation," in anthropologist Alexei Yurchak's words. According to Yurchak, the common identity of this generation was "formed by a shared experience of the normalized, ubiquitous, and immutable authoritative discourse of the Brezhnev's years." In contrast to preceding and subsequent generations, all of which had an "inaugural event" that defined their generational identity (e.g., World War II, the denunciation of Stalin, and the collapse of the Soviet Union), the defining "non-event" of this generation was *zastoy* [stagnation], as the Brezhnev period later came to be defined when compared with Gorbachev's perestroika. As Yurchak argues in his study, members of this generation "became actively engaged in creating various new pursuits, identities, and forms of living that were enabled by authoritative discourse, but not necessarily defined by it."[4] This kind of creative engagement, combined with active estrangement from "official" Soviet culture, shaped the outlook of these four writers and continues to occupy a prominent place in their post-Soviet work. Despite the upheaval of recent decades, their Soviet past retains a strong hold on their imaginations.

In 1992, at the high point of the "great *aliyah*," the mass Jewish immigration from the disintegrating Soviet Union, the Tel Aviv Russian magazine *Zven'ia*

[Links] published an exchange between two recent immigrants. Seventeen years later, in 2009, its successor *Zerkalo* [Mirror]—arguably one of the best Russian small magazines outside Russia—republished this exchange as an important document in the history of the Russian-Israeli intelligentsia. The author of the first essay was Evgeny Steiner—an art historian and critic specializing in medieval Japan and the Russian avant-garde who, prior to his emigration, belonged to the privileged circles of Moscow's intellectual bohemia. In "Apologiia zastoinogo iunoshi" ["Apology of a Young Man of the Stagnation Period"], he describes the cultural and anthropological type of the "para-Soviet man." This type is a product of a particular time and place, namely, Moscow and Leningrad of the 1970s–1980s, a "mutant of the Soviet system with the negative experience of estrangement from the dominant socio-cultural situation but with no positive experience of integration into any other macro-system."[5] Neither a loyal Soviet citizen nor an active dissident, such a person is an eternal outsider unwilling to participate actively in any other form of social life, and is, perhaps, incapable of such participation. The *zastoy* of the Soviet system fostered such a suspended existence; it demanded little ideological commitment or work productivity but provided, at least in Moscow and Leningrad, a certain modicum of material comfort, which even included such "luxuries" as relatively cheap books, concerts, and travel.

Although people of Jewish origin made up a significant part of this "para-Soviet" group, most of them regarded their Jewishness as a negative signifier of "otherness," which strengthened their status as outsiders rather than offering a positive form of identification along religious, cultural, or ethnic lines. Steiner explains that the emigration of many members of this group at the turn of the 1990s was due to the loss of their sense of security and comfort during the Soviet collapse. He concludes his essay with an open question: "To what extent will this group be able to use the baggage which they had accumulated in the specific hothouse of the Soviet animal farm?"[6]

Steiner's impressionistic image of the "para-Soviet" man anticipates Yurchak's more conceptualized notion of "de-territorialized milieus," which he regards as a specific late-Soviet socio-anthropological phenomenon. As Yurchak explains, these milieus consisted of groups of people who positioned themselves outside the forms of social life officially approved and promoted by Soviet authorities. They lived as if "suspended simultaneously inside and outside" of the "authoritative discursive regime."[7] Yurchak claims, projecting his personal experience in Leningrad's bohemian circles onto the entire Soviet society, that this kind of lifestyle was "a central and widespread principle of living in that system."[8] In his acceptance speech for the Hilde-Domin-Preis in Heidelberg, Oleg Yuryev described his Soviet childhood in Leningrad in similar terms: "For me, the entire Soviet reality was not real—a cloudy film wrapped around real life, genuine existence."[9] By their social and educational background, Yurchak and Yuryev belonged to the "para-Soviet" milieu of Leningrad and shared a common attitude to the surrounding Soviet reality. They also used similar strategies of survival in that reality that enabled them to create and preserve their independence without openly confronting the dominant order. Like Steiner in Moscow, they inhabited a "de-territorialized" social space that was broad enough to accommodate informal groups with diverse, sometimes opposing interests, ranging from Russian nationalists to Zionists, devout Christians, and hippies.[10]

Steiner's respondent was Alexander Goldshtein, who came to Israel from the less liberal, less comfortable provincial city of Baku. His experience of the Soviet collapse was much more dramatic. The violent anti-Armenian pogroms in Azerbaijan pushed him into emigration, an experience that haunted him for the rest of his life. Goldshtein responded skeptically to Steiner's "apologia," arguing that the difference between this imagined "para-Soviet" community and the Soviet environment was illusory. He suggests that, unable to create anything new and original, these "para-Soviet" men languished on "cultural rent" provided by the Soviet state. Anticipating Clark's argument about the "global intellectual economy" as a challenge to the Russian intelligentsia's sense of uniqueness, Goldshtein concluded, "And then we left and came to Israel. And it turned out that there was more 'reality' here, and that it was harder and more 'real.' And this means that it will be more difficult for us to fit into this reality, let alone to get to 'love' it. But, fortunately, there is less and less demand for 'love' recently."[11] Both Steiner and Goldshtein acknowledged that their emigration to Israel meant an end to the "de-territorialized" social life they had enjoyed between the wide cracks of the Soviet system. Still, their subsequent milieu can also be termed another "de-territorialization" of the Russian Jewish intelligentsia in the open world of immigration.

In the Soviet Union, Steiner and Goldshtein belonged to different social and cultural environments and were unlikely to engage in a public dialogue or even have their works published by the same press or periodical. While Steiner enjoyed the life of the Muscovite bohemian elite, building his reputation as an expert in the arcane but fashionable field of medieval Japanese cultural history, Goldshtein was eking out a living as a copy editor at an academic press in Baku. Though cosmopolitan and exotic—a meeting point of European and Islamic civilizations with an admixture of Judaism—Baku was nevertheless a backwater compared to Moscow and Leningrad. It was only after their emigration that Goldshtein and Steiner could open a dialogue with each other that could cross borders from Tel Aviv to New York to Moscow. After a few years in Israel, Steiner went on to pursue new academic opportunities in the United States and England; Goldshtein worked his way through the labyrinth of the Israeli Russian press to emerge as its leading intellectual voice. Both remained regular contributors to *Zerkalo*, and both published their books with the Moscow NLO Press.

In the 1990s, *Zerkalo* became an outlet for elitist and highbrow culture with its center in cosmopolitan Tel Aviv. The magazine was created by a group of artists and writers that coalesced around the artist and poet Mikhail Grobman

(b. 1939)—the charismatic self-styled leader of the so-called "second avant-garde" who immigrated to Israel in 1971. Thanks to active international cooperation with the NLO Press, in the early 2000s, the *Zerkalo* group was able to reach a wider audience. The editorial foreword to the anthology *Symbol "We": A Jewish Anthology of the New Russian Literature*[12] proclaimed the advent of a new era in Russian literary history, "free not only from the antagonistic division between the literatures in Russia (*rossiiskaia*) and abroad (*zarubezhnaia*), . . . but also from the hierarchy of subordination in accordance with the geographical belonging of the text and the author."[13] The anthology included twenty items of prose and poetry from authors (not all of whom were Jewish) from Israel, the United States, the Czech Republic, and Russia.

One should also mention two other Russian-Israeli periodicals, perhaps less vocal in their ambition to represent the "new" Russian Jewish culture, but not inferior to *Zerkalo* in their quality and originality—*Solnechnoe spleteniie* [Solar Plexus] (focusing on cultural criticism and literary history) and *Dvoetochie* [Colon] (a poetry-oriented review). The more conventional *Ierusalimskii zhurnal* [Jerusalem Journal] deliberately follows the traditional model of the Russian "thick journal" and serves a wider audience of aging Soviet-Jewish intelligentsia, publishing works written in a more accessible and familiar realist style. Among the regular contributors to this publication are such popular writers as Dina Rubina, Igor Guberman, and Alex Tarn, whose books have been published by major commercial Russian presses such as AST and EKSMO in editions, reaching 100,000 copies that reach a mass Russian-speaking audience in Russia and abroad. Moreover, all four periodicals are freely available online at the site of *Russkii zhurnal* [Russian Journal], which, until recently was sponsored by the Russian President's Administration.[14]

The fact that Goldshtein was the only author who had two items included in *Symbol "We"* indicates his position as the leading critical and intellectual voice of the *Zerkalo* group. As literary editor of the biggest Russian Israeli newspaper *Vesti*, Goldshtein had to churn out newspaper articles on many different themes. His meager income enabled him to survive in shabby rented flats in poor immigrant neighborhoods of Tel Aviv and adjacent towns. Success in Russia came to Goldshtein after his first book—the collection *Farewell to Narcissus*, which appeared in 1997. Penned in the early 1990s in Israel, this book is highly sophisticated in style and method. It represents an extended post-mortem analysis of the "Narcissus of the Russian Literary Civilization of the Twentieth Century," a cultural phenomenon that Goldshtein described as an "absolutely self-sufficient and highly intense [spiritual]" product of Russian imperial development.[15]

Virtually unknown in Russia until then, Goldshtein managed to win two prestigious awards at once: the Russian Booker Prize and its anti-establishment alternative, the Anti-Booker Prize. Paying tribute to Goldshtein in a conversation with Radio Liberty, Irina Prokhorova, the editor-in-chief of the Novoe Literaturnoe Obozrenie press, characterized this book as a "self-description of a generation, which is my generation," a generation that now has "to find its place in a foreign environment, trying to apply a survival strategy that had been worked out in previous years."[16]

To understand Goldshtein's special position in contemporary Russian culture, one has to keep in mind that he never resided in Russia proper and became famous only after—and largely thanks to—his emigration to Israel. Muscovite and Leningrad intellectuals such as Steiner portrayed emigration to Israel as relocation from a center to the remote periphery of the Russian cultural universe. Goldshtein, on the other hand, imagined his emigration as a move from one corner of a large "oriental" province to another. The "carefree, cynical, cosmopolitan, hard-boiled Soviet and yet anti-Soviet through and through, warm, marine and fruity, charmingly ambiguous" Baku of his youth was a "micro-civilization" that fell victim to the new reincarnation of the ancient Oriental barbarism.[17] As Goldshtein portrayed it, the post-Soviet nationalism of the Caucasus is but another reincarnation of the ancient Oriental tradition of tyranny; it is "dark as the history of the Medeans." This transformation is both terrifying and exciting, and as Goldshtein adds, "maybe that's why it's so interesting."[18]

Seen from this Orientalist perspective, Baku and Tel Aviv share some similarities. Both are bustling, cosmopolitan, European seaport cities, located in the heart of the Islamic Middle East, not unlike Cavafy's Alexandria—an unsettling parallel that appears frequently in Goldshtein's writing. What attracts him in Tel Aviv is not its glossy Western surface but its seedy underside. Residing in squalid rental accommodations in South Tel Aviv and Lod, Goldshtein was fascinated by the population of drug addicts, beggars, prostitutes, migrant workers, and déclassé Soviet immigrants, which created a "white Nairobi" at the very heart of the "secular capital of the Jews." The "role of nairobis is tremendous, independent, historic"; these are "magic spaces which do not allow the city to gain the rhythm of bourgeois respectability."[19]

From his position, deliberately maintained on the Mediterranean periphery of the Russian cultural universe, Goldshtein came out of the "unappetizing idea of literary unity" of transnational Russian literature, which smacks of Moscow-centric cultural imperialism. "It is not important . . . where the author is located, be it in Moscow, Tel Aviv, or New York (presumably one has to live in Moscow, but this is not always said, taking pity on foreigners), the main thing is that his work flow into the common river."[20] Instead he championed the concept of a decentralized and diversified literature that he called "imperial." He explains,

> An imperial literature, which Russian literature ought to be, should look favorably at otherness, diversity of its expressions. . . . For the sake of its own, I stress, its own interest, the culture of a cooling-down empire must tell its diasporic writers: "your literature is not Russian but Russophone, and this is good, that's what is needed now. It exists, it makes sense. Aspire to get as far away as possible from the mother

country [*metropoliia*] of the language, cultivate your foreign provincialism. I need you as you are, you are dear to me as a remedy against autarkic insularity."[21]

In this spirit, Goldshtein's ornate and viscous prose, with passages overburdened with metaphors, allusions, and slow rhythms, boasts a distinctly Oriental flavor. As in the previous quote, Goldshtein called upon the imaginary Russian diasporic writer to look for inspiration among postcolonial cultures, such as the Francophone writers of the Maghreb or Anglo-Indian writers.

Three major intellectual concerns inform Goldshtein's writing: the ability of culture to transcend its temporal and spatial limitations and to reach an audience beyond a particular time and space; the "clash of civilizations" between East and West (in particular the precarious position of Westernized minorities, such as Jews and Armenians, in the Islamic Orient); and the mystery of death. The mystery of death was a theme that became painfully pertinent to his own situation during the last two years of his life, as he was fighting lung cancer.

For Goldshtein, emigration was not a matter of personal choice but the result of tectonic shifts in history, which remain beyond the comprehension of its participants and observers. "It was your broken-up empire that performed your battle march by you and for you . . . people rarely recognize their fate by sight."[22] The irony of the historical power that plays with the lives of individuals and nations is particularly evident in the Orient, where "nations fight over primogeniture and miseries," and every Oriental nation takes a "savage pride in disaster."[23] A lesson learned in Baku is relevant for Israel: "There is no word more powerful than nation. . . . It gave blood to the veins, semen to the scrotum, vision to the eye, and I am a voluntary debtor to its generosity."[24] From this viewpoint, Western civilization is merely a dream, in which he sees himself "strolling, like a rootless vagabond in some Pax-Atlantic city . . . and, opening a hotel door, to announce hastily my rootless name to the concierge. For half a century, I wanted to wander from one hotel to another, making a sour face when asked about roots: it has become irrelevant long ago."[25] But as soon as he wakes up, he condemns this dream as a sin.

Goldshtein's opponent, Steiner, approaches the same concern differently. He describes his emigration experience via a loose collection of excerpts from letters, e-mails, academic essays, memoirs, and meditations, arranged against the background of a dramatic conflict between the author and his ex-wife.[26] Most of the texts were literally written "in space," during the author's many flights among America, Europe, Israel, Japan, and Russia, in 1992–2002. Writing in the confessional mode serves a therapeutic purpose; it liberates the author's inner self from the burden of the past by turning his painful experience into a text: "the living participants turn into literary characters—and what can you demand from them . . . and the story comes to an end. And life goes on. Another life. In another space."[27]

In the introductory essay, "Reflections of a Japanologist (Confession of the Century's Mamzer)," Steiner situates himself in the contemporary cultural landscape (he uses the English word "mindscape"), which he imagines as a multi-layered "magic mountain" where everything has already been said. The only thing left is endless reflection and commentary. The foundation of this "magic mountain" lies in the Soviet past, which offered an opportunity to live in the "conjunctive mood" by maintaining only partial contact with reality.[28] One of the devices that made this possible was the imaginary construction of the "Orient." Located in medieval Japan and China, it was one of the products of "para-Soviet" intellectual fantasy, of "playful ironic self-modeling." A kind of "elective affinity" drew many Soviet "rootless cosmopolitans" to *"japonisme"* as a way of aesthetically deconstructing Soviet reality from a position of self-imposed, exoticized marginality. Steiner explains that the special attractiveness of Japanese culture for Jewish intellectuals lies in its intense preoccupation with its own uniqueness and its constant efforts to redefine the essence of "Japaneseness." This imaginary "Far-Eastern spiritual experience" taught Soviet intellectuals how to live outside their unpleasant everyday reality by replacing it with a meditative "Glass Bead Game"—the title of the novel by Hermann Hesse that was particularly popular among the Soviet intelligentsia in the 1970s. This game of aesthetic escapism helped many intellectuals accept the collapse of the Soviet Union with meditative calmness, but it was far less useful for surviving in a new reality—be it the "phantasmagorical" post-Soviet life or emigration to the Israeli Near East or the American Wild West.[29]

Unlike Goldshtein, Steiner did not establish a firm residence in any of those regions. After several years in Israel, he moved to the United States where he held a few temporary university positions. Predictably, "real" Japan, where he spent many months working on the history of the Russian cemetery in Yokohama, turned out quite differently from the "fairytale country of the old days," and the dissonance irritated Steiner "immensely."[30] In his words, studying the lives of Russian emigrants who were buried in that forgotten place became a "handbook for comprehending my own alienation in the world."[31] His prolonged absence from his wife and son who remained in New York contributed to the breakup of his marriage and led to depression, which darkened the narrative mood and made the death motif increasingly prominent in his work. The memory of the 1970s, with their "sad and alluring aroma," became the only real presence in his life, but even this illusion came to an end with the death of the poet Bulat Okudzhava in 1997. As long as Okudzhava was alive, Steiner wrote, "our old world was still preserved, or, perhaps, some illusion of it."[32]

The contrast between Goldshtein and Steiner's images of the Soviet past—as a modern reincarnation of ancient Oriental despotism and as a harmless, benign social structure conducive to various "de-territorialized" forms of existence—exemplifies two opposite ways of appropriating the Soviet experience.

FROM MEMORY TO THE NOVEL: OLEG YURYEV AND ALEXANDER ILICHEVSKY

Born in Leningrad in 1959, Oleg Yuryev began to publish his poetry and prose in Leningrad in the late 1980s and immigrated to Germany in 1991. Today, he is better known in Germany than in Russia, thanks to the translations of his prose from Russian along with his poetry and journalistic articles written in German. In a loose trilogy of novels—*Poluostrov Zhidiatin* (2000), *Novyi Golem, ili voina starikov i detei* (2004), and *Vineta* (2007)—Yuryev attempted to portray the historic transformation of Russia by reinterpreting the foundational myths of European culture in the tradition of the modernist epics of Herman Melville, James Joyce, and Thomas Mann.[33] His mastery of the Russian language in its different stylistic registers enables him to fuse street vernacular and intellectual discourse, producing a variety of effects, from grotesque comedy to epic narrative. As Harriet Murav states succinctly, "His use of language produces the experience of the crash of the Soviet Union as an effect of reading."[34] Yuryev's most recent novel *Vineta* (in German translation, *Die russische Fracht*) is a twenty-first-century revision of the myth of a submerged city that remains intact somewhere at the bottom of the Baltic Sea, a trope common to both Germanic and Slavic folkloric traditions.

Its main character, a rather ordinary Leningrad Jew named Veniamin Iazychnik [Benjamin the Pagan], is the grown-up protagonist of the first part of the trilogy, *Poluostrov Zhidiatin*, who sets off on a ship carrying frozen dead bodies from St. Petersburg to Lübeck in search of Vineta. The details of this phantasmagoric, yet naturalistically portrayed journey form a dense multi-layered narrative, evoking *The Flying Dutchman*, *Moby Dick*, the Soviet war classics *The Living and the Dead* and *Some Like It Hot*, to name a few of the most obvious sources. The rough reality of post-Soviet decay is transformed, without losing its coarseness, into a mythological quest modeled after Joyce's *Ulysses*. A merciless postmodernist caricature of the post-Soviet reality serves as a foil for the ancient mythological story about a lost paradise and the eternal human struggle against the destructive power of fate.

Mockingly referring to Joseph Brodsky's famous self-definition as "a Jew, a Russian poet, and an American citizen," Yuryev once described himself as "a Jewish nationalist, a Russian patriot, and a German liberal," but he refuses to be categorized as a "Jewish writer," claiming that "nobody thinks of Racine as an ancient Roman or ancient Greek author because he uses characters and stories from that life." He held "Jewish building material ... in abundance" due to his "origin [and] biography, as well as by his interests outside of literature."[35] Yet the Russian critic Valerii Shubinskii convincingly argues that each novel of the trilogy lays out a different option for Jewish existence in the diaspora: withdrawal from the impurity of the world into a secluded and self-sufficient Jewish space in *Poluostrov Zhidiatin*; an endless expansion and dilution of the limits of Jewishness, so that it ultimately includes the entire world in *Novyi Golem*; or a quest for Vineta, a mythological space located nowhere and everywhere, which would enable Jews to interact with the world without jeopardizing their own Jewishness.

Yuryev does not give a definitive answer to this dilemma. As Shubinskii argues, for the author the question is more important than the answer: "Yuryev is an artist, not an ideologue."[36] Yuryev's literary identity is not ethnic but aesthetic; it is defined not by theme but by style, namely, by his self-affiliation with modernism as a "culture aware of its own tragedy," as opposed to the avant-garde, which, in his view, "lacks a spiritual foundation."[37] In his capacity as a literary expert, he serves as a custodian of the web-based project *Novaia kamera khraneniia* [The New Baggage Storage], which is dedicated to collecting, preserving, and canonizing Russian modernist literature. He uses his monthly column in Berlin's *Tagesspiegel* "Jurjews Klassiker," as a construction site for his personal canon, which includes figures as diverse as Serge Gainsbourg and Nathaniel West, Meister Eckhart and John Milton, and Charles Dickens and Henry Fielding.

Yuryev's cultural horizon is emphatically Western and he seems to be immune to the charms of Orientalist exoticism—indeed, the world east of St. Petersburg seems to be of no interest to him. Instead, Yuryev has his equivalent of Morgenland—an imaginary magic space located underground. In *Novyi Golem*, Yuryev describes the mysterious *Judenschlucht* [Jewish Gorge] on the German-Czech border, a kind of Central European Hades inhabited by shadows of dead Jews. In *Vineta*, he utilizes a secret, Israeli submarine named *Prophet Jonah Aleph II*. In a postmodernist remake of the Jewish folkloric belief that the bodies of dead Jews painstakingly make their way from their graves through secret underground passages to Jerusalem,[38] the submarine sails through those passages, collecting dead Jewish passengers along the way: "Jewish submarines don't sail [...] under water. They mostly sail underground, along twisted subterranean passages, along glowing cave lakes, along frightening blue rivers leading from every place to Jerusalem, to a huge lake under the Mount of Olives."[39]

The imaginary Vineta and Jerusalem, and the real St. Petersburg/Leningrad, turn out to be two sides of one "mirror chronotope," a peculiar literary lens used by Yuryev to demonstrate the congruity between myth and reality. Both sides of this mirror reflect, in different ways, the "absolute objectivity" of the twentieth-century world. Yuryev, as the artist, positions himself on the border between reality and myth, functioning as an observer and archeologist of Soviet civilization, which has so rapidly sunk into the sea of time, leaving behind a mere mythological reflection.

Alexander Ilichevsky (b. 1970) belongs to the youngest cohort of the "last Soviet generation," and, unlike the other three writers, he chose to return to Russia after seven years in Israel and the United States (1991–1998) but has recently moved to Israel again. He abandoned his career in theoretical physics and dedicated himself to literature. Today, he is one of the most successful and critically acclaimed "highbrow" Russian writers. Since 1996, he has published over a dozen books of poetry, prose, and essays. His lengthiest, most ambitious, and arguably best, novel to date is *Pers* [The Persian] (2010). The action of this dense and complex novel moves between California and Iran, spanning most of the past century. Set largely in Shirvan, a remote corner of post-Soviet Azerbaijan near the Iranian border, the story is narrated by a former scientist turned freelance oil trader, Ilya Dubnov, who returns from California to the land of his childhood in search of his old friend.

As Ilichevsky explains in an interview, Dubnov shares the narrator's childhood experience of growing up on the Caspian coast, but otherwise, they have very little in common. Dubnov's friend, Hashem,[40] whose father is an officer in the Iranian Shah's secret police, found refuge from the Islamic revolution in Soviet Azerbaijan. He withdrew from the world to an abandoned nature reserve and assumed the roles of a Sufi sheikh and commander of a small paramilitary unit named after Velimir Khlebnikov, a Russian futurist poet.

The adventure's plot, which even includes a detailed depiction of the assassination of Osama bin Laden by an American task force (two years before the actual event!), is interlaced with elaborate discussions of geophysics, bioinformatics, ornithology, Islamic theology, oil extraction, and the history of Russian futurism. Like most of Ilichevsky's works, *Pers* possesses a mythological quest for truth, authenticity, and immortality, repackaged as an intellectual thriller. He insists that the complex, multilinear narrative, with its numerous digressions, repetitions, and circular subplots, is absolutely necessary: "It's all made in such a peculiar way that all details remain in close focus, whichever way you turn it and from whichever side you look at it."[41]

Like Yuryev, Ilichevsky would probably not describe himself as a "Jewish" writer, but Jewish motifs and concerns play an important role in the novel. Named after a famous Russian Jewish historian and ideologue of diaspora nationalism, Dubnov embodies the transnational character of contemporary Russian Jewry. A cosmopolitan professional nomad, he remains under the spell of his Soviet past and finds himself drawn to the miserable, oil-soaked sands that were his childhood paradise. The secondary Jewish characters have somewhat similar functions as spiritual and intellectual mediators who convey pieces of important wisdom to other characters but remain on the periphery of the action, thereby corresponding to the role accorded to Jewish intellectuals in German and Russian discourse in the early twentieth century. Among them is a Baku *tzadik* named Meyukhes [Hebrew, a person of good provenance] who instructs Velimir Khlebnikov in the basics of the Kabbalah. Another important figure is Shtein—an engineer at an oil-processing plant and director of an amateur youth theater that becomes the site of a life-changing experience for Dubnov and Hashem. The figure of this provincial Jewish intellectual seems to come straight from the world of Goldshtein's youth. An admirer of the Russian avant-garde and American jazz, he staged plays by Tom Stoppard and Gogol with his teenage actors and captures their imagination through incredible stories about the Baku sojourns of Yakov Blumkin—a notorious left socialist revolutionary turned CheKa agent—and Velimir Khlebnikov, who was sent by the Soviet government to export the revolution to Iran. Like his radical heroes, Shtein believes that the "avant-garde is the way of controlling the future."[42] His dream is to escape from the dullness of Soviet life, since "from the point of view of civilization, this country ceased to exist several decades ago,"[43] and become a Sufi dervish in Iran. Instead, he immigrates to America and ends his life in a secret opium den on the Mexican island of Tiburon.

Both Yuryev and Ilichevsky created post-Soviet versions of the ancient quest myth by using their experiences of Soviet childhood and emigration as building materials. Soviet civilization, which appeared relatively stable and secure, quickly crumbled and disappeared before the eyes of an astonished world. The sudden collapse of the Soviet prison house left the protagonists to their own devices, and they set off to roam the world. Yet the demise of the Soviet universe also burdens them with memories that they must carry until death. In this situation, Jewishness acquires a new significance; from a mark of difference, it becomes a mark of a new certainty. In the post-Soviet vacuum, the protagonist-narrator revisits (or recovers) a sense of identity that helps to define his position in the global world. By coming to terms with their Jewish "roots," these characters overcome their loneliness and join an imaginary "Soviet Jewish" community. In a rather paradoxical way, the formerly antagonistic concepts of "Soviet" and "Jewish" merge into a new synthetic "Soviet-Jewish" identity.[44] The relationship between the two components remains strained, and "Jewish" memory constantly exercises critical authority over its "Soviet" counterpart. Jews of the "last Soviet generation" still remember various forms of discrimination during the Soviet era, which prevents them from participating in the increasingly popular trend of idealizing the Soviet epoch. However, with time, the two elements become inseparable, forming the foundation of a Soviet-Jewish "usable past." This Soviet-Jewish subjectivity of the post-Soviet intelligentsia is a highly complex and eclectic mixture composed of such "Jewish" elements as the Bible, Israel, anti-Semitism, and, by way of "elective affinity," avant-garde and jazz, Sufism and Zen, and even Christianity. At the same time, the Soviet-Jewish intelligentsia has a problematic relationship with its own roots and is anxious to distance itself from everything that smacks of *kleynshtetldikayt* [provincialism], which includes Yiddish language and culture.

CONCLUSION

This chapter has focused on four male writers of the "last Soviet generation" who came to occupy an important position in contemporary Russian culture. Their immediate audience is limited to a relatively small circle of cosmopolitan intellectuals in Russia and abroad who debate continuing the high modernist tradition in Russian culture during the age of postmodernist consumerism. An ambivalent insider/outsider status makes these authors easy targets for criticism by more "conservative" intellectuals who are keen on protecting their territory from "foreign" influence, sometimes with anti-Semitic overtones (despite the fact that some of them are themselves Jewish). On the other hand, the very visibility of these four authors' names on the contemporary Russian cultural horizon—as indicated by publications with prestigious presses, literary prizes, interviews, and critical responses—serves as proof that diaspora literature in general, and its "Jewish" segment in particular, no longer lies on the periphery of Russian literary discourse. While publishing and distribution of books and periodicals becomes increasingly concentrated in Moscow and St. Petersburg, the production of Russian culture is becoming increasingly decentralized, with Jerusalem, Tel Aviv, Berlin, Frankfurt, New York (as well as Kiev, Kharkov, Odessa, Vilnius, and other former Soviet cities) occupying a prominent place on the new "post-Soviet" map of Russian culture.

Of course, understanding post-Soviet diaspora culture in its entirety would require a comprehensive study of its segments, including popular commercial fiction. As I have tried to demonstrate in this case study of a self-proclaimed "high" segment, the phenomenon of Russian Jewish culture remains diverse, complex, and fluid. Rooted in the Soviet past, it undergoes constant revision and re-imagining in accordance with varying aesthetic patterns, ideological commitments, political goals, and commercial interests.

NOTES

1. For example, Masha Gessen, *Dead Again: The Russian Intelligentsia after Communism* (London: Verso, 1997) or Katerina Clark, "The King Is Dead, Long Live the King: Intelligentsia Ideology in Transition," in *Conference on Russia at the End of the Twentieth Century: Culture and Its Horizons in Politics and Society*, ed. Gregory Freiden (Stanford University, October 1998), http://www.stanford.edu/group/Russia20/volumepdf/clark_fin99.pdf.
2. Clark, "The King Is Dead."
3. Dina Rubina, the prolific Russian-Israeli novelist, undoubtedly holds these distinctions; she has published numerous books with major Moscow presses and has become highly popular among Russian readers.
4. Alexei Yurchak, *Everything Was Forever, Until It Was No More: The Last Soviet Generation* (Princeton: Princeton University Press, 2006), 31–32.
5. Yevgeny Steiner, "Apologiia zastoinogo iunoshi," *Zven'ia* 6 (1992), reprinted in *Zerkalo* 33 (2009), http://zerkalo-litart.com/?p=3042 (accessed on July 15, 2014).
6. Ibid.
7. Yurchak, *Everything Was Forever Until It Was No More*, 130.
8. Ibid., 128.
9. "Für mich war die ganze sowjetische Realität unwirklich—ein trüber Film, der das wirkliche Leben, die reale Existenz umhüllte," *Neue Zürcher Zeitung*, December 1, 2010, 19.
10. Among those groups was the Jewish movement, which by the late 1970s, consisted not only of would-be emigrants (many of whom became stuck in the Soviet Union when immigration was curtailed between 1980 and 1986) but also of people interested in Judaism and Jewish culture who weren't necessarily planning to emigrate. As Mikhail Chlenov, one of the informal leaders of that movement, remembers, "Those who came here were ordinary people. They did not come to fight, they came for a certain way of life. In this sense the Jewish movement was very different from the dissidents. The dissident movement aimed to change the situation in the Soviet Union. But the Jewish movement did not set such a goal. They did not do it on principle

and openly declared it." It is important to note, however, that none of the writers discussed in this chapter belonged to this movement or had much interest in Jewish matters at that time. See Mikhail Chlenov, "U istokov evreiskogo dvizheniia," May 18, 2011, http://www.polit.ru/article/2011/05/18/chlenov/.

11. Aleksandr Goldshtein, "Na tu zhe temu," *Zven'ia* 7 (1992), reprinted in *Zerkalo* 33 (2009), http://zerkalo-litart.com/?cat=38 (accessed on July 15, 2014).

12. Irina Vrubel'-Golubkina, ed., *Simvol "My": Evreiskaia khrestomatiia novoi russkoi literatury* (Moscow: Novoe Literaturnoe Obozrenie, 2003).

13. Ibid., 6.

14. Even a superficial survey of these publications would take us far beyond the limits of this chapter.

15. Goldshtein, *Rasstavanie s Nartsissom: Opyty pominal'noi ritoriki* (Moscow: Novoe Literaturnoe Obozrenie, 1997), 8.

16. Elena Fanailova, "Pamiati pisatelia. Aleksandr Goldshtein: ot knigi 'Rasstavanie s Nartsissom' do knigi 'Spokoinye polia,'" December 12, 2006, http://www.svobodanews.ru/content/transcript/366618.html.

17. "Na tu zhe temu. Konets odnogo panteona," *Znak vremeni* 2 (1992), reprinted in *Zerkalo* 33 (2009), http://magazines.russ.ru/zerkalo/2009/33/go8.html (accessed on August 29, 2011).

18. Ibid.

19. Goldshtein, *Spokoinye polia* (Moscow: NLO, 2006), 58.

20. Goldshtein, "Tri darovaniia," in *Vid na zhitel'stvo*, by Aleksandra Petrova (Moscow: NLO, 2000), http://www.vavilon.ru/texts/prim/goldstein1.html (accessed on August 29, 2011).

21. Ibid.

22. Goldshtein, *Spokoinye polia*, 77.

23. Goldshtein, *Pomni o Famaguste* (Moscow: NLO, 2006), 20.

24. Ibid.

25. Ibid., 21.

26. Evgeny Steiner, *Pis'ma iz prostranstva* (Moscow: NLO, 2006).

27. Ibid., 590.

28. Ibid., 55–56.

29. Ibid., 249.

30. Ibid., 177.

31. Ibid., 159.

32. Ibid., 346.

33. The trilogy structure was suggested and convincingly argued by Valerii Shubinskii in his article "Chast' ili tseloe: evrei i evreistvo v knigakh Olega Yuryeva," *Narod knigi v mire knig* 77 (December 2008), http://www.narodknigi.ru/journals/77/chast_ili_tseloe_evrei_i_evreystvo_v_knigakh_olega_yureva/. The first novel, *Poluostrov Zhidiatin*, is analyzed by Harriet Murav in *Music from a Speeding Train: Jewish Literature in Post-Revolution Russia* (Stanford, CA: Stanford University Press, 2011), 338–341. The second novel of the trilogy, *Novyi Golem, ili voina starikov i detei*, is discussed in my article "'An Invisible Decade': The 1990s in the Russian-Jewish Imagination," *East European Jewish Affairs* 34:1 (2004): 2–6.

34. Murav, *Music from a Speeding Train*, 337.

35. As quoted in Shubinskii, "Chast' ili tseloe."

36. Ibid.

37. Annotation to the almanac *Kamera khraneniia*, vol. 2, ed. D. M. Zaks and O. A. Yuryev (St. Petersburg: Assotsiatsiia sovremennoi literatury, 1991).

38. This belief is likely to have been appropriated from Agnon.

39. Oleg Yuryev, *Znamia* 8 (2007): 72.

40. In Hebrew, *hashem* means "the name," which is a traditional substitute for "God" in Judaism, though the significance of this connection in Ilichevsky's writing remains unclear.

41. Aleksandr Ilichevsky, "Byt' persom—funktsiia stanovleniia," *Chastnyi korrespondent* 9 (August 2010), http://www.chaskor.ru/article/aleksandr_illichevskij_byt_persom_—_funktsiya_stanovleniya_19045 (accessed on August 30, 2011).

42. Ilichevsky, *Pers* (Moscow: AST, 2010), 315.

43. Ibid.

44. As one Russian-Israeli blogger stated in his post, "I am a Soviet Jew (hopefully, an intelligent one), who moved at a conscious age from Lviv to Ofakim and learned Hebrew. My tastes and interests [*pristrastiia*] have been formed in my childhood. . . . I do not consider myself an Israeli." This post generated a heated discussion that was taken over by other bloggers. As the author of this statement clarified, he immigrated to Israel in 1990 at the age of fourteen. See "O grazhdanstve i samooschuschenii," posted August 18, 2011, http://shaulreznik.livejournal.com/1860116.html and "O 'russkikh' i izrail'tianakh," posted August 18, 2011, http://o-aronius.livejournal.com/582555.html.

16 · POETS AND POETRY IN TODAY'S DIASPORA

On Being "Marginally Jewish"

STEPHANIE SANDLER

To be Jewish in the contemporary Russian-speaking diaspora no longer means, for poets, to wear a yellow star as a blazing badge of identity. Being Jewish or identifying with stories from Jewish experience remains a vivid, valuable mode of expressing the disorienting experiences of diaspora, but it is no longer a way of being in the world that excludes all others. There are exceptions—poets for whom Jewish identity has become an organizing moment in their lives far from Russia, for example, Marina Temkina. Still, there are also those for whom an outburst of Jewish self-exploration has yielded to a firm and sustaining embrace of Russian Orthodoxy, for example, Boris Khersonskii. Both of these poets, as well as the broad spectrum between them, inhabit a vast and little understood terrain of what I will refer to as the "marginally Jewish." In adopting this term, I have deliberately revised the more common phrase "barely Jewish" in order to emphasize the metaphor of spatial location on the periphery and to retrieve as usable and as value-neutral a phrase that can have a demeaning glow to it. Jewish identity, like so much else that marks us in our mutable world, is a capacious and rapidly shifting category, and I do not invite judgment regarding degrees of Jewishness. The borders of Jewish identity are permeable, and its embrace increasingly loose.

Most Soviet Jews had so little knowledge of Judaism and so little access to religious practice that a strong presence of fervent believers could not be a defining feature of post-Soviet life. Yet surprisingly, connections to and explorations of Jewish experience, history, ritual, and custom all linger, less often forming the core of identity than contributing to a set of ideas that help people in diaspora locate and sustain themselves. This set of ideas is made by and in the margins, and thus, it is an experience of "marginal" Jewishness that is doubly telling.

Poets whose attitude toward Jewish identity fluctuates provide the most piercing articulations of diasporic dislocation and constitute the vast majority of contemporary Jewish poets. The Nazis would have exterminated these poets, to use a crude description; the writers acknowledge this terrible connection of blood and birth, but they barely register that recognition in the vast bulk of their writing. I shall focus on four such poets: Boris Khersonskii, Marina Temkina, Mikhail Gronas, and Ilya Kaminsky.

I want to acknowledge, by way of preamble, the tremendous achievements of a much larger group of poets that I will hardly mention in this chapter. These include a large group who settled in Israel (Gali-Dana Singer, Leonid Shvab, the late Mikhail Gendelev, and others who passed through Israel long enough for it to deeply imprint their work, such as Alexandra Petrova). To be "marginally Jewish" in Israel is potentially a different matter entirely, but I think the idea of diaspora is different there, as well. I have also relegated to a few endnotes the absorbing, demanding work of Anna Glazova and Sergei Magid. But I mention these poets to make clear that there are a surprisingly large number of poets who inhabit the middle ground of the "marginally Jewish." This alone, I believe, gives this term relevance to a significant segment of the current intellectual life of Russian poetry. Marina Tsvetaeva thought that all poets were Jews (or, as her words might be more accurately translated, Yids); to all poets, the experience of marginality and of diminished cultural status was powerfully available. My question is how a poet might make something but not everything of that experience—how, in a sense, the burden of Jewish identity as an overwhelming fact of lived experience might be lightened, but not shed. What results, I argue, are freer and perhaps deeper acts of self-creation.

Why poetry, you may ask. The simplest answer is that this is the material I know and love; it is what I work on and what I believe to be one of our most important forms of artistic creation in Russia and in many other places in the world. Yet another answer should be offered, one truer to the material itself: because I am arguing that forms of self-expression change—that sometimes poets delve into Jewish experience, and sometimes they don't—the material of poetry is especially appropriate to reveal such variation. In a sense, a poet starts over with every poem, creating a world and a language with each poetic utterance. More than is the case with long fiction or vast canvases, poetic texts offer the poet something of a quick-change opportunity, a provisional act of self-expression that can be displaced by the next poem or the next book. Poets who produce a lot, such as Boris Khersonskii, do this more elaborately than those who write very little, such as Mikhail Gronas, but the variability persists. The kind of poems I am looking at, then, are like an artist's drawings—a way of seeing the world that is sketched, provisional, and often self-conscious of its distance from more central, more fully assured visions.

PRAYER, RITUAL: BORIS KHERSONSKII

For many of the poets I treat here, being a Jew, once a marker of separateness, now eases connection and similarity to new environments. The tragedy of modern Jewish history still resonates, but it is assimilated into a view of the contemporary world as itself tragic, if not apocalyptic. Elena Fanailova, a Moscow poet, expresses her view more vulgarly: "*Eto ne istoricheskii krizis, eto pizdets*" [colorfully translated by Matvei Yankelevitch: "It's not a historical crisis, it's a fucking apocalypse"]. On the one hand, the contemporary world has brought freedom of movement, freedom to create an easy relationship to space and place that is not exile, not tortured, not weighted down by nostalgia for a lost Russia. On the other hand, freedom of movement brings many poets to see the surrounding world as a political, economic, ecological, cultural, and/or psychological disaster.

The most stunning example of this is in the book that brought immense attention to Boris Khersonskii (b. 1950)—a poet who had been publishing quietly and prolifically in Odessa for quite a while. When *Semeinyi arkhiv* [*Family Archive*] was released in 2006, his readership exploded, and his presence now looms much larger both on his blog (where he seems to publish a new poem daily) and in his frequent readings in Moscow, Europe, and New York.

Khersonskii's family album is a mesmerizing cultural history of the Jews in and around Odessa: photographed individuals surrounded by books and artifacts that embody their whole lives; families seeking news of missing relatives, recounting their own narrow escapes from invading Germans; children studying Yiddish and adolescents seeking admission to St. Petersburg State University; and victims of marital betrayal and woe who turn to rabbis only to receive enigmatic commentary in reply. The narrative is peculiarly relaxed. The poet slowly unfolds one story or image after another, as if it were the most natural thing in the world for the Russian language to accommodate these names, their diminished dreams, and distant longings. Khersonskii's book is not the first to tell such stories, but it is unusual in its matter-of-fact, calm tone, resistant to both sentimentalism and sensationalism. The poet anchors the stories in objects (photographs, postcards, and auction lots of Judaica), and he gives these objects a strange unconscious life through his use of dreams and fantasies.[1] This isn't just history as event; it is history as imagination, and thus, there is not so much forward movement in the tales as there are multiple, relentless, repeated rhetorical structures.

Family Archive is organized around a number of repeated poem titles or forms, giving it the air of a ritual. The trope of repetition is structural as well as lexical. There are multiple poems about auctioned items of Judaica, several with the subtitle of "dream" [*snovidenie*] or "dictum" [*izrechenie*] that come to feel like anchors holding the history of the twentieth century in place. The sense of history comes from poems with place names and dates as their titles: for example, Odessa, July 1954; Berdichev, 1911—Odessa, 1986; Kremenets 1942—Odessa, 1973; and Bessarabia, 1935, to name only a few. Repetition shapes the geographic and chronological landscape, and Khersonskii links locations as Jews disperse across Ukraine, western Russia, and eastern Europe, making their way in later poems to Israel and New York, thus rehearsing the pathways of the twentieth-century Jewish diaspora.

Here is a typical example. It is the second part of a longer poem called "Dve fotografii" ["Two Photographs"], in which we see the structure of rabbinical conversation. It also reports on family life, the way in which preserved objects call up the entire memory of a person, and the emphasis on learning and love of Torah.

> Rabbi Itzhak Levi used to say,
> "It's no surprise that the Jews
> have mastered secular wisdom
> and aroused the envy of their neighbors.
> When they abandoned Torah,
> the hole in their hearts and minds
> was so vast that you could put
> there anything at all."
> And Rabbi Schraga Mendlovich
> would reply,
> "There is nothing to be surprised at
> and, alas, nothing to be proud of.
> Would Jeremiah be proud
> if he were told
> that Jewish sculptors
> had carved a golden idol
> of Ba'al-Pe'or better
> than the Canaanites?"
> Their friend Aaron ben Riven
> was silent for a moment, then answered,
> "Well, anyway, whatever you say,
> my son graduated with honors
> from St. Petersburg University
> and is being published in the capital papers."
> Aaron takes from the inkpot
> the tiny carved ivory lid
> (which even then was probably covered
> with a fine web of cracks)
> and turns it over in his hands—a habit.
> The inkstand has been preserved.[2]

This strangely evolving tale sees adaptability and change as blasphemy—effectively the same thing as being able to create the best pagan idols. Khersonskii twists his tale of three rabbis into an enigmatic chain of readings and events that produce nothing but the capacity to create fresh texts, to use the inkset that time has miraculously preserved.

More interesting still are Khersonskii's prayers. Listen to his Russian rendering of the *shehekheyanu* prayer, the traditional praise of God for keeping us alive and allowing us to celebrate a happy event:

A Prayer
Blessed art Thou, Lord, our God,
King of the Universe,
Who has kept us and protected us,
and supported us until this day
it would be better we had never seen.
You deprived us of nothing,
neither despair nor dejection,
nor monotonous dull hope.
You are always the same, Holy One,
and we few haven't changed much, either.[3]

The first four lines reprise the familiar and beloved blessing, but the last line bespeaks a darker sentiment—that the day one has lived to see is a source of pain and grief. Rather than the gifts of God's generosity, the poem chronicles the sources of pain that God has not spared His people. In place of personal, domestic happiness, Khersonskii substitutes a shared history of despair and dim hope. The last lines confirm the relentless nature of that cycle, affirming the sameness and unity of God and of His people, few though their numbers be.

Another of the book's prayers reaches a similarly bleak tone; it is, in fact, the final poem and thus the note on which *Family Archive* ends:

A Prayer
And Thou art faithful to Thy promise
to raise the dead.
Blessed art Thou, o Lord
our God, King of the Universe,
who raises the dead,
if only in our fragile memory,
if only now and then.[4]

Khersonskii's God is one who keeps His promises, who keeps faith with His people Israel, but whose people feel their memories weakening beneath His gaze. That memories grow faint is yet another woe, perhaps the greatest tragedy to befall the Jewish people, this poem suggests. Khersonskii's entire project is devoted to the preservation of memories; it is an album created from poems and photographs, but it also records loss. Thus, it features recurring poems about auctions of Judaica, about selling off the tangible objects of a people's legacy. Khersonskii emphasizes the spiritual value of these auction lots. He begins one of the auction poems with the first words of the *Sh'ma*, in this case not translating the Hebrew words into Russian—as he did with the *shehekheyanu* prayer—but, instead, rendering them separate words as they might be chanted in prayer, a pause after each one, and also as foreign, yet familiar sounds. Khersonskii substitutes one name of God, *Hashem*, for another, *Adonoi*, thus doubly honoring that name for God which is itself often written in substituted lettering (as the Tetragrammaton, spelled as YAHWEH). His poem, however, does not leap from auctioned items into the mystic contemplation of God's names. Instead, it yields to a few words from the prayer that follows the *Sh'ma* and then immediately becomes a kind of estranged midrashic commentary on words and variants. Rather than names for God, we get the name of an ordinary Jew, Chaim (which means *life*, as the poem itself explains). Here is most of the poem, beginning from line 9:

Judaica Auction
Lot 6: Mezuza, Silver, Niello. Early twentieth century. Galicia
[. . .]
The sole God of the Jews is life—chaim
("Hey, Chaim, get outta here!")—life, in spite of it all,
in spite of everything: for the gates of Jewish cemeteries
are adorned with the inscription "Bet Chaim"—that is, the "Dwelling Place of
    Life." Who else
could come up with such a thing?
Actually, the One God
of the Jews, perhaps only He Who
divided the darkness from the light, and all
that happened afterward in the breach between white and black,
including the lines of black written on white
calf hide, on the smallest piece of it,
the prayer for mercy, rolled up like a snail
in its casket shell (Sh'ma Yisroel)
of blackened silver. Actually it's this very object
that is exhibited for sale, empty of its contents.
This is an auction of Judaica, a Judaica
auction. Do you hear the groaning
souls brought back to their dwellings now reduced to dust,
displaying the loss of everything,
everything, even the objects themselves,
lost to the touch: for there is only one
thing that cannot be felt to the touch—the cross, on which You are crucified.[5]

Khersonskii puns and plays on the Hebrew word *chai*/"life," turning it into the name Chaim and then using that name to castigate and send away the Jew, and further rendering *chai* as the name of a cemetery—as "Bet Chaim," the house where the dead live on (Bet Chaim [the house of the living] is a common euphemistic name for cemeteries). What lives on in the physical world may be only the words inked across the parchment of the Torah or the tarnished silver objects of ritual celebration. But by its end, the poem trades Judaica and all such acts of naming for the supreme symbol of Christianity, the crucifix. In one sense, the transformation is motivated by biography: a converted and openly committed Orthodox Christian, Khersonskii here turns the poet's gaze at the objects and stories of the Jews toward the enigmas of a suffering Christ. It is as if he proclaims—hear, O Israel—not that God is one, but that he has moved beyond his comprehension of God's unity toward the incomprehensible miracle of Jesus's passion. In that last image, Khersonskii takes the stories of suffering that make up *Family Archive* to their logical extreme. What is the point beyond which Jewish identity can no longer account for suffering? In asking that question, the poet is pointing the way toward the "marginally Jewish" forms of self-expression that dominate his next books. The template of Judaism serves as Khersonskii's Old Testament—as the foundation on which he will build a new set of truths about God.[6]

Khersonskii is not alone among contemporary poets for whom a double vision of Judaism and some form of Christianity coexist; the remarkable Sergei Magid, who lives in Prague, traces a similar path in his poetry, which is more concentrated and more thoroughly theological in many ways.[7] This similarity demonstrates the far broader universe in which contemporary poets think about and situate any sense of Jewish identity. Such broadness is itself an effect of the diaspora, I would argue, and of a movement toward the peripheries of Jewish experience in which alternatives, even theological alternatives, can be contemplated and in some cases even embraced.

MUSEUMS OF DAILY LIFE: MARINA TEMKINA

Far less tragic than Khersonskii in her worldview is the New York–based poet Marina Temkina (b. 1948). She identifies herself half-jokingly but also entirely seriously as a "Russian-Jewish-Immigrant-Woman Poet."[8] And to a certain extent, she would qualify as what Elena Nosenko-Stein calls a "new Jew."[9] Temkina's fourth book of poetry is entitled *Canto immigranto* [*Canto Immigrant*] (2005), a splendid way of revealing the foreignness through which she imagines her relationship to poetry. Temkina is known as a forthright, bold writer, and feminist scholars celebrated her terrific "Kategoriia lifchika" ["Category: Brassiere," 1994].[10] A poet who could produce an encyclopedic account of the varieties of breasts has an unyielding sense of humor, which also lightens the poetry of *Canto immigranto*. Temkina has gained a broad knowledge of the *émigré* experience:

she led the creation of New York's Archive for Jewish Immigrant Culture, managed projects that collected oral histories of Jews from the Soviet Union, and has become an activist who speaks about the experiences of Jews in New York living alongside émigrés from many other parts of the world.[11] Her activism is that of a person who has experienced the diaspora, and who wishes to chronicle and preserve that history, even as she recognizes the many features that make the Jewish experience of immigration similar to that of other foreign groups.

What is striking about her work—particularly in comparison with Khersonskii's more oratorical, ritualized style—is its commitment to daily life, to prosaic details like bras and breasts, to cataloguing museum exhibits and using that structure to reimagine a slow movement through cultural space. This is a kind of normal everyday life in which the poet luxuriates: as she has written, in an English-language poem, "What Do You Want, M & M?": "What do you want, Michel? / —To repair my house in Villarcoin and build a studio there. / What do you want, Marina? / —I want to pay high taxes and have a pension plan."[12] Many other desires follow in this poem: for publications, gallery space, and fellowships. The point of the sequence is its location in the everyday life of an artist or poet, not the symbolic or the sublime. Her turn toward writing in English and toward the production of an artist's book shows Temkina's adept capacity to move far beyond the confines of Russianness and assimilate in ways that Khersonskii's rabbis would lament when they refer, in "Two Photographs," to the son who has gone off to Petersburg to study.

Yet glimmers of a world where daily pleasures are impossible sometimes invade Temkina's poems, and this impossibility is most often represented not by the Soviet Union she left behind but by the Holocaust. In a 2002 poem from *Canto immigranto*, we find the following:

Aurora Borealis
Tea bearing the label "Morning Thunder"
recalls the squabbles of Turgenev and Fet
and the hasty tears of my mother, saying:
"Get up, we're going to be late,
hurry up, we're already late."
So you live, never pausing, always in a rush,
unable to make memories, gobbling up time
that runs out as from a wound. You pay your taxes,
pay off debts, you can end your days
in an almshouse with an ocean view, getting
your research experience, learning how to die.
The horoscope reads: "Take care
of your childish pain and pay it off
as the northern lights give off their flashes and sparks

by means of electromagnetic energy."
In the dictionary, it's always there, between *Aurora*
and *Auschwitz*, or, as we say, *Avrora* and *Oświęcim*.[13]

October 2, 2002

Auschwitz comes into this poem as an accident of the alphabet, a result of a glance in the dictionary that is no more ominous than a glance at the horoscope. There is something Proustian about the poem in the way it begins with a cup of tea and a memory of the mother's voice, but the particular course of thought—from the tea brand name and a catalogue of daily life as paying taxes and paying debts, to aging and the electromagnetic fields of the Northern Lights—is not so rarified as Proust's memories of Combray or Odile. Auschwitz looms, a word in two languages that cannot be escaped.

Another poem, printed just after "Aurora Borealis" in *Canto immigranto*, takes up the inescapability of Jewish experience as suffering in a different way; it offers a glimpse into one specific life, shown as if a museum exhibit.[14]

Franz Kafka: An Exhibit in the Jewish Museum
Two brothers died in infancy, three sisters
in Auschwitz. After the fall of Austria-Hungary
he was not fired; the insurance agent Frantiszek
knew Czech, and tried to improve the insurance
policies against catastrophic losses in the factories,
he sympathized with minorities, defended
"lesser" Czech literature. Anarchists,
Marxists, socialists, Zionists, atheists.
He is a vegetarian. Café "Argo," Café "Savoy."
The empty Judaism of his father is a formality.
Thoughts about authenticity. Tuberculosis is linked
to Jewish mysticism. The influence
of the Yiddish theater, but not sure on what.
One hundred Hassidic tales, collected by Martin
Buber. Bohemia, Moravia, Galicia, Pomerania, etc.,
the countries that disappeared from imperial maps.
America, he wrote, is a country where they disappear.
A first: *Popular History of the Jews*, Leipzig,
1888; before that, Jews had no history, only
religion. Another first: *History of German
Jewish Literature*, but it appears for some reason
in Paris, 1911. At the end of life, he studies Hebrew,
dreams of leaving for Palestine, perhaps the dream
also fuses with the hope that the local climate
might cauterize the gaping holes in his lungs. A sanatorium

in the Tatras, starving himself so as not to suffer for long,
refusing even water, and dying in only a few days.[15]

November 17, 2002

Temkina reprises a story here that is at once familiar and shockingly strange. The gesture is not unlike Khersonskii's, although, rather than compounding many individual stories into one huge tale of multiple generations, she offers up the life of a famous individual, shown as if on display in a museum. With some changes and omissions, she reprises the story of Kafka's siblings' deaths, his work in the insurance industry, his attraction to Yiddish theater, and his death. By leaving out the thing for which we know Kafka, his strange and beautiful writing, Temkina makes him into any other person whose life could be told in the Jewish Museum. And yet her account is true to what we know of Kafka's lived biography, one marked by literary fame that came only after his death.

Were she a different poet, we might think her point is a critique of the way such museums represent lived experience, how they cannot account for the way some Jews turn out to be Kafka. But her goal is not that of critique. Rather, from Kafka's life, she pulls out a parable of place and change. Note her list of place names:

Bohemia, Moravia, Galicia, Pomerania, etc.,
the countries that disappeared from imperial maps.
America, he wrote, is a country where they disappear.

The places that have disappeared from the imperial maps of the world are those where Jews have lived, and where Jews have also disappeared. Kafka, too, has disappeared in the process, but was it in order for Temkina to ask what it means that America is a place into which people disappear? The grammatically logical subject for "*ischezaiut*," actually, is not persons but places—America is a country into which Bohemia, Moravia, Galicia, and Pomerania have disappeared. Temkina's poem laments not the loss of persons, and not even or only the sad fate of Franz Kafka, but of the places in which those people perished. Hers is not a poem of diaspora but of its reverse: Jews didn't disperse across the globe; they were sucked into a smaller number of luckily hospitable places, but in the process the great diversity of locales of Jewish past lives has been reduced.[16]

THE METAPHYSICS OF RUIN: MIKHAIL GRONAS

Mikhail Gronas's encounter with places and identities that are distinctly Jewish is far less explicit, and in his work we squarely confront the presentation of self as "marginally Jewish." Gronas (b. 1970) is twenty years younger than Khersonskii and Temkina, and the poetics of his writing differ substantially. Their work feels almost extravagant compared to his; he writes little, and his jagged poems can be short and fleeting, as if the texts aspired to the impermanence that is so often his subject. The tonality can plunge readers into a more intense sensation of loss, and when diaspora is so obviously the backdrop for his thinking, one perceives it as a kind of verbal pun. The self is dispersed as much as personhood is displaced, and no fantasy of lost homeland or distant stabilization anchors the work.

It bears mention, as something of a paradox, that Gronas has an almost alternative persona as a writer; he is a scholar whose work goes in directions one would never predict from his poetry. Usually there is more continuity among writers' professional endeavors. Khersonskii is a well-established psychologist, whose experiences can be felt in the way his poems use dreams and explorations of identity. He has lived his whole life in Odessa, a place often tangible in his work. Temkina's museum and archival experiences are present in her work, as is New York City, where she mainly lives, and France, the country of her husband and a place where she spends a significant amount of time. And Gronas? One would never suspect from his poems that he is a tenured professor at Dartmouth College; a man who was born in Tashkent, educated in Moscow and Los Angeles; and the author of a witty, brilliant book about literary mnemonics and of studies in cognitive poetics, reader preferences, and epistolary experiments in the Pushkin period. His is, in some ways, a more mutable writerly identity, at once curious about both market forces and about states of mind.

Only that mutability would predict what we find in his astonishing, prize-winning poetry. I begin with the untitled poem that opens his one small book, *Dorogie siroty* [*Dear Orphans*] (2002). Across his work, Gronas presents the poet as an orphan of place (rather than parents).[17] In this poem, the speaker has survived a fire at home and seems surrounded by survivors. The poem abjures any lament for lost property, even asking ironically what difference it would make to have a house, offering instead a condensed, lyrical song about the experience of being bereft of shelter. I present here only the last two quasi-stanzas:

> houses on houses people on people hand on hand by the way in our language forget means begin to be forget means begin to be no there is nothing brighter and I must go but now in parting several times I repeat so that you forget once and for all:
> forget means begin to be
> forget means begin to be
> forget means begin to be[18]

Let us take only the last two quasi-stanzas, one more bizarre than the other. What kind of lines are created by this sequence of, first, nouns alone: the words I render as "houses on houses . . ." are similarly just a string of words, without punctuation, in the original: "*doma o domakh liudi o liudiakh ruka o ruke.*" All could be taken to be direct objects of a missing verb, perhaps the verb from the previous stanza, which is essentially a future infinitive of a verb meaning "to remind" ["*budet napominat'*"]. Even if we were to supply the verb, the tautologies abound, and there is still a sense that logical explanations are missing. Does the house call to mind a house? Do persons cause us to remember people? The hand calls up its own image? That endless circle yields to an even stronger syntactical enclosure, one resolved in the closing three poetic lines. Literally, forgetting is said to mean starting to live, as if the burning of a fire (which is what the earlier stanzas of the poem describe) leaves all of the past in ruins, freeing survivors for a new life. However, nothing but futility has pervaded this poem; there is no renewal in lines that describe neighbors who have little confidence in a rebuilding project. Nor is there anything new brought to mind by fresh sights or objects: people lead to people, hand leads to hand. Is it a hand that builds or a hand that writes? We do not know, but we do know that it is a mind that thinks in deeply linguistic terms.[19] The last lines of the poem constitute an etymological pun. If we look at the Russian word meaning "forget" [*"zabyt'"*], we are reminded that the prefix *"za"* often marks the initiation of an action, so that *"zabyt',"* even as it means "to forget," as *"za-byt',"* could suggest the moment when the action of living is begun or, as the poet writes, "to begin to be." To begin life on such a burned-out foundation is to do the work of creation not in a divinely ordered universe, but in a place abandoned.

In the next poem in *Dorogie siroty*, Gronas represents that abandoned world as if seen from distant outer space, but also as if experienced from within. This short poem is also untitled:

autumn
the broken world cools on its side
no one will set it right
no one will right the axis
instead:
sit and nod
while words about you are spoken on high
by kinship and orphanhood
while they bestow on each other all manner of gift[20]

The themes of repair and ruin, of orphanhood and kinship, and of gift-giving as a spectacle performed before one who is curiously left out of the circuits of exchange, connect this poem to the main preoccupations of *Dear Orphans*. Yet the strange glory of the poem is its remarkable sound orchestration (in Russian, the "os" sound connects the words for "autumn" and "axis": *"osen'"* becomes *"osi"* and then, in line 5, it echoes in *"prosto,"* rendered here as "instead"). Lexical contrasts are also starkly wonderful: the plain-spoken imperative to "nod" is *"poddakivai,"* and it appears in parallel position to the glorious Slavonicism that commands speech, *"razglagol'stvuiut."* (This is what makes Gronas impossible to translate, I have found—the task seems as if it should be easy; it isn't.)

When Gronas speaks of a broken world, he is exemplifying a larger sense of ruin, something that goes well beyond the experiences or history of the Jews, in or out of diaspora. Here is a poem, written slightly later (2006), in which that history is explicitly addressed. Do not be put off by its apparently scientific tone, its apparently decisive twist toward numerical precision, or its teetering balance between tautology and infinite gestures of differentiation:

> This poem was written by the author at night.
> It is the eight million nine hundred and fifty three thousand one hundred and eighty sixth poem after Auschwitz (a rough estimate).
> It expresses such feelings as longing for homeland, love for loved ones and friendship amongst friends
> By words and then ends.[21]

Gronas may be sardonic about Adorno's declaration that poetry after Auschwitz cannot be written, about the millions of poems that have in fact been written, and about the pieties of nation, love, and friendship such poems may exude. But there is no contempt toward the words that constitute this poem, nor toward the slyly obvious last sentence that reminds us that poems are built of words, words already used millions of times elsewhere.

In a sense, Gronas has written this poem already—which is to say that a poem about endless iteration is itself a repetition and rewriting of something the poet himself has already created. Compare this text from *Dorogie siroty*, its third poem, and notice its strange spacing—a technique Gronas uses to slow down our perception of the poem, making it occupy more space on the page and thus in our minds:

> the receiver no one picks up but oh how it blasts and shrieks can you imagine it?
> but no one
> actually I was calling to say precisely
> what the receiver said:
> four six eight twelve sounds
> indistinguishable one from the other
> one no more important than another
> precisely this—nothing else[22]

Numbers again, we realize: not the number that quantifies poems written, but the numerical code that produces a telephone connection. The poem's deadpan articulation is thus nothing more than an announcement that the speaker is inducing a connection to another; he is indulging in a speech act as a form of address. But in the post-Auschwitz poem, the focus is not on the act of listening or reading (a reception theory moment that has to be a near-constant in diaspora poetry, the "is-anyone-out-there moment" of Brodsky's abandoned dog circling in the cosmos)[23] but rather on the sheer accumulation of text. Gronas, the reluctant publisher of his own work (and a rare example of a contemporary poet who, on principle, does not give public poetry readings), recedes behind the ruin of text accumulating before him. He is like Walter Benjamin's angel of history, "where a chain of events appears before *us, he* sees one single catastrophe, which keeps piling wreckage upon wreckage and hurls it at his feet . . . the pile of debris before him grows toward the sky."[24]

To compare Gronas's poetic persona to Benjamin's angel is to place him in the "marginally Jewish" context I have been suggesting. Perhaps we should consider whether anything makes this particularly Jewish. It is distant from the prayers and lived experiences of Khersonskii and Temkina, closer to a metaphysical, cosmic evocation of abandonment that Jews may feel is quintessentially familiar. This has been expressed eloquently and succinctly by the poet, critic, and editor Alexander Skidan, who said, "On a more metaphysical level, what Jewishness is for me is an experience of going astray, of being lost in the desert, and also of the endless experience of finding a way, of finding a thread, to escape."[25] Mikhail Gronas is that poet in contemporary Russia who, perhaps more than any other, threads his way through landscapes of loss.

ESCAPE INTO ENGLISH, AND INTO PRAISE: ILYA KAMINSKY

An alternative way to locate the same thread is to escape into a different language. That has been the choice of Ilya Kaminsky (b. 1977), a poet whose family left Odessa for the United States in 1993, when he was a teenager. One of Kaminsky's books in English is entitled *Dancing in Odessa*; it appeared to tremendous acclaim in 2004. He has published poems from his next book, *Deaf Republic*, and they have won prizes as well. He lives in California, has American bachelor's and law degrees, and teaches in the MFA program at San Diego State University. He lives the life of an American poet in many ways, and American poets are his milieu, but he occasionally writes in Russian and translates from Russian to English. Kaminsky speaks Russian comfortably, in some ways more so than in English, but for a curious reason—he has been deaf since early childhood. Thus, unlike others, who might have switched to compose in the new language that surrounded them upon emigration, Kaminsky's ear is not inundated with the sounds of English. He hears it in his head, and knows an immense amount of poetry in English, but I would argue that his writing constitutes a continuation of Russian poetry, simply by other means.

His contribution to the theme of diaspora is thus quite special. Kaminsky leaves aside none of the terrifying experience of violence and catastrophe that defined Jewish identity in the twentieth century, but brings it into his poems surreptitiously. His work exudes a rare and strangely beautiful feeling of joy. In a poem written as he was preparing *Dancing in Odessa* that did not make it into that collection, Kaminsky creates that enjoyable flush of pleasure out of the material of elegy. In the passage below, he refers to Ovid's lines written in exile, *Tristia*, a quotation that also closes this passage. The poem is a long sequence entitled "My Father Says Yes and No," and includes this evocative segment:

> As the night uncurls we discover light
> falling on the walls, from where?
> "Go into exile—write your Tristia," a Gypsy fortune-teller laughs
> opening her dress.
> I recall her vowels filled with the rain.
> I escaped, yes—a butterfly in a parking lot
> or man in a parking lot, his chest full of yellow wings.
> I lived as though the city was on fire—faces from the metro followed me to the
>   house and upstairs.
> There I sat, cataloging memories
> fragile as chrysanthemums on a wind.
> I turn back, laundry flattens on the balconies like sails,
> mornings full of light make my hands harden with language.
> It's August. The sun begins a routine narration, whitening their bodies—mother,
>   father dancing, moving as the darkness speaks behind them.
> It's August. Light washes the balconies. August,
> the speech in my mouth thickens as a pear, dark sister of sweetness. I
> retell the story a light etches
> into my hand: *Little book, go to the city without me*.[26]

To live as if the city were aflame is to live as if in an emergency, but the action of this poem—as so often in Kaminsky's work—is lushly slow: night uncurls, light falls, vowels fill with rain, memories are catalogued, and speech thickens. This imagistic richness is a large part of Kaminsky's appeal as a poet, bringing into English poetry a set of qualities that seem as if they originate elsewhere. Readers turn to Kaminsky as they would toward a translation, I suspect, finding in his work a set of places, names, sights, and smells that feel foreign, as if they were emerging from a darkness that the poetry itself evokes.

Oddly, the references to Jewish experience and the evocations of great Russian writers feel familiar, nearly all of their names also synonymous with the fates of exile, violence, and suffering: in the cycle "Traveling Musicians," for instance, we find poems about Brodsky, Babel, and Tsvetaeva, to whom the great German (Jewish) poet Paul Celan is added, in accordance with the same logic of traumatic heritage.[27] In "Musica Humana," the myths and fantasies around Mandelstam are central. In the long title sequence that opens *Dancing in Odessa*, Kaminsky more directly evokes the very material that is the stuff of Khersonskii's *Family Archive*— but how much lighter is his touch. There are terrible moments of shattering violence, nearly all rendered with brief and sexual specificity so that the harm flashes against the most intimate sense of self—a grandmother raped, a grandfather whose genitals are singed as he saves a pregnant woman from a fire—but these are brief, stark moments, single lines in poems that otherwise evoke tomatoes and apples, ponies on balconies, and couples dancing on rooftops.

Here are some segments from this longer poem—quoting one of the individual parts would not do it justice, nor convey its texture and pace. First, a portion of the envoi in prose that sets *Dancing in Odessa* in motion:

> In a city ruled jointly by doves and crows, doves covered the main district, and crows the market. A deaf boy counted how many birds there were in his neighbor's backyard, producing a four-digit number. He dialed the number and confessed his love to the voice on the line.
>
> * * *
>
> But in the secret history of anger—*one man's silence*
> *lives in the bodies of others*—as we dance to keep from falling,
> between the doctor and the prosecutor:
> my family, the people of Odessa,
> women with huge breasts, old men naïve and childlike,
> all our words, heaps of burning feathers
> that rise and rise with each retelling.
>
> (from "In Praise of Laughter")
>
> * * *
>
> What is memory? what makes a body glow:
> an apple orchard in Moldova and the school is bombed—*when the schools are*
>   *bombed, sadness is forbidden*
> —I write this now and I feel my body's weight:
> the screaming girls, 347 voices
> in the story of a doctor saving them, his hands
> trapped under a wall, his granddaughter dying nearby—she whispers *I don't want*
>   *to die, I have eaten such apples.*
>
> (from "Maestro")
>
> * * *
>
> In a soldier's uniform, in wooden shoes, she danced
> At either end of day, my Aunt Rose.
> […]
> She hung her husband's
> Picture on a wall in her apartment. Each month
> on a different wall. I now see her with that picture, hammer
> in her left hand, nail in her mouth.
>
> (from "Aunt Rose")

Kaminsky, like a novelist filling in the life of a family through telling details, zeroes in on that nail temporarily lodged between Aunt Rose's lips as she rehangs her husband's picture; it is an emblem of fierce devotion. Kaminsky creates a lost world as surely as Khersonskii does in *Family Archive*, but in a kind of miniature, sketched-in format, as if trying to recreate the improvisational quality of lived experience. And the bodies in his descriptions are weightier, more substantial. We have a richer sensory impression of his world than is suggested by the largely visual imagery of Khersonskii. Not for nothing do so many people in this book dance.

In the final poem in the sequence, time has passed, and August has become April. The poet sets sail for unknown lands, more Odysseus than Ovid:

Dancing in Odessa
We lived north of the future, days opened
letters with a child's signature, a raspberry, a page of sky.
My grandmother threw tomatoes
from her balcony, she pulled imagination like a blanket
over my head. I painted
my mother's face. She understood
loneliness, hid the dead in the earth like partisans.
The night undressed us (I counted
its pulse) my mother danced, she filled the past
with peaches, casseroles. At this, my doctor laughed, his granddaughter
touched my eyelid—I kissed
the back of her knee. The city trembled,
a ghost-ship setting sail.
And my classmate invented twenty names for Jew.
He was an angel, he had no name,
we wrestled, yes. My grandfathers fought
the German tanks on tractors, I kept a suitcase full
of Brodsky's poems. The city trembled,
a ghost-ship setting sail.
At night, I woke to whisper: yes, we lived.
We lived, yes, don't say it was a dream.
At the local factory, my father
took a handful of snow, put it in my mouth.
The sun began a routine narration,
whitening their bodies: mother, father dancing, moving
as the darkness spoke behind them.
It was April. The sun washed the balconies, April.
I retell the story the light etches
into my hand: *Little book, go to the city without me.*[28]

To repeat, as Kaminsky does, the assertion that the city "trembled" like "a ghost-ship setting sail," is to personify the place, then to give it a capacity to defy death as if it were more than a person—something like a spirit. The city as ship calls to mind Odysseus setting sail, a connection that might seem arbitrary were it not for Kaminsky's writing in another poem of the name for his native city, Odessa: "I was born in the city named after Odysseus."[29] So many of the details in "Dancing in Odessa" could seem whimsical and fantastic, but the German tanks, the tractors, and the suitcase of Brodsky's poems all take the poet back to the ghost-ship on which he left the Soviet Union. His voyage is toward an America whose name he praises in the final poem in this book, a word he puts on the page and calls "my keyhole."[30]

Praise is a key word in Kaminsky's vocabulary. Given his admiration for the work of Joseph Brodsky, Kaminsky's reverence may remind us of the paradoxical insistence at the end of Brodsky's 1980 birthday poem that, until the end of his days, for all the sufferings of his lifetime, he will voice only gratitude ("May 24, 1980").[31] Kaminsky, too, is unsparing in his record of violence and loss, but he never dwells on this pain and he seems not to despair. His presence as a poet, as those who have heard him read can testify, is positively radiant. He has less metaphysical angst, in fact, than we find in Brodsky's work, and that may in part be a gift of his having found his way to poetry in English, rather than in Russian.

The one who sets sail with a suitcase full of poems, however, remains a vivid emblem for the Russian poet in diaspora. All is in motion; even the poet's creative psyche is ready for flight. Kaminsky's work replaces the worldly possessions of Khersonskii's poems—the Judaica, the photographs—with the bits of paper on which poems would be written. As if not trusting his own memory, he holds fast to the papers on which words are imprinted. What results are not the prayers of Khersonskii's best efforts in *Family Archive*, nor the minimalist constructions of Gronas, nor the museum-like exhibits of Temkina's verse. Instead, something else emerges: a sensory world of past and present and a celebration of the human capacity to hold those pains and their pleasures long in the mind.

I end with Kaminsky, then, whose work has moved us from prayer, often uttered in despair in Khersonskii's work, to words of praise; from burnished silver ritual objects sold off in desperation or confiscated, through the curious museum exhibits of Temkina, past the burned out words of Gronas, toward the dancing exhilaration and determination of Kaminsky's English. Of all these poets, Kaminsky is the one who has found an admiring audience in the United States, who was asked to edit an anthology of world poetry, and is often featured in journals and poetry festivals. That happy fate makes him less marginal in the country in which he now resides, but it is his capacity to make use of material from the margins of Russian life that has made for his American success. At this moment, early in the twenty-first century, when Russian poetry flourishes in many places around the world, poets of Jewish descent play a strong role in giving to Russian poetry its distinctive, border-crossing, wall-tumbling, boundary-shifting identity.

NOTES

1. Khersonskii is a practicing psychologist, which no doubt influences this perceptive rendering of mental processes through tangible symbolic formations. He makes no reference to the work of Christopher Bollas, but I see some remarkable similarities to Bollas's *The Mystery of Things* (London: Routledge, 1999). See also Bollas, *The Shadow of the Object: Psychoanalysis of the Unthought Known* (New York: Columbia University Press, 1987).
2. Cited, although with a number of modifications, from Boris Khersonsky, *Family Archive*, trans. Ruth Kreuzer and Dale Hobson, http://www.dalehobson.org/khersonsky/boris5.html (accessed on March 18, 2015). For the original, see Boris Khersonskii, *Semeinyi arkhiv* (Moscow: Novoe literaturnoe obozrenie, 2006), 21.
3. Ibid.
4. Ibid. For the original, see Khersonskii, *Semeinyi arkhiv*, 149.
5. Khersonskii, *Semeinyi arkhiv*, 140.
6. Khersonskii's blog posts would provide ample material here—to take a vivid example, see the poem posted on July 10, 2011, "Pisano v pisaniiakh: vo vremena ony," http://borkhers.livejournal.com/, which begins with an Old Testament scene of the pharaohs and Moses in Egypt, only to open out onto a vista of Jesus's wanderings. Also of great interest are the poems in his later book *Spirichuels* (Moscow: NLO, 2009); they range from the sights and sounds of Brooklyn to saints' lives and spirituals reprised.
7. For the poetry, see Sergei Magid, *Zona sluzhen'ia* (Moscow: NLO, 2003) and Magid, *V doline Elakh* (Moscow: Vodolei, 2010).
8. In her English-language "almost artist's book," as she described it, Marina Temkina, *What Do You Want?*, 1st ed. (Brooklyn, NY: Ugly Duckling Press, 2009).
9. See her article "'Lost Jews,' 'Chimeras,' or 'the Hope of the Nation'? Jews, Russia, Mixed Marriages, and Historical Memory Revisited," *Anthropology and Archeology of Eurasia* 48.1 (Summer 2009): 39–66.
10. Marina Temkina, *Kalancha: Genderhaia lirika* (New York: Slovo-Word, 1995), 24–31.
11. See the short biography written up at the time of her Revson Fellowship, 2001: http://www.revson.columbia.edu/meetthefellows/fellow/marina_temkina. For more information about the archive, see http://artsites.ucsc.edu/faculty/efimova/archive/about/about.html.
12. Temkina, *What Do You Want?*, 49.
13. Marina Temkina, *Canto immigranto* (Moscow: Novoe literaturnoe obozrenie, 2005), 92; my translation.
14. The idea of the museum is a long-standing one in Temkina's poetry. See, for example, "Muzeinye eksponaty," in Temkina, *Kalancha*, 32.
15. Temkina, *Canto immigranto*, 93; my translation.
16. This account of Marina Temkina's work is expanded and revised in Sandler, "Marina Temkina and Marginally Jewish Russian Poetry," *New Studies in Russian Literature: Essays in Honor of Stanley J. Rabinowitz*, ed. Catherine Ciepiela and Lazar Fleishman, Stanford Slavic Studies, vols. 45–46 (Oakland, CA: Berkeley Slavic Specialties, 2014), vol. 46, 338–350.
17. In a review of this book, Anna Glazova astutely notes that it isn't just the people in it who are orphaned, but the words themselves. See Anna Glazova, "Vyrazhenie slov: O stikhakh Mikhaila Gronasa," *TextOnly* 29 (2009), http://www.litkarta.ru/dossier/expressionofwords/.
18. Mikhail Gronas, *Dorogie siroty,* (Moscow: OGI, 2002), 5; my translation. Note that the comma is part of the book's title; Gronas suggests that the two-word title is a greeting in a letter.

19. Thinking in linguistic terms presents a subtle point of continuity to other aspects of Gronas's life: in Moscow, he studied as a linguist, and his USC dissertation was supervised by a linguist-turned-literary scholar, Alexander Zholkovsky.
20. Gronas, *Dorogie siroty*, 6; my translation.
21. Gronas, "Eight million nine hundred and fifty three thousand one hundred and eighty sixth poem after Auschwitz," trans. Christopher Mattison with the author, *Jacket* 36 (2008), http://jacketmagazine.com/36/rus-gronas-trb-mattison-author.shtml. For the original, see *Vozdukh* 2 (2006): 33. The original is untitled, and the precise numbering of which poem this is after Auschwitz is different, which surely adds to the poem's insistent arbitrariness in enumeration.
22. Gronas, *Dorogie siroty*, 7; my translation.
23. In "The Condition We Call Exile." See Joseph Brodsky, *On Grief and Reason: Essays* (New York: Farrar, Straus and Giroux, 1995), 32.
24. Walter Benjamin, *Selected Writings*, ed. Marcus Paul Bullock, et al., trans. Rodney Livingstone and E.F.N. Jephcott, vol. 4 (Cambridge, MA: Belknap Press, 1996).
25. Joshua Cohen, "Aleksandr Skidan Sees 'Red,'" *Jewish Daily Forward*, February 8, 2008, http://www.forward.com/articles/12618/. An interesting poem of Skidan's to consider in this context is "'Delirium' / Fragmenty," with its strange evocation of Lot and his daughters. The poem appears in his book *Delirium* (St. Petersburg: Mitin Zhurnal, 1993), http://www.vavilon.ru/texts/skidan1.html#32.
26. Cited from *Adirondack Review* 3.2 (Winter 2002), http://adirondackreview.homestead.com/featuredkaminsky.html (accessed on July 15, 2011).
27. The role of Paul Celan in the imagining of Jewishness for Russian (and not just Russian) poets is a large topic. Gronas concludes his book of poems with several translations from Celan. Anna Glazova, a Russian poet, translator, and scholar of comparative literature, has translated and written about Celan; see, for example, her "Poetry of Bringing about Presence: Paul Celan Translates Osip Mandelstam," *Modern Language Notes* 124 (2009): 1108–1126. This essay used as a point of entry into Glazova's poetry would make a further extension of my argument here: her approach is phenomenological, making of Celan a poet who creates an ethical, temporalized relation between speaker and listener that has much in common with the core ideas of Lévinas and Derrida. Her key phrase is that the poet brings "the balance of justice to the grammar of poetry" (1117). For Glazov's Celan translations, see *Tselan, govori i ty* (New York: Ailuros, 2012).
28. Ilya Kaminsky, *Dancing in Odessa* (Dorset, VT: Tupelo Press, 2004), 5–12.
29. Ibid., 56.
30. Ibid.
31. For his translation of the poem into English, see Joseph Brodsky, *Collected Poems in English*, ed. Ann Kjellberg (New York: Farrar, Straus and Giroux, 2000), 211. For the Russian original, see Joseph Brodsky, *Sochineniia Iosifa Brodskogo*, ed. Gennadii Komarov, et al., 2nd ed. (St. Petersburg: Pushkinskii fond, 1998), vol. 3, 191.

17 · TRIPLE IDENTITIES

Russian-Speaking Jews as German, American, and Israeli Writers

ADRIAN WANNER

Since the turn of the millennium, an increasing number of Russian-Jewish émigrés have become successful writers in the languages of their host countries.[1] By using German, English, or Hebrew as their medium of literary expression, these authors have acquired a triple transnational identity that combines a Russian linguistic and cultural origin, a Jewish (generally secular) "ethnicity," and a German, Austrian, American, Canadian, or Israeli nationality. While these writers have received a warm, even enthusiastic response from readers and critics in their countries of residence and elsewhere, the reception of their books in their country of birth has been indifferent at best, hostile at worst.[2] To some extent, the negative Russian reaction may have been triggered by wounded national pride. Writing in a language other than one's native tongue involves a radical act of assimilation to a new culture, which can offend some who view the abandonment of one's mother tongue as "tantamount to matricide."[3] For those who follow Johann Gottfried Herder in romanticizing language as the ultimate carrier of a national essence and "soul," forfeiture of a native tongue entails a serious loss of national identity. Of course, as Jews, these writers never truly qualified as "genuine Russians" in their country of birth. Yet, one could also argue that, paradoxically, by writing in a language other than their native Russian, they have made a commodity of their "Russianness." In this chapter, I explore these issues by studying a few leading, contemporary trans-lingual Russian-Jewish writers living in Germany, Austria, the United States, and Israel.

RUSSIAN IMMIGRANT WRITERS IN GERMANY AND AUSTRIA

In the years since reunification, Germany has become home to over 200,000 Russian-Jewish *Kontingentflüchtlinge* [quota-refugees]. One of these immigrants, Wladimir Kaminer, is currently one of Germany's most popular writers. Born in Moscow in 1967, Kaminer trained as a sound engineer and studied at a theatrical institute before serving two years in the Soviet military. Remarkably, he knew no German before he immigrated, at age twenty-three, to what was then the German Democratic Republic. After working various odd jobs in Berlin, including stints as a cabaret and club performer, in 1998 he began to write in the language of his adopted homeland. Kaminer's first book, *Russendisko* (2000)—a collection of vignettes of Russian émigré life in Berlin—became a surprise hit and turned the author into a new "shooting star" of German literature. Kaminer has since published nineteen more books in rapid succession.[4] By 2004, his works had sold over 1.2 million copies and had been published in fifteen countries.[5] In addition to print editions, Kaminer is also doing a brisk business in audio versions of his books. Moreover, he writes columns for a number of German newspapers and magazines, runs a weekly radio show, tours Germany and other countries for public readings, and, last but not least, he serves as the DJ in his Russian Disco in former East Berlin, which has become a legendary fixture of Berlin's night life, attracting large crowds of Germans, Russian immigrants, and tourists.[6] For many Germans, Kaminer has come to represent the "quintessential Russian," a role that he has learned to play to perfection with a tinge of self-conscious irony.

As the title of his first book indicates, Kaminer's Russian identity looms large in his literary self-fashioning. Russianness is signaled from the outset in a conspicuous, if hackneyed, manner via graphic elements such as *matryoshka* dolls and the Soviet Star. Kaminer skillfully capitalizes on German clichés about the Russian national character by playing on such stereotypes as the Russian penchant for hard drinking, sentimentality, and chaotic spontaneity, which are antagonistically opposed to notions of German neatness, dullness, and pedantry. It is no accident that the audio CDs of his book, which showcase Kaminer's thick Russian accent, enjoy a particular popularity with the German public. Kaminer's radio programs and public readings also hold the same "exotic" appeal. He frequently refers to himself as *"der Russe vom Dienst"* [loosely translated: "the Russian from central casting"], and his public performances are announced with phrases like *"Der Russe kommt!"* ["The Russian is coming!"]. By contrast, Kaminer's Jewish background appears in a much more muted form. While he does not hide his Jewishness, Kaminer prefers not to dwell on it. "Russian," rather than "Jewish," is the common denominator he uses for the immigrants from the former Soviet Union. Nevertheless, an important, unmentioned factor contributes to his popularity with the German public: he is a Jew who has happily embraced the German language and culture and, thus, can burnish the image of the new Germany as a philo- rather than an anti-Semitic nation.

Given the large number of Russian-speaking immigrants in Germany and the success of Kaminer's Russian brand, the pool of potential "new Kaminers" is vast. One of Kaminer's "competitors" is the Leningrad-born Lena Gorelik. Like Kaminer, Gorelik is a Russian-Jewish "quota refugee." Unlike Kaminer, she left Russia when she was still a child. Born in 1981, she immigrated with her parents to Germany in 1992. She grew up near Stuttgart and graduated from the German School of Journalism in Munich. In 2006, she obtained a graduate degree in East European Studies from the University of Munich with a thesis devoted to the representation of Russian-Jewish immigrants in the German media. Since 2004, Gorelik has published six books—*Meine weißen Nächte* [*My White Nights*], *Hochzeit in Jerusalem* [*Wedding in Jerusalem*], *Verliebt in Sankt Petersburg: Meine russische Reise* [*In Love with St. Petersburg: My Russian Journey*], *Lieber Mischa* [*Dear Misha*], *Sie können aber gut Deutsch!* [*Your German Is Really Good*], and *Die Listensammlerin* [*The Collector of Lists*]. Her books have been favorably reviewed in the German press, and she has received several literary awards. The autobiographical heroine in all of Gorelik's novels is a young Russian-Jewish woman who came to Germany at age eleven and leads a happily integrated life together with her extended family. Although Gorelik acknowledges her Jewish heritage more openly than Kaminer, she also relies on her Russianness as a tool of self-identification and self-promotion.

Both Kaminer and Gorelik present themselves as culturally assimilated, secular, "nonthreatening" immigrants who entertain the German public with humorous, tongue-in-cheek stories about their culture of origin. Part of their success is that they manage to present themselves as both Russian and German simultaneously. The double performance as a "typical Russian" and a "typical German" is a key ingredient of Kaminer's strategy, which allows him to assume a perspective that is both foreign and domestic at the same time. As the Austrian scholar Eva Hausbacher has noted, "[Kaminer] speaks as a Russian about Germans and has simultaneously already become a 'German writer,' he speaks as a 'German writer' about Russians and is (still) 'der Russe vom Dienst.'"[7] Similarly, in her book *Verliebt in St. Petersburg*, Gorelik presents her city of birth to a German friend by assuming the role of tour guide and cultural mediator who is both an insider and outsider in Russia. Unlike the situation in Gorelik's first two novels, the heroine's triple Russian-Jewish-German identity is reduced here to a Russian-German binary. The heroine's relatives appear as paradigmatic "Russians" without any reference to their Jewish background.

Interestingly, in her fourth book, Gorelik performs the opposite operation by focusing squarely on her Jewish identity. She writes *Lieber Mischa* in the form of a letter to her newborn son. The baroque subtitle strongly hints at the book's satirical tone: "Dear Misha . . . whose name almost would have been Schlomo Adolf Grinblum Glück, I am so sorry I couldn't spare you this: You are a Jew. . . ." Adorned with Talmud-esque side glosses and oscillating between Jewish pride and Jewish self-mockery, the book runs through numerous clichés ranging from the Jewish nose, to the Jewish mother, to the Jewish world conspiracy. The book's jacket blurb states, "Lena Gorelik belongs to a new generation of Jews in Germany who wants to define itself via the future, not via the past." Gorelik seems to be most annoyed by German philo-Semites rather than by German anti-Semitism. She reserves her particular scorn for those who convert to Judaism in the belief that they will be somehow absolved from German collective guilt if they become "super-Jews" [*Überjuden*]. What these converts do not understand, according to Gorelik, is that "while one can convert to Judaism, one cannot become a Jew."[8] Rather than tying Jewishness to the observance of religious rules, her definition of Jewishness rests on a sense of belonging and solidarity and on a self-ironic sense of humor—something that, in Gorelik's judgment, some Germans sorely lack.

The conundrum of being a Jewish writer in post-Holocaust Germany is of little concern to Kaminer and Gorelik. Anti-Semitism, if mentioned at all in their stories, is presented as a Russian rather than a German phenomenon. This certainly has facilitated their status as "model" German Jews. Kaminer has been put on display in Daniel Libeskind's Jewish Museum in Berlin, which has become a major tourist attraction in the new German capital. In a room devoted to contemporary Jewish life in Germany, visitors can pick up earphones in front of Kaminer's photograph and hear him reminisce about his life as a Jew in the Soviet Union. He talks about receiving his first passport at age sixteen and being teased by his classmates because of his Jewish nationality. Later, he discovered that "being a Jew could be fun" when he joined a gang of hippies who irritated the KGB with public demonstrations on Jewish holidays, overturning police cars, and demanding the right to emigrate to Israel.[9] Tellingly, he has nothing to say about his life as a Jew in Germany. Gorelik does address the topic of German-Jewish relations, as we have seen, but anti-Semitism plays almost no role in her fiction. Interestingly, the few people who treat her Russian-Jewish immigrant characters with condescension are primarily German Jews. In *Hochzeit in Jerusalem*, Russian newcomers are snubbed as socially undesirable elements during an event at the Jewish Community Center. By contrast, the heroine's family is moved to tears by a German ceremony of public contrition commemorating the anniversary of the "Reichskristallnacht."[10] The implication is that secular, modern, and tolerant Germany provides a more accommodating home for Russian Jews than the narrow-minded Jewish religious community.

To be sure, this philo-Germanism is not shared by all Russian-Jewish immigrants. Vladimir Vertlib is a different example of a Russian Jew who has become a successful writer in German. Born in Leningrad in 1966, Vertlib settled in Austria at age fifteen after a ten-year odyssey that involved numerous border crossings and residence in multiple countries, including Israel, Holland, Italy, and the United States, where he and his family lived in New York's Brighton Beach neighborhood and later in Boston before they were deported as illegal aliens.[11] Vertlib's literary persona is that of the alienated outsider rather than the happily integrated immigrant. Unlike Lena Gorelik's protagonist, who displays her patriotism by rooting for the German soccer team at the world championship, the German-Jewish hero of Vertlib's novel, *Letzter Wunsch* [*Last Wish*, 2003], has a more complex attitude. When simple-minded souls subject him to an inane loyalty test by asking which side he would support in a hypothetical soccer match between Germany and Israel, he varies his answer according to the questioner. To Germans, he invariably replies, "Israel," but if the questioner is a foreigner, especially a Jew, he says "Germany."[12]

Becoming a writer in German, a language to which he only gradually developed a more positive attitude, finally freed Vertlib from the compulsive need for further emigration as he explained in a 2004 interview.[13] Nevertheless, Austria has not become an unproblematic "home" for him. Unlike Kaminer and Gorelik, who tend to avoid the topic of German anti-Semitism, Vertlib is well aware of the baggage that he carries as a Jewish author writing in German, especially in a country that has been reluctant to confront its Nazi past. The Jewish-German protagonist of the novel *Letzter Wunsch* shocks the teacher of his provincial school when he suggests that, in the interest of historical truthfulness, the local Horst-Wessel-Strasse and the Hermann-Göring-Platz should have kept their names and the Hitler monument should be restored to its former location in front of the town hall. Placed in a double bind, neither the teacher nor the classmates dare to object, because "how can you respond to a Jew who pleads for the erection of a Hitler monument without inevitably saying something wrong?"[14] Vertlib's account suggests that the conspicuous philo-Semitism of the Germans masks an underlying unease. The feisty protagonist of the novel, *Das besondere Gedächtnis der Rosa Masur* [*The Special Memory of Rosa Masur*, 2001], who is modeled on Vertlib's own grandmother, observes, "as we know, the Germans nowadays love the Jews, at least as long as the Jews don't behave as Jewishly as they believe Jews are capable of but should rather not."[15]

The hallmark of Vertlib's own identity remains an uneasy sense of being in-between. He resists being categorized or showcased as a representative of a specific ethnicity. Like Kaminer, Vertlib undermines essentialized notions of ethnic identity by turning them into an ironic performance. His autobiographical novel *Zwischenstationen* concludes with the narrator's arrival in Salzburg—his new permanent home in provincial Austria. The first thing he does after leaving the train station is to purchase a Tyrolean hat and break into a cheerful yodel. Thus, his multinational odyssey ends on a faux note of Austrian folklore. Overall, however, Vertlib's attitude toward his own identity, in spite of a subtle and acerbic humor, is far removed from Kaminer's postmodern play and its clichés. Instead of assuming the role of the stereotypical Russian, he prefers to keep his distance from any facile attempts at multicultural tokenism. While Vertlib is certainly no less Russian than Kaminer or Gorelik, perhaps to his credit, he has refused to play the "Russian card" in any systematic way, making it instead a component of a more complex and conflicted cosmopolitan identity.

RUSSIAN-AMERICAN WRITERS

Gary Shteyngart's novel *The Russian Debutante's Handbook*[16] launched the genre of contemporary Russian-Jewish immigrant fiction in the United States. In some respects, Shteyngart's self-ironic performance of his ethnic identity resembles that of Kaminer. Unlike Kaminer's integrated foreigner and ironic model immigrant, Shteyngart (like Vertlib) cultivates the persona of a culturally alienated outsider. While Kaminer tends to downplay his Jewish background, Shteyngart foregrounds his (secular) Jewishness as an additional alienating factor. Like the Russian-German immigrant writers, Shteyngart embraces an anti-essentialist cultural hybridity, though less extremely and consistently than Kaminer. When Kaminer was asked by *Deutsche Welle* in 2003 whether he sees himself primarily as a Russian, a German, or a Jewish writer, his response was: "I understand that for others this is an important distinction. But personally I don't give a damn about it [*mir selbst ist das schnurz*]."[17] By contrast, Shteyngart's "hyphenated" status still presumes a composite of underlying "real" ethnicities. In spite of his irony, he also displays something resembling a residual ethnic pride. In a 2005 Russian-language interview with Radio Liberty, he claimed that Russian literature occupies the "first place in the world,"[18] and in a conversation with Natasha Grinberg, he declared that he is "proud to be a secular Jew" even though he does not seen himself as a "flag waver in any way."[19]

Like Kaminer in Germany, Shteyngart has become a trailblazer for an entire generation of Soviet-born immigrant writers in North America, including David Bezmozgis, Lara Vapnyar, Ellen Litman, Anya Ulinich, Olga Grushin, Sana Krasikov, Irina Reyn, Mark Budman, Keith Gessen, Michael Idov, Michael Alenyikov, Maxim D. Shrayer, Nadia Kalman, Boris Fishman, Yelena Akhtiorskaya, and Kseniya Melnik. In recent years, these authors have come to form a vibrant subgroup of contemporary American fiction, and have made Russianness a sought-after commodity on the U.S. publishing market. As Masha Gessen observed, with only a slight touch of hyperbole, in the Russian magazine *Snob* in 2009: "It is fashionable to be 'Russian,' it is fashionable to write about it, it is fashionable to be the editor or agent of a 'Russian-American writer.' Or, rather, for an American writer today, it is best to be Russian."[20]

Comparing Russian-German immigrant writers with their Russian-American counterparts, we notice that both groups employ similar strategies to turn their Russianness into a marketable commodity for their local target audiences. They all deploy clichés associated with Russian culture both as a marker of ethnic distinction and, in some cases, as a self-ironic means of auto-exoticism. A *matryoshka* doll, a quintessential symbol of Russianness, appears on the covers of books by such diverse authors as David Bezmozgis, Wladimir Kaminer, Lena Gorelik, and the Russian-Israeli writer Boris Zaidman.[21] Capitalizing on the prestige of Russian high culture and exploiting the totalitarian mystique of the Soviet Union and its former status as a rival superpower have provided additional layers to the promotion of Russian cultural products in the United States and other Western countries.

Nevertheless, there are some important differences between Russian-German and Russian-American writers, which stem from the different nature of their respective host societies. In the United States, the immigrant experience lies at the core of the nation's self-image and cultural mythology, allowing Russian newcomers to insert themselves into a long tradition of immigrant and Jewish writing in America. As an intriguing new ethnic brand, Andrew Furman argues, Russianness can help revitalize Jewish-American literature and assure Jews their rightful place in the multicultural canon.[22] The situation is very different in Germany, a country that has defined itself traditionally as an ethnically homogenous *Volk* and that only recently (and reluctantly) has begun to grapple with the fact that it has become a destination for immigrants. Kaminer's depiction of German society as a vibrant multicultural mix counters the stereotypes of Germans as a homogeneous mass of Teutonic bores or Nazi thugs. One wonders whether Kaminer and Gorelik's success is not also boosted by the fact that they remove the guilt from their host society's hegemonic sense of superiority by impersonating "subalterns" who happily glorify the dominant culture.[23] Kaminer's benevolent depiction of Germany has a greater appeal to the German public than the more subversive writings of Vertlib, who continues to raise uncomfortable questions about German xenophobia and anti-Semitism. Kaminer's performance of the "cool" yet ultimately harmless Russian, and Gorelik's persona of the female "immigrant overachiever" fit neatly into the utopian projection of the New Germany as a happy, multicultural community.

RUSSIAN WRITING IN ISRAEL

Israel is the country that has received, by far, the most Russian-Jewish immigrants. "Russians" today make up about one fifth of Israel's Jewish population. They have created a thriving subculture with their own food stores, media outlets, political parties, and an extensive output of literature published in Russian. A comparatively small number of these Israeli "Russians" have become writers in Hebrew. Most of these writers have chosen not to dwell on their Russian origins, perhaps out of a desire to gain acceptance as "regular" Israelis. Thus far, the only exception to this rule seems to be Boris Zaidman, whose novel *Hemingway Ve-Geshem Ha-Tziporim Ha-Metot* [Hemingway and the Dead-Bird Rain], published by Am Oved Publishers in 2006, explicitly addresses the protagonist's dual identity as a Russian Israeli.

Zaidman was born in 1963 in Kishinev and immigrated to Israel with his parents when he was thirteen. Like most Third Wave immigrants arriving in the 1970s, the family sought to shed its Russian identity as quickly as possible and to assimilate to the Israeli mainstream. Trained in visual communication, Zaidman worked as an art director and manager of an advertising agency before publishing his first novel in 2006. It was hailed as one of the five best books of the year and has since been translated into several languages, although not into English.[24] Its hero, Tal Shani, like the author himself, came to Israel at age thirteen and, now in his thirties, lives the life of a "normal Israeli." However, he is suddenly confronted with his past when he receives an invitation from the Jewish Agency to participate in a Festival of Israeli Culture in his Ukrainian city of birth. During the plane ride from Tel Aviv to the (fictitious) Ukrainian town of Dnestrograd, he begins to reminisce about his childhood in the Soviet Union. The narrative becomes a journey backward in time as Shani mentally relives his former existence when he was still known as Tolik Schnaiderman. The novel consists of a series of loosely connected novellas relating various episodes from Tolik's former life in the Soviet Union, his emigration, and eventual arrival in Israel.

Zaidman's narrative posits a certain symmetry between the life of a Jew in the Soviet Union and that of a "Russian" in Israel. In both cases, the relevant ethnic identity confers an outsider status that is treated as a "dirty secret." Because Zaidman represents both the Soviet Union and Israel with irony and sarcasm, depending on the reviewers' own attitude and ideology, *Hemingway and the Dead-Bird Rain* has been interpreted as a denunciation of Soviet totalitarianism and anti-Semitism, or conversely, as an expression of disillusionment with the Israeli reality resulting in nostalgic feelings for Russia.[25] Both interpretations are equally one-sided. In reality, Zaidman's book evokes the duality typical of any immigrant existence. The novelty of his approach in an Israeli context lies in questioning the assimilationist, or "absorptionist," myth of the Israeli melting pot by showing the traumatic consequences of an abrupt, forced identity change and the residual, indelible Russianness that marks even a seemingly completely assimilated immigrant.[26]

Reverence for canonical Russian literature distinguishes Russianness from other immigrant ethnic brands. The Russian newcomers to Israel, in Zaidman's account, bemoan the natives' "illiteracy with regard to everything concerning Pushkin, Lermontov and Dostoevsky."[27] The fetishized essence of Russianness manifests itself in the worship of its literary classics. Young Tolik visualizes rows of collected works on bookshelves as powerful military phalanxes fighting a symbolic battle for world domination. One can find a similar attitude among Russian-Jewish immigrant writers elsewhere. For example, Gary Shteyngart's novels, like those of many of his colleagues, are peppered with allusions to the Russian classics. In some cases, the entire plot of a story or novel is "borrowed" from a canonical Russian literary source. Such is the case with Shteyngart's story "Shylock on the Neva," a rewriting of Gogol's tale "The Portrait,"[28] or with Irina Reyn's novel *What Happened to Anna K*,[29] a transplantation of Tolstoy's *Anna Karenina* into the Russian-Jewish immigrant milieu of New York. For many Russian Jews, identification with canonical Russian art, music, and literature has become a sort of secular *ersatz* religion. As Larissa Remennick put it in her study of Russian Jewish émigrés in Israel, North America, and Germany, "if they had any deities at all, these were Pushkin and Chekhov, Pasternak and Bulgakov."[30]

CONCLUSION

Of course, there are important and significant differences among Russian Jews who have become authors in other languages. A few pertinent generalizations can nevertheless be made. Even though they all have multilayered identities, most of these writers foreground their Russianness in their writings. Paradoxically, as Jews they managed to become fully recognized as "Russians" only outside of Russia. This situation creates the unenviable predicament of the eternally denigrated "Other," the alienated migrant who is a stranger both at home and abroad. The "dirty Jew" in Russia becomes a "dirty Russian" in Israel, America, or Germany. On the other hand, an outsider status involving multiple identities can of course become a precious resource for a creative writer, especially in an environment that validates "multiculturalism" or "hybridity," in whatever guise. It is important to stress that this Russian identity does not automatically emerge as a result of a writer's ancestry, language, or country of birth. Simply having been born in the Soviet Union and speaking Russian as one's native language are not sufficient to constitute an author's Russianness. Rather, this identity is actively *created* through a process of literary self-invention.[31] Possibly as compensation for the loss of Russianness implied in the shift to another language, the characters and setting of these authors' fiction tend to be Russian immigrant communities, the former Soviet Union, or contemporary post-Soviet Russia. Furthermore, their stories frequently feature protagonists serving as the authors' alter egos who engage in self-reflective musings about their own conflicted identity.

These writers depict their Jewishness in a wide variety of ways. While almost none is an "observant" Jew,[32] their attitudes toward Judaism range from a sort of melancholic nostalgia (as in the case of David Bezmozgis),[33] to Vladimir Vertlib's earnest grappling with the Judaic tradition, to indifference (the most common stance), to irony and overt hostility. The latter position is the one taken by Gary Shteyngart. Misha Vainberg, the hero and first-person narrator of the novel *Absurdistan*, presumably echoing Shteyngart's own opinion, calls Judaism "a codified system of anxieties" devised "to keep an already nervous and maligned people in check," and he insists that "the very best of Jews have always been assimilated and free thinking."[34] The decision to emigrate was prompted in most cases by the promise of economic advancement or fear of anti-Semitism, rather than by the desire to practice Judaism. The patronizing American Jew who expects gratitude for having rescued his brethren from Soviet captivity and tries to impose a Jewish religious identity on the Russian newcomers appears as a figure of satirical derision in several of the books by Russian-American writers.

Rather than their Jewishness, then, it is their Russianness that has made these writers stand out. That is how their publishers have promoted them, and this is the identity that many of them have foregrounded in their own fictional self-representation. One banal reason for this decision may be that Russianness sells better than Jewishness in the current fiction market, where a title like *The Jewish*

Debutante's Handbook would not have the same resonance as *The Russian Debutante's Handbook*. For a Russian-Israeli writer like Boris Zaidman, Russianness is the only distinguishing ethnic identity that he can claim.[35]

As immigrants become integrated and assimilated, they eventually cross a threshold when their foreign roots become a distant memory rather than a lived reality. The immigrant experience, therefore, may not provide a life-long inspiration for fiction writing. If it does, there is a risk that the result will be a form of ethnic kitsch. As Val Vinokur writes, "In some ways, this is the problem for assimilated immigrant writers (and for Jewish writers in particular, since the Jewish experience in America is so well-trod): how do you let go of the ethnic material once it is something that no longer owns you (when you're fresh off the boat) as much as you are now trying to own it (as some sort of internal heritage tourist)?"[36] Several of these writers have indicated plans to move away from Russian subjects in their coming works. In spite of such pronouncements, however, given the lucrative market for Russianness, it seems doubtful that these authors (or others) will stop playing the "Russian card" anytime soon.

NOTES

1. For a general discussion of contemporary translingual Russian literature in French, German, Hebrew, and English up to 2010, see my book, *Out of Russia: Fictions of a New Translingual Diaspora* (Evanston, IL: Northwestern University Press, 2011).
2. Only a few of these writers have been translated into Russian. Among the books discussed here, Wladimir Kaminer's *Russendisko*, Gary Shteyngart's three novels, and Vladimir Vertlib's *Zwischenstationen* have been published in Russia. None was a commercial success. In the Russian blogosphere, one can find occasional comments denouncing Russian-Jewish émigré writers as pseudo-Russian purveyors of ethnic kitsch. See, for example, the discussion "Opiat' ob Gogolia," November 12, 2004, http://gem.livejournal.com/213405.html, attacking mainly Lara Vapnyar, but also David Bezmozgis and Gary Shteyngart. The only writer who fared somewhat better in Russia is Michael Idov, whose novel *Ground Up* (2009) was published in the author's own Russian translation as *Kofemolka* (Moscow: Korpus, 2010).
3. Steven G. Kellman, *The Translingual Imagination* (Lincoln: University of Nebraska Press, 2000), ix.
4. *Frische Goldjungs* (an edited volume containing stories by other writers in addition to Kaminer's own, 2001), *Militärmusik* (2001), *Schönhauser Allee* (2001), *Die Reise nach Trulala* (2002), *Helden des Alltags* (2002), *Mein deutsches Dschungelbuch* (2003), *Ich mache mir Sorgen, Mama* (2004), *Karaoke* (2005), *Küche totalitär: Das Kochbuch des Sozialismus* (with Olga Kaminer, 2006), *Ich bin kein Berliner: Ein Reiseführer für faule Touristen* (2007), *Mein Leben im Schrebergarten* (2007), *Salve Papa!* (2008), *Es gab keinen Sex im Sozialismus: Legenden und Missverständnisse des vorigen Jahrhunderts* (2009), *Meine russischen Nachbarn* (2009), *Meine kaukasische Schwiegermutter* (2010), *Liebesgrüße aus Deutschland* (2011), *Onkel Wanja kommt: Eine Reise durch die Nacht* (2012), *Diesseits von Eden: Neues aus dem Garten* (2013), *Coole Eltern leben länger* (2014). Kaminer's books are published by Goldmann/Manhattan in Munich, a subsidiary of Random House.
5. Random House press department e-mail to author, June 8, 2004. The only book available in English is Wladimir Kaminer, *Russian Disco*, trans. Michael Hulse (London: Ebury Press, 2002).

6. See www.russendisko.de for pictures, sound samples, and updated information.

7. Eva Hausbacher, *Poetik der Migration: Transnationale Schreibweisen in der zeitgenössischen russischen Literatur* (Tübingen: Stauffenburg Verlag, 2009), 256. All English translations are my own. Whether this bifocal gaze actually qualifies Kaminer as an inhabitant of a subversive postcolonial "in-between space," as Hausbacher believes, must remain questionable, given that Kaminer both deconstructs and confirms national stereotypes. As Hausbacher herself acknowledges, Kaminer's success rests on the wholesale reproduction of clichés, which allows for divergent and mutually contradictory modes of reception. Ultimately, the meaning of his oeuvre depends on "where the reader wants to stop the pendulum swinging back and forth between deconstruction and affirmation of stereotypes" (Hausbacher, *Poetik der Migration*, 249).

8. Lena Gorelik, *Lieber Mischa* (Munich: Graf Verlag, 2011), 119.

9. The complete text can be found in Kaminer, *Es gab keinen Sex im Sozialismus* (Munich: Goldmann/Manhattan, 2009), 126–134. The version presented at the Jewish Museum includes only the first half of the story. The second half is devoted to a Jewish hippie who ends up emigrating to Israel but finds no happiness there—the climate is uncongenial, there are no "funny demonstrations," and all neighbors are Jews, which is "not all that great either" ("auch nichts Besonderes," 131). He moves on to California, later to Berlin, and finally returns to Moscow.

10. Gorelik, *Hochzeit in Jerusalem* (Munich: Diana Verlag, 2008), 61–62.

11. This episode inspired Vertlib's first book, the novella *Die Abschiebung* [*The Deportation*] (Salzburg: Otto Müller Verlag, 1995). Vertlib's second book, the autobiographical novel *Zwischenstationen* [*Intermediate Stations*] (Vienna: Franz Deuticke Verlag, 1999), provides a fictionalized account of his wanderings between continents and languages. In the meantime, Vertlib has published six more books.

12. Vladimir Vertlib, *Letzter Wunsch: Roman* (Munich: Deutscher Taschenbuch Verlag, 2006), 231.

13. Vertlib, *Spiegel im fremden Wort: Die Erfindung des Lebens als Literatur: Dresdner Chamisso-Poetikvorlesungen 2006* (Dresden: Thelem, 2007), 209.

14. Vertlib, *Letzter Wunsch*, 246.

15. The sentence sounds better in the German original: "Die Deutschen lieben ja heute die Juden, zumindest solange die Juden sich nicht so jüdisch benehmen wie sie glauben, daß sich Juden benehmen könnten, aber nicht sollten." Vladimir Vertlib, *Das besondere Gedächtnis der Rosa Masur: Roman* (Munich: Deutscher Taschenbuch Verlag, 2003), 227.

16. *The Russian Debutante's Handbook* (New York: Riverhead Books, 2002).

17. "Eine sehr skurrile Gemeinde," February 10, 2003, http://www.dw-world.de/dw/article/0,,657365,00.html.

18. Aleksandr Genis, "Benar-Anri Levi ob Amerike. Novaia kniga Kamilly Pal'i. Gost' nedeli: Zvezda amerikanskoi prozy Gari Shteingart," Radio Svoboda, April 19, 2005, http://www.svoboda.org/content/article/127943.html.

19. Natasha Grinberg, "Can't Live Long Without Writing. A Conversation with Gary Shteyngart," Del Sol Literary Dialogues, http://www.webdelsol.com/Literary_Dialogues/interview-wds-shteyngart.htm (accessed on April 28, 2011).

20. Masha Gessen, "Inostrannaia literatura," *Snob* 8 (May 2009), 103.

21. See David Bezmozgis, *Natasha* (New York: Farrar, Straus and Giroux, 2004); Wladimir Kaminer, *Ich mache mir Sorgen Mama* (Munich: Manhattan, 2004); Lena Gorelik, *Meine weißen Nächte* (Munich: Diana Verlag, 2006); and Boris Zaidman, *Safa Shesu'a* (Tel Aviv: Zmora-Bitan, 2010). Sana Krasikov revealed in an interview that her publisher wanted to put a *matryoshka* doll on the cover of her book, *One More Year*, but she was able to veto the idea. See Masha Gessen, "Inostrannaia literatura," *Snob* 8 (May 2009), 111. A matryoshka doll also graces the cover of a volume of essays on Russian-French writers: Murielle Lucie Clément, ed., *Autour des écrivains franco-russes* (Paris: L'Harmattan, 2008).

22. See Andrew Furman, "The Russification of Jewish-American Fiction," *Zeek* (April 2008), www.zeek.net/804furman/. For a more skeptical view, see Adam Rovner, "So Easily Assimilated: The *New* Immigrant Chic," *AJS Review* 30.2 (2006): 313–324. A more comprehensive discussion of this issue can be found in my article "Russian Jews as American Writers: A New Paradigm for Jewish Multiculturalism?" *MELUS* 37. 2 (Summer 2012), 157–176.

23. It should be noted that Gorelik has taken a much more critical stance in her recent writings. Her book *"Sie können aber gut Deutsch!"* bears the polemic subtitle, "Why I don't want to be grateful anymore for being allowed to live here, and why tolerance doesn't help us further." In particular, Gorelik expresses resentment at her own status as a *Vorzeigeausländer* (a term with similar implications as the American "model minority"). She resents being complimented for her good German and makes clear that she has become fed up with being touted as a role model for other immigrant groups, mainly Muslims, who are judged to be insufficiently willing to integrate.

24. A brief excerpt in English, translated by Sondra Silverston, has been published in *Zeek* (Spring/Summer 2008): 59–64. The novel has appeared thus far in German, French, and Italian. Given my own poor command of Hebrew, I have been consulting the German edition: Boris Saidman, *Hemingway und die toten Vögel*, trans. Miriam Pressler (Berlin: Berlin Verlag, 2008).

25. For an example of the first view, see Vladimir Balzer, "Tote Vögel: Als Jude in der Sowjetunion," *haGalil*, July 29, 2008, http://buecher.hagalil.com/2008/07/saidman/. For the second, see Sigrid Löffler, "60 Jahre Israel: Seht nur, was geschehen ist," *Literaturen* 5.8, http://literaturen.partituren.org/de/archiv/2008/ausgabe_0508/index.html?inhalt=20080421135344 (accessed on February 24, 2009).

26. In the meantime, Zaidman published a second novel, *Safa Shesu'a* (Tel Aviv: Zmora-Bitan, 2010), which continues his investigation of linguistic hybridity. Literally, the title *Safa Shesu'a* means "harelip" or "cleft lip." In Hebrew, the word "lip" also means "language," so the name of the book refers, of course, to the author's and hero's bilingualism. The book relates Tal Shani's military service during the first Intifada and his trip to France together with his girlfriend, who is of French origin. The linguistic situation becomes more complex as the hero finds himself torn among three languages—Russian, Hebrew, and French. I am indebted to my colleague Amit Schejter for this information. Zaidman himself is married to an Israeli woman of French origin and holds French citizenship (see his interview with *Le nouvel observateur*, March 13, 2008, http://bibliobs.nouvelobs.com/2008/03/13/boris-zaidman-lhomme-qui-venait-du-froid).

27. Boris Saidman, *Hemingway und die toten Vögel*, 40. Complaints about foreign ignorance of Russian literature can also be found in Lena Gorelik's novels. Her fictional alter ego observes with some irritation that Germans seem convinced that all Russians are drunkards, but "hardly anyone has read Dostoevsky," and she resents having to explain that "Pushkin is a poet and not a vodka brand" (Gorelik, *Meine weißen Nächte*, 26, 29).

28. See my article, "Gogol's 'Portrait' Repainted: On Gary Shteyngart's 'Shylock on the Neva,'" *Canadian Slavonic Papers* 51.2–3 (June–September 2009): 333–348.

29. Irina Reyn, *What Happened to Anna K* (New York: Simon and Schuster, 2008).

30. Larissa Remennick, *Russian Jews on Three Continents: Identity, Integration, and Conflict* (New Brunswick, NJ: Transaction, 2007), 48–49.

31. Not all trans-lingual Russian writers necessarily construct themselves as "Russians." Iegor Gran, for example, the son of Andrei Siniavsky, has become a successful French novelist using the last name of his wife as his *nom de plume*, but he does not address his Russian origin in his writings. Similarly, the Moscow-born Keith Gessen, author of the novel *All the Sad Young Literary Men* (New York: Penguin Books, 2008), does not dwell much on his Russian origin, and the novel has not been marketed as a "Russian" product. The same is true for Michael Idov's novel

Ground Up (New York: Farrar, Straus and Giroux, 2009). See my article "Moving beyond the Russian-American Ghetto: The Fiction of Keith Gessen and Michael Idov," *Russian Review* 73.2 (April 2014): 281–296.

32. Perhaps the only exception is Maxim D. Shrayer, who considers Judaism an essential part of Jewish identity. Several of his fictional plots in the collection *Yom Kippur in Amsterdam: Stories* (Syracuse, NY: Syracuse University Press, 2009) revolve around the moral dilemma of a Jewish male who has fallen in love with a *shiksa*. It is hard to imagine any of the other Russian immigrant writers taking up such a topic except as satire (as Shteyngart does in *The Russian Debutante's Handbook*, where the Russian-Jewish protagonist ends up marrying his gentile sweetheart from the American Midwest).

33. On the role of Judaism in Bezmozgis's work, see Bettina Hofmann, "David Bezmozgis—Muscles, Minyan, and Menorah: Judaism in *Natasha and Other Stories*," *Studies in American Jewish Literature* 25 (2006): 101–111.

34. Gary Shteyngart, *Absurdistan* (New York: Random House, 2006), 88, 251.

35. David Laitin has argued that Soviet Jews in Israel stress their Russian identity, whereas in America they emphasize their Jewishness, given that being Jewish carries more political clout in the United States than being Russian. See David D. Laitin, "The De-Cosmopolitanization of the Russian Diaspora: A View from Brooklyn in the 'Far Abroad,'" *Diaspora* 13.1 (2004): 5–35. This seems to contradict my observation that Russian-Jewish immigrant writers in the United States and elsewhere tend to foreground their Russianness. However, one could argue that while Jewishness may be a more advantageous identity politically, Russianness is more helpful in the literary marketplace.

36. Val Vinokur, "New Jews from the Old Country," *Boston Review* (February/March 2005): 7.

AFTERWORD

The Future of a Diaspora

ZVI GITELMAN

Like immigrants past and present, many Russian-speaking Jewish immigrants are saddened by the prospect that their culture will be lost in coming generations that will adopt the ways of their countries of immigration. Today and in the past, others are eager not only to forget the "old country" but to abandon its ways, including its language. This difference in attitudes may correlate with education and vocation along a spectrum ranging from rejection to preservation. It is likely that the more education one received in the "sending" country and the more one was involved in its culture, the more reluctant one would be to abandon it, or see it neglected or rejected by one's progeny. By contrast, people for whom language was merely an instrument of communication and, moreover, have no love for the sending country and its people, are likely not to have been "producers" of the former culture and to have "consumed" it without passion. Obviously, writers, dramatists, and devotees of Russian culture are apt to be more attached to it than workers, technicians, engineers, or those who were not regular theatergoers or readers of literature. As in all emigrations, there are those who are so intent on rejecting the old country and "making it" in the new that they do not transmit their former cultures across the generations. My impression is that Russian-speaking immigrant parents are more committed to speaking Russian to their children than the Yiddish-speaking immigrants of several generations ago were to speaking Yiddish. The earlier immigrants were much more anxious to become "Yankees," and less receptive to the idea of bi-culturalism. Abraham Cahan, the longtime editor of the most widely circulated Yiddish newspaper in America, *Forverts*, used the paper to spread knowledge of American ways and even "anglicized" the Yiddish language in order to teach his readers English.

On the other hand, in the early twentieth century, some immigrant Jewish intelligentsia did set up networks of—mostly secular—supplementary Yiddish schools, even teacher-training institutes, in Europe and in North, Central, and South America. Today, Russian-speaking immigrants, not all of them Jews, have established supplementary Russian schools in Canada, Israel, and the United States. Camps, family gatherings, and weekend retreats reinforce language competence and familiarity with the culture. The very presence of other Russian speakers no doubt mitigates feelings of peculiarity and isolation that immigrants and their children may experience.

Israel has received more RSJs than any other country. Most arrived when Israeli culture was moving away from an exclusivist insistence on Hebrew (one that achieved what no other people has done—revive a dead language) and as their insecurities about molding a nation from a very variegated immigrant population faded. Many Israelis have made their peace with cultural pluralism. They accommodate—some celebrate—linguistic and ethnic diversity, though, ironically, native Israeli Arabs have not benefitted from this shift as much as immigrants. Russian speakers are in a particularly good position to benefit from the change since they embody a relatively high prestige culture (though not as high as English-speaking "Anglo-Saxons"), have a very large number of speakers of their language, and, as Gur Ofer's chapter demonstrates, clamber rapidly up the socioeconomic ladder. Moreover, they fit relatively easily into the predominant Israeli conception of Jewishness. Israelis acknowledge the religious foundations of their ethnicity, but they are confident that they have transformed themselves into a modern nation. They have all the requisites of a nation and a state: a distinct (even unique) language, culture, territory, and sovereignty. The fact that most of Israel's neighboring states reject their very existence as a people and a state in no way diminishes their certitude of nationhood. Religious belief and practice are optional, though most Israelis—and their Supreme Court—reject the idea that Jewish identity is compatible with Christian or Muslim practice. Yet, one need not be Jewish to be Israeli—indeed, over a fifth of the population is not Jewish but is Israeli.

RSJs fit comfortably into this paradigm of Jewishness. In the Soviet Union and its successor states, they were a "nationality." In Israel, they move up the scale of ethnicity and become part of a "nation." At last, they have met even Joseph Stalin's criteria for nationhood: in Israel, Jews are a "historically constituted, stable community of people, formed on the basis of a common language, territory, economic life, and psychological makeup manifested in a common culture."[1] Ironically, Stalin denied that the Jews are a nation; yet, it is people from his state who constitute the single largest group to join the Jewish state and solidify its claim to nationhood. More than any other Jewish community in the world, the State of Israel accommodates a secular, ethnic understanding of Jewishness, precisely the one most RSJs bring with them.

In the Jewish diaspora, RSJs fit less well into Jewish institutions and self-conceptions. Ever since the Emancipation of European Jews, they and their descendants have managed to craft a dual identity by proclaiming at least their citizenship, and often their nationhood, to be that of the state in which they live. Their Jewishness is encapsulated in their religion, even if they don't practice it. RSJs are, for the most part, people without religion. Upon arrival to their new country, primarily the United States and Germany, beyond immigrant resettlement organizations, they encounter the synagogue or temple. It may be that for most diaspora Jews, Judaism is a façade for ethnicity. One sociologist asserts, "Jewish self-definition is that of a religious group but few Jews are believers in any significant way. As a Reform rabbi stated the problem, 'Prayer is still the pretext, but the justification of the act, the real purpose, is now achievement of community, the sense of belonging.'"[2] In Britain, too, "a feeling of belonging, rather than belief in God, is the driving force behind synagogue attendance."[3] Nevertheless, RSJs at first take the "religious façade" at face value and, for the most part, they are not attracted to it. Perhaps over time, immigrants, and more likely the next generation, will become comfortable with the religious forms that unite Jews, whatever their deep beliefs are.

A critical difference between these generations of immigrants from the FSU and those who came earlier from the Russian Empire and Eastern Europe—"Yiddishland"—is that the RSJs have an existing homeland that continues to produce culture and sustain language. Yiddish-based secularism in the countries of immigration faded and has nearly disappeared because Yiddishland and its inhabitants were murdered by the Nazis and their collaborators. Moreover, Yiddish was overwhelmed by the more powerful English, French, and Spanish. True, the Yiddish motherland had orphaned children all over the world, and so some of its culture—especially religious practices and traditions in food and music—live on. But there is no further source of nourishment.

Today, traditional Yiddish culture is celebrated, not lived. Those who live "in Yiddish"—*haredim* ("ultra-Orthodox")—see no intrinsic value in it. Celebrations of Yiddish culture, in literature, art, drama, "cultural festivals," concerts, and museums (most recently and prominently in Moscow and Warsaw), are homage to the past and stimuli to interest. The culture they celebrate is history. Surely, it is being remade, but it will not reappear in its original form.

The same may hold for Russian-Jewish culture. Elements of it are being absorbed into common speech, the arts, and "higher" culture, just as its bearers become discernable but embedded parts of their new countries' mosaics.

NOTES

1. Joseph Stalin, *Marxism and the National and Colonial Question* (New York: International Publishers, n.d.), 8.
2. Paul Ritterband, "Modern Times," unpublished paper, March 1991, 22–23.
3. Stephen Miller, "Changing Patterns of Jewish Identity among British Jews," in *New Jewish Identities: Contemporary Europe and Beyond*, ed. Zvi Gitelman, Barry Kosmin, and Andras Kovacs (Budapest: Central European University Press, 2003), 200.

NOTES ON CONTRIBUTORS

OLENA BAGNO-MOLDAVSKI is a research fellow at the Institute for National Security Studies in Israel. She is interested in the political behavior and socialization of immigrants and ethnic minorities. Her most recent work, forthcoming in *Politics and Religion*, studies the effect of religiosity on political attitudes in Israel. Her work published in *Russie.Nei.Visions* analyzes the behavior of distinct minorities, elites, and diaspora organizations during security crises.

ELIEZER BEN-RAFAEL is a professor emeritus of sociology, Tel-Aviv University. His areas of research are ethno-cultural cleavages in Israel, collective identities, the sociology of languages and linguistic landscapes, and the sociology of the kibbutz. He was awarded the Landau Prize for lifetime achievement in sociology, and served as president of the International Institute of Sociology, the Israel Sociological Association, and the Israel Language and Society Association. He has published *Confronting Allosemitism in Europe: The Case of the Belgian Jews* (2014), *Sociologie et Sociolinguistique des Francophonies Israéliennes* (2013); *The Risk of Enduring* (2011); *Jews and Jewish Education in Germany Today* (2011); and many other works.

JONATHAN DEKEL-CHEN is a senior lecturer in modern history at the Hebrew University of Jerusalem. His publications include *Farming the Red Land: Jewish Agricultural Colonization and Local Power in Soviet Russia, 1924–41* (2005) and the coedited volume *Anti-Jewish Violence: Rethinking the Pogrom in East European History* (2010).

NELLY ELIAS is an associate professor in the Department of Communication Studies, Ben-Gurion University of the Negev. Among her main research interests are media and migration and media and children in changing technological environments. Recently, she published an edited volume, *Ethnic Minorities and Media in the Holy Land* (2015).

ZVI GITELMAN is a professor of political science and the Preston R. Tisch Professor of Judaic Studies at the University of Michigan, Ann Arbor, where he has served as director of the Center for Russian and East European Studies and of the Frankel Center for Judaic Studies. Gitelman is the author or editor of sixteen books. In 2012, Gitelman published *Jewish Identities in Postcommunist Russia and Ukraine: An Uncertain Ethnicity*. His book *A Century of Ambivalence: The Jews of Russia and the Soviet Union* (1988, 2001) has been translated into Japanese and Russian.

STEVEN J. GOLD is a professor and associate chair in the Department of Sociology at Michigan State University. His interests include international migration, ethnic economies, qualitative methods, and visual sociology. The author, coauthor, or coeditor of seven books, he has conducted research on Israeli emigration and transnationalism, Russian-speaking Jewish and Vietnamese refugees in the United States, ethnic economies, and conflicts between immigrant merchants and their customers.

MIKHAIL KRUTIKOV is a professor of Slavic and Judaic Studies at the University of Michigan, Ann Arbor. He is the author of *From Kabbalah to Class Struggle: Expressionism, Marxism and Yiddish Literature in the Life and Work of Meir Wiener* (2011). He is also the coeditor of *Children and Yiddish Literature: From Early Modernity to Post-Modernity* (2015).

JULIA LERNER is a senior lecturer at the Department of Sociology and Anthropology, Ben-Gurion University of the Negev. Her research interests are in the anthropology of knowledge and the sociology of migration. At the intersection of these fields, she explores the relocation of individuals and the translation of ideas both in post-Soviet Russia and in the Russian-speaking collective in Israel. Currently, she is working on two projects: one of them analyzes the modes of adaptation of therapeutic culture in the popular discourse in post-Soviet Russia; and the other seeks to explain the new immigrant religiosity among "Russians" in Israel. Lerner has published her work in different languages (English, Russian, Hebrew, and French) in international academic venues.

ELENA NOSENKO-STEIN graduated from the History Department of Moscow State University. At the Russian Academy of Sciences, she is a senior researcher at the Institute of Oriental Studies and Institute of Ethnology and Anthropology, where she is also the head of the Research Center for Disability Studies. Her fields of research are contemporary Russian Jewry, Russian-Jewish intermarriage, Reform Judaism, Jewish identity and cultural memory, sudden disability, and the social and cultural adaptation of disabled persons. Nosenko-Stein is the author of numerous publications in these fields.

GUR OFER is a professor emeritus of economics and Russian studies at the Hebrew University of Jerusalem, Israel. He received his PhD at Harvard. In addition to extensive publications on the Soviet economy, he has published in the areas of immigration, the welfare state, and health economics in Israel. Ofer was among the founders of the New Economic School in Moscow and was chair of its international advisory board 1991–2004. During 1995–2007, he served as head of the Israel National Institute for Health Policy and Health Services Research. He was president of the Israeli Economic Association (1998–99).

HANNAH POLLIN-GALAY was the Heideman Research Fellow at the Mandel Center for Advanced Holocaust Studies, United States Holocaust Memorial Museum, and at the Herbert Katz Center for Advanced Judaic Studies, University of Pennsylvania. She has published articles in journals such as *Holocaust and*

Genocide Studies, Jewish Social Studies, and *Prooftexts.* She is currently writing a book on language, place, and Holocaust testimony.

UZI REBHUN is an associate professor and the head of the Avraham Harman Institute of Contemporary Jewry at the Hebrew University of Jerusalem. He holds the Shlomo Argov Chair in Israel-Diaspora Relations. His areas of interest are Jewish migration, Jewish identification, the Jewish family, Israeli-Diaspora relations, and population projections. His forthcoming book, by Columbia University Press, is titled *Jews and the American Religious Landscape.*

SVETA ROBERMAN is a research fellow at the Research Institute for Innovation in Education at the Hebrew University of Jerusalem. She is also a lecturer at the Gordon College of Education in Haifa. She has published articles in *Ethos, Qualitative Anthropology, Social Identities,* and *Social Anthropology.* She is the author of *Memory in Migration: WWII Red Army Soldiers in Israel* (in Hebrew), and the recently published *Sweet Burdens: Welfare and Communality among Russian Jews in Germany* (2015).

YAACOV RO'I, a professor emeritus of history at Tel Aviv University, is the author of *The Struggle for Soviet Jewish Emigration, 1948–1967* (1991) and editor of *The Jewish Movement in the Soviet Union* (2012). He has authored and edited many other books on Islam in the USSR, Soviet Jewry, and Soviet-Israeli relations. Ro'i edited a Hebrew-language curriculum at Israel's Open University: "The Jews of Russia in the Twentieth Century" (2014).

STEPHANIE SANDLER is the Ernest E. Monrad Professor in the Slavic Department at Harvard University. Her publications include *Commemorating Pushkin: Russia's Myth of a National Poet* and translations of contemporary poets: Elena Fanailova's *The Russian Version* and Olga Sedakova's *In Praise of Poetry.* She is completing *The Freest Speech in Russia: Poetry after 1989.*

MARINA SAPRITSKY is a visiting fellow at the Program for the Study of Religion and Non-Religion and the Anthropology Department of the London School of Economics. Her research focuses on social relations, city life, religious revival, and community-building in the former Soviet Union and abroad. Her current project, *New Directions in Transnational Jewish Identity: Russian-Speaking Jewry in London,* is sponsored by a Brandeis-Genesis Faculty Grant. Her latest publications include "Negotiating Cosmopolitanism: Migration, Religious Education and Shifting Jewish Orientations in post-Soviet Odessa" in *Post-Cosmopolitan Cities: Explorations of Urban Coexistence* (2012), edited by Caroline Humphrey and Vera Skvirskaja.

ANNA SHTERNSHIS is the Al and Malka Green Associate Professor of Yiddish studies and acting director of the Anne Tanenbaum Centre for Jewish Studies at the University of Toronto. She is the author of *Soviet and Kosher: Jewish Popular Culture in the Soviet Union, 1923–1939* (2006). Her second book, tentatively entitled *When Sonia Met Boris: Jewish Daily Life in Soviet Russia*, is forthcoming in 2016. Shternshis is coeditor-in-chief of *East European Jewish Affairs*.

MARK TOLTS is senior research associate in the Division of Jewish Demography and Statistics at the Avraham Harman Institute of Contemporary Jewry at the Hebrew University of Jerusalem. He has written widely on the demography of the former Soviet Union and, in particular, on Soviet and post-Soviet Jewry.

ADRIAN WANNER served as head of the Department of Germanic and Slavic Languages and Literatures at the Pennsylvania State University. He has published numerous articles in Slavic and comparative literature journals and is the author of three monographs: *Baudelaire in Russia* (1996); *Russian Minimalism: From the Prose Poem to the Anti-Story* (2003); and *Out of Russia: Fictions of a New Translingual Diaspora* (2011). In addition, he has published six editions of Russian, Romanian, and Ukrainian poetry in his German verse translation.

INDEX

Page numbers in italics indicate figures; those followed by T denote tables.

Die Abschiebung (Vertlib), 296n.11
"absent presences," 192
Absurdistan (Shteyngart), 294
acculturation, linguistic, 15, 175, 177, 177T
adaptation: and change, as blasphemy, 269; family and gender, by RSIs in U.S., 108–109; by RSJ children in U.S., 107–108, 115–116; through role-playing, 191–192
Adorno, Theodor, 278
Afghanistan, Soviet invasion of, 10
age: of German Orthodox Jews, 47, 181; and integration into German society, 175, 176T; of *olim*, and difference in meaning of "Russia," 85; and television watching by immigrants, 176T
Agnon, Shmuel Josef, 264n.38
Akhtiorskaya, Yelena, 247, 291
Al Aqsa Intifada, 108
Alenyikov, Michael, 291
alienation: from host society, 221–222; from Jewish tradition, in Soviet Union, 190, 199
aliyah/olim, 83, 104, 139; of 1971–1988, 9, 11, 21, 143, 156–158; age difference in, 85; biblical basis, 16n.9; eligibility under Law of Return, 25 (*see also* Law of Return); failed, 61, 62–63; from FSU since 1989, 9, 16n.5, 143, 156–158, 252; by Odessans, 66; pre-Holocaust, 78–79, 82; "Russian," 149, 151
Aliyah party, Israel, 130, 137n.11
Alliance Israelite Universelle, 78, 81, 87n.20
ambivalence: about identity, of Jews resident in Eastern Europe, 99–100; of Israelis in America, 103; in transitional Jewish self-identification, 202
Andrschek, Shaul, 233
Antall, Jozsef, 8
"antidos," blogger, 231–232; and antireligious propaganda of 1920s and 1930s, 236–237; and critique of Judaism, 232–236; Internet and real-life, 240–242
anti-Semitism: in Austria, 290; "new" Jewish self-identification not dependent on, 205; in RSJ novels of present-day Germany, 289;

290; in Soviet Union, 12, 105, 142, 199, 201, 219, 232, 244n.14
Arab-Israeli wars of 1967 and 1973, 156
Arabs, Israeli, 154n.35, 300
Archive for Jewish Immigrant Culture, New York, 273
Argentina, Jewish *gauchos* of, 82
Ari, Lev, 106
Ashkenazi: communities: Eastern, self-description as, 199–200; *vs.* non-Ashkenazi, in Israel, 85
Asian republics, 45–46; emigration from, 26T; immigration to Israel from, 25. *See also individual nations*
Assembly of Captive European Nations, 8
atheism, 211, 222; as modernism, 146
attachment to Israel, 22, 45; among return migrants, 55, 69–70; of RSIs, 42, 51–52; time factors, 42–43
attachment to Jews and Jewry, and length of stay in Germany, 179
Aussiedler, 184
Australia: Odessans, returnees from, 62; percentage of world post-Soviet Jewish diaspora population, 36
Austria: anti-Semitism in, 290; Vertlib's novels about, 289–290
Averbach, Efrat, 164
Azerbaijan: anti-Armenian pogroms in, 254; "core" Jewish population, 35T, 37n.1

ba'alei teshuvah, 64, 212, 234; on antidos blog, 235–236; and online "virtual village," 242; Russian, 231, 232; within Ultra-Orthodox society, 239
Babel, Isaac, 280
Baltic republics, immigration to Israel, 26, 26T; Soviet annexation of, 11. *See also* Estonia; Latvia; Lithuania
baptism, 203, 219, 219n.19
bar/bat mitzvah, of RSJ immigrants' children, 146
Barth, Fredrik, 155n.53

307

Batory, Agnes, 18n.35
Belarus, 7; "core" Jewish population, 35T; emigration from, 26T, 31
Belensky, Misha, 72n.22
Benjamin, Walter, 279
Ben-Rafael, Eliezer, 6, 172
Bessarabia-Bukovina, Soviet annexation of, 11
Betar, 72n.23
Bezmozgis, David, 2, 247, 291, 294
Birobidzhan, 3, 154n.34
blogging: Jewish/Russian identity discussions via, 265n.40; by Khersonskii, 284n.6; and Russian *ba'alei teshuvah*'s "virtual village," 212, 231, 242 (*see also* "antidos")
Blumkin, Yakov, 261
Bodemann, Michal, 184
Bollas, Christopher, 284n.1
books, secular, religious limitations on, 240
boundaries, ethnic, 155n.53
Boyarin, Daniel, 3, 69, 84
Boyarin, Jonathan, 3, 69, 84, 90
Bradatan, Cristina, 16n.2
"brain drain": from Israel, 61; from Russia, 6
Breytenbach, Breyten, 247
Brezhnev period, Soviet Union, 252
Brodsky, Joseph, 252, 259, 278, 280, 283
Brym, Robert J., 40n.40
Brzezinski, Zbigniew, 7
Budman, Mark, 291
Bukharans, Jewish culture of, 143
Bulgakov, Mikhail, 293
Bulgaria, 7
Bundists, 3
Bunin, Ivan, 247
Bush, George W., 116

Cahan, Abraham, 299
Canada, 31, 146, 55, 36, 46; Ukrainians in, 8
Canto immigranto (Temkina), 272
Celan, Paul, 280, 285n.27
Central Asian republics. *See* Asian republics
Central Bureau of Statistics, Israel, 157
Central Council of Jews, Germany, 174
Chabad, 47, 65, 73n.28, 93, 116, 205, 238; Berlin synagogue, 174; online religious citations from, 234. *See also* Lubavitch organizations
chai, 272
Chandler, Daniel, 188
Chanukah, 48, 50, 59n.26, 114, 206, 207
Chekhov, Anton, 293

Chlenov, Mikhail, 263n.10
children, RSJ: acquisition of German culture by, 177, 177T, 178; adaptation by, in U.S., 115–116; education of, 153n.24 (*see also* education); family size, in U.S., 105, 107; and fluency in Russian, 299; immigrant, self-ghettoizing of, 154n.49; Jewishness of, importance to parents, 183; perceived promise for, in German society, 177, 177T, 178; role of elderly in care of, 107; safety and opportunities for, greater in U.S. than in Israel, 108; youth movements, 45
China, and offshore citizenship rights, 8
Christianity: conversion to, 22, 201, 216, 248; immigrant churches, in Israel, 217, 218–221, 222–223; "new" Russian Jews' preference for, 219n.19; postwar Soviet availability of information about, 199; reinforcing national identity of immigrants to Israel, 219–220; "undeclared" category, among immigrants to Israel, 222. *See also* Russian Orthodox Church
circumcision, among RSJ immigrants to Israel, 146, 153n.28
citizenship, 5–6, 18n.35; dual, 8, 119; FSU, while living in Israel, 55; Israeli, vs. Ukraine, 73n.27, 73n.32; multiple, 8; in new country of residence, 54
civic vs. ethnic nationality, 22
"civil" religion, 206; Judaism as, 148, 202–207
Clark, Katerina, 251, 254
Clifford, James, 70
Cohen, Robin, 5, 16n.1
Cohen-Goldner, Sarit, 164
collectivism, Soviet, and religion, 216
community: identity, bases for, 19n.52; imagined, 70; and immigrant church, 221, 229; local Jewish, participation in social and cultural events, 48–49, 65–67; overstatement of numbers, 192–193; religious, among immigrants to Israel, 215, 217; of RSJs in Germany, 178–179; among worldwide Jewry, 173
compatriots, 18n.32; post-Soviet definition of, 7
Conservative Judaism, 47, 114, 116; in Russian urban centers, 205
consumption patterns, among immigrants to Israel, 165–166

conversion: to Christianity, 22, 201, 216, 248; to Judaism, 148, 214, 289
Crimean Tatars, 81
Croatia, 7
cultural associations, Jewish, in Soviet Union, 142
culture, 84; of Lithuanian Jews, 98; political (*see* political culture); Russian, 166; of "sending" countries, 299; "thick" *vs.* "thin," 14, 85, 124, 139–140 (*see also* "thin" Soviet Jewish culture). *See also* acculturation
cyberspace, 14–15, 41

"Dancing in Odessa" (Kaminsky), 279, 282–283
Deaf Republic (Kaminsky), 279
Dear Orphans (Gronas), 276–277, 278–279
Dekel-Chen, Jonathan, 13, 75
"Delirium/Fragmenty" (Skidan), 285n.25
Democratic Choice party, Israel, 130
demographics, RSJ: of emigration from FSU, 23–28, 24T, 26T, 27T, 28T; of immigrants to Germany, 174–175
The Deportation (Vertlib), 296n.11
diaspora, 69; Armenian, 75; biblical basis, 2, 16n.9; definitions, 1, 16n.1; diaspora-homeland relations, 17n.26; ethno-national, 43; *fin-de-siècle* Jewish, 78–79, 87n.20; "homeland" relations to, 6–8; as imagined community, 70; internal Jewish, 84; maintenance of identity in, 19n.52; Muslim, 77; network approach to, 78–79; of RSIs, 45–46, 70; of Russian speakers, 70, 78–79, 167; secondary, destination countries as, 90; as state of mind, 84–85; terms for, 3; theoretical considerations, 43–44; transnational structures of, 185
diaspora studies, 77, 90
"disruption" model of migration-identity relationships, 56
dissident movement, Soviet Union, 263n.10
Dizhik, Alina, 1
Dorogie siroty (Gronas), 276–277, 278–279
Dreizin, Felix, 192
dual citizenship, 8; Israeli-U.S., 119
Dubnov, Shimon, 3
Dufoix, Stephane, 16n.1
dukhovnost', 216

Eastern Ashkenazi: East European/Yiddish way of life, 13; foodways, 204; self-identification as, 199–200, 208
East Germany, Jewish immigration to, 174
economics: and engagement, 132; of Israeli immigrants' work life in U.S., 111–112; of Jewish rescue and resettlement, 80–81; of RSJs' work life, in U.S., 109–111; status of immigrant *vs.* veteran Israeli populations, 156–167
education: church's role in, 221; in countries of origin, and commitment to its culture, 299; ESL classes, in U.S., 113; gender-egalitarian, in FSU, 110; Israeli options for immigrants' children, 153n.24; Jewish, 49, 59n.26, 182T, 183, 183T, 185, 206, 223; overall high level of, among RSIs, 45; religious, disconnection from, 223; "Russian" preschools, in Israel, 150; and sense of political efficacy, 133; strong attainment among RSJs in U.S., 107, 110; supplementary Russian schools, 300; Yiddish schools, early twentieth century, 299–300
efficacy, 127–128, 130, 132, 133, 134
Ehrenberg, Ilya, 145
Einseln, Aleksander, 9
emigration: of Lithuanian Jews, 92–93, 98–100, 102n.35; and resettlement in diaspora country, 42; right of, 9, 82; from Soviet Union, 9, 23–28, 24T, 26T, 27T, 28T, 142, 190, 195n.13; and "tectonic shifts" in history, 257; and ties with native land, 18n.37
Enlightenment, Jewish, early nineteenth-century autobiographies, 241–242
entrepreneurship: among returnees to FSU, 67; in U.S., by Israelis and RSJs, 110, 111
Epstein, Mikhail, 222
ESL classes, in U.S., 113
Estonia: "core" Jewish population, 35T; immigration to Israel from, 39n.18
Ethiopian Jews, 153n.31
ethnicity: and homeland attachment in diaspora, 43; "hyphenated American," 107; and immigrant churches, 218; malleability of, 171; and mixed families, 148, 214, 219, 224, 225n.1; re-affiliation of FSU non-migrant, mixed-origin people, 32; re-identification, among emigrants, 32–33; and symbolic religiosity, 48

Evangelical Christianity, among immigrants to Israel, 217, 224

family/families: immigrant church as, 221; mixed-ethnicity, 148, 214, 219, 224, 225n.1; size of, among RSJs, 105, 107; ties among RSJ immigrants to Israel, 221
Family Archive (Khersonskii), 268–272, 280
Fanailova, Elena, 268
Feingold, Henry, 80
Feldman, Elizar, 61
Feuchtwang, Stephan, 70–71
Feuchtwanger, Leon, 145
Fielding, Henry, 260
Finkel, Evgeny, 71n.10
Fishman, Boris, 247, 291
Fitzpatrick, Sheila, 191, 192
Foreigners' Advisory Councils, Germany, 135
Forverts newspaper, 299
The Free World (Bezmozgis), 2
FSU (former Soviet Union): aging of Jewish community in, 77–78; core Jewish population, 17n.16, 32, 33–34, 34T, 35–36, 35T; destinations of emigrants from, 45; as diasporic "center," 167; economic crisis of 2009, 25, 31; ethnic re-affiliation of mixed-origin people in, 32; immigration to U.S. from, 23–28, 24T, 26T, 28T, 103, 106; Jewish communal structures, 59n.24; Jews free to redefine selves, 172; percentage of world post-Soviet Jewish diaspora population, 35T; political culture of, 125, 135; repeat migration from, via Israel, 31T; returnees to, 30, 30T, 70 (*see also* returnees); RSJs' attachment to culture in, 13–14; table of RSJ emigration, 1970–2009, 24T
Furman, Andrew, 292

Gainsbourg, Serge, 260
Gans, Herbert, 15, 48
Gaon of Vilna, 97
Geertz, Clifford, 139, 152n.2
Geguzhinskis, Meishe, 95
Gemeinschaft vs. Gesellschaft, 17n.25
Gendelev, Mikhail, 267
Gentiles: halakhically defined, 152n.14; marriage to, 180, 182, 182T (*see also* mixed-ethnicity families)
Georgia: "core" Jewish population, 35T; as Soviet ethnicity, 154n.35; "thicker" Jewish culture in, 143

Georgiou, Myria, 19n.52
Germany: culture of, acquisition by RSJs' children, 177, 177T, 178; as destination for emigrant Ukrainians, 126; diversity within, immigrants' culture shock at, 146; facilitates immigrant socialization, 134; Foreigners' Advisory Councils, 135; immigration law changes of 2005, 12; instrumentalizing Jewishness in, 191–194; language proficiency, and immigrant acculturation, 175, 177, 177T; multicultural, depicted by Kaminer as, 292; percentage of world post-Soviet Jewish diaspora population, 35T, 36; political engagement of immigrants in, 135; political environment, 128, 129T; postwar return of ethnic Germans to, 80; "quota-refugees" in, 287; returnees from, 62; RSJ immigration to, 10, 11, 24, 24T, 25, 26, 26T, 28, 28T, 72n.22, 190–191; RSJ writers in, 287–289, 290; self-identification as Jewish in, 173; study population for political socialization, 131
Gessen, Keith, 291, 297n.31
Gessen, Masha, 291
Gitelman, Zvi, 145
giyur. See conversion: to Judaism
glasnost, 21, 211–212
Glazova, Anna, 267, 284n.17, 285n.27
globalization, 1, 16n.2, 143–144, 173. *See also* transnationalism
Gmelch, George, 68
Goffman, Erving, 187
Gogol, Nikolai, 192, 261
Golbert, Rebecca, 90
Gold, Steven, 76
Goldberg, J. J., 104
Goldshtein, Alexander, 252, 254, 255–257
Gorbachev, Mikhail, 21, 142
Gorelik, Lena, 248, 288–289, 291, 297n.23, 297n.27
Goren, Rabbi Shlomo, 97
Gran, Iegor, 297n.31
Grand Duchy of Lithuania, 100–101n.6
"Great *Aliyah*" (1989–1999), 9, 156, 157–158, 252; 1990–1991 peak, 143
Grinberg, Natasha, 291
Grobman, Mikhail, 254–255
Gromyko, Andrei, 3
Gronas, Mikhail, 248, 267, 275–279, 284–285nn.17–19, 285n.21

Ground Up (Idov), 295n.2, 297–298n.31
group identification and identity, 43, 55, 57
Grushin, Olga, 291
Guberman, Igor, 255

halakhah, 203, 236; and definition of Jewish identity, 33, 39n.28, 83, 152n.14, 180, 214, 219; and matrilineality, 225n.1
half-Jews, 197, 198
halyava, 193–194, 195n.20
haredim, 153n.30, 157, 235; antidos critique of, 238–240; lifestyle of, 233, 301 (*see also* Ultra-Orthodox Jews); marriage of *ba'alei teshuvah*, 239; misbehavior of, discussed on antidos blog, 237
hasidic groups: in Israel, 47; in Lithuania, 93. *See also* Chabad; Ultra-Orthodox Jews
Haskalah, 242. *See also* Enlightenment, Jewish
Hausbacher, Eva, 288, 296n.7
Hebrew: acquisition by immigrants to Israel, 145–146, 157, 158, 161, 163; after-school courses and scouting activities in, 115; cultivated by young Odessa returnees, 65; cultural consumption requiring, 52, 117; fluency in, 50–51, 54; instruction of children in, 108; Israeli revival of, 300; linguistic borrowings into RSJs' Russian, 147; and the "new" Russian Jew, 144, 203
Hebrew Immigrant Aid Society (HIAS), 81, 82
Helsinki Accord, 9
Hemingway and the Dead Bird Rain (Zaidman), 292–293, 297n.24
Herder, Johann Gottfried, 286
Herzl, Theodor, 101n.20, 149
Hesse, Hermann, 258
High Holy Days, 48, 59n.26
hilonimyi, 232. *See also* secularism
Hochzeit in Jerusalem (Gorelik), 288
holidays, Jewish, observance of, 65, 148. *See also* High Holidays; *individual holidays*
Holocaust: central in RSJ solidarity, 15; in discussions by Lithuanian Jews, 101n.35; and Jewish immigration to Germany, 187, 191; memory of, 176T, 177, 178; "milking" of, 193, 194; "new" Jews' ignorance about, 204–205; and self-identification, among Eastern Ashkenazi, 15
home: blurring of image of, 43–44; *vs*. center, 90; failed, Lithuania as, 91; Israel as, for RSJ immigrants, 17n.26; Lithuania as, 93–96; as

mental construct, 15; as place of familiarity and discovery, 62; as state of mind, 84–85; as territory of belonging, 70–71; virtual, Internet as, 230
homecomings, by returnees, 68
homeland, 69; church perceived as piece of, 222–223; colonial surrogates for, 2–3; and diaspora, 6–9; failed, 98; identification with, 43, 180T, 181; Israel as, 56; multiple, 69; national, and indigenous nation, 147; old and vanished Lithuania as, 100; as primary locus of cultural identity, 89. *See also* country of origin
homeland-diaspora relations, 17n.26, 180T, 181
Homo Sovieticus, 123, 142
Horn, Gyula, 18n.35
Hovanissian, Rafi, 9
human capital, 163
humra, 235, 236
humus, 204, 219n.24
Hungary, 7, 8; cultural programs among coethnics abroad, 8
hybridity, 294
"hyphenation" of identity: and ethnic membership in U.S., 107; Russian-Jewish-Israeli, 150

identification: cultural, role of homeland in, 89; with homeland, 43, 180T, 181; with Israel, 50–54; multiple, 99–100; of self as Jewish, 42–43, 46, 49–50, 55, 152n.8 (*see also* Jews: halakhically defined)
identity: collective, of RSJs in Germany, 179–183; created through literary self-invention, 294; crisis of, among immigrants to Israel, 220, 222; dual, 300; ethnic re-identification, and migration, 32–33, 37; ethno-national, 56; and geography, 84–85; group, 43, 55, 57; "Israeliness" and Jewishness, 108–109, 114, 146; Jewish (*see* Jewishness); maintenance of, in diaspora, 19n.52; migrant, "disruption" model, 56; modern national, *vs*. globalization, 143–144 (*see also* transnationalism); multiple, 41–42, 43–44, 85, 218, 294; religious, 37, 47–49, 83, 116, 215; "Russian," persistence of, among RSJs, 81, 113; and serial migration, 79
Idov, Michael, 291, 295n.2, 297–298n.31
Ierusalimskii zhurnal magazine, 255
Ilf, Ilya, 186

Ilichevsky, Alexander, 252, 260–262
immigrant churches, in Israel, 217, 218–221, 222–223
immigration laws: German, 12; U.S., 11, 12, 25, 78, 105
immigration to Israel, 3, 4; and consumption patterns, 165–166; cultural and psychological baggage of RSJs, 135; and earnings, 162–163; first wave (1968–1971), 156; general demographics, 158, 159T; as "home" to RSJ immigrants, 17n.26; labor force absorption and participation, 158–162; and occupational downgrading, 163–165; and political socialization, 134, 135; and postwar Jewish resettlement deals, 80; religion as path to belonging, 212, 213, 225; repeat vs. return migrants, 22; RSJ demographics of, 24, 24T, 25, 26, 26T, 28, 28T; RSJ writers in, 286, 292–293; second wave (1989–1999), 156 (see also Great *Aliyah*); tenure in, 42–43, 45, 54; and "thin" Jewish culture among immigrants, 140–142; trust, efficacy, and protest, in political culture, 133; visits by RSIs abroad, 51–52, 53, 54. See also aliyah/olim; Law of Return
income, median: of Israeli immigrants to U.S., 111; of RSJs in U.S., 109
Income Surveys (Israeli Central Bureau of Statistics), 157, 162
India, and citizenship rights, 8
individualism, 173
Industrial Removal Office, 82
inostranki Internet community, 230
"In Praise of Laughter" (Kaminsky), 281
"insertion" into society: vs. integration, 173; of RSJs, in Germany, 175–178
integration: vs. insertion, 173; of RSJs into Israeli culture, 219; in tension with separatism, 140, 231
intelligentsia, Russian: conversion of, to Orthodox Christianity, 216; "death" of, 251; and Jewish *kulturnost*, 140–141; Jews internalize characteristics of, 151
Intermediate Stations (Vertlib). See *Zwischenstationen*
Internet: immigrant use of, 229; as RSIs' source of information on Israel, 52. See also World Wide Web
Israel, State of: absorption of immigrants into labor market, 158–160; American emigrants from, 76; Ashkenazi vs. non-Ashkenazi communities in, 85; attachment to, 22, 42–43, 45, 51–52, 55, 69–70; "brain drain" from, 61; Central Bureau of Statistics, 157; "demographic wars," 214; as destination for emigrant Ukrainians, 126; German RSJ solidarity with, 179, 180–181, 184; Jewish self-distancing from, 4; as Jewish state, 108–109, 147; labor force participation, by immigrants, 160–162; language courses, 8 (see also Hebrew); Law of Return (see Law of Return); migration of Lithuanian Jews to, 92–93; Ministry of Immigrant Absorption, 44, 157; multiculturalism in, 143, 146; national religion as collective identity, 144, 215–216; official definition of Jewish identity by (see *halakhah*); outmigration of FSU immigrants, 28–32, 29T; percentage of world post-Soviet Jewish diaspora population, 35T, 36; "personal status" in, 83; political environment in, 129T; support for, by "new" Russian Jews, 206, 207
Israeli Arabs, 154n.35, 300
Israeli immigrants to U.S., 46, 76, 103, 104; community life in U.S., 117–118; demographics of, 106; disenchanted with current society, 105; economic adjustments, 111–112; family and gender patterns among, 106, 108–109; naturalized, 118; relations with native-born U.S. Jews, 114–115
Isurin, Ludmila, 17n.26
Italy, cultural programs among coethnics abroad, 8

James, William, 187
Jehovah's Witnesses, in Israel, 218
Jewish Agency for Israel, 12, 66, 72n.23, 217
Jewish Benevolent and Education Society, 131
Jewish Club for the Elderly, Odessa, 63
Jewish Colonization Association, 82
Jewish Communal Centers (JCC), in U.S., 59n.24
Jewish Community of Lithuania (JCL), 89, 92, 96
Jewish education, 49, 59n.26, 182T, 183, 183T, 185, 223
Jewish movement, in Soviet Union. See Soviet Jewry movement
Jewish Museum, Berlin, 289

Jewishness: behavioral expectations of, 145; encapsulated in RSJs' religion, 301; enhanced sense of, since immigration to Israel, 154n.45; ethnically defined, in Soviet Union, 145, 149, 214, 219; as "floating" signifier, 188; geographical variants in, 199; in Germany, 179, 180–183, 180T, 183, 184, 187–188; importance of, for children of RSJs, 183; instrumentalization of, 191–194; Israeli conception of, 300; and marginalized religious frameworks, 216; as negative signifier of Otherness, 253; of non-halakhic Jews, 148; performance of, 172, 187–188
Jewish organizations, 196, 209n.19; in Germany, extraction of benefits from, 192–193
Jews: archetypes of, in Germany, 192; of Argentina, 82; "communal deviants" from Russia or Israel, 104; communal structures in U.S., Western Europe, and FSU, compared, 59n.24; core population, 17n.16, 32, 33–34, 34T, 35–36, 35T, 37, 39n.23; cultural dominance of, in Israel, 108–109; and diaspora studies, 77; Ethiopian, 153n.31; full, 197; of Germany, 5–6, 72n.22 (*see also* RSJs: in Germany); halakhically defined, 33, 39n.28, 83, 152n.14, 180, 214, 219; half, 197, 198; Lithuanian (*see* Lithuanian Jews); native-born U.S., and relations with RSJ and Israeli immigrants, 112–115; "new" (*see* "new" Jew); old *vs.* new immigrants, 82–84; post-Soviet, 85; Russian Orthodox Christian (*see* conversion: to Christianity; Russian Orthodox Church); Russian-speaking (*see* RSJs); self-identification as, 42–43, 46, 49–50; shetl, 189, 190; "Sovietization" of, 117; spectrum of observance, 48–49, 54, 64, 65; veteran Israeli, 157; world population changes, 3–4; youth movements, 49
"Judaica Auction" (Khersonskii), 271–272
Judaism: "civil," 148, 202–207; Conservative, 47, 114, 116, 205; conversion to, 148, 214; "empty," 184; as façade for ethnicity, 301; and Israeli collective identity, 144, 215–216; low significance of, for Jews in Russia, 203, 205; observant, among returnees, 65, 73n.28; Orthodox, 47, 72n.24 (*see also* Orthodox Judaism); as path to belonging, in Israel, 212, 213, 225; preferences within, in Russia, 205–206, 206T; Reform, 47, 114, 116, 205; as religious identity, 116;

Ultra-Orthodox, 47–48, 153n.30 (*see also* Chabad; hasidic groups)
jus sanguinis: in Germany, 128; in Israel, 129T
jus soli, in Germany, 128

Kafka, Franz, 274–275
Kalma, Nadia, 291
Kaminer, Wladimir, 248, 287, 288, 291, 295n.2, 295n.4, 296n.7, 296n.9
Kaminsky, Ilya, 248, 267, 279–284
Karpinovitch, Avraham, 92
Kass, Dora, 104
"Kategoriia lifchika" (Temkina), 272
Kazakhstan, 7; "core" Jewish population, 35T
Khersonskii, Boris, 248, 266, 267, 268–272, 273, 276, 280, 284n.1, 284n.6
Khlebnikov, Velimir, 261–262
Kissinger, Henry, 7
Kittner, Ierakhimiel, 233
Kornblatt, Judith Deutch, 201
Krasikov, Sana, 291, 296n.21
Krutikov, Mikhail, 5, 247
Kunstman, Adi, 231

labor force participation: gendered, by Israelis in U.S., 112; by immigrants to Israel, 160–162
Labor Force Surveys (Israeli Central Bureau of Statistics), 157
labor market, Israeli, immigrant absorption into, 158–160
Laitin, David, 298n.35
landsmanshaftn, 13, 78–79. See also settlement houses
language: proficiency in, and acculturation, 15, 146, 175. See also *specific languages*
Larom, Tali, 164
Latvia: "core" Jewish population, 35T; emigration from, 31
Laub, Dori, 102n.35
Law of Return, Israeli, 12, 25, 36, 83, 128, 143
Lazarus, Emma, 81
Lederhandler, Eli, 14
length of residence, RSJs': in Israel, 46, 54; in Germany, 175, 179
Lerner, Julia, 212
Lestchinsky, Jacob, 18n.37
Letzter Wunsch (Vertlib), 290
Levin, Evgenii, 233
Lieber Mischa (Gorelik), 288–289
"life cycle" socialization model, 125–126
Lipphardt, Anna, 92

Lipset, Seymour Martin, 104
Die Listensammlerin (Gorelik), 288
Lithuanian Jews: affirmation from "abroad," 96–98; "core" population, 35T, 75; demographics, 92–93; emigration from Israel to, 31; emptying out of core community, 98–100; immigration to Israel, 92–93, 102n.35; Jewish Community of Lithuania, 89, 92; "Litvak" identity and heritage, 75, 101n.6; Memel refugee crisis of 1869–1870, 81; oral histories of, 91–92; prewar, 91; religious life, 95; return and rehabilitation stories of, 91
Litman, Ellen, 291
The Little Golden Calf (Ilf and Petrov), 186
LiveJournal, 212, 230, 232–233, 242
The Living and the Dead (film), 259
Long, Lynellyn, 68
Lubavitch organizations: Chabad Lubavitch, in Russia, 205; Lubavitch Community, in Lithuania, 93; outreach by, in Israel, 232

"Maestro" (Kaminsky), 281
Magid, Sergei, 267, 272
Mandelstam, Osip, 280
Mann, Thomas, 247
"marginally Jewish," 248, 266–267, 275, 279
Markowitz, Fran, 113
marriage: of *ba'alei teshuvah*, 239; early, among RSJs in U.S., 107; endogamy vs. exogamy, among RSJs in Germany, 181–183, 182T; to a Gentile, by children of German RSJs, 180, 182, 182T; interethnic, in Soviet Union, 141 (*see also* mixed-ethnicity families); to other RSJs, 15; preference for fellow Jews, by "new" Russian Jews, 207
Marxism-Leninism: effect on Soviet religiosity, 146, 211, 216; Soviet code of civic ethics, 188
matrilineality, and halakhic validation of Jewishness, 225n.1
media: Jewish, exposure to, in Germany, 178; Russian-language, 150. *See also* television-watching
median income: of Israeli immigrants to U.S., 111; of RSJs in U.S., 109
Meese, Edwin, 9
Meine weißen Nächte (Gorelik), 288
Melnik, Kseniya, 291
"melting pot": Israel as, 143, 165; Soviet trope of, 142

memory: collective Jewish, in Russia, attenuation of, 205; and community, 19n.52; of the Holocaust, 176T, 177, 178; in Khersonskii's poetry, 270–271
Mesamed, Vladimir, 38n.11
messianic groups, among immigrants to Israel, 217
Mickiewicz, Adam, 247
migration: circular, 42; "disruption" identity model, 56; early vs. late, FSU to Israel, 42; of Lithuanian Jews to Israel, 92–93; motives for, 24–25, 41, 75, 78, 81, 105; repeat (*see* repeat migrants); return (*see* returnees); within Russian-speaking space, 84; serial, 78, 79; transnational, dynamics of, 41
Milton, John, 260
Ministry of Absorption, Israel, 157, 217
mixed-ethnicity families, 148, 214, 219, 225n.1; and collective identity preferences, 181–183; and religious weddings, 224
mobility, socioeconomic: blocked in Soviet Union, 105; downward, for immigrants, 124
Moldova/Moldavia: "core" Jewish population, 35T; emigration from, 26T; tenure of emigrants in Israel, 46
Moscow, emigration from, 26, 27, 27T
multiculturalism, 294, 300; German, 292; Israeli, 143, 151; official, 19n.40
multilingualism, 289, 297n.24
multiple citizenship, 8. *See also* dual citizenship
multiple identities, 41–42, 43–44, 85, 294
Murav, Harriet, 259
"Musica Humana" (Kaminsky), 280
"My Father Says Yes and No" (Kaminsky), 280
myths of return, 93–96

Na'aleh, 72n.23
Nabokov, Vladimir, 247
names: of ethnicities, persistence of, 155n.53; Jewish, as markers of ethnicity, 14–15, 145, 206, 207, 1152n.14
nationalism, post-Soviet resurgence of: in the Caucasus, 256; Russian, 142; in Ukraine, 19n.40
nation-state, "container" view of, 17n.25
Nesbitt, Laura, 187
networks: analytical approach to, 75; Internet, 229 (*see also* blogging); and the Russian Jewish diaspora, 78–79; among RSJs in

U.S., 106, 114; and Ukrainian homeland-émigré ties, 87n.13
Nosenko-Stein, Elena, 5, 172, 272
noshrim, 105
Novaia kamera khraneniia (curatorial web project), 260
Novyi Golem (Yuryev), 259, 260
Nudel'man, Misha, 137n.11

occupational distribution: of Israeli emigrants to U.S., 111T; of RSJs in U.S., 110T
occupational downgrading of immigrants to Israel, 163–165
Odessa: ambivalence about return, 68; department for diaspora relations, 8; exploratory visits to, 67; reintegration into Jewish life, by returnees, 65–67; returnees to, 22, 62–63; RSIs in, 72n.24; "Worldwide Club of Odessans," 18n.37
Ofer, Gur, 124, 300
Ohr Sameach, 73n.28
Okudzhava, Bulat, 258
olim. See aliyah/olim
One More Year (Krasikov), 296n.21
Operation Birthright, 4
Orange Revolution, Ukraine, 31
Orientalism, in Goldshtein, 256–257
Orleck, Annalise, 117
Orthodox Judaism, 47, 72n.24; and age of German RSJs, 47, 181; likened to Soviet Communism, 237–238; in Odessa, 72n.24, 73n.23; Ohr Sameach, 73n.28. *See also* Chabad; *haredim*; hasidic groups; Ultra-Orthodox Jews
ORT (Obshchestvo Remeslennogo Truda), 82
Oxfeld, Ellen, 68

Pale of Settlement, 197
Palestine: under British Mandate, 80, 82; Ottoman, Russian emigration to, 79, 82, 87n.20; as Zionist homeland, and ancient Israel, 2. *See also* Yishuv
Pamyat', 142
"para-Soviet man," 253, 254
Passover, 206, 207. *See also* seder attendance
Pasternak, Boris, 293
perestroika, 11, 21, 81, 199, 212, 252
Pers (Ilichevsky), 261
"persistence model" of early-life socialization, 127

"personal status" in Israel, 83
Petrov, Evgeny, 186
Petrova, Alexandra, 267
philo-Semites, German, 289, 290
Piatigorsky, Reuven, 233
Pinto, Diane, 184
pluralism: ethnic and nominal societies tolerant of, 15; religious, among RSJs, 213. *See also* multiculturalism
poets: and marginality, 267 (*see also* "marginally Jewish"); of the new diaspora, 266; in Russian, of Jewish descent, 248. *See also individual poets*
Poland: cultural programs among coethnics abroad, 8; and postwar Jewish resettlement deals, 80
Pollin-Galay, Hannah, 75
political culture, 127–128, 130, 133, *134*
political socialization: in early life, 125–126, 127; "life cycle" model, 127; "lifelong" model, 135; as lifelong process, 126, 127; in USSR, and experientialist model, 130
politics: of diaspora and resettlement, 79–82; engagement with, 132, 135; of host country, and change in RSJ outlooks and behaviors, 123; power of FSU emigrants in Israel, Germany, and Ukraine, 129; U.S., "soft" power of Jews in, 80, 87n.13
Poluostrov Zhidiatin (Yuryev), 259
Portes, Alejandro, 119
"The Portrait" (Gogol), 293
"Poster" (Rubin), 146
post-Soviet Jewish identity, multiple, 85
post-Soviet religiosity, 216, 225; and the "supermarket of religions," 224
Prashizky, Anna, 214, 216
"A Prayer" (Khersonskii), 270
pripiski, 192–193
Prokhorova, Irina, 255
propiska, 64
protest, in political culture, 127–128, 130, 132, 133, *134*
Pushkin, Alexander, 293
push-pull motivators in migration, 24–25, 41, 75, 78, 81, 137n.13
Putin, Vladimir, 7, 8

Rabin, Yitzhak, 6, 104
Rebhun, Uzi, 22, 60, 106
reciprocity, 127; under Soviet civic ethics code, 188

Reed-Johnson Act of 1924, 78
"Reflections of a Japanologist (Confessions of the Century's Mamzer)" (Steiner), 257–258
Reform Judaism, 47, 114, 116, 205
refugee status of RSJs, U.S. change in, 11, 12, 25, 105
refuseniks, 113
re-identification, ethnic, and migration, 32–33, 37
reintegration into Jewish life, of Odessan returnees, 65–67
religion: "civil," 206 (*see also* "civil" religion: Judaism as); identification with traditions of, 14, 144; and identity, among RSIs, 47–49 (*see also* religious identity); as Marxist "opiate of the people," 211; newly observant Jews, 64 (*see also ba'alei teshuva*); post-Soviet secularism, 85; and sociopolitical belonging, 212, 213, 225; symbolic affiliation with, and ethnicity, 48; universalist understanding of, 149. *See also* Judaism; Russian Orthodox Church
religiosity: among Russian Jews, 204T; false, 232; of immigrants to Israel from FSU, 146, 214–215, 223–225; and integration into German society, 175–177, 178–179; post-Soviet, 216, 225; self-reported, of M70 vs. M90 immigrants, 158; youth's spiritual search, in Israel, 221–223
religious education, Jewish, 49, 59n.26, 182T, 183, 183T, 185, 206; disconnection from, 223
religious identity: of converts to Christianity, 248; fostered by Israel, 108–109; and immigrant churches, 218; Judaism as, 116; of new immigrants to Israel, 215
Remennick, Larissa, 14–15, 144, 146, 214, 216, 244n.14, 293
repeat migrants, 22, 31–32, 31T, 42, 78; Internet use among, 230; *vs.* returnees, 42; of West-Central Europe, 55
resettlement: politics of, 79–82; religion as conduit of Israeli resources, 214–215
returnees, 22, 28–29, 29T, 30, 30T, 31, 42, 60–62; Barbadian, 68; Crimean Tatar, 81; failure narratives, 93–94; from Israel to FSU, 78; Jewish identity and attachment to Israel among, 55; narratives of, 63–65; to Odessa, 62; *vs.* repeat migrants, 42; secularism among, 47. *See also aliyah/olim*

Reyn, Irina, 291, 293
rights: of emigration, 9, 82; of Jews in the East, Western advocacy of, 9; political, of immigrants, in new states, 152n.2
Ritterband, Paul, 113, 116
ritual observance, 48–49; among *ba'alei teshuvah*, 235; among naturalized Israelis in U.S., 114; by West-Central European RSIs vs. FSU returnees, 54; women's stronger commitment to, 50
Roberman, Sveta, 6, 172
Ro'i, Yaacov, 124
Roman Catholicism, among immigrants to Israel, 218
Romania, 7; and postwar Jewish resettlement deals, 80; revival of Hungarian revisionism in, 8; Soviet annexation of Bessarabia-Bukovina, 11
Rosh Hashanah, 207
Rothschild, Nathan, and family, 81, 82
RSIs (Russian-speaking Israelis), 22, 56, 70, 84; as community within Israel, 145–150; creation of the diaspora of, 45–46; fluency in Hebrew, 50–51; Jewish identification, 42–43; in Odessa, 72n.24; orientation toward Israel, 42–43, 51–53; out-migration of, from Israel, 28–32, 29T, 71n.10; religious identity and denominational preference, 47–49
RSJs (Russian-speaking Jews), 2, 4–5, 11, 15, 23, 116, 137n.13; children's adaptation, in U.S., 107–108, 115–116; community life in U.S., 115–117; cultural status in Israel, 300; debates over "Jewishness" of, 83; defined, 153n.18; demographics of emigration from FSU, 23–28, 24T, 26T, 27T, 28T; and diaspora studies, 77; directions of emigration, 11–15; economic adjustment, in U.S., 109–111; educational attainment of immigrants to U.S., 107, 110; family and gender patterns, among immigrants to U.S., 106–108; in Germany, 173–195; immigration of, to Israel (*see aliyah/ olim*; immigration to Israel); Internet use, 230–232; politics of diaspora and resettlement, 79–82; relations with native-born U.S. Jews, 112–114; and religion, 213, 214, 216; U.S. experience, *vs.* Israelis', 76; U.S. shift on refugee status of, 11, 12, 25; writers (*see* writers)

Rubina, Dina, 146, 153n.29, 255, 263n.3
Rudling, Per, 8, 19n.40
Russendisko (Kaminer), 287, 295n.2, 295n.5
Russia, imperial: emigration from, 78–79, 82; Jewish life in, 13
The Russian Debutante's Handbook (Shteyngart), 291, 294–295, 298n.32
Russian Federation: authoritarian culture of, 136; as "center" of diaspora, 167; "core" Jewish population, 34, 35T; emigration from, 26T, 27, 27T, 32, 38n.11, 45; Jewish self-identification in, 196–197, 198, 200–201; return migration to, 30T, 61
Russian immigrant enclaves, in U.S., 115
Russian intelligentsia, 140–141, 151, 216
Russian-Jewish-Israeli identity, 150
Russian language: and culture, German RSJ identification with, 179–180, 180T; fluency in, 37n.1, 299; Jewish speakers of (*see* RSJs); media, 150; preservation of, by RSJs in Israel, 147; supplementary schooling in, 300
Russianness: created through literary self-invention, 294; as marketable commodity, 295, 298n.35; sense of one's own, 152n.8, 154n.39
Russian Orthodox Church: ethnic Jews worshiping at, 37, 63, 200–201; intelligentsia's conversion to, 216; in Israel, 37, 218
Russkii zhurnal magazine, 255

sabbath observance: in new "civil Judaism," 114, 206; parents noncompliant with, 234
Sachar-Gertner, Sheina, 93–94
Safran, William, 19n.52, 42
Sandler, Stephanie, 5, 248
Sapritsky, Marina, 22
Satanovsky, Yevgeny, 61–62
Schejter, Amit, 297n.24
Schiff, Jacob, 81
Second Lebanon War, 31
secularism: antireligious propaganda of 1920s and 1930, 236–237; among post-Soviet Jews, 85; among RSJs, 47; of urban parents, 234; 240, Yiddish-based, 301
seder attendance, 48, 50
self-employment, in U.S.: among Israeli immigrants, 111; among RSJs, 110
self-identification, Jewish, 208n.5; as ambivalent/transitional, 202; as Eastern Ashkenazi, 199–200, 208; in Germany, 173; negative, of Russian Jews, 201–202; as "new" Russian Jew, 202–208; as Russian, 200–201
Semeinyi arkhiv (Khersonskii). *See Family Archive*
separatism: among children of immigrants, 154n.49; *vs.* integration (*see* integration); among RSJs in Israel, 140, 147
serial migration, 78, 79. *See also* repeat migrants
settlement houses, 113. *See also landsmanshaftn*
Seventh Day Adventists, in Israel, 218
Shapiro, Vladimir, 203
Sharansky, Natan, 149
shetl Jews, 189, 190
Shoah. *See* Holocaust
Shokin, Samantha, 2
Sholem Aleichem, 141, 247
Shrayer, Maxim D., 291, 298n.32
shtadlanim, 81, 82
Shternshis, Anna, 14–15, 212
Shteyngart, Gary, 247, 291–292, 293, 294, 295n.2, 298n.32
Shubinskii, Valerii, 259
Shumsky, Dimitry, 148, 154n.35
Shvab, Leonid, 267
"Shylock on the Neva" (Shteyngart), 293
Silverston, Sondra, 297n.24
Singer, Gali Dana, 267
Siniavsky, Andrei, 297n.31
Six-Day War of 1967, 156
Skidan, Alexander, 279, 285n.25
Skolnik, Jonathan, 72n.22
Slavic republics, Jewish immigration to U.S. from, 11–12
Slezkine, Yuri, 142
Slovakia, 7; revival of Hungarian revisionism in, 8
Slovenia, 7
Smith, Timothy L., 224
Snob magazine, 291
snowball sampling, 185n.9
social and cultural events, of local Jewish community, participation in, 48–49
socialization, 127
Social Survey (Israeli Central Bureau of Statistics), 157, 162
social ties, of RSJs in U.S., 114. *See also* networks
Sokhnut. *See* Jewish Agency
Solnechnoe spletiniie magazine, 255

Some Like It Hot (film), 259
Sonderbehandlung, 10
Soviet Jewry movement, U.S., 82–83, 104, 263–264n.10
Soviet Union: atheism of, and ethnic classification of Jewishness, 116; Brezhnev period, 252; code of civic ethics in, 188; collapse of, and "vacuum" for Jewishness, 262; emigration impeded from, 21; invasion of Afghanistan, 10; Jewish emigration from, 9–11, 10T, 82, 105 (*see also* RSJs: direction of emigration); Jewish life under, 85; Jewish movement of late 1970s, 263–264n.10; Jewishness ethnically defined, 214, 219; Jews as ethnicity, 171; last literary generation, 262–263; as refuge for socialist fringe, 87n.11; Yiddish antireligious propaganda of 1920s and 1930s, 236–237
Stalin, Joseph, 300
Steiner, Evgeny, 252, 253, 254, 256, 257–258
Stoppard, Tom, 261
St. Petersburg, emigration from, 26–27, 27T
structural equation modeling (SEM), 132–133
study groups, religious, among immigrants to Israel, 217
Sukkot, 238
Superfin, Uri, 233
"super-Jews," 289
symbolic religiosity and ethnicity, 48
Symbol "We" anthology (*Zerkalo* group), 255
synagogues: attendance, 48–49, 59n.26, 64, 65, 113, 182, 182T; as focal point of communal affiliation, in U.S., 59n.24; of Kovna, 97; in postwar Vilna, 95; of present-day Berlin, 174

Tadzhikistan, "core" Jewish population of, 35T
Tarn, Alex, 255
Tatars, Crimean, 81
"tele-presence," 19n.52
Temkina, Marina, 248, 266, 267, 272–275, 276, 284n.14
tenure in Israel, 54; and place of birth, 46
Territorialists, 3
"thick" culture: of Georgian and Bukharan Jews, 141; Russian, of Soviet Jews, 141, 148; *vs.* "thin," 14, 85
"thin" Soviet Jewish culture, 124, 139–141, 150–151; modification of, in 1980s, 141–142
Tishkov, Valery, 6–7

Tolts, Mark, 4, 5, 16n.5, 21, 61
Torah and Talmud studies, 206, 207
traditions: popular, among *ba'alei teshuvah*, 235; positive relation to, 144; of religion, identification with, 14
Transcaucasia, emigration from, 26T
transmigrants, 63, 66
transnationalism, 1, 16n.2, 17n.25, 90; of diaspora structures, 185; and dynamics of migration, 41, 43; of identity, asserted through religion, 215; and Internet communities, 229; of Israelis, 118–119; multiple identities of writers in diaspora countries, 289
trust, in political culture, 127–128, 130, 132, 133, *134*
truth-telling, 127
tsimmes, 204, 219n.25
Tsvetaeva, Marina, 267, 280
Turkmenistan, "core" Jewish population, 35T
Tur-Sinai, Aviad, 164
"Two Photographs" (Khersonskii), 269–270, 273

Überjuden, 289
Ukraine, 7; "core" Jewish population, 34, 35T; destinations of emigrants from, 45; diaspora members in Canada, 8; emigration to Israel from, 26, 26T, 31, 38n.11; homeland-émigré network, 87n.13; immigrant political socialization in, *134*; multiculturalism and revival of nationalism, 19n.40; political environment in, 128–129, 129T; returnees to, 61–69; as Soviet ethnicity, 154n.35; trust, efficacy, and protest, in political culture, 133; visa requirement, and Israeli citizenship, 73n.27; visits to, by emigrants, 62
Ulinich, Anya, 247, 291
ulpanim, 157
Ultra-Orthodox Jews, 47–48, 153n.30; *ba'alei teshuvah*, 64, 231, 232
Union of Progressive Jews synagogue, Berlin, 174
United States: associational nature of Jewish communities in, 59n.24; emigrants from FSU to, 23–28, 24T, 26T, 28T, 103, 106; experience of Israelis *vs.* RSJs, 76; family and gender patterns, among RSJs, 106–108; immigrants' culture shock at diversity of, 146; Israeli immigrants to (*see* Israeli immigrants to U.S.); as multicultural society,

55; percentage of world post-Soviet Jewish diaspora population in, 35–36, 35T; Reed-Johnson Act of 1924, 78; returnees from, 62; reversal in RSJ immigration policy, 11, 12, 25, 105; RSJ writers in, 286, 291–292; Soviet Jewry movement, 82–83
USSR. *See* Soviet Union
Uzbekistan, "core" Jewish population of, 35T

Vapnyar, Larisa, 247, 291
Verliebt in Sankt Petersburg (Gorelik), 288
Vertlib, Vladimir, 248, 294, 295n.2, 296n.11
Vertovec, Steven, 100
Vīķe-Freiberga, Vaira, 9
Vilnius/Vilna: as center of Lithuanian Jewish community, 89, 92; Gaon of, 97; postwar synagogue, 95
Vineta (Yuryev), 259
Vinokur, Val, 295
virtual communities, Jewish topics in, 231
"virtual villages," 230, 242
volunteerism, eschewed by RSJs in U.S., 116
vyzovy, 142

Wanner, Adrian, 5, 248–249
West, Nathaniel, 260
Western Europe, Jewish communal structures in, 59n.24
"What Do You Want, M & M?" (Temkina), 272
What Happened to Anna K (Reyn), 293
women: egalitarian education system, in FSU, 50; occupational downward shift, as immigrants to Israel, 164; percentage in labor market, among Israeli immigrants to U.S., 112; stronger commitment to ritual practices, 50; years of education, among immigrants to Israel, 161
Woolf, Virginia, 16
work: downward mobility in prestige of immigrants' occupations, 124; employment distribution of RSJs and Israeli immigrants to U.S., 110T, 111T; median U.S. income, RSJ and Israeli immigrants, 109, 111; occupational downgrading of immigrants to Israel, 163–165; opportunities in U.S., 108; self-employment, in U.S., 110. *See also* economics
"Worldwide Club of Odessans," 18n.37
World Wide Web, 14. *See also* Internet

writers, RSJ: in Germany and Austria, 286, 287–290; in Israel, 286, 292–293; in U.S., 286, 291–292. *See also* poets

Yandex, 230
Yankelovitch, Matvei, 268
"Yekkes," prewar, 5
Yeltsin, Boris, 7
yeridah/yordim, 61, 62–63, 69, 71n.9, 74n.9, 104. *See also* failed *aliyah*
Yiddish: associated with *kleynshtetldikayt*, 262; cultural transmission via, 146; dwindling numbers of speakers of, in Lithuania, 99; among earlier Jewish émigrés, 13–14; among Eastern Ashkenazi self-identifiers, 199, 200; and Eastern European way of life, 13–14; identified by RSJs as Jewish national tongue, 153n.29; indifference of "new" Russian Jews to, 203; Lithuanian touring troupe, 93; schools, in early twentieth-century U.S., 299–300; speakers of (*yidn*) vs. German-speaking *yahudim*, 83
yiddishkeit, 200. *See also* Jewishness
"Yiddishland," 13, 301
Yishuv, 82, 83
Yisrael Ba'aliyah party, 130, 147–148
Yisrael Beiteinu party, 130, 148
Yom Kippur, 48, 49–50, 114; among "new" Russian Jews, 206
Yom Kippur in Amsterdam (Shrayer), 298n.32
Yom Kippur War of 1973, 156
youth movements, Jewish, 49
Yurchak, Alexei, 252, 253–254
Yuryev, Oleg, 252, 253–254, 259–260

Zaidman, Boris, 291, 292–293, 295, 297n.24, 297n.26
Zak, Khatzkel, 97
Zapadniki, 11
zastoy generation, 252–258
Zerkalo magazine, 252–253, 254–255
Zevelev, Igor, 18n.32
Zholkovsky, Alexander, 285n.19
Zionism, 2, 3, 80, 90, 93, 101n.20, 104
Zionist organizations, German Orthodox Jewish membership in, 180
Zven'ia magazine, 252–253
Zwischenstationen (Vertlib), 290, 295n.2, 296n.11